BROADWAY BABIES

Broadway Babies

THE PEOPLE WHO MADE THE AMERICAN MUSICAL

ETHAN MORDDEN

OXFORD UNIVERSITY PRESS

New York   Oxford

Oxford University Press
Oxford   New York   Toronto
Delhi Bombay Calcutta Madras Karachi
Petaling Jaya Singapore Hong Kong Tokyo
Nairobi Dar es Salaam Cape Town
Melbourne Auckland

and associated companies in
Berlin   Ibadan

First published in 1983 by Oxford University Press, Inc.,
200 Madison Avenue, New York, New York 10016

First issued as an Oxford University Press paperback, 1988

Oxford is a registered trademark of Oxford University Press

Library of Congress Cataloging in Publication Data
Mordden, Ethan
Broadway babies.
Discography: p. Includes index.
1. Musical revue, comedy, etc.—United States.
I. Title.
ML1711.M73   1983   782.81'0973   83-8132
ISBN 0-19-503345-0
ISBN 0-19-505425-3 (ppbk.)

2 4 6 8 10 9 7 5 3 1
Printed in the United States of America

To my brothers—
Ned, Jim, Andrew, Tony

The author wishes to acknowledge the very crucial guidance of his editor Sheldon Meyer and the expert polishing of Leona Capeless. Kenneth Mandelbaum and Larry Moore expanded the possibilities of research with arcane matter and sharp queries; Harvey Evans, Jack Lee, Pamela Sousa, and Lewis Stadlen enlarged on the backstage structure of the profession (with great loyalty to their colleagues, I should add); and the once-and-future Dorothy Pittman sustained, considered, and prodded, as ever before.

Contents

BROADWAY BABIES

Introduction
Broadway, 1900

Convention ruled. One composer sounded much like another, lyricists came in one color only (dull), and scores were made of genre songs like the animal fable or the ethnic pastiche—"The Serenades of All Nations," say, taking one through Irish, Spanish, Chinese, French, and ragtime imitations. The powerful music publishing industry, centered on vaudeville (where the new hits were plugged), fostered the practice of the interpolation, a Hit Tune calculated to stimulate the public rather than to relate in any way to a musical's plot or characters.

A Hit Tune might be a strophic story ballad ("After the Ball"), a rhythm number ("Yip-I-Addy-I-Ay!"), a nostalgic strain ("Love's Old Sweet Song"), a spoon ditty ("Shine On, Harvest Moon"), or a coon song* ("Under the Bamboo Tree"). Self-contained and having its own character rather than assimilating that of the show it invaded, the Hit Tune typifies the early musical as a performer's rather than an author's art. The Broadway Babies with the clout were the earthy singers who commissioned and put over the interpolations; the star comics, patrolling tradition for "business" and out-of-context quips; the vivacious prima donnas of operatic vocal commitment; and The Girls, perhaps the oldest element in the musical comedy handbook.

Yet most musicals were not revues. They told stories, took place, covered a beginning, middle, and end in that order. There were four basic types of musical: British musical comedy, American musical comedy, comic

---

* This objectionable term will offend readers, but I think it better to accept the past as it was, warts and all, than to forgive it, inadvertently, with euphemisms.

opera, and extravaganza. The British musicals were the Gaiety shows, named after the London theatre managed by George Edwardes. Gaiety style favored unpretentious, modern-dress plots, shopgirl heroines, noble suitors, American (usually villainous) millionaires, fashionable, even fashion-setting costumes, a dignified chorus line, and story-oriented scores. *Florodora* (1899) is a notable example (though it belonged neither to the Gaiety Theatre nor to Edwardes), even more influential in America than England.

American musical comedy preferred exotic settings wherein an American comic could suffer culture shock and comment on mores—*The Sultan of Sulu* (1902), for instance. Gaiety shows were light, crisp, and pretty; the American model was heavier, louder, sloppy. Both *Florodora* and *The Sultan of Sulu* are set in the Philippines, yet *Florodora*'s score, riddled with interpolations, nevertheless held to a firm sound style while *The Sultan of Sulu* gloried in incongruous coon songs.

Extravaganza, related to British pantomime, was sloppiest of all, virtually written by its director, designer, and performers. *The Wizard of Oz* (1902), from L. Frank Baum's book, is the classic entry, the most popular musical of its era—over a year in New York and Brooklyn and six years on tour. Yet its score came from so many different sources that no one publisher could bring out a piano-vocal score, and for all its popularity it cannot be revived, as it was all tricks and the secrets are lost today. Who was in charge of *The Wizard of Oz?* Not Baum, who wrote the original libretto, nor his composer Paul Tietjens, but Julian Mitchell, who rewrote the script and staged the production, and Fred Stone and Dave Montgomery, who played the Scarecrow and the Tin Woodman.

Musical comedy and extravaganza relied on "theatre" voices, capable of sending a Hit home. Comic opera needed real singers, for where musical comedy emphasized fun in an irreverent worldview, comic opera emphasized musical richness in a world ruled by romance: Reginald de Koven's *Robin Hood* (1891), for instance, once a perennial of the touring troupe, the amateur theatrical, and the home singing soirée at the piano. As of the death of farce and burlesque, two forms depending entirely on interpolations, musical comedy and comic opera remained the two major unlike forms, confronting each other through the decades with their respective qualities of satire and romance. Musical comedy became *Oh, Kay!*, *The Boys from Syracuse*, *On the Town*, *Annie Get Your Gun*, *Li'l Abner*, *Anyone Can Whistle*, *Chicago*, *42nd Street*. Comic opera became *The Desert Song*, *Music in the Air*, *Carousel*, *Fanny*, *Juno*, *The Rothschilds*, *A Little Night Music*.

As we begin, then, Broadway's Babies are Montgomery and Stone, or the singing beauty Lillian Russell, or Julian Mitchell, not composers and lyricists; and Broadway's great event is not a triumph of authorship, but a big number, like *Florodora*'s Sextet, "Tell Me, Pretty Maiden." Staging matters: steps in time, a twirl of parasols, gala gowns. The Sextet is more than a number. It serves as the show's signet, an essence of its experience, a key moment: a *numbo*. It is a ground zero of super showmanship. Yet someone wrote the words; someone set them to music. There are authors, and they will take power. Would Ethel Merman have been able to project her unique character so fully without Cole Porter and Herbert Fields to style her? Would Agnes de Mille have taught so much about dance without Rodgers and Hammerstein to inflect? Shortly after *The Wizard of Oz* opened on Broadway, the first of the truly great Broadway composers emerged in a *Wizard* imitation, *Babes in Toyland,* to articulate form and substance in the musical. He is in some ways the greatest of all: for he did nearly everything first.

I

The Score

Victor Herbert, born in Dublin, was trained in Stuttgart and Vienna. As a cellist, bandmaster, and symphony conductor, he had no apparent calling for the theatre. Yet when he turned to the stage he wrote with such authority that his versions of the available genres became the models all other artists painted from. Because few people today have access to Herbert's oeuvre in full, their impression of his work comprises waltzes and love lyrics, plus some military boom-bah with a thin soprano riding over the chorus. Because two of his most admired scores, *Naughty Marietta* and *Sweethearts,* were given the Jeanette MacDonald-Nelson Eddy treatment at MGM in a highly distilled operetta of gala costumes, mannered acting, butchered scores, and sweet mysteries of life, he is thought a florid composer. Because today the librettos he set sound antique at best and at worst really dumb, he is cornered by camp collectors. Because the major opera companies that stage his pieces cannot handle the pop-theatre aspect of his shows and smaller groups are weak in vocal casting, Herbert revivals argue a poor case for the composer who was considered the giant of the early 1900s. Posterity still listens to Herbert, but only in part: it cannot comprehend him.

In fact, Herbert wrote all kinds of theatre songs, for all the genres, for voices operatic to comic. He stressed compositional unity, crowding out the vaudeville interpolation. He formalized the sometimes accidental use of pastiche, making it an active element of satire or scene-setting. He wrote for any kind of singer, cutting through the genre code to allow for a more *musical* comedy in the comedy musical and more comic naturalism in the musical musical. When he came upon the scene, there were certain kinds of shows uncertainly written. Herbert gave them commitment, made them certain. Then he shuffled their parts, creating equally certain hybrids. A practical idealist, Herbert revealed the musical's possibilities.

Take for instance *Miss Dolly Dollars* (1905), a musical comedy with a Gaiety savor. Librettist Harry B. Smith took a look at fortune-hunting among impoverished British nobility and title-hunting among the American nouveaux riches. Keeping to Smith's musical comedy slant, emphasizing satire over romance, Herbert favored waggery rather than sweep in his tunes. In fact, the show's one hit, "A Woman Is Only a Woman (but a good cigar is a smoke)" is that rare Herbert number whose lyrics were as well liked as its melody.

Miss Dolly Dollars was a star vehicle, for the somewhat less than formidable singer Lulu Glaser. She was a roguish comedienne of great beauty—her head shots on the sheet music cover look like the treasured photograph of someone's madcap mother in her youth. Glaser dominated *Dolly Dollars* as Dorothy Gay, entering in muffler and goggles to sing of automobile joyriding, stalling and teasing her greedy suitors, delivering the animal fable in "The Moth and the Moon," leading the chorus in an eleven o'clock song, "Queen of the Ring," and getting engaged to the only lord in sight who prefers true love to riches. Her risible family and a few guests led the comic scenes, her brother Guy delivered the dainty more-or-less title song, "Dolly Dollars," and five of the comics gathered together for the evening's best number, "American Music":

> Oh, I love those songs where "honey"
> Is the only rhyme for "money."
> They are better than old *Parsifal* to me.

It's ragtime, of course—especially endearing when the chorus takes the tune in four-part harmony.

Only two years after *The Sultan of Sulu*, *Miss Dolly Dollars* shows American musical comedy midway between derivative adolescence and early maturity. There are throwbacks—two Eton Boys are trouser roles for The Girls, Dolly's hero is so ambiguously characterized in the book scenes that his romantic solo, "My Fair Unknown," has no commitment, some of the comedy songs still deal in the outdated 6/8 hopalong, and heavy choral frolics open both acts on the conventional up note that tells us more about the authors' opinion of the audience's mood than about the show itself.

However, otherwise Herbert and Smith try to fit conventions into the piece or forgo them altogether. *Miss Dolly Dollars* isn't about love; it's a social satire. So all the songs follow the theme. Thus, Dolly's auto number, "Just Get Out and Walk," nicely introduces the wild heiress:

When at first we started, the speed would make you dizzy;
All along our route every hospital was busy.
Bzzzz! I made the people scurry!
But still I always spare their lives unless I'm in a hurry.

Even the overture is made to matter, to prepare the ears for the mode of
the piece. Herbert sends us off in high spirits, laying out the parts of excitement and irony that make up most of the action. His imaginative orchestration, of course, is famous. Trained musicians generally did their
own, but Herbert's stood out, not only for craftsmanship but bizarreries.
Today, he is too often heard in the lush gloop of MacDonald-Eddy or a
Kostelanetz "pops" medley, but the original was lean, perky. Even more
remarkable than his scoring was Herbert's phrasing, the rubato that taught
his colleagues how to slide into and out of strict rhythm to suggest ecstasy
in a love song or to quibble in a charm song. (The Herbertian rubato was
popularized in the "hesitation" waltz, but Herbert used it in any rhythm,
even marches.)

As the first decade of the century wore on, Herbert began to seem like
the master of the musical, especially after achieving outstanding popular
successes in comic opera with *Mlle. Modiste* (1905) and in musical comedy
with *The Red Mill* (1906). Carrying on his tour through format, Herbert
tackled burlesque in *The Magic Knight*, first given on a double bill with
Dream City in 1906. This pair makes an odd statistic. *Dream City* is musical comedy, a spoof of land development and class snobbery ending with
the inhabitants of the planned paradise, Dreamtown, bound for the opera.
The *Magic Knight* is the opera they see: *Lohengrin* in lampoon.

It was a daring project, for while Lew Fields's former partner Joe Weber
played the lead in *Dream City* as a Long Island farmer scoffing at Dreamtown's swank, *The Magic Knight* had no popular call. On the contrary,
only operagoers—preferably Wagnerians—could get it. So Weber's following, at ease with *Dream City*, would be scoffing (and worse) at *The Magic
Knight*. One has to admire Weber for producing and Herbert and librettist
Edgar Smith for writing *Dream City* and *The Magic Knight*, for this double bill may well be the first commercially doubtful American musical. In
Herbert's age, a good musical was a successful musical; a flop musical was
a poor musical. A musical should please the public at large—not just hope
to please, but *ought* to please: or why do it? But like such later unusual
shows as *Johnny Johnson, Beggar's Holiday, Ballet Ballads,* and *Pacific
Overtures, Dream City* and *The Magic Knight* were written and produced
because they were too interesting not to be. Such corollary premiums as a
road tour, a film sale, a strut along the hit parade were not taken into

account. Who even knew if these works would prosper in New York? Indeed, none did.

Still, this long forgotten experiment by Weber, Herbert, and Smith makes a fascinating study. The composer was secure by now in American song so he made *Dream City* something of a musical burlesque in itself, slipping tintypes of the Hit Tune in between the plot numbers. There are loving takeoffs on the Florodorian sextet ("Down a Shady Lane"), on the animal fable ("The Ravenous Rooster"), on the New York anthem ("A Shy, Stubborn Maid"), on the telephone ditty ("Love by Telephone"), on rag ("Hannah"). The prospect of an extended *Lohengrin* spoof is enticing, at least for those of us who don't think the opera is already loony as it stands. But Herbert's digs at the pop tune are more enjoyable than his jibes at Wagner. Who is Herbert to spoof operatic procedure after having used so much of it in his comic operas? Opening choruses, dopey kings, impedient rackets, recitative . . . Herbert has prayed in this church himself, for comic opera was not that much different from opera in the long run. And Herbert demonstrated how close they are—but this time with real elan—in *Algeria* (1908).

Algeria was the first operetta in the modern sense, comic opera's major breakaway from musical comedy. Till now, American comic opera was like a way station between opera and musical comedy: a silly opera, a grandiose musical comedy. Now, in *Algeria,* operetta mixes its Aristotelian compound, and what comes out of the workshop is neither silly nor grandiose. It is unlike opera. It is like musical comedy, but more romantic, more musical. *Much* more: it is almost nothing but music and romance.

Algeria's recipe held fast as the mandate of American operetta for thirty years: exotic rather than familiar locale, sublime love lyrics for impassioned singers, strong choral work, ambitious dance and pageantry, comedy relegated to a few characters in a few numbers, as little contemporaneity as possible, and adventure to the nth degree in fury, danger, nostalgia, gallant men and reckless women. *Algeria*'s heroine, Zoradie, the Sultana of the Barakeesh tribe, is typical. She has sworn to wed a man she has never met, the author of a poem called "Rose of the World." *Algeria*'s hero is of course the poet, a handsome Captain in the Foreign Legion. He has sworn to marry a woman he *has* met, a fortune-teller he encountered in the marketplace. And who is the fortune-teller? Zoradie, in disguise.

Oaths, poems, sultanas, handsome captains, masquerades—this with comparable substitutions is the operetta of the future, right on to *The Desert Song* and *Kismet*. It would all be silly if the music lacked fervor or majesty, but Herbert is eloquent. He has the melody, of course, and craft. But more: he has the idealism operetta requires; he believes in oaths and poems. This, we shall see later in the chapter, his contemporaries of 1908 did not have. They mustered melody and craft and wrote away. But one has the impression, in their operettas, that they think a poem is silly. Not till Rudolf Friml and Sigmund Romberg inherited Herbert's operetta would it blaze with rekindled idealism.

Don't let the comedy run out of control, Herbert warns us—comedy keeps us from believing in oaths and poems. So *Algeria*'s comedy lay mostly in the book scenes and was entirely subsidiary. The reason for this show was its score. From the first notes, flowing strings over a pulsing bass of ambiguous intent—protection? harm?—we are in another world. The curtain rises almost immediately, no overture, and, as the Legion post's trumpet calls a warning, the marketplace begins to swarm with beggars, merchants, tourists, and our fortune-telling Sultana, all suggesting the importunate menace of desert places. From number to number, the music and romance conspire. Everything is a gesture, as in the hero's reminiscence of "The Boul' Miche" in his Parisian youth, the devil-may-care of the Latin Quarter conjured up in a lovely waltz followed by a can-can. Or take his insouciant "Love Is Like a Cigarette (a cigarette may last as long)": after the verse, the orchestra sounds a tango-like vamp while the hero rolls a cigarette. *Then* he goes into the chorus, smoking. Or the Sultana's flamboyant court procession; or, generally, the evocative modal feeling of the African desert, which taught Romberg how to harmonize *The Desert Song*.

At the center of this new operetta aesthetic is the music for Zoradie. She is a Brünnhilde of operetta, a lover *and* a fighter. Her first solo, the fortune-telling episode in the opening, is lavish and sweet, but, like herself at the time, in a kind of disguise. We don't really meet her till, revealed as the Sultana, she repeats the poem that has entranced her. This number, "Rose of the World," begins in stillness, the halting tune suggesting a recitation. But the poem has amazed her, and as she reaches the line, "My life, I love thee," her calm pulls to passion over churning strings. The words begin to entreat, the music to soar, and gradually we lose our ironic resistance to her fey dream of finding and adoring the poet. The music believes; so we must. The music pounds, and it fears, too, for operetta is as vulnerable as it is bold. At the end of Act I, in the midst of a storm, Zoradie begs the Captain to let her through the locked city gate, but he refuses to let her brave the desert in bad weather. "Why do you hold me prisoner?" she cries, the voice shooting up to high notes few musical comedy heroines needed. Why? Why else? As "Rose of the World" sneaks in under a violin tremolo, the hero and heroine confront each other, and romance, and fate, all—through Herbert's music—merged. The storm breaks wild, the fainthearted dash for cover, and Zoradie and her cigarette-rolling poet stand transfixed as "Rose of the World" crashes into glory in the orchestra and the curtain falls.

Algeria has light numbers as well, but they carry more of a lilt, less of a slambang. A comic solo for the Captain's General uncle, "I've Been Decorated," sounds exactly like something Sullivan might have composed for Gilbert, the vintage allusion further removing *Algeria* from the modernday immediacy of musical comedy. Operetta is now definitively set apart from musical comedy on a plan that may be summed up in a line from *Naughty Marietta:* " 'Tis love and love alone the world is seeking."

Herbert was so sure he had something special on his hands that he termed *Algeria* a "musical play," advanced nomenclature not to catch on till the 1940s. Sadly, the project was sabotaged by the feckless Glen MacDonough, who needed tight and passionate and came up with lax and dreary. *Algeria* failed. Lew Fields was so impressed by the music that he had MacDonough revise the book, dropped one minor song, added two others equally minor, and restaged the piece as *The Rose of Algeria* (1909). Its bad reputation dogged it, and the revision failed too.

Herbert helped establish yet another genre, the dance musical, the form that was eventually to produce *On The Town, West Side Story,* and *Pippin.* For his base of operations, he used extravaganza, the form most hospitable to dance—but here, too, he has to revise the formula. Despite his success with *Babes in Toyland,* Herbert regarded extravaganza as outmoded. He took his music seriously; extravaganza took only comedy seriously. Accordingly, each time he tried extravaganza he changed it, squeezed it, shaped it. *Wonderland* (1905) stressed plot and character numbers, a sort of comic opera with a fairytale setting. *Little Nemo* (1908) was virtually a revue, a cartoon musical to suit its source, Winsor McKay's celebrated comic strip about the boy who nightly dreams his way to Slumberland. And *The Lady of the Slipper* (1912) was the dance show.

The Lady of the Slipper was one of Herbert's biggest hits. On closing, it vanished, not even leaving a love-song hit to recall it. As the title implies, the subject was *Cinderella,* but the stars, Montgomery and Stone and Elsie Janis, lacked vocal heft. So Herbert avoided romanticizing the tale. Cinderella's entrance at the ball was a ravishing moment, a violin line with choral oohs and ahs highlighting the Prince's little solo. But this was the utmost of the magic, for Cinderella's succeeding waltz, "The Princess of Far Away," is home-simple and the lovers' duet, "A Little Girl at Home," is oldtime soft shoe.

In other hands, *The Lady of the Slipper* might have been just another extravaganza. R. H. Burnside, a man in the Julian Mitchell tradition, was the director, and the three stars were all exponents of the topsy-turvy style in entertainment. However, Herbert and his partners, Anne Caldwell and Laurence McCarthy on book and Caldwell's husband James O'Dea on lyrics, laid out a musical comedy with certain extravaganza investments. The pantomime animal was present (Mouser, the Cat, who sings only "Meow" syllables in a duet with the heroine), but the "principal boy" trouser role was gone and the story told fairly and clearly—it's not nice to fool around with *Cinderella*. True, Montgomery and Stone pulled their stunts as Punks and Spooks. But as Cinderella the charming Janis stuck to plot songs, and the other characters—Fairy Godmother, stepsisters Dollbabia and Freakette, Prince, and court—played appropriate parts in script and score.

The astonishing amount of dance music sets the show apart. Dance in the average musical was tidbits, a waltz clog or tap tacked onto the end of a song. Here Herbert constructs whole dance scenes. Except for the big one at the ball, they don't relate strongly to the story, but their variety is impressive, ranging from hoofing and "eccentrics" to ballet, the instrumentation varied to suit each turn—a xylophone solo, say, for Montgomery and Stone's follow-up strut to "The Garden Party," a punning account of Ima Bean's coming-out ball. Producer Charles Dillingham even made an attempt to include the latest in stepping by hiring Vernon and Irene Castle, fresh from Paris and just on the verge of American fame, to introduce their lively ballroom style. Their duet spot was dropped during the Philadelphia tryout when Mrs. Castle decided to introduce a little trick she had picked up in Paris, pulling up her skirts to exhibit what Janis recalled as "the shortest pair of 'shorts' ever glimpsed."

Not all of Herbert's work was experimentation. Some of his best scores simply defined established forms. *Algeria* played with operetta's possibilities; *Sweethearts* (1913) classified operetta as it stood, blending the elements but underlining romance as the essential ingredient. (In terminology, Herbert reverted to the designation "comic opera" in the published score: operetta per se does not yet exist.) Thus, though the action takes place in 1913, the setting is Bruges, a city that hasn't changed in 500 years, and the kingdom of Zilania, another of those lands found only in the atlas of operetta. There is a prince, a foundling princess, and a lot of talk about the nature of love. "We don't love because we *should*," the heroine explains. "We love because we *must*."

She must love the prince (incognito, the best kind), and this is considered controversial until it is revealed that she is the long-lost heiress to the throne of Zilania. That is the European view of things; the American musical, later operetta included, prefered democratic overturn of the Cinderella type: love levels rank. No sooner has heroine Sylvia reached the stage than she is telling everyone about the conquering power of love; for proof, she makes that entrance riding in on a dogcart pursued by rowdy beaux. "Pretty goings on, I must say!" intones her foster mother. But is it Sylvia's fault that all the boys clamor for kisses? Love is in the operetta air: "It takes you by surprise." And she is into the title song, a wide-spanned arc of waltz lines, each next one developing the last. It's the kind of thing no one did as well as Herbert, and presents a grand opportunity to the soprano who plays Sylvia. Christie MacDonald, the first to do so, is one of those fabled Broadway dainties who won the hearts of the day. To judge by the *Sweethearts* recordings she made, she was no Farrar, her voice unsupported and her phrasing labored. She was no damozel, either, by 1913—seven years later she was closing her career as the husband-hungry widow in the Shubert revival of *Florodora*.

On the other hand, Herbert's lovers are often less pedantically Romantic than such later tillers of the field as Jeanette MacDonald and Nelson Eddy would have us believe. With them, operetta shatters the piñata and a thousand doilies float down; the true Herbert operetta usually has a lot of musical comedy in it. *Sweethearts'* prince, for example, is only relatively Byronic, making his entrance in riding habit, yes—but calling for his laundry. Though royal, he's a good sport:

> PRINCE: If ever I am King of Zilania . . . I shall consider only the happiness of the people.
> MIKEL: That's what they all say before they get in.

Yet the Prince, like Sylvia, must register his tribute to romance. "Sweethearts" for her; for him, "Every Lover Must Meet His Fate."

Revolutions in musical comedy are made by collaborators, not just composers; here Herbert was at a disadvantage. He worked with the best librettists of his time, but the best were seldom good enough. The banal pleased them, for all the big hits were imitations, and no one could even remember where it all started. Why Herbert did six shows with Glen MacDonough, for instance, is a mystery, for a MacDonough book has more holes than a colander, and his lyrics were no prize, either. One can see why Herbert worked most often with Harry B. Smith, for while Smith is a favorite target of historians, he was at least dependable: fast and solid. Amazingly prolific, Smith worked with most of the early giants, from Reginald de Koven and Ludwig Englander in the late 1800s to Jerome Kern and Sigmund Romberg in the 1910s and 1920s. He was not an inspired writer, but his stuff holds up today in the natural survival of the workmanlike. Beverly Sills revived a song from a forgotten Herbert show, *The Enchantress* (1911), with Smith lyrics, "Art Is Calling to Me." Sung by a character who wants to be an opera star, it has stock rhymes ("propriety" and "society" or "viva" and "diva"), and, once it states its proposition ("I want to be a prima donna, donna, donna") never goes anywhere. Yet it's a fine song, the kind you want to hear again immediately after the first runthrough. Obviously, Sills's singing it, diva to "diva," gives it an extra layer of fun, and she sang the hell out of it; also obviously, Herbert's swank tune is going to factor the fun. But, even so, Smith has done his job. The words have point and vigor and they sing easily. The first Broadway librettist to publish a collection of his lyrics, Smith enjoyed a fine reputation, a man in demand. But he was not a maker of waves. Smooth rowing was not merely good box office; it was sensible theatre.

Yet in *The Enchantress* Herbert made public his intention to Americanize comic opera: "I determined . . . to disregard absolutely every foreign impulse and to write in a frank, free, American style." Strange. Herbert had been doing this for years, and in scores—*The Red Mill,* for instance—of greater native oomph than the Continentally placid *Enchantress.* Smith's libretto, with its Zergovia, Prince Ivan, court intriguers, and opera-singer heroine revealed as being of noble birth in time to become Ivan's queen, was hardly the medium in which to try naturalizing the European style in the American musical.

A more likely partner in such an undertaking was Henry Blossom, a librettist of some finesse and even zing—he once broke his leg dancing the tango. It cannot be accidental that two of Herbert's most successful entries in straight format, *The Red Mill* (musical comedy) and *Mlle. Modiste* (comic opera), had Blossom librettos; that the composer's favorite among his forty-six scores, *Eileen* (1917), was likewise Blossom's work; nor that Herbert's two most brilliant formal experiments were made with Blossom. These last two, both huge hits, affirmed Herbert's vitality and spoke to his successors. Moreover, they marked a high point in the revolution of Authors' over Performers' Rule. Yet scarcely anyone mentions them today: *The Only Girl* (1914) and *The Princess "Pat"* (1915).

The Only Girl is a real surprise, a "musical farcical comedy" that preceded the legendary Princess shows* of Kern, Bolton, and Wodehouse in the use of a naturalistic story, a small cast, modest decor, and songs strongly keyed to character. *The Only Girl* doesn't even have a chorus line. There are four male principals, sworn singles; four woman principals, who one by one partition the bachelor fraternity; one man's valet; a comic soubrette; six women to fill out the ensemble; and that's the cast. The scene plot is the next thing to a bare stage: the hero's living room and dining

* See Chapter 6.

room. The action is artless: hero Kim, a musical comedy librettist, partners Ruth, a composer, in a strictly business arrangement. Of course they fall in love, and the fourth bachelor resigns.

This chamber plot is unusual in a musical of 1914; even more unusual is Blossom's book, sound theatre of itself. It had to be—Herbert wrote his leanest score for *The Only Girl*. There is a bit of music to get the curtain up on, but no opening number, and Act I has only four songs, the last a compact duo of celibate "understanding" between Kim and Ruth: "Just two machines and nothing more!" He has heard her playing a lovely theme on the 'cello, and wants it for his show; she in turn will get her first professional break. "I'll write the book!" he exults, "I'll write the score!" she agrees, and the curtain falls on the most concisely *narrated* first-act finale in musical history. No recitative, no choral commentary, no dance diversions. What we have here is a play with certain songs: the right ones.

The Princess "Pat" sallied into form more complexly, meshing elements of comic opera into a musical comedy framework. The Princess of the title suggests Ruritania, but note the "Pat": the action is set amid the Long Island country club set. The former Pat O'Connor has married an Italian prince who is losing interest in her, and her best friend is being courted by a rich, coarse German. The three acts comprise the two women's successful plot to respark the old marriage and arrange a new one between the friend and the German's handsome son.

The frame is musical comedy, a Gaiety show removed to the Hamptons. What is *The Princess "Pat"* about?: sexism in marriage. The stage is filled with arranged couples, spatting couples, fiancés, and remarried spouses. So the songs reflect this *by gender,* some lines—such as Pat's "Now, while men marry whom they will and woman whom they do"—comparing men's freedom of movement with women's societal obligations.

Harry B. Smith practiced convention; Henry Blossom finished it off. There are no animal fables here, no story ballads, no sequential pastiche. Much as one may love, for instance, *Sweethearts'* "Jeannette and Her Wooden Shoes" as a song (and it is well crafted, a sharp tune cut to the beat of a clopping clog), as a theatre number it is a boilermaker in a milk bar. The ingenue says—why? because it's there—"I know a girl who got into a lot of trouble by wearing wooden shoes," and gboing! we're into the saga of Jeannette, which has about as much to do with the scene, the ingenue, and *Sweethearts* in general as the Kol Nidrei does. That's the Smith style. (He collaborated on the *Sweethearts* book and his brother Robert wrote the lyrics.) Blossom, by the time of *The Princess "Pat",* patterned each show's libretto individually, and this show's songs all deal with courtship and marital problems: "Allies," "Make Him Guess," "I'd Like To Be a Quitter," "Love Is the Best of All," "For Better or for Worse,"

"I Wish I Was an Island in an Ocean of Girls," "I Need Affection," "In a Little World for Two," "The Shoes of Husband Number One."

For his part, Herbert wrote for a sly combination of true singers and "Broadway voices," averaging out operetta's grandiosity and musical comedy's throaty howling. Pat, the key figure, is a soprano with showbiz juju. She gets the full star entrance, soaring over the chorus on an "ah" vowel, but she must put over gritty comic tunes as well. Herbert was lucky: Eleanor Painter was available. Too often, after losing the services of Alice Nielsen and Fritzi Scheff, he had to make do with singers of tertiary mettle. Some of the failure of *Algeria* and *The Rose of Algeria* must be ascribed to their leading women, neither of whom could hurdle the music, though in their defense it must be said that Herbert cast the part for a singer with the delicacy of Mozart's Susanna and the arrogance of Tosca. The authors billed *The Princess "Pat"* as a "comic opera," but it's more a *musical* musical. Herbert had proposed to kiss his elbow—and succeeded.

If there is one major theme in Herbert's career, it is the insistence on liberating the music: from bad habits, sloppy performers, the humdrum. The American musical is reckless; Herbert did not tame it. Nor should he have done. He wanted the music to match the recklessness . . . and the romance, and the whimsey, and the bizarre, and the nostalgic.

Herbert was a leader in extracurricular activities as well. As conductor of the Pittsburgh Orchestra he was the first composer to bridge the classical and Broadway spheres, to the latter's benefit. As the first musician to challenge in court the corrupt editor of the *Musical Courier*, Marc Blumenberg, Herbert broke a web of blackmail and intimidation that musicians of greater reputation had feared to cut.* Most importantly, Herbert was a prime mover (over dinner at Lüchow's) in the founding of ASCAP, the American Society of Composers, Authors, and Publishers, designed to protect creators from exploitation. Composer Raymond Hubbell, a specialist in revue scores and best remembered today for "Poor Butterfly," was the true instigator, but in later years he was to credit Herbert's comradely zeal as the crucial factor in getting organized.

All of this indicates a man determined to nurture the integrity of the

---

* The case was a libel suit brought against Blumenberg for an article that began more or less exulting in the London failure of *The Fortune Teller,* then went on to attack Herbert's Pittsburgh appointment: "Great symphony conductors are not drafted from the ranks of composers of the shoddy American farce operas, alias leg shows." Particularly galling was a slash at Herbert's originality: "Everything written by Herbert is copied; there is not one original strain in anything he has done." The trial stood the bar in October of 1902. Herbert's attorney made hash of Blumenberg and his witnesses, Herbert won damages of $15,000 (reduced by two-thirds on appeal), and the music world cheered. The trial did more for Herbert's prestige than his shows—his early hits *Babes in Toyland, The Red Mill,* and *Mlle. Modiste* were still before him.

score, and this was Herbert's great achievement. He not only developed the forms of the musical; he made this work so important that the musical *became* important. As vaudeville, it could never be more than product, something to sell. When Herbert finished with it, it was art. Few called it that—many resented the dignity the word "art" implies. These were, after all, leg shows, as Blumenberg said, shoddy farce operas. Yet, undebateably, the musical first entertained ideals in the prime Herbert years, roughly 1903–1915. Perhaps his great innovation was self-respect, his great concept that of the "artistic success" that is worth staging regardless of how well it comes out financially. The picture of a Luders or Caryll show being restaged, as *Algeria* was, because the score was just too good to lose is not easy to conjure up.

Herbert had no comparable rival. Reginald de Koven was written out of first-rank tunes when Herbert was just getting going, John Philip Sousa lacked versatility, and the other names of the time—Gustav Luders, Julian Edwards, Gustave Kerker, Ludwig Englander—are justly forgotten today. The one standout in the group is Ivan Caryll, Belgian-born and French in feeling, though he got his training in the Gaiety school. Caryll was less finicky than Herbert about the innate consummation of a score composed by one man. Where Herbert's contracts forbade interpolations, Caryll's merely forbade the interpolators' getting credited. After all, as a Gaiety veteran, Caryll was an interpolator himself.

Caryll was eclectic, drafting the major accounts in the musical's history—Gilbert and Sullivan and Offenbach, naturally, but the later Viennese leaders as well. No one learned better than Caryll the lesson that Lehár taught in *The Merry Widow* that a musical can use all the comedy, prancing, nostalgia, pastiche, and anything else it likes, as long as it expresses romance with eloquence and sweep. And, like Lehár's librettists, Caryll's were worldly, racy. In Caryll's two standout hit musical comedies written for Broadway, *The Pink Lady* (1911) and *Oh! Oh! Delphine* (1912), everybody is a card, every exchange farcical. The love plots peak in sumptuous waltzes designed to share the amorous urbanity of Lehár's trendstyling "Merry Widow Waltz," but the action is far more sophisticated—adulterous, literally—than anything Herbert set. Herbert's projects were fairy tales, spoofs, and lessons in monogamous courtship. *Oh! Oh! Delphine* shows how the times were starting to replace Herbert. The musical's title derives from the favorite cry of the heroine's parrot; it seems she's always getting into trouble and needs chiding. She does have her problems. A former beau has turned up (a sculptor, by the way; and you know what they sculpt) begging for a return engagement, and Delphine's soldier husband has gotten in dutch with his commanding officer, who will forgive the offence on the condition that Delphine rendezvous with him at the Villa Primrose.

It's a sly show. No sooner has the curtain gone up than the officers and their wives complain to the audience that Colonel Pomponnet demands great decorum from married couples, yet that worthy promptly marches in and, to a hopping 6/8 meter, makes the men turn their backs while he kisses the women. It's a naughty show: the sculptor goes everywhere accompanied by six gorgeous models, his face one big smirk. It's a daffy show: the parrot not only cries "Oh! Oh! Delphine" constantly, but actually launches the title song, to the consternation of Delphine's husband—*now* what is she up to? It's a wild show, too, its third act curtain rising on a scene of near pandemonium in a ballroom—"Since Pavlova bowled us over," the chorus explains, "everyone's got to dance!" It's a bizarrely imperious show: Delphine enters the ballroom atop an elephant named Toodle-Doo who, she says, has a sensitive ear and will trample anyone who sounds a false note in the refrain. And it's a reckless show, for by the final curtain Delphine's husband decides to join the flirting, since he can't beat it. "I was a lamb domestic," he notes. "Now, little girls, I'm not!"

By about 1915, Herbert found himself beginning to be overtaken: by younger colleagues and subject matter. Moreover, producers resented the artistic musical with its plot songs that didn't sell in the millions the way "After the Ball" and "Under the Bamboo Tree" had done. Vaudeville was dying and the musical had taken over its commercial functions, so Broadway was now the place in which to launch a song hit. But Herbert had banned the interpolations. He had killed the story ballad, with its self-contained, take-home entertainment package. He had committed art in the marketplace. "Songs from successful plays are printed in great numbers and are the source of great profits," he said in 1920. "In order that these songs may sell, they must have words that are independent of the play—that is, on some general theme and attractive to the person that has not seen the play."

With misgivings, Herbert tried to oblige. A man who can write coordinated musicals can certainly write a string of pop tunes. Sure enough, the eighteen songs in *Angel Face* (1919), to Harry B. Smith's book and brother Robert's lyrics, tell the uninformed nothing of what *Angel Face* might have been about. Everything's general—"Sow Your Wild Oats Early," "Tip Your Hat to Hatty," "A Man Should Have a Double When He's Single," or the hit, "I Might Be Your Once-in-a-While." *Angel Face* wasn't about much of anything; Herbert and his partners had anticipated the 1920s, a golden age of pointless musicals. The *Angel Face* songs are a treat, as creative as ever—a ragtime lullaby, for instance, called "Bye, Bye, Baby." But it seems that Herbert had already made all the innovations possible given production and performance technology and what the public would bear. He had defined an American style for musical comedy and operetta alike. What more could he do? He died in 1924, just before his financially most successful creations were heard: *Rose-Marie, The Student Prince, The Vagabond King, The Desert Song, The New Moon.*

Rudolf Friml and Sigmund Romberg composed them: but Herbert designed them. His two successors worked, like him, in musical comedy as well as operetta, but where Herbert mixed the styles, inventing and replacing parts according to the challenge in each next story, Friml and Romberg grew out of musical comedy into operetta, where they expunged as much of the musical comedy as possible.

It's not easy to tell Friml from Romberg. Friml could—he said Romberg was the derivative one (of Friml, particularly). Their heroes are interchangeable, likewise their heroines, their settings are old and foreign, their musical structures invariable from show to show, with standard scene-laying choruses, finales, and big-tune reprises. Actually, the two men's similarity ends at the close of their heyday in the 1920s, for thereafter Friml began to retire, disappointed at the eclipse of his brand of operetta, while Romberg kept at it, moving back into musical comedy and turning out a lively score (completed at his death by orchestrator Don Walker) for *The Girl in Pink Tights* in the early 1950s. Still, it is in their big operettas of the 1920s that Friml and Romberg made their mark, and it is here that they prove Herbert's contribution to the style we call operetta. In one work alone, Herbert organized the form so perfectly that Friml and Romberg drew on it again and again; not coincidentally, it is the score that operetta buffs often rate as Herbert's masterpiece: *Naughty Marietta* (1910).

Opera impresario Oscar Hammerstein produced the piece, using singers, musicians, and staff freed from his Manhattan Opera Company. The Metropolitan Opera had offered Hammerstein a fortune to desist because New York could not support two full-size operations indefinitely and Hammerstein's people put on finer art than the high-hat Met. Hammerstein accepted the deal (the Manhattan had nearly bankrupted him anyway) and took his troupe to Broadway. *Naughty Marietta* would be comic opera then, on the musical bias: a coloratura soprano heroine (Emma Trentini), a Wagnerian tenor hero (Orville Harrold), a hefty contralto second woman (Maria Duchène), a lavish baritone villain (Edward Martindel), a rich choral ensemble, and an orchestra that does not merely set rhythm and keep melody in key but helps tell the story. The comedy was definitively set to one side, the hero's sidekick providing most of the laughs in the book scenes (his two songs are more character novelties than comic numbers), and altogether Rida Johnson Young's libretto reveled in costume and nobility and sweeping gestures, in superb personalities and sudden adventure and disguises. The locale alone implants an operetta atmosphere: New Orleans in the eighteenth century.

The story and characters also established a model for twenties operetta in its capricious heroine, stolid and idealistic hero, lacey bad-guy courtier, and highly politicized background of imperialism and egalitarian upheaval. Only in operetta would a heroine pin her romantic yearnings on the man who can complete a "dream melody" known only to her, as Marietta does; only in operetta would that man be a buckskinned vigilante, making an attractive coupling of his backwoods majesty and her aristocratic daring. It runs the other way, too, for in *The Desert Song* we learn that romance is "a prince who tells a country maid 'I love you!' " Romberg's and Friml's operettas doted on social misalliance, in *The Student Prince* (prince and waitress), *Princess Flavia* (princess and impostor prince), *My Princess* (heiress and immigrant, though he turns out to be a prince), *The New Moon* (great dame and revolutionary), *The Vagabond King* (princess and thief), *The Wild Rose* (princess and gambler), or *The White Eagle* (Indian maid and English aristocrat).

The music makes the form: this, too, is Herbert's discovery, and *Naughty Marietta* reveals it at its best. "Tramp! Tramp! Tramp!" gives us Captain Dick's swagger, "The Italian Street Song" presents Marietta's dash, and all the major songs look at love—its power, its crushing grandeur, its deceptiveness, its intoxication. And of course the dream melody, "Ah, Sweet Mystery of Life," hymns its searching intimacy and universality: " 'Tis love and love alone," remember, "the world is seeking." With its impulsive approach-avoidance love plot, slimey noble villain, aristocratic dance divertissement, democratic politics, sidekick comic, key love theme, waltz numbo, colorful choral opening, and its ban on ragtime, novelty dances, and other musical comedy conventions, *Naughty Marietta* set a form that held the stage for two decades. Herbert made the first step toward taming performer power, and pointed the way in all the forms of American musical theatre. But, in particular, bigtime American operetta, and the belief that a great musical needs great music, is his invention.

2

The Urban Ethnic Emergence

The American stage was largely an English stage—or French, in translation—until New York secured its position as the nation's theatre capital by the 1850s. Manhattan's cosmopolitan savor slipped into the industry most effectively in the work of Harrigan and Hart, developers of the downtown school of playwrighting, with immigrants for characters, mixed-race casts, eminently hummable tunes, and farcical adventures drawn from life in the cold-water flats of "Five Points," the notorious junction of Baxter, Park, and Worth Streets. Edward Harrigan was a native of New York, Tony Hart an interloper from Massachusetts, and their house composer, Dave Braham, came over from England. With their relatives and friends they staged charades that, in little more than five years changed the face of—the faces in—American drama.

William Dean Howells thought Harrigan an American Aristophanes; the music publisher Edward B. Marks saw Hogarth and Dickens in him, and the celebrated Irish-American playwright Dion Boucicault told Harrigan, "You have done for the Irish in New York what I have done for the Irish in Ireland." WASP reactionaries disdained Harrigan. One A. M. Palmer, noting Harrigan and Hart's Irish, German, and black characters, asked how such casting could produce an American play. Who's American? Harrigan's answer: "Whoever votes the Republican or Democratic ticket in these United States."

Harrigan's people tended to vote Democratic. They were, in Howells's description, "the street cleaners, the contractors, the grocery men, the shysters, the politicians, the washerwomen, the servant girls, the trashmen, the policemen, the rising Irishman and Irish woman." These formed the

Mulligan Guard, originated in 1873 as a vaudeville sketch portraying the regimental fraternities popular among New York's working class. The subject itself was unusual, for while the Irish had been standard characters on the stage, it was only in minor parts as brainless drunkards. Harrigan portrayed them culturally, and with zest, especially in his rousing theme song, "The Mulligan Guard":

> We shoulder'd guns, and march'd, and march'd away,
> From Baxter Street
> We march'd to Av'nue A;
> With drums and fife, how sweetly they did play,
> As we march'd, march'd, march'd in the Mulligan Guard.

By 1879, after Harrigan and Hart had opened their own theatre at Broadway and Spring Street, the sketch had grown into *The Mulligan Guard Ball,* a play rippling with life: Harrigan as Dan Mulligan, Annie Yeamans as his wife Cordelia, Hart in blackface as the maid Rebecca Allup, various neighbors, and the rival Skidmore Guard, a black club which provides the plot action by hiring the same hall as the Mulligans for the Skidmore Ball—on the same night. The manager of the hall, typically, was a German immigrant, and the outcome of the double booking an absurd disaster. The Skidmores move up to the second floor and their dancing so punishes the building's hinges that the Skidmores crash through the ceiling on to the Mulligan celebration. (Harrigan staged it with dummies.) A *Mulligan* series ensued, all comedies sprinkled with songs.

Harrigan and Hart wrote the scripts, Harrigan handled the lyrics and staged the shows, and a look at the staff roster of Harrigan and Hart's Theatre Comique proves how much a family affair this was. Harrigans, Yeamanses, and Cannons (Hart's kin) predominate, and Harrigan rounded it all out by marrying Braham's daughter Annie. Thus, the enterprise never fell into the hack professional groove worn thin by routine. Harrigan and Hart found their own way, their bungling but hearty honesty. They owed something to the informal Irish variety nights called "Hibernicons," but these were seen only within the parish. Harrigan and Hart were open to the public, who thought them inseparable and were stunned to hear they were parting in 1885. Hart was already suffering an advanced stage of the syphilis that would kill him in 1891. Harrigan and Braham went on without him, but the house style had peaked and was over. Gilbert and Sullivan's works had first come here during the early Harrigan-Hart glad season, whetting theatregoers' taste for better lyrics than Harrigan's and smarter music than Braham's. The Mulligan Guard broke up.

When Harrigan conceived the title role in *Reilly and the Four Hundred*

(1890), his last success, he played with the idea of making its pawnbroker protagonist not Irish but Jewish: *Moses and the Four Hundred*. He had feared staling in his specialty, and was proud of his work in *Mordecai Lyons*. Annie Harrigan talked him out of it—but by coincidence the legitimately Jewish counterparts of Harrigan and Hart were just coming into fame. Like him, they dealt in stereotypes; still, they broke the monopoly that names such as as Douglas, Booth, Kemble, Payne, and Forrest had held in main-stage American theatre.

"Don't poosh me, Myer!" the little fat one would moan, but the tall thin one would poosh him, and on they came, Mike and Myer: Joe Weber and Lew Fields. Natives of the ghetto in Manhattan's Lower East Side, they had started in vaudeville in a "knockabout" act, acrobatic stunts in an atmosphere of love-you-hate-you physical assault. Gradually, they worked into verbal comedy with the same attitude, discovered the appeal of spoof, and stood, by 1900, among the most popular comedians in the theatre.

It is not clear how many tickets they could have sold, for in their prime as a team they worked in an extremely small house, the Weber and Fields Music Hall on Broadway and Twenty-ninth Street. But in fame they led the top rank, and broke a major racial bar by succeeding directly through rather than around their ethnic basis. Weber and Fields didn't trim their Jewish accents down to some "polite" minimum. They overplayed, mangling English with fake German versions. The style was dubbed "Dutch comedy" (from *Deutsch* = German), but this is a euphemism. Weber and Fields were the advance guard of the Jewish performing brigades who would take in Eddie Cantor, Al Jolson, and Fanny Brice among others.

Try a sample of Weber and Fields's famous pool sketch, from their vaudeville days. Myer, the bully and cheat, is teaching the game to Mike the dupe:

> MYER: Vell, vell! Tell vot you is playing.
> MIKE: Pool, ain't it?
> MYER: Vat *ball?* Vat *ball?*
> MIKE: Ah! So I got to play a ball?
> MYER: How many times got I to tell you you got to name vat ball you shoot?
> MIKE: Good! I name this one Rudolph.

Burlesque was the Weber and Fields specialty, and they happened into it by accident. Working for Oscar Hammerstein at his Harlem Opera House in 1894, the two stars found their pool skit elbowed out of honors by an imported novelty, Signor Fregoli, a quick-change artist. Fregoli performed a multi-character melodrama by himself, taking an exit through one door, jumping out of costume with the help of an army of assistants, and entering moments later through another door. Resentful of Fregoli's fascination yet amused by his stunt, Weber and Fields found two men who resembled them and presented a lampoon of his act on the same program, shortly after Fregoli and on his own set. In their version, Weber and Fields exited through one door and their two lookalikes entered through another—at *precisely* the same moment. Fregoli was already a bit screwy; by taking him just a bit farther, the two comics reduced him to the bottom of silliness while they came off as kings of the absurd.

The absurd lampoon became their métier. No sooner had a new hit opened than the Weberfields troupe, as they were known, would look it up, memorize its tics, and smash it in takeoff: a Gaiety musical, *The Geisha,* became *The Geezer.* The big scene in *Zaza* was faithfully reproduced; as in the play, the actress heroine storms the home of her married lover and is disarmed by his little daughter. Weber and Fields made one substitution: the child's lines were spoken by a very large French poodle.

Harrigan and Hart worked in original farces with songs, Weber and Fields in burlesque with songs, plus an act of vaudeville. Harrigan and Hart started with a script; the Weberfields company improvised. Harrigan and Hart ran a quasi-amateur group, not unlike Hollywood's Mickey and Judy gang who put on the show; Weber and Fields gathered veterans, from director Julian Mitchell to leading women Fay Templeton and Lillian Russell. Harrigan and Hart's songs were fresh in the theatre context, while the Weberfields tunes, set by house composer John Stromberg, accorded with the standard forms of the time, coon songs especially favored. As a revolution, then, Weber and Fields were both more and less than Harrigan and Hart: less artistically in that they popularized an old form, but more socially, in that their distinctly ethnic endeavor played to a more general public.

It is notable that the influence of Harrigan and Hart and of Weber and Fields grew strong *after* each team left vaudeville for the full-length Broadway evening, for the history of the musical in those years features the book show's struggle to purge itself of "variety." Typical of the war between vaudeville and musical comedy was George M. Cohan, who started in variety, promoted himself to Broadway, and wrote shows with so little vaudeville in them that he inadvertently aided the revolution in naturalizing musical comedy. A fascination for character songs and smallish chorus lines suggests that his early successes, such as *Little Johnny Jones* (1904), are the first real Princess shows, beating Herbert's *The Only Girl* and the Princess shows themselves by a decade. Not that *Little Johnny Jones* is conceived for straight-on, no-idylls-permitted storytelling. The adventures of an American jockey falsely accused of throwing the English Derby, it delights in grotesquerie, as in a mysterious comic who wanders in and out of scenes, identifying himself late in the action after a number of exchanges like this one:

> WAITER: Do you feel like a cup of tea, sir?
> COMIC: No, I don't feel like a cup of tea. Do I *look* like a cup of tea?

or this:

> WAITER: Is there anything else I can do, sir?
> COMIC: If there was, you wouldn't be a waiter.

In surprising other ways, however, Cohan did turn around the habits of his time. A fanciful playwright while a conventional songwriter, he put on a strong value on a solid book where his colleagues preferred a solid score. Pacing was his obsession. Keep it going, keep it . . . American: innocent, youthful, ambitious, heedless. Cohan had no need for a Sulu or the Gaiety resorts. Americans were his kind, the men straight-shooting, city-bred dandies, the women gallant, gentle but plucky. If the songs are simple in layout and run thin about the rhymes, they have a very taking directness. No decoration, no ethnic pastiche, no legit voices even in supporting parts—not even a full score, in the earlier titles, if Cohan thought six or seven songs would do it. This was Yankee art, lean and unpainted. Fresh. Critics couldn't understand why the public ignored their irritated reviews and acquired the taste for Cohan. Couldn't they see it?

They saw it plain, and liked it. Cohan has been accused of milking applause through patriotism; more likely, he was celebrating a native revolution in popular art. He didn't Americanize musical comedy; others had begun to do so before him. He completed the job—not by perfecting the form, but reducing it to its essentials. That's what made it fresh.

George M. was also the first legendary personality in the musical, the first person many people knew well for things he said and did. There are biographies of Harrigan and Hart, and of Victor Herbert; but the men themselves don't figure much in theatre lore. Has anyone heard a good story about Ivan Caryll? Or Harry B. Smith? Even Julian Mitchell, for all his historical links, is recalled merely as a quiet gentleman who went into directing because deafness impeded his career as an actor. Weber and Fields were legendary, yes; but they parted nearly eighty years ago, their scripture has faded away, and all we have now are photographs of men mugging in crazy suits.

Cohan is still around. His survivors tell Cohan stories yet, and the tales are an informative treat, starring a figure as generous and multi-talented as he was unforgiving and set in his tastes. Everything with Cohan was a personal matter. The long-lived producing firm of Cohan and Harris let Sam Harris hawk the business end, for George saw the world entirely as loyalty versus betrayal, star turn versus walk-on, slicker versus hick, or "ruben," or "jay." And when Cohan and Harris broke up, it was for personal, not business, reasons; and they stayed friends, ironically, for those same reasons.

Men are what they do. If they're gifted they do show business. Cohan was most gifted of all, in his instinctive distillation of the banal universal into a unique moment—a song admiring the unpretentious name Mary, say, or a few lines of script on the excitement in the word "Broadway" that only an American can register. His most personal gift was his morality, something the musical didn't have till Cohan got hold of it: be honest and fair, be pals with good men and worshipful of women, don't worry about money, cultivate confidence, and take pride in your people. In Cohan's America, this *was* the morality; no wonder he was so well liked. In today's America such an approach is at best corny and at worst politically incorrect, and when the Goodspeed Opera revival of *Little Johnny Jones* was brought to Broadway in 1982 with Donny Osmond as the jockey, theatre critics understood it as their assignment to attack the piece. Though preview audiences had been extremely enthusiastic, the blanket of bad notices closed the show on opening night.

Too bad; too bad for us all. The revival was quite well staged and, with some revision, held up well. There were changes in dramaturgy—the hero no longer had to hold at gunpoint an enraged British mob on the dock at Southampton; he had nothing worse to face down than persnickety porters. There were more numbers, from other Cohan shows. Osmond's hero, clearly, defied authorial tradition, the television star's sweet voice and western openness adding up to a Johnny different from the one Cohan played, a mixture of cheek and Gaelic smarts spilling out of a crooked grin. Still, the experience was authentic Cohan, from the hero's "Hello, everybody!" on his entrance, as he shakes hands with hotel bellboys, and his key line a bit later, "Do you think I'd marry an heiress for her money? What do you take me for, an Englishman?" to his even more pungent line, "There's not much you can say to a loser"—not to mention the huge flag that swooped down on the back of the stage in the finale. In Harrigan and Hart, the Irish were culturally displaced, a clan in a strange land. Cohan assimilated the Irish. His musicals were not pure Yankee: they were symbolic of a time in which the Yankee melting pot yielded a richer stock from its infusion of races. One of the reasons he got such a bad press in his early years is the sociological impact of his shows. They celebrated racial integration; this was a controversial topic in the early 1900s.

Cohan didn't just write and perform musical comedy; he *was* a musical comedy. He believed its tales of guts and gifts winning through to a fluke success, of making a hit on Broadway. After all, he originated them. The self-affirmation that the audience discovered in Cohan, Cohan himself discovered in show biz. In his versatility he had become The Man Who Owns Broadway, even writing himself into a play by that title, though he let Raymond Hitchcock play the part. In 1919, when an actors' strike pulled so many big and little names out of work that virtually every theatre in the nation closed down, Cohan joined the managers, despite the education they had given him, when he was nobody and they owned Broadway, just what management consisted of.

But then Cohan as manager was just and open-handed, a handshaker with a bond, and he took the strike personally. He swore that if the actors won he'd leave the business and run an elevator rather than join their union. To which Eddie Cantor, a strike leader and a Cohan chum, replied, "Somebody better tell Mr. Cohan that to run an elevator he'd *have* to join a union." And Equity hung a sign from its office window: "WANTED— ELEVATOR OPERATOR—GEORGE M. COHAN PREFERRED." Equity won the strike, sat down with management at the bargaining table, and all the actors joined the union. All but one.

Cohan never retired. He made a kind of peace with the new Broadway in the 1930s, playing scripts written by men who replaced him in drama (O'Neill) and the musical (Kaufman-Hart and Rodgers-Hart). And he understood show business too well for the avant garde to correct him absolutely. Rehearsing his penultimate production, *The Return of the Vagabond* (1940), Cohan put on his oldtime three-cornered hat to write, direct, and star. During rehearsals, ingenue Celeste Holm asked him about her "motivation" in a particular scene. The old grads in the cast were convulsed; Cohan was patient. Motivation? "Why not just say, 'Why?'" he asked her. "Why?" has a simple answer: "My dear, you'll find out your motivation on opening night before an audience." The one thespian Cohan regarded as an equal was Noël Coward, comparably actor, writer, director, songwriter—and just as traditional in getting it on.

Cohan's own motivation was clear: he was wild about theatre. He not only spent his entire life in it—literally—but saw it as the boiled-down decoction of life. He was forever confusing the two, commentatively crossing them, as in his occasional character who enters to speak not only lines but stage directions ("He was a man of medium height, say forty years of age . . . As he stepped from the cab and approached the Court Portal, a bellboy appeared and said . . ."); or in the set to *Popularity* (1906), a backstager that uses the real backstage of whatever theatre it plays in; or in the script-like "scenes" he uses in his autobiographical narratives. He actually gave his regards to Broadway, leaving what was to be his death-bed to ride through his old demesne and take in a few minutes of his Hollywood biography, *Yankee Doodle Dandy*. His last words, however, spoke to a personal matter: "Look after Agnes"—Agnes Nolan Cohan, his second wife.

Besides his contributions in aesthetics, Cohan did one extremely crucial favor for musical comedy. He defined the urban, upstart, immigrant, egal-itarian character that was to see it through its golden age. The Cohan musical is a New York show, and that is what musical comedy is: fast town, hip characters, innocents getting wise, applying grit to make it. In their heart of hearts, *Annie* and *42nd Street* are Cohan musicals. The no-tion of an Eddie Cantor or a Bert Lahr as the hero of a book musical is implausible without the prior arrangement of the immigrant upstarts.

The upstarts all came from vaudeville, an international bazaar compared to Broadway's WASP enclave. But one class of graduates vaudeville could not send to the big time: black performers were banned from taking any major part in a white show. However, *In Dahomey* (1903), the first full-length musical written and staged by black talent on Broadway, intro-duced the former vaudeville team of Williams and Walker, a smooth duo playing city con man (George Walker) and lazy rural simpleton (Bert Wil-liams). The personae were traditional, as was the dialect, but otherwise the team laid its own traces. Williams used blackface makeup, standard even for black performers; Walker went on as was. Both were rather good-looking for jesters, Walker cutting a natty figure offstage. Their songs in particular belonged more to popular music in general than to the coon song—and when they included one of these it would be so keenly charac-terized that it would suggest a new genre, or perhaps simply a black en-tailment on a non-racial idea. Thus, their cowritten vaudeville number, "I Don't Like No Cheap Man," uses the dialect, rag accompaniment, and Bill Johnson and Miss Simpson of the white-born coon song yet lacks the whites' ersatz rowdydow. Coming by local color naturally, Williams and Walker don't trouble to paint it; they're dealing more with a certain char-acter and situation: a coon song with the coon cut out of it. A black song, on Johnson's efforts to date Miss Simpson without devastating his wallet, and her efforts to devastate it. Williams and Walker were perfect transi-tional figures, standing halfway between black stage tradition and white. And when Walker was pulled off the boards by the same disease that had incapacitated Tony Hart, Williams made a historic leap into the biggest thing on Broadway, Florenz Ziegfeld's *Follies*. It was the first mixed-cast star presentation in the American theatre.

Ziegfeld did not make Williams a star; he already was one. During the turn-of-the-century Tenderloin race riots that inspired many blacks to resettle in quiet Harlem, white mobs looking for scapegoats would scream, "Let's get Williams and Walker!" Brother, that's fame. Anyway, it appears that Ziegfeld sought Williams out because he had heard that Belasco was negotiating with him. So the importance of Williams's integrating the Broadway musical lies not in any gala success story, but in the influence Williams exercised as a Ziegfeld star, in 1910 and five later editions, including the key one of 1919. The *Follies* were not just big Broadway gifts to city folk, but big road items, national art. And what this very general public saw in Williams was neither offensive white stereotyping nor self-aggrandizing black rebuttal, but a total dismissal of both approaches for something honest, amusing, and artistic. Raceless, it was. "The colored man has never successfully taken off his own humorous characteristics," Williams said, "and the white impersonator often overdoes the matter," to say the least. Williams proposed to ignore the middle era of liberation in which sensitivities are cultivated. He progressed to a true equality in which everybody is ripe for satire. It seems amazing that he brought off something so avant-garde, but apparently his talent was irresistible. As the hapless clown he was moving, as in his mournful theme song, "Nobody" (to his own music):

> When winter comes with snow and sleet,
> And me with hunger and cold feet;
> Who says, "Here's two bits, go and eat"?
> Nobody!

Weber and Fields founded a school of ethnic humor; Williams refounded another one; Cohan assimilated himself. An interesting alternate approach also worked well, but only once, for it was so preposterous and psychologically contradictory that it couldn't be imitated. This was Al Jolson, all of the above on any list: Jewish, black, Irish, German, American, northern city boy, Dixie redneck, ecumenical, local, profane, sacred, satiric, sentimental, winner, loser, lover, fighter. Like Cohan he lives in legend, but unlike Cohan's the backstage sections of Jolson's legend are seedy. Onstage he was almost disreputably warm, exhorting the public, loving and thrilling them, so crazed to please that he'd break into a dance step during an already wildly demonstrative routine, as if every piece of him had to be going at once. And, yes, the crowd responded to Jolson as to no other. But offstage, where only his colleagues could see, he was a megalomaniac who changed a word in every lyric he sang, thereby "earning" byline credit and royalties; who feared rivals like Eddie Cantor as a witch fears water in Oz; who reportedly maintained the most rapacious audition couch in show biz; who, in his prime, had anyone who showed a glimmer of talent fired out of his shows. Few performers so popular onstage were so hated off it.

It's all in the vantage. A famous story has Jolson rising from his seat in the auditorium to sing "Liza" to his wife Ruby Keeler in *Show Girl.* The received interpretation is: Keeler, not the world's most confident performer, is flustered, and husband Al, to cheer her on, sang to her to rouse the spectators into thinking they were in on a hit—wow! spontaneous Jolson! Try another reading: Keeler is nervous not in general but because husband Al has been driving her crazy with his unemployment panic—he is between shows, and, as always, acts as if he'll never be hired again. Rather than let her fill *her* spotlight in *her* show, he jumps uninvited into her big number, leaving her to smile and tap it away as best she can.

Spontaneous Jolson!: but there was no other kind. It is demonstrably true that Americans are impressed by performers who are willing to wreck themselves for applause; the work ethic promises rewards for hard labor. Jolson labored. Buffs argued his merits with Cantorites, and critics picked up the debate. However, all had to agree that in terms of sheer energy Jolson took the prize. He had precision and stamina: precision to decorate the songs with pantomime and stamina to pour them out in a flood. Jolson sang as if his songs could stop a war. He threw a whole person into his numbers, committed, ironic, overthrowing the vaudeville tradition of presenting songs without overt emotional involvement. Nora Bayes presided over a tune; Jolson occupied it. In "Row, Row, Row" he did row. The effort winded him, but still he sang, and pulled, and pulled, and even thought to pluck a splinter out of his pants (the precision). In "April Showers" he mesmerized himself into visualizing the transcendent splendor of the green world (the commitment). In "Where Did Robinson Crusoe Go with Friday on Saturday Night?" he had to chuckle at the way of the world (the irony), for Crusoe is surrounded by "wild men in cannibal trimmin' "—and where there are wild men, of course, "there must be wild women." The voice was not remarkable. The delivery was—the hysteria, really: for Jolson would be adored or he would be nothing. So, for stamina, he would on occasion literally dismiss his supporting cast, with the audience's "approval," and hold forth in concert till the public was as exhausted as he. And if he spotted a single person leaving the theatre before Jolson left the stage, he wouldn't sleep that night.

His character is hard to place. Part comic, part singer, he never played anything as written and slid in and out of plots with reference to whatever was on his mind. He was colloquial, sensual, a joker, a preacher. In blackface makeup, he would sing of mule and mammy, then suddenly throw off a joke in Yiddish that most of his audience couldn't catch. The very idea of a Jewish émigré from Russia singing "Down Where the Swanee River Flows," "I'm All Bound Round with the Mason-Dixon Line," "Coal Black Mammy," or "Rock-a-Bye Your Baby with a Dixie Melody" is gruesome—and Jolson didn't just sing them, remember. He exalted them. Yet, sure as he was of a solid song, he distrusted the musical, eyeing his colleagues with suspicion, browbeating writers, ignoring directors, and viewing each work as the sabotage of his one-man show. By the late 1910s, Jolson was the king of a hybrid form crossing extravaganza's incoherent structure with burlesque's gimcrack fun. The Shuberts paid for it, but no one made it: a group of people made musicals for Jolson and Jolson unmade them. There was one influential innovation in his form, a runway (inspired by the Kabuki-style *hanamichi* which Max Reinhardt had introduced to New York in *Sumurun* in 1911) that allowed Jolson to go forth and seek his public cheek to cheek, thereby combining the hugeness of a big Broadway house with the intimacy of his personal address. It must have been quite some adventure for Jolson's admirers. Others found it too much of a good sing. And the shows themselves, built as they were around Jolson and further amplified by the star through Performers' Rule as the run progressed, were mere launching pads.

In *Robinson Crusoe, Jr.* (1916) Jolson was a chauffeur who becomes Friday in his employer's dream. In *Sinbad* (1918) Jolson was a janitor who travels the world for reasons never made clear. In *Bombo* (1921) Jolson was a deckhand on Christopher Columbus's ship. All three had story scores by Sigmund Romberg and Harold Atteridge, but you'd never know it from the interpolated concerts Jolson would give. *Robinson Crusoe, Jr.* at least threw in a number related to the subject in "Where Did Robinson Crusoe Go with Friday on Saturday Night?." But the exotic *Sinbad* featured such homey selections as "Why Do They Take the Night Boat to Albany?," "Hello Central, Give Me No-Man's Land," "I'll Say She Is," "Swanee," and "You Ain't Heard Nothin' Yet," the last a spinoff of Jolson's habitual promise to his public. (He once uttered it strutting onstage in a benefit gala—just after Enrico Caruso had finished singing.) *Bombo* was so dizzy it thought nothing of having one of Columbus's seamen sing "California, Here I Come." You know which one.

Speaking artistically, Jolson gave nothing to the musical; he took from it. Harrigan and Hart gave it realism. Weber and Fields gave it a screwball innocence it has been using for eighty years. George M. Cohan gave it ethics, a sense of structure, and a new approach to musical composition. Bert Williams gave it a kind of pathetic comedy that previously had been the province of the silent clowns of pantomime and showed how it might be sung. But Jolson? All he had to give was ego, and ego cannot share. Not till he came to California to help inaugurate the movie musical was he forced to accommodate the demands of written, fixed art.

Still, in his day he was Broadway's biggest Baby, perhaps the last defender of the performer's autocracy. And speaking sociologically, like Harrigan and Hart, Weber and Fields, Cohan, and Williams, Jolson forced the issue of social integration onto the culture through the musical. From now on, the musical would be as cosmopolitan, as racy, as venturesome—literally, as sophisticated—as New York is itself.

3

The Great Glorifier

The producer is the least important element in musical comedy production. He raises money, sees to the logistics of rehearsals, tryouts, and the run, hires and fires. He has opinions, and might exercise them to the point of improving or marring a piece. Still, he does not touch it the way its authors, stagers, and performers do.

One doesn't speak of many musicals as having "the style of" a given producer. There are Gershwin shows, or Rodgers-Hart shows; or Merman or Astaire shows; or Robbins or De Mille shows. *Lady in the Dark* might be seen as a Gertrude Lawrence show, or a Kurt Weill show, or a Moss Hart show, or a Hassard Short show, depending on what aspect of its production is under scrutiny. But one would hardly speak of it as a Sam H. Harris show, though Harris was one of the best-known producers in the musical, gathering in such historical points as the Cohan revolution (*Little Johnny Jones*), the Princess influence (*Going Up*), the smart revue (the *Music Box Revues*), and political satire (*Of Thee I Sing, I'd Rather Be Right*).

One producer, however, is strongly identified as an artistic creator: Florenz Ziegfeld. He had a style, no question. And its elements influenced the repertory so fully that reverberations are still being felt. The very word *"Follies"* conveys a sense of era, a kind of show, an opinion about décor and women's looks, and even an attitude toward life that the word did not have before Ziegfeld seized it. It's true, of course, that few producers worked as hard to put their name before the public. (One worked harder, Billy Rose.) Ziegfeld's name not only arose in PR stunts and at the head of big-news productions but gripped his titles as a clamp wherever those titles appeared, even on the labels of recordings. Florenz Ziegfeld, Jr., did not just present. He presented *a Florenz Ziegfeld, Jr. production.*

His lifetime production, the *Follies,* is his most obvious contribution, for in devising a unique and extremely popular revue format, Ziegfeld gave vaudeville a venue of esteem next to rather than within the musical. While Victor Herbert was purging the musical of vaudeville numbers, while George M. Cohan was purging it of storyless comics, while Henry Blossom was purging it of go-nowhere lines, Ziegfeld gave their victims a place to land and a workshop for their traditions. The *Follies* were by no means the first American revues—the minstrel show preceded them by some seventy-five years. However, all revues before Ziegfeld were little better than vaudeville with a title. The *Follies* gave revue dignity and latitude. They weren't vaudeville's exile, but vaudeville's apotheosis.

Chicago-born, Ziegfeld dismayed his cultivated German émigré parents by getting involved in show business's seamy edges, in Buffalo Bill's Wild West Show and various carnival midways. His first notable coup was the promotion of "the modern Hercules," Sandow. Ziegfeld thought up spectacular tricks for Sandow to pull off, but he also applied the velvet touch in leading society women backstage to feel Sandow's muscles. Without Ziegfeld, Sandow was an imposing hunk; under Ziegfeld's care he became, for those Who Counted, Collectable. A more appropriate attraction for Ziegfeld, in the light of his later endeavors, was Anna Held, a star of European music halls whom Ziegfeld saw in London. Other producers might lure, bribe, or impress a potential client. Penniless and unknown, Ziegfeld courted Held, literally: she was to become his first wife. A more exacting theatre would have found her wanting, for her soprano was thin, her line reading spiritless, and her dancing an oblique walk. But she was something to see, with huge eyes and the tiniest waist in the West. She was a toy woman; it was past closing time in the toyshop, and she had come out to play.

Sandow had been the first Florenz Ziegfeld, Jr., production, but Held was the key one, pivotal, regenerative, doctrinal. Sandow was a glamorized freak turn, a "silent act" like those that opened vaudeville bills, one with the acrobats and animals. Held was the central figure in Ziegfeld's experiments in form. She was not The Ziegfeld Girl—rather, that would be Marilyn Miller, fair, confident, and plumb American. But Ziegfeldian touches pressed Held's first years in America. There was, first, the PR notoriety anent Held's milk baths (which Ziegfeld fabricated) and the theft of her jewelry case (which Ziegfeld arranged). Or consider the astonishingly lengthy and suspenseful buildup to Held's entrance in *Mam'selle Napoleon* (1903), a choral piece replete with rave reviews:

Salvos greet in every tier.
Brava! Brava! Brava! Brava!
Clamoring that she appear.
Brava! Brava! Brava! Brava!
Cries of Brava! rent the hall.
Brava! Brava! Brava! Brava!
There's another curtain call!
Brava! Brava! Brava!

The drum-rolling, chorus-carolling, audience-baiting star entrance is a Ziegfeld invention; it cannot be found in scores for shows predating *Mam'selle Napoleon.* Yes, the star entrance qua se was ancient by then. But Ziegfeld's orchestration of these elements was innovative. Similarly Ziegfeldian is the use of a song's topic as the concept for its staging. In *The Parisian Model* (1906), there is a simple application of this in "A Gown for Each Hour of the Day," in which Held popped in and out in half-a-dozen sumptuous dresses. A defter application, in the form of a pun, is found in "I'd Like To See a Little More of You," by itself a suitor's plea for time, but staged as a hot flash: artist's models disrobed behind easels, simulating nudity. (They were dressed; but the easels hid the clothed parts and stroked the imagination.) *

Another Ziegfeldian quality already operative in the Anna Held days is his complete lack of engagement with the process of composition. To Ziegfeld the musical was staging, décor, and performers, whether comic opera, musical comedy, or revue. Historians ask, "Who wrote the songs?" Ziegfeld asked, "Who will put them over, and let me see the dress against the backdrop." As we shall see, Ziegfeld worked at one time or another with virtually all of the top-rank composers and lyricists and mounted some highly well-written shows, including the single greatest American musical, *Show Boat.* So he must have had a taste for good writing—just no interest in it. His insistent use of the alcoholic hack William Anthony McGuire produced a series of incoherent books which destroyed shows with scores by Romberg, Gershwin, Rodgers and Hart, and Vincent Youmans. Even when Ziegfeld employed the best, or his dependable company men, the chaos he would radiate like a vain god at a festival utterly defeated them.

You're a songwriter. Ziegfeld shows you a set design, a field of white

---

* This conceptual staging caught on immediately, and hit its apex in the big Busby Berkeley numbers in the Warner Brothers backstagers of the 1930s. A song called "The Words Are in My Heart" inspires a Piano Number: fifty girls in white playing fifty dancing white pianos against a black background. Or "All's Fair in Love and War" shows courtship and sex war, the boys and girls on gigantic rockers, then hitting the trenches for battle, the women fighting with spray-top perfume bottles.

roses attended by a pair of bees. Ziegfeld wants a song to go with the set, and you oblige with "Summer's First Roses," a nostalgic ballad with a bounce so The Girls can wander through the scene in rose costumes. But when you hand it in, Ziegfeld announces that he has ordered bee costumes for The Girls. He needs a Bee Number. Back to the piano, and voilà!: "A Bee Gets Busy in the Springtime," a slightly screwy gavotte. You hand it in, and Ziegfeld is delighted with it—just the thing for a slightly screwy comic he has just hired, on the advice of house lyricist, talent scout, and idea man Gene Buck. "What about the flower set?" you ask. "A song for the flower set?" Oh, forget it—Ziegfeld never liked that set, anyway. But he does need a song for a Venetian tableau, with The Girls floating through on gondolas. You write a barcarolle, "The Gondola Glide." Ziegfeld loves it; but where can he use it? "The Venetian Number," you stammer. What Venetian number? Oh, that's out. Ziegfeld didn't like the lighting. But the dancing star needs a tap number. Fresh out of tunes, you speed up "Summer's First Roses" and put new lyrics to it as "Travelin' Toes." It works beautifully. As you play it over one last time, five pages' worth of telegram arrive from Ziegfeld, whose only message is that the dancer has left the show. Late that night the phone rings you awake; it's Ziegfeld, with another idea, a Sports Number, with The Girls coming in and out attired for tennis, polo, and so on. Quick, a sports song. "The Gondola Glide" becomes "Pour le Sport"—but now Ziegfeld wants to do it in front of a meadow set, with The Girls dressed as . . . Do we still have the bee suits? "No," says Buck. "We sold them to the Shuberts." Flowers, then. Roses. Ziegfeld asks you if you have something for a Rose Number.

Typically, then *Mam'selle Napoleon, The Parisian Model,* and Ziegfeld's other Held shows are horribly mediocre as works, despite the constant novelty of French phrases (sometimes a whole verse of a song) so the Polish Held could radiate her Gallic élan. *Mam'selle Napoleon,* drawn from a French musical with wholly new music by Gustav Luders, is worse than mediocre; it celebrates convention on the cult level. Of course a Luders score would have its animal fable, but in this one Held sings *two,* "The Lion and the Mouse" and "The Cockatoo and the Chimpanzee." And the pastiche number, "The Language of Love," is perhaps the worst of its kind, with lame looks at courtship in Tyrolean yodel, Japanese wicki-wacki, and a Spanish waltz. Even Held couldn't make this kind of thing fun.

Yet Ziegfeld was careful in production, reckless about cost but nonetheless painstaking in details of costume and dance. A gambler, a spendthrift, a womanizer, and a show-off, Ziegfeld should have been simply a money-raiser, maybe, or a designer. How can someone so oblivious to the intent of creation be so successful a showman? Yet he was *the* showman, at least partly because he drummed it into the nation's ears that Ziegfeld was the best: so all the best talents wanted to work for Ziegfeld. Catch-22.

Talent in profusion was one of the special qualities of the *Follies*. Before Ziegfeld, one or two stars were the maximum. Ziegfeld observed the practice in his Held musicals, but broke ground with the *Follies,* stuffing four or five star performers, his incredible Girls, the stupendous designs of Joseph Urban, and a score by Irving Berlin and Victor Herbert among others into one evening. The *Follies* started small, however, and were only overseen, not entirely devised, by Ziegfeld. The year is 1907. The idea is Held's—copy the Parisian style of revue, with its elaborate décor, smart tone, top-class comedians, and showgirls. The title is Harry B. Smith's—borrowed from his newspaper feature, "The Follies of the Day." The staging is Julian Mitchell's—the expert of extravaganza here converting to a different kind of spectacle, one grander in line and body language yet more intimate in overall appeal.

Even the hiring and firing was not Ziegfeld's, but Marc Klaw and Abe Erlanger's. These Syndicate producers engaged Ziegfeld to produce a revue in the huge nightclubby loft atop the New York Theatre, and the results were so promising that the show was moved to a legit theatre on street level. Immediately, the profits fell, proving that Ziegfeld would have to wean his public on the new idea of full-price, evening-length vaudeville that was at least as entertaining as a book show. *The Follies of 1907* was succeeded by *Follies* in 1908, 1909, and 1910, each edition giving Ziegfeld a little more practice room. Who should occupy the star parts? Singers? Dancers? Anna Held? Must the hoofing chorus look as sensational as The Girls? Will an evening of acts hold together on sheer energy, or should there be an overriding theme? What kind of comedy, who writes the songs, how long is enough?

By 1915 the tinkering was over. The 1910 edition introduced the most intriguing Ziegfeld star, Fanny Brice. The 1911 edition established a new and permanent title: *The Ziegfeld Follies*. The 1913 edition took over the New Amsterdam Theatre, the choicest house on Broadway. The 1915 edition introduced Joseph Urban, the Austrian designer whose bold color schemes and stylistic approaches, lit with advanced Continental technology, made the *Follies* the best-looking show in town. Where the early *Follies* counted two or three star turns, 1915 disclosed Bert Williams, Ed Wynn, W. C. Fields, Leon Errol, Ina Claire, Ann Pennington, and Mae Murray. 1917 was even more impressive, with Fanny Brice, Eddie Cantor, Will Rogers, and Lilyan Tashman joining Pennington and Fields. Throughout the series, from 1907 to 1931, there was billing for only one star: Florenz Ziegfeld, Jr.

No one seems to have known how the show worked. Journalists assessing the Ziegfeld Touch would dance around the famous good Ziegfeld taste but never land on anything concrete; even Gilbert Seldes, a pioneer in the serious appreciation of pop art, wrote an article on Ziegfeld without saying a single thing about him. Yet, once he got his bearings, Ziegfeld kept his *Follies* trimmed on very certain lines. These were, roughly: (1) Sex is suave, (2) Song and dance may be competent, but comedy must be unique, (3) Tap is nice but ballet is swank, and (4) A show is for looking, and one had better see sights. Of a sort, Ziegfeld created the American revue, because the strong conceptual architecture of an *As Thousands Cheer* or a *Call Me Mister*, the pride in the look of *The Band Wagon,* and the cut of talent involved in *At Home Abroad* are Ziegfeld's legacy.

Most Ziegfeldian of all, of course, were The Girls. This was the most primitive element in the American musical. The first shows in the era of *The Black Crook* enjoyed sensations for the dancers' limb-revealing tights, and the British actor-manager Lydia Thompson, of the same era, won renown for her burlesques with nearly all-women casts—trouser parts, pastel tights, kick lines, the whole peacherine socko. Theatre was notorious, for a roughhouse audience. Actors, too, were rough: Thompson publicly horsewhipped and then, onstage, sang to ridicule the editor of the *Chicago Times* who dared to arraign the "immorality" of her art. Few women who minded what was said of them would be seen in a theatre of any kind. Actresses were prostitutes, to general belief: men went to the theatre to look over the market. But Tony Pastor's explicitly bourgeois approach to vaudeville in the 1880s and the institution of "ladies' nights" tamed the public, integrated it sexually. Ziegfeld helped, with his society women calibrating the symmetry of Sandow. By the time the *Follies* was inaugurated in 1907, theatregoers were no longer mostly men gentlemanly agreed on the use of the stage as an arena of lubricious agenda.

Then why retain The Girls? It is one of the musical's unanswered questions. Ziegfeld's Girls were the best, to be sure—at The Walk, back hard and breasts thrust forward; with The Look, into an imaginary mirror, content; in The Dress, skimpy at the flesh but detailed in headdress or cape. The numbers that framed them might look silly today, with some mouthy tenor paying out a theme song such as "A Pretty Girl Is Like a Melody" or "The Girl of My Dreams" and the orchestra simply restating the tune while The Girls had their parade down a staircase. But Ziegfeld exercised that famous taste; and beauty does not lie.

"Ziegfeld can dramatize girls the way no other producer can," wrote critic George Jean Nathan. "He can take a various assortment of them, most of whom naturally or in other hands wouldn't be worth a second glance, and with that peculiar cunning of his convert them into what appear to be lovely and glamorous creatures," It wasn't that Ziegfeld had better taste than other producers, Nathan concluded, but that only he knew how to bend the tricks of stagecraft to "create the illusion of feminine beauty even where beauty isn't." The Girls, then, were neither like a melody nor of dreams; Ziegfeld played the melody, spun the dreams.

The Girls, in fact, were human; oddly, it seems that Ziegfeld had been hoping they wouldn't be. The *Follies,* he advertised, were by way of "glorifying the American girl," and a Ziegfeld Girl was a Chinese box of tropes: a historical remnant, a reconstruction of same, an ideograph, a proper noun, a decoration. When Ziegfeld wasn't looking, however, they were something else: people. If the *Florodora* Girls were a shock for their bad marriages and indiscretions, the Ziegfeld Girls were *expected* to marry cads and make gossip. Will Rogers, playing his lariat, would explain to the audience that half the showgirls would mysteriously disappear as the *Follies* toured the nation after the summer-fall run in New York. "It seems they're all marrying millionaires," says Rogers. He throws out a whistle noose, pulls it into a Chippewa shank, and drops it loose with a nod. "But . . . they generally catch up with us again a few weeks later."

Ziegfeld hoped his Girls would stay out of the papers, yet he was purveying a sexual tease that was bound to encourage stage-door corruption. Ziegfeld displayed his Girls as a pieman might his ware—who was Ziegfeld then to despair of sordid sequellae? He himself dipped into the stock. After all, it was his taste, his truth of beauty that he was glorifying. With access to so many champion examples of his type, what man would deny himself? Ziegfeld planned for discretion in these matters, but while he married women of poise, some of his personal favorites among The Girls had, shall we say, extra pepper. Let one example suffice: Lillian Lorraine.

Lorraine was the best known of Ziegfeld's showgirls, the most beautiful perhaps and the most reckless. She was born to nothing in San Francisco in 1890, named Eulallean de Jacques, rented to her first sexual partner by her father when she was barely nubile, and grew up into a breathtakingly voluptuous woman who destroyed Ziegfeld's first marriage, made her debut in *The Follies of 1909* high in the air in a little biplane while down on the stage the chorus sang "Up, Up in My Aeroplane" and girls costumed as flying machines sashayed here and there, went through jewelry as others do cigarettes, dominated the fastest parties (at times in the nude), got mixed up with the basest men available, and caroused her fame into a shambles of alcoholic poverty. Lorraine closed her public career, years after Ziegfeld despaired of saving her, at the reopening of the Ziegfeld Theatre in 1933 (as a movie house). All the Ziegfeld veterans on hand were invited up to the stage to take a bow and do a turn; Lorraine's was to be "By the Light of the Silvery Moon," her old *Follies* number. But, came the vamp, Lorraine could not utter a sound. All she produced were tears.

It seems churlish to dwell on these women's misfortunes, but it is relevant to any study of the Ziegfeld style, for while he did much to purge the chorus line of its smutty hangover from the Lydia Thompson days, he could not contain the steamy atmosphere in the end. Because he designed it. The very act of "glorifying" women in the near-nude is, however tastefully handled, a whetting of humankind's Dionysian appetite. Today, a reenaction of the Ziegfeldian Girl loitering in her amazing sequins is a wild card, a face without eyes. The Stephen Sondheim musical *Follies,* an epic about who we were and what we've become, had only to raise its curtain on a Girl posed on a rubbled stage in darkness to ghostly music to transport us back to Ziegfeld's time with the question, "What was it for?" And the show's title tells us.

For all the weight Ziegfeld put on The Girls, few of them were promoted to the front lines, though many of them went on to a form of greatness in Hollywood. The true *Follies* stars were the singer-comedians, the names that resonate today. There was Nora Bayes, who helped kick off the first two *Follies,* thereby proving the revue's close association with vaudeville (and putting a kink in the career of Sophie Tucker, who was so good that Bayes had her fired). There were Bert Williams, Fanny Brice, Eddie Cantor, the team of Gus Van and Joe Schenck, or Marilyn Miller (mainly a dancer, but she did everything at all times). Others were strictly comedians, like W. C. Fields and Will Rogers, or strictly singers, like Ruth Etting. Ziegfeld seemed to prize especially those who could rise to a multiple occasion—which is what the *Follies* in effect was, the revue solid in all its parts.* Take *The Ziegfeld Follies of 1919,* generally cited as one of the best of the series. The name talent took in Miller, Cantor, Williams, and Van and Schenck. All, except Miller, had their variety spots, basically open turns in which they could pull out old standbys and any new items as fancy prompted. This is vaudeville at its essence: you're alone on stage with nothing but your material and nerve. As in vaudeville, 1919's score was a grabbag, mostly by Ziegfeld's house songwriters Dave Stamper and Gene Buck (plus a "Circus Ballet" for Miller by Victor Herbert) but including numerous contributions, more and more as the New York run and the tour went on. Naturally, there were the plain-old dressy-tenor-and-showgirl numbers—this is the *Follies* in which John Steel sang Berlin's "A

---

* Strangely, Ziegfeld seems to have had a distaste for comedy; some of his jesters made the *Follies* not on Ziegfeld's hunch but on Gene Buck's, followed by Buck's protection when Ziegfeld wanted to fire them in rehearsals. He didn't understand comedy till he heard the public roar.

Pretty Girl Is Like a Melody," then ripped into a medley of familiar classical melodies as The Girls came in in appropriate costumes. However, certain topics, such as Prohibition and minstrelsy, ran through the show in sketches, song lyrics, and dances; and as always Urban designed by scheme.

This revue, then, is a *matched* patchwork, most Ziegfeldian in the episodes which called all the *Follies* forces into play—stars, assistants, chorus, and Girls. The first-act finale, a miniature minstrel show, involved everyone, with Cantor and Williams as the end men, a harmony quartet of Eddie Dowling, Steel, and Van and Schenck, and Miller dancing to Berlin's "Mandy," the whole thing situated on a stage-wide stairway and colored in pink, silver, and white. (The set must have stuck in some memories: the minstrel reconstructions in MGM musicals favor the tiered look.) Later, in Act II, Dowling as Father Time introduced a Prohibition Number against an envisioning of the Manhattan skyline draped in mourning. Songs, dances, and a sketch entitled "A Saloon of the Future" commented on the national disaster as bartender Cantor offered his patrons children's drinks and the showgirls glided in—yes!—as lemonade, juice, pop, and such. Miller topped it off with tap in Berlin's "A Syncopated Cocktail."

If the *Follies* specialty was the wild, versatile comic, then Fanny Brice is the key *Follies* star. Bert Williams appeared in more of them than she did, Ann Pennington and W. C. Fields in as many, and it is worth remarking that when Ziegfeld made an all-out effort with the 1927 *Follies,* knowing that the series had lost its fix on contemporaneity, he built it around Eddie Cantor, one of the few performers with energy enough to carry a three-hour show via almost nonstop singing, dancing, mugging, cringing, and pranking.

Yet it was Brice whom Ziegfeld most meticulously plucked from obscurity, nurtured, and gave to stardom. After all, Williams was already famous before he joined the *Follies,* Pennington went to work for the competition (George White took her with him when he left the *Follies* to organize the *Scandals*), Fields is better known for his movie work (and he too went on to the *Scandals;* the *Vanities* as well), and Cantor was so successful in his annual Goldwyn musicals, in the early years of the talkies, that his history gets fragmented. But Brice, who also worked for other revue producers while the *Follies* was still going, was the most Ziegfeldian of them all, the most drastic, the most versatile. She was old, old *Follies*— she joined the lineup in 1910—and, when the Shuberts attempted to revive the *Follies* after Ziegfeld's death, using his widow's name as an affidavit, it was Brice whom they turned to for authenticity. "I could never write the story of my life," she once said, "without half of it being Ziegfeld."

Brice is bigger than Ziegfeld. She is all show biz, from vaudeville to Broadway, thence to film and radio and at last into "documented" legend as the subject of the Barbra Streisand vehicle *Funny Girl*. She projected a contradictory personality, now a hoyden, next a hooker, then a hausfrau. She plied the heaviest Jewish accent in the business and depended far more than Jolson or Cantor on Jewish content in her songs—think of "Second Hand Rose" or "Rose of Washington Square." Yet she could drop it in a torch song, spirit away the Jewish Brice and turn into a stranger you knew intimately. In the 1921 *Follies*, she appeared alone in shabby finery before Urban's stunning view of Paris at night. The vantage is that of the Seine embankment under the arch of a bridge: gray and brown stone and, beyond the arch, the yellow-white glow of the Eiffel Tower looming over the roofs and spires of the Left Bank. Even Urban's evocation cannot make a French tart of Second Hand Rose.

But Brice can. "Costs me a lot, but there's one thing that I've got . . ." The tune is tawdry, the lyrics are bathetic, and the situation (of the woman we learn nothing about except that she's wild for her no-good lover) is *usé*. Kurt Weill and Bertolt Brecht, in "Surabaya Jonny," could animate this genre of song through the force of their originality. Brice has much less to work with, and the creepy violin figure of the introduction sounds more comic than plaintive. Yet Brice made the song tell, by the force of *her* originality. She was the first torch singer to act the lyrics line by line, the way actors play character, as opposed to the usual torch approach of acting the idea of the song as a whole, the way vaudevillians play themselves. By rules of composition the song has no right to be moving, but Brice is unnervingly complete in it; it's as if the sound had a heartbeat, veins, blood. He cheats her, exploits her, beats her, yet she can't pull away: she knows she'd only return on her knees. As she begins the second chorus, she falls behind the orchestra, runs out of voice, as if "Oh, my man I love him so" were too bitter a statement to make—as if singing the lyrics were to confront the story they tell. Yet she rallies at the end, strong in sorrow, archetypally womanly and self-dramatizing at once. "Just being miserable gives her a thrill," runs another of her torch songs, "When a Woman Loves a Man."

Symbolistic Brice, individual Brice, tragic and comic Brice. She was not only bigger than Ziegfeld, but bigger than the size of American entertainment. She overpowered everything she was in, even her follow-up to Jolson's *The Jazz Singer, My Man* (1928). Warner Brothers built the film entirely around Brice, giving her all the advantages of the primitive, unreasonable, gloriously candid early talkie. Yet Brice was too paradoxical a personality to succeed in film, even a candid one. When she did well on radio, it was for one piece of herself, as the Baby Snooks who sneers, coos, whines, and otherwise bedevils the adult world. It's typical of what Ziegfeld did for Broadway that the only format able successfully to take all that Brice could give was the *Follies.* She was so rich that Hollywood couldn't make money on her. She puzzled the national audience that reveled in Jolson. What was she, a romantic clown?

That's just what she was: the last of the "serio-comics." This old show biz term used to refer to the repertory of songs not specifically ballads—comic songs, rhythm numbers, novelties, what have you. By extension, the term came to cover women who sang these songs, any woman who wasn't by looks and tone limited to playing heroines. Serio-comics were game ingenues, nutty best friends, interested widows, prim teachers, villains: versatile as a rule. Their songs took them into a wider range than a heroine's usually did, and the era of story songs was their golden age. Let Lillian Russell stick to her Offenbach and Gilbert and Sullivan and ragtime ballads. Nora Bayes, queen of serio-comics, spanned a much broader range—and Brice pushed that range to its extremes. The very term "serio-comic" was dying by the time Brice came along, for the growing characterological integration of the musical was beginning to ask more of its heroines, more in the way of what the serio-comics used to do. Brice would never be a heroine in a musical till *Funny Girl* told her story, but she could do everything else so well that by her example versatility became something everyone should shoot for. Yet, ironically, what could be more limited than a romantic clown?

Some things limit as they liberate. As the most New York of personalities, Brice was free to express herself in the sophisticated entertainment New Yorkers had developed. But, out of the parish, Brice mystified regional America's villager mentality. No wonder, then, that she rose in the *Follies,* most New Yorker of musicals, a melting pot that took in Bert Williams and Will Rogers, plumed itself on beauty and money, and dictated town topics to the nation. Brice held the *Follies'* center as the element in the pot that would not melt: she was already distilled. Even Bert Williams was not as distinctive. In 1919's big minstrel number, he would be just another blackface specialist. Brice stood alone with her anomalies of type, a Rose growing in a place like Washington Square. Anything she touched grew smaller: she was that large. Even an old-line institution like the *Florodora* Girls slipped into Brice's pocket when she took it on, in the 1920 *Follies,* in "I Was a Florodora Baby" (in honor of the Shubert revival of the old Gaiety warhorse, still running when the *Follies* opened). It seems that Brice was the only one of the sextet who didn't make the most of their notoriety. Gaiety Girls conventionally made wild marriages, so "Five darn fools got married for money," Brice tells us. But *"I got married for love!,"* the voice wry with the pathos of human frailty. Twenty years after, the Girls have finally become human.

Ziegfeld never put Brice into a book show—too much of a challenge, perhaps. Given the strait patterns for heroines, Ziegfeld would have had to invent a new compositional approach to fit Brice into a story—and if composition was the least important facet of a Ziegfeld show, challenge was downright wasteful. Why strive when the talent was ready for the picking—Held, Miller, Cantor, Errol, Durante for personality, Urban for design, and The Girls for the rest? On the few occasions when Ziegfeld produced a work by authors rather than a vehicle for performers, he felt hemmed in, as with Noël Coward's *Bitter Sweet* (1929), which came over from London fully written and escorted by an author defiant of Ziegfeld tampering.

Rio Rita (1927) was the kind of show Ziegfeld could really *produce,* a big nothing made experiential by Urban's panoramas, by Albertina Rasch's choreography, by shtick comedy, by a Tune here and there. A notable moment in a notable musical is that wherein character and music fuse so consequentially that one is swept into the piece willing or not—when Marietta sails her reckless high notes over the "Neapolitan Street Song," or when the Fiddler plays a last few notes for the emigrating Tevye, or when Egerman takes Desirée in his arms to the swelling rhapsody of "Send in the Clowns." A notable moment in *Rio Rita* was the Shawl Number, a set-changer in which a singer delivers a song so putrid it doesn't even bother to rhyme where it's supposed to ("shawl" and "dull") while a mixed chorus glides now here, now there till the next set is ready and the restatement of the song's main strain can come in just as the curtain flies up to expose the full stage, dressed and posing. ¡Caramba!

Yet *Rio Rita* and comparable monstrosities cannot be called typical Ziegfeld shows, because there were none. *Sally, Whoopee, The Three Musketeers,* and *Show Boat* are all key Ziegfeld entries, all identified with the Touch; yet *Sally* is Cinderella derived from Gaiety-Princess formulae, *Whoopee* a snazzy comedy musical, *The Three Musketeers* do-or-die operetta with a solid story score; and *Show Boat* one of a kind. They have nothing in common. There is no typical Ziegfeld show because Ziegfeld was not a tutor to material, not a benefactor of the *literature* of American popular art. He was concerned with the adventure of having a hit—marketing special personalities, calling for numbos, planning, junking, and replanning the décor, and spending the money. This was the age when the notable musicals were notable fun, and Ziegfeld had amazing abilities in organizing that fun. He was slick. Yet he produced *Show Boat* despite his

certain fear that it would bring respect without profit. *Show Boat* promised to end Ziegfeld's age, to restructure the Broadway musical from Performers' Rule to Authors'. Why did Kern and Hammerstein offer Ziegfeld
first dibs on it? Why did Ziegfeld produce it? Because he spent the money?
No: because this Broadway Baby had show biz genius. Ziegfeld spent more
than money: he spent ideas. The *Follies*, Brice, Cantor, Rogers, Williams,
Fields, Miller—these were Ziegfeld innovations, or properties, or developments, and each of them was not the best of a kind, but the example
without kind, unique. It makes sense that Ziegfeld produced *Whoopee*, for
it called for keen show biz sensibility. *The Three Musketeers*, too, fits in:
for that was show biz sensibility admiring a noble strain in pop theatre.
But *Show Boat* also fits in: that was Ziegfeld's nervy interest in the unique.

Ziegfeld's most immediate effect was the proliferation of revue, at first
in imitation of the *Follies*, later in reaction against their utter hugeness.
Jake Shubert ran the annual *Passing Shows* at the Winter Garden starting
in 1912, George White launched his *Scandals* in 1919, Earl Carroll instituted the *Vanities* in 1923. All three series were successful, show by show:
but none really rivaled the *Follies*. The *Passing Shows* had too much oldtime burlesque in them; where the *Follies* were sumptuous and recherché,
these were dated and tuneless. Carroll's shows were smutty, lacking Ziegfeld's finesse; and his scores were as vapid as those in *The Passing Show*.
White came off best. The *Scandals* were light and fast, with a lot of fine
hoofing and belting, and George Gershwin composed five of the editions,
De Sylva, Brown and Henderson succeeding him on four. Of big variety,
the choice events were the four *Music Box Revues*, 1921 to 1924. These
were the most like the *Follies* in their elegance and dash. Ziegfeld was
worldly, and his creation was worldly. The *Vanities* and the *Passing Shows*
were smarmy and the *Scandals* were snazzy.

Still, it was the *Scandals* that most irritated and threatened Ziegfeld, for
they became better and better just when the *Follies* seemed to be drained
of juice. It was probably the excellence of the 1926 *Scandals*, the one with
"The Birth of the Blues," "Black Bottom," and "Lucky Day," that
prompted Ziegfeld to make an all-out effort on the 1927 *Follies*. Sometime
before that, he had offered White two thousand dollars a week to return
to the fold. White countered by offering Ziegfeld three thousand dollars a
week if he and Billie Burke would join the *Scandals*.

There was room for just so many big revues. John Murray Anderson
devised intimate variety in *The Greenwich Village Follies* in 1919: soigné
subject matter in a nightclub aura on a small stage. One thing the big
Follies couldn't be was deft; Anderson was deft. His show gave way in
1924, the year in which the British impresario André Charlot presented

his revue, with Gertrude Lawrence, Beatrice Lillie, and Jack Buchanan. The *Passing Shows* gave up in 1924, the *Scandals* would last out through 1931 (with two final tries at intervals thereafter), the *Vanities* would survive into 1933 in a book format as *Murder at the Vanities* (with a terminal try in 1940). But *André Charlot's Revue* had pointed the way of continuity in the smallish revue, with wit and personality replacing spectacle and comic shtick and The Girls gently let go.

The high point of this format was reached in *The Band Wagon* (1931), in most details the least Ziegfeldian of revues but, taking the long view, the logical consequence of the *Follies,* given the changing taste of the times. Ziegfeld had decreed that the performing talent must be rich, the design superb, and The Girls stupendous. Take away The Girls and add a great score and you have *The Band Wagon.* The fledgling Max Gordon produced it, retaining the key creative elements of his revue of 1930, *Three's a Crowd*: Arthur Schwartz and Howard Dietz for the songs, Dietz for the sketches, Hassard Short for direction, Albertina Rasch for choreography, Albert Johnson for the sets, and Kiviette for the costumes. *The Band Wagon* was not an intimate revue—it occupied the New Amsterdam, former home of the *Follies.* But it followed intimate procedure in finding its dimensions in the range of talent involved rather than in size and numbers. *The Band Wagon* had no overriding concept, but Johnson's ingenious designs, based on the innovative use of two revolving stages, made for a little unifying suspense as the audience waited to see how each new number used the revolves.

In the *Follies,* a lot of things contributed to success. In *The Band Wagon,* two things were essential (besides Johnson): the cast and the score. No *Follies,* no *Scandals,* no *Vanities* ever had a score of the literacy and urbanity of *The Band Wagon*'s—there Ziegfeld notably failed. In the fatalistic "Dancing in the Dark"; the exuberant "New Sun in the Sky," harmonized with absurd altered notes; the helplessly amiable "Sweet Music (to worry the wolf away)"; the Parisian Katzenjammer "Hoops"; the German pastiche "I Love Louisa," oafish as a beer hall; the chaste "High and Low," clean as bells in the hills; the slyly risqué "Confession"; and the dazzling jive of "White Heat"—in all this, Schwartz and Dietz styled a sound for the revue, touching a round of emotional bases distinctively rather than expectably.

Three's a Crowd had proposed a well-rounded cast for revue: a dry comedian (Fred Allen), a debonair song-and-dancer (Clifton Webb), a torch wailer (Libby Holman), and a ballerina (Tamara Geva). *The Band Wagon* improved on the card with a dizzy comic (Frank Morgan) and a dry comic (Helen Broderick) and two debonair song-and-dancers (Fred and Adele

Astaire), besides the ballerina (Tilly Losch). With the Astaires as the devilish tots in "Hoops," a merry-go-round for "I Love Louisa," the hats and the tails for "White Heat," George S. Kaufman assisting Dietz on the sketches, and a fresh idea for the opening—curtain already up, cast ushered onto onstage seats, muttering threats and pleasantries ("You have a nice face"—"I made it myself") and breaking into "It Better Be Good"— the evening provided a culmination for the revue. Many aficionados insist it was the best there ever was.

Even if *The Band Wagon* is seen as the antithesis of the *Follies* (in its subtle score and lack of showgirls especially), still Ziegfeld haunted the revue in general, large and small, after his death in 1932. The showgirl staircase was on view as late as in 1956 in a *New Faces* (albeit for purposes of spoof), his experiments in design never lost their instruction, and his employees haunted productions. Whatever the precise extent of Ziegfeld's artistic domain, it is certain that Broadway was obsessed with him. Because he spent the talent.

4

The Heroine

Women were pretty, capricious, torrid. Men were intrepid, but a little like trees, planting themselves in a love lyric with branches fixed whereas women were at ease in a song, rhapsodic. Vaudeville was where all this began: all the great vaudeville singers were women, except for a few Irish tenors like Chauncey Olcott. As recordings attest, women like Nora Bayes and Sophie Tucker had not only solid instruments to work with, but The Gift—vigor, pathos, and a sense of structure. They could sing sweet, coy, mean, sexy, pathetic, or ironic; what could Chauncey Olcott do but sing sweet?

In the musical, song was character. You are what you sing. So the women who were not comedians got more to do than the men who were not comedians. The women got all the fun stuff, the dressing up, the leading of the troops in travesty, the dancing of a jig, the giggling, the pining, and the scheming. The men got the athletic stuff—but there isn't that much in the way of sports in the average musical. So the men who were not comedians got less to do than the women who were not comedians.

So the women were the romantic stars and the men stars were comics. However, while there was a variety in the types of romantic women (in looks, dress, vocal apparatus) and a variety in the types of men comics (mainly in their personal patented "business"), there were virtually no male romantic stars and no crudely comic women, not in the musical. The men's parts just weren't interesting enough to bring anything out in personality, and women comics were saucy, not zany.

The exceptions to the rule are so few they stand out in bold. Donald Brian was a romantic lead, something of a headliner, possibly even a box-office draw. But his status owes a lot to his having played the unprece-

49

dentedly flavorful Prince Danilo in the original Broadway production of *The Merry Widow*. When he made his debut in 1901, Brian wasn't an aspiring matinee idol, but a hoofing juvenile, the sidekick type. The hedonistic Danilo relaunched him, not only because the part suited him, but because *Merry Widow* mania led producers to hire him to authenticate their imitations. In the years when the form we call operetta was still called comic opera, Donald Brian was something of a name. However, though he was the best-known male in romantic leads, he was nowhere near as big a star as the women names—Anna Held, Christie MacDonald, Marie Cahill, Fritzi Scheff, Elsie Janis, Julia Sanderson, Fay Templeton. Brian had reputation enough to secure sole top billing in Victor Herbert's *Her Regiment* in 1917—but when Carolina White joined the cast during the tryout tour, Brian's name was shoved over to the right of hers. Nor did Brian have the staying power of the women stars. Europe's prominent Danilos are famous for aging gracefully; Johannes Heesters played the role well into his sixties, brilliantly. But by 1920 Broadway's Danilo had dropped to the second rank to play operetta revivals for the nostalgia set, to replace younger men near the ends of Broadway runs, to land the dancing lead in *No, No, Nanette* in a touring cast; and to be fired from *Hit the Deck* during the tryout. Too old or something.

Brian was the only romantic leading man of note till Dennis King, who enjoyed a matinee idol's fame in the mid-1920s and early 1930s. Yet King worked far more as a speaking actor (despite an outstanding singing voice) than in musicals. And before Brian and King there was only Henry E. Dixey, eminent in the title role in *Adonis* (1884). Dixey, who died at the age of eighty-four, outlasted everybody. Already a stage veteran when he played *Adonis,* he closed his career taking over George M. Cohan's role in *The Merry Malones* in 1928. Dixey's years as a romantic avatar were over by the time Brian played Danilo, so that gives us, counting Chauncey Olcott, only four men headliners in the musical over a period of fifty years.

No, wait. There were also George M. Cohan and Al Jolson. Both played love-plot roles. But neither, really, was known for Getting the Girl, and when they did it was mainly out of a sense of obligation to the stage, like eating dessert on a full stomach just to please a hostess. Nor were either Cohan or Jolson specifically complementary to the alluring Held, the radiant MacDonald, the tumultuous Scheff, the elfin Janis, the robust Templeton. Herbert wrote *Sweethearts* for MacDonald and couldn't wait to hear what his tunes would sound like. Would he or anyone else have written a *Sweethearts* mainly for the tenor or baritone who would play the Prince? Such visions of an operetta ideal collected around a soprano as a rule. And musical comedy relished its buffoons, not singing heroes. It relished few women buffoons, though again there are exceptions, such as

Marie Dressler and Charlotte Greenwood. What the musical wanted was Lillian Russell.

She was supple and ample, a comic opera soprano more dreamy than haughty, but very firm about taking center stage for her solos in spectacular gowns. Russell presided over the American musical in its crucially formative period, when Gilbert and Sullivan, Offenbach, vaudeville, and burlesque gradually gave way to narrative formats in the native idiom. By 1912, when Russell was reunited with her old employers Weber and Fields for a good-old-days monster rally, she was obsolete. Her clothes had led fashion; now, she might have joined a museum. Her habit of breaking contracts and missing performances once made her a silly darling; now, a more settled profession thought her self-indulgent. Her songs were the old sentimental songs; they sounded all the older now that Irving Berlin's "Alexander's Ragtime Band" had come forth.

Actually, Russell was neither silly nor sentimental. Offstage she was outspoken in her politics. She advocated woman suffrage, but also wanted to see men *lose* the vote. "Absolute suffrage for women and the withdrawal of the power and the reins of government from man's hands," she said in an interview in the New York *Morning Telegraph*, "will give men themselves a fuller opportunity to play the games in which they have been most successful." Let them tend to their specialties, cutthroat business and warmaking, and women will guide the social estate. The implication is that, with women in charge, there wouldn't be any more wars in the first place.

This is stimulating commentary from a woman whose own game on stage was to provide decoration. Her comic opera roles and her stints with Weber and Fields seldom gave her the chance to portray the independent and well-reasoned person she appears to have been. About the only daring thing Russell ever did on stage was to puff a cigarette during her Weberfields period—this only affirmed the conventional view of actresses as joyriding outlaws. And the most famous thing she ever did on stage was to break down on opening night of *Twirly-Whirly*, the Weberfields show of 1902, during the number "Come Down, Ma Evenin' Star." The song's composer, John Stromberg, long associated with Weber and Fields, had killed himself to escape an agonizing illness, and the manuscript of the song was found in his coat. A typically oblique cue led Russell to the tune: "The life of a society star is not a path of roses," she observes. Of herself! the public decides, of herself! "I envy the little stars up there. They can stay out every night and not lose their sparkle." The orchestra begins the introduction, *moderato espressivo,* and Lillian begins the verse:

> When from out de shades ob night
> Come de stars a-shinin' bright . . .

Another coon song. But this one is tender, with a shimmering finish. Lillian almost didn't reach it. At some point in the verse she gave way to tears and the show stopped till she could master herself. The public wept along with her, though not, probably, for Stromberg. They cried for all that Russell represented—the glory of American beauty and glamor and frailty. Russell was a Ziegfeld Girl with a voice and a thorough wardrobe. She had spirit, but she was vulnerable. She would melt. That was the part they liked best.

Russell passed her information on to those who succeeded her. Anna Held had a smaller version of her figure, Christie MacDonald her grace, Edna May her voice, Marie Cahill sang the same repertory and broke down in public (during her quarrel with Victor Herbert on *It Happened in Nordland*). Those who didn't at least approach the model were bucking the system—Sophie Tucker, for instance, whose suggestively aggressive comic numbers and Jolsonesque sell-it! style in Dixie songs kept her busier in vaudeville than in musicals. It is notable that, at her peak with Weber and Fields, Russell shared the stage almost exclusively with comics and "the Weberfields Beauty Chorus." These were the essentials of the musical circa 1900: a singing heroine, jokes, and The Girls.

However, the rage for ballroom dancing that dominated the 1910s withered the story ballad, nurtured ragtime, and introduced a new set of voices equipped to handle the spilling lyrics and earthy élan of the pushy rhythm songs. Heroines now were less rural (or national) than Russell, trimmer and gutsier. They didn't need the voice to sing comic opera; musical comedy had taken over the field work. By about 1915, a heroine was something of a jazzy Cinderella. *Irene* (1919) is the transitional piece, in a contemporary setting steeped in nostalgia for old manners, old morals, old things. Its centerpiece was the heroine's "Alice Blue Gown," an A-prime moment of characterological stimulation. After it, musical comedy heroines would need a special song like this one, early in the evening, to propound their qualities of self-belief and positivism. "I once had a gown, it was almost new . . ." and we are on Irene O'Dare's side at once—her treasures came second-hand, yet they gave her joy. The gown is long gone, the allusion to Alice Roosevelt Longworth's debutante years adds a patina of vanished grace, and the simple waltz has the tidy old-time sweep. However, lest we dream too much, Irene goes on to catalogue the gown's features, speaking over the music. It's wistful, but factual as well, a touch realistic. "Aw gee," she sighs, "it was nifty!" The world of the feather boa and the staircase entrance—of Lillian Russell—is now urbanized. *Irene* has feather boas, but only for satire: they are designed by a humbug who bills himself as "Madame Lucy." And instead of posing on a staircase, Irene hangs out on a tenement fire escape.

Unpretentiously staged, with a book by James Montgomery and score by Harry Tierney and Joseph McCarthy, *Irene* broke Broadway's long-run record in the musical at 670 performances and made Edith Day the heroine of the moment. Her style might have become *the* style, but Day, like her predecessors, was primarily a singer. The new heroine of the 1920s didn't need melody as much as she needed rhythm, hotcha, pizazz. So, a few months after Day had left to play Irene in London, Florenz Ziegfeld, Jr., unveiled his choice in the heroine style. And Ziegfeld, Broadway knew, made right choices.

"She does her hair all wrong," said Ziegfeld's wife Billie Burke. "She isn't costumed properly. She has a sweet voice but not much of it and I've seen better dancing . . . but . . . a delightful thing *happens* when she comes on stage." So began the rise of Marilyn Miller, whom Burke had recommended to Ziegfeld after catching her in *The Show of Wonders,* a Shubert revue of 1916. Burke herself notes the irony in having been the one to tout Miller to Ziegfeld, for of the showman's attachments to his Girls, this was the alltime hot one. Later, when Ziegfeld's involvement with Miller became public, many thought that Miller was willing and able to wreck the Ziegfeld home, daughter Patricia and all. Able Miller was, but only Barkis was willing, for Miller seems to have put up with Ziegfeld only for professional purposes. She was a dedicated performer, and Ziegfeld truly loved performing; they had that in common. But why should they share anything else? After all, Ziegfeld was the man who murdered her first husband.

Miller started with her family in vaudeville, reaching the big time in the Shubert Winter Garden revues. (She was called Marilynn then; Ziegfeld trimmed it.) You could have filled a billboard listing the talents she didn't have; but she had It and her dancing, *contra* Burke, was strangely delightful. Most significantly, she could bridge the transitional gap between Lillian Russell's good old days and the jazz era. She looked elfin prim but danced chastely hot, pulling the old information into the new times. "Ev'ry small town girlie," she sang in *The Passing Show of 1915,* "has a big town way." They were pure; now they're flashy; but they're still pure. They're bold. To put it in the words of Harbach and Hammerstein in *Sunny,* "You've no less a share of Jack than Jill." Miller was a playful sweetheart, the sum not of idealized parts but of unique ones. *The Passing Show of 1915* styled its performers into archetypes of romance, and Miller was cast as First Love. Perfect casting—a generation of boys was going to idolize her as the Indiana girlie with the New York way. Ziegfeld dressed her, gave her Kern tunes, aimed an entire cast at her to teach the public how to grovel before a once-in-a-lifetime star, and set her in a plot that climaxed with her Cinderella trip from helpless waif to *Follies* star. It isn't clear whether the life or the art came first, but that was Ziegfeld's plan. Miller is playing Miller: in theatre, to make magic is to be magic. After two years in the *Follies,* Miller literally became what her first Ziegfeld book show was about, the girl of the century in the show of the age: *Sally* (1920).

What's a star without a star entrance? In life, Ziegfeld gave Miller the best there was: the *Follies.* In *Sally,* Ziegfeld gave her a better one yet, sneaking her onstage in a plain frock amid a group of tykes on a day trip. As Irene had done, Sally sings a kind of motto song, evocative of the old morality of self-reliance sustained by optimism. "Remember," Sally advises, "somewhere the sun is shining," in one of the silkiest, most serene melodies ever composed, a seamless line so perfect it needs no harmony. All of *Sally* is like that, all expert, all the top: for what creative wit could not devise, Ziegfeld's money could simply buy into existence. *Irene* was the work of one pro (the book) and two neophytes (the songs), featured no headliners, and got by on looks. *Sally* was the work of champs, starred the odds-on favorite as the Lillian Russell of the 1920s, and had Joseph Urban's sets plus costumes by a host of couturiers. Strangely, it is not a big show. It is a show made big.

It started as *The Little Thing,* a miniature that Guy Bolton and P. G. Wodehouse had planned with Jerome Kern in their Princess days and never got around to finishing. Ziegfeld had been looking for a setting for his new gem, and *The Little Thing* sounded right: waif heroine, can dance, will travel uptown. Bolton, Wodehouse, and Kern set to turning *The Little Thing* into *Sally,* broadening, lengthening, above all *centering.* Princess shows were stories—but Ziegfeld shows were spotlights. From a dishwashing job in Greenwich Village to a ritzy party disguised as a ballerina on to the *Follies* in a ballet numbo, Sally passes the heroine test question: she is lowly but proud, can tap it slick or toe it in a tutu, can mix with the bloods while preferring her Village comrades, and can make it because she believes that somewhere the sun is shining. It sounds simple? It is simple— except that by the time Ziegfeld got it onstage, the little Princess show had acquired three extra wordsmiths (mainly Clifford Grey, also B. G. De Sylva and Anne Caldwell), a second champ composer (Victor Herbert wrote the *Follies* ballet, as he had done in several real *Follies*), the indispensable Ziegfeld Girls; and the action was divided into a rather grand three acts. Ziegfeld believed in the safety of numbers, and in this case it paid off, making Miller the musical's supreme star and Ziegfeld the musical's greatest begetter. *Sally* stood so sacred in theatregoers' memories that when they got a chance to see it again in a revival in 1948, almost nobody went. Such magic must not be made twice.

However, it was not the luxury that made *Sally,* but Miller and the score. Utilitarian in the set-up numbers, the two narrative act finales, and the comedy songs, it springs to wild life in Sally's part, treating her optimism, ambition, mystery, and susceptibility in incantatory melody that has never been surpassed for the utter rightness of its line. Much of *Sally's* magic danced in the spell that Kern wove. This much the other Cinderella shows—little *Irene,* middle-size *Mary,* jumbo *Manhattan Mary*—could not share. Their composers could garnish them. Kern authenticated *Sally.* "Joan of Arc" treats Sally's strong sense of motivation ("You can't keep a good girl down!"), and, as "Look for the Silver Lining" tells us of her unaffected charm, "Wild Rose" layers that charm: in a costume among Society, Sally has allure and remoteness ("You're like a splendid flower," the men tell her, "not from our domestic clime"). The stag line cannot reach her; one man only will meet her on her level of tiny yearning wistfulness, outlined in the nostalgic "Whip-Poor-Will."

Intimacy amid luxe was Miller's forte. In her dishwashing rags, her hair every which way, she still glistered. In the ball scene she was a vision. Clothe her in fur, have every character hail her gifts, light her for glory, and she'll turn the whole gala into a one-person numbo. It was partly Miller's exquisite freshness and partly the distinctive dancing, for she wasn't a beauty poured from the mold and had one of those toneless sopranos that hits the notes without ever quite sounding them. Nor did her acting have any particular style or commitment. As Billie Burke noticed, a delightful thing *happened* when she came on stage. Edith Day would have played Sally more appropriately, perhaps, and would certainly have had an easier time in the songs. But Miller danced the role as no one could. Besides Herbert's "Butterfly Ballet," there are dance sections for "Joan of Arc," "Look for the Silver Lining," the title song, "Wild Rose," and in the second-act finale. Edith Day would have been perfect for *The Little Thing*— But *Sally* was for Miller. She so impressed the nation in it, for three years in New York and on tour, that when Hollywood went into regular sound production, one of its major projects was to film Miller's *Sally* in Technicolor.*

After all this, relations between Ziegfeld and his wild rose were tense, and it was not clear whether they would follow *Sally* with a joint enterprise of any kind. The trouble had begun with the 1918 *Follies,* when Miller had taken up with a fellow *Follies* performer, Frank Carter. Though

---

*A silent *Sally* was filmed in 1925 with another key twenties Cinderella heroine, Colleen Moore. Leon Errol was retained from Broadway, and there were dance sequences. Still, without the full musical treatment, it was hardly right for Miller. Moore's version is lost; Miller's survives in one black-and-white print in Wisconsin.

Ziegfeld jealously harassed them, Miller married Carter in the spring of 1919. This was just before the 1919 *Follies* was to go into rehearsal—the 1919 *Follies* which Ziegfeld had planned as the first major sortie in Operation Miller. So, should he drop her, forgive her and accept the *fait accompli*, or wait for her to tire of Carter? It happens. Ziegfeld liked the last possibility the best, but decided to help her forget Carter rather than wait it out. He hired them both for the 1919 *Follies*—then fired Carter during the out-of-town tryout. Clever: now Carter was out and Miller, by contract, must stay in. She stood the separation, seething. But while in Boston with the show she learned that Carter had had a fatal auto accident. Miller collapsed. Ziegfeld attempted to console her; of such moments great reconciliations have been forged. But it was Ziegfeld who had broken their pairing in the first place: who sent Carter off to his accident.

Miller never forgave him. The extent of their involvement is not known, but whatever détente they had enjoyed when Ziegfeld first proposed to glorify his protégée beyond the others was now shattered. *Sally* enters here, as the big one that no one, no matter how embittered or disgusted, could turn down. But it did not save Ziegfeld's relationship with Miller. She married again, again offensively: Jack Pickford, the man who had taken showgirl Olive Thomas from Ziegfeld. And she returned to Broadway under the management of the producer thought to be Ziegfeld's only rival, Charles Dillingham.

Dillingham's *Sunny* (1925) might be called a *Sally* without Ziegfeld. This, too, was built entirely around Miller-as-waif, with Kern tunes and the New Amsterdam, house of hits, to host. Some of *Sally*'s most potent imagery was lacking. There was no "silver lining" motto tune, no big ballet, no sense of the girl's ambition fulfilled. So Miller made her peace with the one man who could utterly present her, in *Rosalie* (1928) and *Smiles* (1930). In the event, only the first succeeded, and there was nothing on Broadway as resounding as a Ziegfeld flop, especially with Miller as its star. Nor did her three Hollywood musicals affirm on film what was thought to be the most appealing woman stardom in the theatre.

From *Sally* in 1920 till her death in 1936, Miller only appeared in five shows. Her last, *As Thousands Cheer* (1933), is utterly unlike *Sally* in every respect. A revue of the kind in which everyone does everything from dominate a number to impersonate a celebrity of the day, *As Thousands Cheer* might have put Miller at a disadvantage. Not only would versatility overextend her, but she had to sing on the same stage as Ethel Waters and test her comic aplomb against that of Clifton Webb and Helen Broderick. Not since the 1919 *Follies* had Miller any competition from her colleagues, and at that Ziegfeld protected her from trying to match Cantor's sinewy vocals or Williams's portraiture. *Smiles* put Miller side by side with the Astaires, but as all three were best known for dancing, this was more a festival than a contest. Moreover, *As Thousands Cheer* turned up in times vastly different from *Sally*'s effervescent 1920. Ziegfeld and the bankrolls were gone, the Depression seemed here to stay, and the advent of Clara Bow and Joan Crawford in Hollywood in the late 1920s had evolved a sexy Cinderella heroine. Sally looked for the silver lining; the new women had bite and looked for the golden checkbook. They were the Ziegfeld Girls that Ziegfeld had been afraid to show publicly—"gold diggers" was the term of the day, and it's a euphemism.

All this points to a bad era for Miller, but *As Thousands Cheer* proved a triumph for her, its pitfalls paradoxically enhancing her image positively. Revue and its all-aroundness, after all, was the medium in which Miller had first made it to Broadway, in the *Passing Shows* and *Follies*. Her threateningly gifted costars did not show her up but accompanied her, Webb's effete irony, Waters's dark, velvety throb, and Broderick's acid being qualities no one ever looked for or wanted in Miller in the first place. And the more worldly Miller of this last show turned out to be the ideal antidote to Sally's by-then outmoded candy-floss outlook. Thus, despite Miller's all-of-a-piece Sally-Sunny-Rosalie chain, she defined the heroine in one period, then saw the character safely into an age that asked more of its guiding personalities—something, say, serio-comic. *As Thousands Cheer* gave Miller the chance to imitate Barbara Hutton and Joan Crawford, to play a society bride waking up in bed with groom Webb on the morning of their wedding day, to dance with the denizens of the comic page in "The Funnies," and to lead an antique rotogravure in "Easter Parade"—a mixture, in all, of the oldtime innocence she had symbolized and the new style of expedient sensuality.

One wonders if Miller appreciated the freedom of *As Thousands Cheer* after having played one role for a decade. Waters did for sure. Garson Kanin tells a story of the show's tryout, a time when a revue is juggling its acts to find tempo, to establish and hold tension from opening to finale. Came the time that "Harlem on My Mind" had to be moved, and the only place director Short could find for it was just after a grand turn by Miller and Webb. Short asked Waters if she'd mind trying to follow them. "Hell, no," replies Waters. "There's nothing I like better than workin' on a *hot* stage!"

5

The Top Banana

History is written by the victors, and it was the Hammerstein generation who wrote the musical comedy histories. In the wake of *Oklahoma!, Carousel, South Pacific,* and *The King and I,* the official line held that a great musical was well-made, diversely and impeccably joined, and if possible well-meaning. By hindsight, a hit show that wasn't integrated or solemn had to be a fluke—no matter how many there were—and we were urged to think exclusively in terms of authorship. But, as Ziegfeld has taught us, the great shows of the early 1900s are not necessarily written well; many are *performed* well, sometimes despite the writers. On our way to Hammerstein, we meet unarguably great Broadway stars who owed little to librettists or composers, and this chapter in particular stands as their private club.

The star comic is the oldest ingredient in the musical. The musical's first star was a comic, George L. Fox, a clown of the pathetic type who dominated the 1870s in "pantomime," fairyland burlesque that was eventually to become extravaganza. But then all brands of musicals counted heavily on their comedians. Farce was nearly all comics, comic opera had its runoffs of Ko-Ko and Major-General Stanley, and musical comedy had sultans of Sulu. Even *The Black Crook,* which emphasized spectacle, ballet, and occult horror, had its joke maker, the asinine valet von Puffengruntz. Not till the Gaiety shows rescaled musical comedy plotting and Victor Herbert's scores invigorated the love plots were there opportunities in quantity for singing actors.

By then the comics had become dominant by seniority. Though most of them enthusiastically shared traditional business old as snakebite, the best of them aimed to be inimitable. There were wild and shy comics, victorious and thwarted comics, acrobatic and uncoordinated comics, dialectitions and native sons, the studied and the improvisors. Some were more actors than comics—Francis Wilson, for instance. Some wielded a fine singing voice—bass De Wolf Hopper, a fixture in comic opera. Some, who failed to become identified with an immortal hit, like James T. Powers, are so thoroughly forgotten now their names don't carry even a hollow echo. And some invariably improvised.

Expert jesters were essential to the musical of 1900 not only because the genres needed them but because libretto writing was so unadventurous as a rule that the comics supplied necessary spontaneity, mischief, something *happening*. When the sweethearts came out on stage, the public might have called out their lines along with them, so ingrained was the ritual. But let a zany toddle out in his freak outfit and the house was stimulated. Comics had trademarks—business, a look, a sound, a character: style. They were familiar and beguiling, familiar because you already knew the style and beguiling because the style was made of surprises.

Montgomery and Stone, the original Tin Woodman and Scarecrow of *The Wizard of Oz,* are classically typical: up from vaudeville, Broadway smash, fame assured in shows tailored to their talents; normal-living, good-looking men who made themselves as weird-looking as possible on stage; consistent personae from show to show of stiffly amenable Montgomery and nimbly screwy Stone, varied only by Stone's acrobatic stunts, a new one in each show. Comic duos were a cliché, but few broke through to really big fame; Montgomery and Stone were the biggest, as popular as Weber and Fields and for a longer period.

Fred Stone was the energy in the act. "The western frontier and I grew up together" is how he begins his autobiography, and he took the mobility, high spirits, and recklessness of the Old West into show business, first in the circus, later in variety. It was a mean life. As a kid trapeze artist he was cheated by managers and harassed by locals, even threatened by a lynch mob in McCook, Nebraska. In vaudeville he learned how quickly one's personal novelty becomes public property. It was, for show biz, the age of tradition and self-reliance, of carrying on in the set attitudes and businesses and trying to hammer out your own entailment on these, nailing down the surprise in the style.

Most comfortable in a double act, Stone worked first with his younger brother Ed, then teamed up with the somewhat pallid Dave Montgomery. Stone thought they were well matched, nasally bellowing advices on survival in a comedy number, pulling off an ethnic burlesque, or having a daydream of glory in remote places, usually in bizarre costumes having no connection with the plot at hand. In *The Old Town* (1910), along with *The Red Mill* (1906) the only Montgomery-Stone vehicles that were not fairytale extravanganzas, they came closest to playing what they were, show-biz vagabonds. Gustav Luders and George Ade wrote *The Old Town,* but of course the big number was an interpolation, "Travel, Travel, Little Star." Toward the end, the music stops so the two can exchange a few sallies on circus life. The conversation turns to the gorilla:

> STONE: When the manager got him he was keeping a saloon on Main Street.
> MONTGOMERY: The gorilla?
> STONE: No, no, no, the manager . . . Of course, once we captured him in Africa and brought him up here, he wasn't acclimated and died.
> MONTGOMERY: The manager?
> STONE: No, no, the gorilla . . . of course, after he died, you know, they skinned him.
> MONTGOMERY: The manager?
> STONE: (*Building to the boffo*) No, no, no, no! (*Socking it home*) You *can't* skin* a manager!

This was stock fun. Stone's acrobatic stunts gave the act its novelty. In *The Red Mill* he made his entrance falling backward down an eighteen-foot ladder trying to escape an unpaid hotel bill and exhilarated the first-act finale by rescuing the burgomaster's daughter from her prison in the top of a windmill by holding her in one arm while he swung down on one of the mill runners. In *The Lady of the Slipper* (1912) Stone introduced "The Punch Bowl Glide," a dance performed on hidden trampolines. The crazy disguises—as many as six or seven in each show—were also a Montgomery-Stone trademark. In *The Red Mill,* as stranded tour guides Con Kidder and Kid Conner, they threw in a Holmes-and-Watson act and an Italian organ-grinder bit. These were worked into the plot—but if someone had a good idea for the team and the story afforded no cue, they did it anyway. As *The Lady of the Slipper*'s second act draws to a close, Cinderella hears midnight sound and runs out, to the Prince's despair. Clearly, the curtain is ready to fall—but suddenly an aide announces "the drums" and Montgomery and Stone stamp merrily in to lead one of the last of the oldtime pastiche sequences, a medley of marches including the Marseillaise, a highland fling, an Indian war dance, "Pop Goes the Weasel," and, the pair in an ecstatic tizzy, "Dixie."

"Dixie" in *Cinderella!* But that was the Montgomery-Stone style, unreconstructed variety and no apologies. Stone's stunts were splendid. Other comics had logged time in the circus, but who else could walk the high

---

* Swindle, defraud.

wire or fake a trick fall? Montgomery's song solos had the carefree camaraderie of the neighborhood talent night. His spot in *The Lady of the
Slipper*'s ball scene, "Bagdad," longs for the dangerous place where "the
women of the harem knew exactly how to wear 'em" with such naïveté
that even the risqué comes off, as Stone would have put it, "clean as a
whistle."

Clean shows, friendly shows: with a few thrills, some hurdy-gurdy slap-
stick, and sweethearts to toodle while the two stars got into another weird
outfit. Montgomery and Stone were the last of the oldtimers, treating a
public that didn't care how a show worked as long as it was fun. The
team entered into a kind of firm with producer Charles Dillingham, director R. H. Burnside, composer Ivan Caryll, and librettist Anne Caldwell, all
of them opening the planning meeting not with "What is the story about?"
but "What stunts is Fred readying for this one?"

Chin-Chin (1914) was the culmination of Montgomery and Stone, of
their extravanganzas the biggest and most tuneful, with all the inane puns,
facetiae, showgirl parades, transformation scenes, irrelevant novelty ditties, and eccentric dances that had been holding the musical back for fifty
years. The Oriental story supposedly casts Montgomery and Stone as servants of a magic lamp against a love plot involving the "Chinese" boy
Aladdin and an American heiress, with a villainous merchant for menace.
But this is so much technicality. *Chin-Chin* was simply the latest version
of *The Black Crook*. There was the invocational magic: the opening scene
presents a toy store come to life, the tin soldiers flirting with the dolls; or
the spectacular first-act finale, a rain of gold granted Aladdin by the Goddess of the Lamp. There were the time-honored one-liners and comebacks.
Given the freedom of the city because of his new-found wealth, Aladdin
frets over his American sweetheart, but his mother points out the advantages of the Orient. "When," she asks, "is the freedom of the city given to
a man in America?" Replies the heroine's father, "When his wife goes to
the country." There was the feckless ramming in of song cues: spang in
the middle of some intrigue about the lamp, Montgomery barges in to say,
"There go those temple bells. They're playing ragtime again," and flips us
into a numbo, "Ragtime Temple Bells." There is the disregard for character in composition, as when the Goddess, whose role has consisted of sto-
rybookland waltzes and dire pronouncement, closes the show with "In
January You May Love Mary (She is your June girl, your honeymoon
girl)." There were the interpolations, including "It's a Long Way to Tip-
perary," and the Stone stunts, including an imitation of Paderewski and a
horse-riding trick in drag as Madame Falloffski. And there was the ami-
cable contempt for storytelling when, at the end, the two comics push the

lovers together without ado and send the villain home. He swears he'll be back—tomorrow at 8:30, matinees at 2:15.

On Montgomery's death, Stone went on as successfully as a solo (and with his daughter Dorothy) but—terrible as it sounds—musical comedy had to get rid of Fred Stone. As performer, the man elaborated on qualities many Americans held as ideal: in his gamey, unpretentious singing style, his "okay! what's next?" practicality, his avoidance of smut, his daredevil gags. But his vehicles sustained qualities some Americans despair of in their art, in their show biz junkorama and their refusal to challenge the public. Extravaganza imploded the moment Stone let go of it, not only because it had outlived its age but because more alert compositional procedures were raising the public's expectations, nurturing a taste for sharp storytelling. Even Stone, with Montgomery at the time of *The Wizard of Oz* and *Chin-Chin* the surest draw in musical comedy, suffered a terrible failure in *Smiling Faces* (1932) and departed the stage to play character parts in Hollywood.

Not all of Stone's generation fell so direly athwart the shifting gears of artistic transformation—but then not all were so dependent on improvisation. Victor Moore trudged another route, as a dumpy little man in pathetic fuddles. Moore grew old playing musicals, for he was happy to work within the bounds of story. True, he was no great help in song and dance. He introduced the title song in Cohan's *Forty-five Minutes from Broadway* (1906) and turned up in shows by the Gershwins, Porter, Rodgers and Hart, and Berlin. Yet while he was a somewhat less than musical comic, his character was unique and made him irreplaceable: as the naïf entangled in a web of deceits and larks who never quite disentangles himself. It was the sort of character the musical could never have enough of, very useful in plotting, and Moore found a niche as foil to William Gaxton, six times. Gaxton would handle the songs, the love plot, and the schemes; Moore would whine and dither. Too, he had a knack for choosing the right properties and good team workers—boxer Bert Lahr in *Hold Everything* (Moore's his manager), wife Sophie Tucker in *Leave It to Me* (Moore's the ambassador to Russia), or Gertrude Lawrence in *Oh, Kay!* (Moore's her assistant bootlegger).

Perhaps Moore's gift was his ability to *listen* to the scripts—Montgomery and Stone were too busy with their business to follow a plot. Moore's scripts reveal a character, no bystander or interferer but someone at the center of the action. Perhaps *Of Thee I Sing*'s Throttlebottom (Moore's most famous role) is accessory. But his Shorty McGee in *Oh, Kay!* is essential to the story scheme and a pleasure for Bolton and Wodehouse to write for. They place his efficient dimness with a droll chic, as when he poses as a butler:

JIMMY: What did you say your name was?
SHORTY: Mr. McGee.
JIMMY: You don't expect me to call you Mr. McGee, do you?
SHORTY: Oh no, Mr. Winter. I've got an alarm clock.

Thus Moore rode into the Hammerstein era, as Stone couldn't. Perhaps it's significant that Moore started with Cohan, the musical's first inner-directed author (or the musical's first performer who cared about the whole rather than his part). But Montgomery and Stone's successors in the vaudeville approach had a bad time of it at length, for Performers' Rule was giving way even as they enjoyed their biggest hits, and they began to slip at the top of their fame. Ed Wynn, Eddie Cantor, Bobby Clark, and Bert Lahr all came to Broadway between 1910 and 1927, a period of great formalistic reinvention, from *Naughty Marietta* to *Show Boat*. But these vaudevillians were each a set format in themselves, not very adaptable.

Lisping Wynn was "the perfect fool," flibberty-gibbet and noted for crazy inventions. Cantor was the kid, duping bullies and lucky in love despite a fiasco in macho. Clark was the girl-chasing con man in painted-on glasses, twirling a cane and chomping a cigar. Lahr spoke for the urban proletariat with knockabout stunts, a bluff exterior hiding sensitivities, even dreams of debonair romance. Each was unique; but each frolicked in a storyless vacuum at a time when the musical was emphasizing story. And they came in at the wrong time: the age of Hammerstein and Kern.

Except for Clark, the whole generation was Jewish, but only Cantor exploited his background onstage. He had a rival in type in the more strongly accented Willie Howard, half of a brother act but most successful on his own as the cab driver Gieber Goldfarb, who attempts the most daring fare in taxi history—nonstop from Manhattan to Arizona—in *Girl Crazy* (1930). Willie and Eugene Howard were strictly New York (like Fanny Brice), supported by the tireless Jewish theatregoing population. Cantor, however, was national (like Jolson). Consider the change in the star-comic vehicle by comparing *Chin-Chin* with Cantor's *Whoopee* (1928). Or was there any change? *Chin-Chin* was put together around Montgomery and Stone by a smart producer (Charles Dillingham), *Whoopee* around Cantor by a smart producer (Florenz Ziegfeld). *Chin-Chin* is a premise (comics cavort in the East) expanded by fun, *Whoopee* a premise (comic cavorts in the Wild West) expanded by fun. *Whoopee*'s book is a *little* more adult than *Chin-Chin*'s and *Chin-Chin*'s score is a *little* more story-filled than *Whoopee*'s. Otherwise, there is no change.

Whoopee was an ideal Cantor show, given his milquetoast style. The cowboys will bully him, the Indians will bully him, his nurse will bully him, and in the end he'll get the best of everybody. The score? Walter Donaldson and Gus Kahn will supply Hit Tunes, and, should they be absolutely needed, a few pieces for atmosphere. The love plot? Romeo Indian loves Juliet white girl, who kicks the plot into gear by ducking out on her wedding to mean Sheriff Bob and appearing to elope with Cantor. The big showgirl number? A cinch, in an Indian mode, so pounding drums and Urban's startling sunset colors can support the effect made by Indian maids entering one by one at equally spaced intervals, on horseback in little more than ceremonial headdress and artfully draped long braids. Cantor will supply so much comedy that the other characters need only hold up the musical end, so there'll be a deputy ingenue who can dance wild, another who can sing sweet, and the hottest band of the day, George Olsen and His Music.

Whoopee was a book musical exempt from responsibilities toward its book. Inspired by the title, Donaldson and Kahn came up with a song called "Makin' Whoopee," cute lyrics, engaging tune: "Another bride, another groom . . ." A sure thing. Now, where to put it? No problem: as wedding bells call the cast to the Juliet's wedding, six Girls enter to dress the stage in John Harkrider's dazzling riding costumes. The Girls look right at home, though they're some little distance from the Piping Rock Club. Enter Cantor, who improvises a salute, takes stage, and puts it over: "Every time I hear that march from Lohengrin . . ." He's singing about a wedding, so the song *seems* integrated, but in fact it isn't remotely connected to the story. It's a Ziegfeld triumph: star comic, Hit Tune, and Girls.

The dancing ingenue is even less smoothly worked into the action. In a brief scene at a gas station, created exclusively for the number "Taps," her brother tells her, "You can dance all night, but you can't walk a mile!" She replies, "Well, I like to dance but I don't like to walk," the brother makes himself scarce, and she goes into her solo. Most sloppy of all is the handling of the featured singer (Ruth Etting), who wanders through the show with literally no part in the story, though some of the other characters address lines to her as if they knew her. Donaldson and Kahn wrote "Love Me or Leave Me" for Etting, but they didn't even bother to tape this one onto the show. In the most bemusing defiance of story since Montgomery and Stone sang the interpolation "Hurrah for Baffin's Bay" and its successor "Football" in *The Wizard of Oz,* out of character without explanation, Etting just comes out and does the number. She does not sneak in on a preposterous song cue. She does not stand around waiting for someone to ask her to sing at a party. She does not show up in a nightclub scene pretending to be a club performer. *She comes out and does the number.*

Nor are Cantor's bits spliced into the story with any care, though they form the core of the entertainment. He spends many jokes vaunting his ailments, fearing women, baiting the cowboy he-men, and satirizing racism. When the Romeo Indian, half white, speaks of his background in "your schools," Cantor cries, "An Indian in a Hebrew school! Tell me, how did you get along?" And of course the inevitable blackface sequence adds to the racial review. Evading a posse, Cantor slips into an oven. "Look over the ranch," the sheriff snarls to his men. "Don't let a white man get by you." The oven explodes and Cantor pops out in his minstrel makeup. He gets by. Claiming to be a "singing waiter," he proves his stuff in a spot left blank for interpolations, one of the last such spots in musical comedy. Cantor would pull them in and drop them at whim: "Hungry Women," "My Blackbirds Are Bluebirds Now," "Ever Since the Movies Learned To Talk," "The Automobile Horn Song," and "I Faw Down an' Go Boom" among others. (The best of the lot, "My Baby Just Cares for Me," was written for the same spot in the film version.)

Cantor's singing set him apart. Wynn and Clark talked their way through their numbers, and Lahr was more a satirist of singing (opera and prissy crooning especially) than a singer. But Cantor's voice exactly complemented his persona of the little guy with energy to spare, bright, well-focused, and loud. This made him the ideal musical comedy comedian, a talent able to accommodate all the parts of format. By comparison, Wynn could at best accompany a musical. No matter how central his role, he was no help in the musical's two crucial elements of song and dance. Cantor could preside over smart shows while Wynn was limited to loose vehicles in the old manner—he actually played the last of the fairyland extravaganzas, Simple Simon (1930).

Alternatively, Bobby Clark might have made the definitive crossover from variety into story, for despite his crude voice he could put a number over and was game for a novelty in dance. But he only played roles that gave him a main chance to work scams, ogle The Girls, break up his colleagues with ad lib gags, and in general work the house to the utmost. Little Clark must have seemed like a dinosaur in the 1940s, when old timers would tout his shows as the kind where a man could count on seeing a lot of leg. "Girls to the right of me, girls to the left of me!" Clark croaked in Mexican Hayride (1944) and, after calling time out for a relatively demure revival of Herbert's Sweethearts in 1947, was back on the old track in As the Girls Go (1948) as the husband of the first woman President. When he did at last play parts rather than himself, he was miscast—as the unworldly genie in the west coast revision of Flahooley, Jollyanna, and as the devil in the national tour of Damn Yankees (1955).

It was left to Bert Lahr to make the needed transition, to put comedy to the challenge of expanding along with the musical rather than containing it. Lahr was a star born in his second show, *Hold Everything!* (1928), as unhinged, mediocre boxer Gink Shiner who takes on the champ. Critics were bewildered but enthusiastic, laughing uproariously without getting it. (It would take years.) Dropping the Dutch accent that had served him in burlesque, Lahr attacked the possibilities with imagination, dovetailing his overkill and paranoia with trainer Victor Moore's little-guy underplaying. Lahr entered riding—actually wrestling—a bicycle. It carried him offstage to a tremendous crash. Staggering back in, he observed, "That's a *hell* of a place to plant a tree."

Too many twenties musicals were not about anything in particular, relying on the eternal boy-meets-girl and some tunes. Topicality crept in in desperation, and *Hold Everything!* offers an instance: boxing. The subject will provide peculiar scenes, songs, and characters. Similarly, Lahr's next show, *Flying High* (1930) tackled aviation. Again Lahr played a back-bench pro, a wrong-way Corrigan who breaks flight records because he isn't quite sure how to land. With his gnong-gnong-gnong coda to jokes and his zesty paranoia, Lahr caught something everyone believes in, the archetype made of clay from feet to brain. Burlesque had taught him that everything is spoofable because almost everyone is a kind of fool. Other star comics worked their personal quirks; Lahr's touched a universal nerve.

He was the happy hooligan only at first. In the 1930s, he began to stretch himself in revues. Elegance fascinated him; just who did the elegant think they were, anyway? Lahr showed, in the tautologically titled *George White's Music Hall Varieties* (1932), wherein he performed a "Chanson by Clifton Duckfeet," a lampoon of the ever-so-thoroughly-finessed style of Clifton Webb. Svelte, polished, clipped of speech, Webb would materialize before the curtain, hands pocketed, serenely to sing. Lahr did, too. Webb would glide through the lines, scarcely touching notes. Lahr glided. Webb would tap a touch, just a touch. Lahr, too. The song, "A Bottle and a Bird," was ludicrous, but otherwise the act did not let down its premise. It did not subvert the debonair with vulgarity; it exposed the vulgar in the debonair.

Comparably, Lahr ripped into the brittle veddy-veddy of the Noël Coward school in the sketch "Chin Up" in *Life Begins at 8:40* (1934). Lahr is the family scion, Richard, about to dress for "dinner with the Duchess." In the constipated, not-a-word-extra manner of *Private Lives,* Richard's father, wife, and mother come in one by one to reveal a faux pas and take poison proffered by the butler, so wise in noble ways that his tray never runs out. The father can't pay a gambling debt, the wife has been unfaithful, and the mother confesses a marital indiscretion: Richard is illegitimate.

RICHARD: (*reeling*) Chin up.
MATER: Chin up.
RICHARD: (*blubbering*) Stiff upper lip. Honor of family.
MATER: Honor of family.
RICHARD: (*recovering himself*) And you?
(*Butler enters with a glass on a tray.*)
MATER: One thing to do.
RICHARD: Right.
MATER: (*Sees butler at her elbow*) This it?
RICHARD: Rather.
MATER: Thanks.

But now Richard is late for dinner with the Duchess. Shocking; one thing to do. He drinks the last glass of poison.

Though his film career was blasted by bad management and luck, Lahr remained a gala name on Broadway. Unlike many of his fellows, he liked a role that tested him. His colleagues had one role each; Lahr amassed an oeuvre. Just as well, for the musical had by the late 1930s outraced the star comic to such an extent that his tradition, its impetuous whimsey along with its routine, was in danger.

DuBarry Was a Lady (1939) is historic in this context, a show halfway between the star-comic vehicle and the book-tight story shows of the post-*Show Boat* era. One can't imagine anyone but Lahr as Louie, the nightclub washroom attendant who loves a singer in vain, tries to slip his rival a Mickey, drinks it himself, and dreams that he is King Louis XV of France pursuing DuBarry, still in vain. The very notion for the show seems to have been adapted from the character Lahr had been featuring in his thirties revues, with its elements of gentleman and bum. This was Lahr's version of the beguiling surprise. *DuBarry* was not Lahr's to mock up, however. B. G. De Sylva and Herbert Fields's book was solid, Cole Porter's score keyed to character, and for his DuBarry, Lahr had to contend with Ethel Merman, the ace upstager of the day. This show, then, was both of the old style and ahead of it. Lahr's part was tailored to his gifts, but the show did not revolve around him to spin limply off course when he made an exit. An essential difference between *Chin-Chin* and *DuBarry Was a Lady* is that in *Chin-Chin* all the elements of entertainment must be in balance with Montgomery and Stone. In *DuBarry Was a Lady* all the elements must be in balance.

The show tantalizes with its riches. Merman sings sweet, friendly, torch, and rouser, but her lines always talk tough; Lahr sings coarse but gushes with generosity when he least expects to. It's not a blend. It's a dead heat. And the setting, whether at the louche Club Petite or at the French court, is so bawdy it gave some critics the jitters. Lahr was the Chaucerian among his peers, man in his bodily functions, changes of heart, and stops in the mind. No show suited him better. Scanning some ladies of the court as they pass in cloaks, Louis coos, "Je vous en pris! And where is this gay little party off to?" They're heading for a rehearsal of some masque. "Would you like the Royal Approval on your costumes?" Obediently, they drop their cloaks, and it's The Girls of yore, wearing maybe three spangles each. "Vive la France!" cries Lahr, examining each in turn. "My, my, ma petite," he remarks of one. "What a lovely costume! Where'd you get that, off a lamb chop? How delicate! How fine! You'll never get pinched for carrying concealed weapons." No one could transform the coarse into the quaint, measure the bum in the gentleman, as neatly as Lahr.

There were the set pieces, to be sure, as when washroom Louie leads his new assistant through a point drill on procedure, or in the famous chase around the bed, Louis XV versus DuBarry, in which the winded monarch falls so behind that DuBarry comes around and passes him. As a full-fledged musical comedy, the show had its ingenue and juvenile (Betty Grable and Charles Walters), its romantic hero (Ronald Graham), its kickline and crazies. But the core of it was Merman, for tunes and wisecracks, and Lahr, for person. His line at the end of the washroom scene, when he realizes he has taken the Mickey himself, is comic genius. Out of town, the authors were stuck for a tag, something to put a button on the gag and set the dream in motion. Lahr considered. It has to be short, it has to be loud, and it has to work. It's simple: "Get me an ambulance!"

None of this was simple for Lahr. "I don't think I've ever worked with a more talented or insecure man," Merman recalls. "I never knew anyone else who took everything so seriously—to the point where he was his own worst enemy." After the first tryouts, when the theatre shook with laughter, Lahr decided the producers had hired a claque. When the show opened in New York it was such a hit that even Lahr had to admit it. "Bert, you're a smash," he was told. "You're in!" "Yeah," he replied. "But what about next year?"

DuBarry Was a Lady was the last really great show of its kind. The 1940s was the decade of *Carousel* and *Allegro,* of *Cabin in the Sky* and *Carmen Jones,* of *Pal Joey* and *Finian's Rainbow:* of idealistic experiments in Americana, in dance, in fantasy, in satire, in naturalism. Of the respected authors, only Herbert Fields and Cole Porter—veterans of *DuBarry*—were willing to proceed in star-comic story vehicles. Of the stars, only Bobby Clark lucked into successful book musicals. By the 1950s, Wynn, Cantor, the Marx Brothers, W. C. Fields, Willie Howard, Jimmy Durante, Joe Cook, Frank Fay, Jimmy Savo, Teddy Hart, and possible other members of the elite of classic early-modern musical-comedy clowns were all out of the musical, some dead, some retired, some in film or television. Only Lahr was left.

What was left him, however, was revue. *Two on the Aisle* (1951), in which he shared honors with singer Dolores Gray, might be thought of as Broadway's last successful try at top-dollar gags, Girls, and tunes variety. Jule Styne, Betty Comden, Adolph Green, and Abe Burrows wrote it, and Burrows directed, all people of acclaim. It looked big and touched bases timeless and contemporary—a love scene in three styles (*á la* burlesque, T. S. Eliot, and Cole Porter), or digs at television. Lahr was supreme as Captain Universe in "Space Brigade," discovering Venus with his Flash Gordon troupe ("Our hearts are full of space" they carol in their anthem). At the top of the scene, Captain Universe struts onto the Venusian landscape and takes his bearings. "What's our stellar orientation? . . . Our orbitary retraction? . . . Our gravitational quotient? . . . Longi-space-itude? . . . Lati-space-itude?" Consulting his instruments, he announces, "Men, as I calculate it, we're in Perth Amboy."

The revue was a moderate hit, mainly because oldtimers talked it up as a welcome return to the good old style. But that was the trouble. The musical had reinvented its styles. Here's a paradox: musical comedy didn't want star comics anymore. "Bert, you came up in this school, and you assume that since everybody in that school did that, everybody is *still* doing it. But you've got to realize that you're the only guy *alive* from *that* school of comedy. Nobody around here can do it, nobody here would do it, and nobody here knows *how* to do it!"

Thus spake Larry Blyden to Lahr while rehearsing Lahr's last book musical, *Foxy* (1964). It sounds a dream idea, Ben Jonson's *Volpone* set in the Alaska gold rush, with Lahr as the miser who pretends to be dying in order to sting his voracious associates. But *Foxy's* creative staff didn't know how to do it. The authors of the book were arrant tyros, the composer nondescript, the director a product of the Hammerstein revival. Not one of them understood or respected the improvisational grasp a practised comic has on the public. Yet that improvisation, humiliated, rewarded, goaded in tryout sessions, is what made musical comedy in the first place. You have Lahr, you don't waste him. Nobody helped him, and *Foxy's* producer David Merrick was busy with other big ones that season, including *Hello, Dolly!*. Yet, when Lahr was in view, *Foxy* roared with glory; and when he was off, it smelled. Lahr didn't just know timing and footwork; he had the unreasonable genius instincts. Once, on stage, he whispered to Blyden, "After the next line, say 'umlaut!' " Blyden said "umlaut!" and the audience screamed. Don't try to figure it out—you had to be there.

That was true of them all. They were an experience, and now they're gone: the integrated musical killed them. It is notable that Phil Silvers, the sole comparable star comic of the generation following that of Wynn, Cantor, Clark, and Lahr, is not correctly comparable at all. Silvers bears some of the characteristics—the training in burlesque, the trademark prop (horn-rimmed glasses), the career-long persona (gauche con man), the expert choices in timing, gesture, business. The man has talent. While his singing won no contests and he scarcely danced, he participated fully in his shows. In *Top Banana* (1951), a takeoff on television, Silvers took four of the funniest minutes in musical comedy history trying to teach a bewildered ingenue how to pull off a commercial, cajoling, hectoring, professorial, puerile, in audition, in tirade. The entire cast is on stage for this, in televisionland regalia, the cameras are ready, and the girl is trying, really; but time stands still for a bit as Silvers does *everything* with this girl but get through. Then, in *Do Re Mi* (1960), a takeoff on the pop music industry, he was truly moving in a final soliloquy, "All of My Life," in which the eternal petty hustler bitterly wondered why his scams never paid off. So Silvers is versatile, top talent.

But he is not comparable to Lahr's generation because Silvers took his first lead role, his second Broadway part altogether, in 1947, well after the fully integrated musical had taken form, and he only did three other shows as a lead, all of them strong story scripts written to be played—as written. To develop the point, Silvers's successor as top banana, Zero Mostel, moved from Pseudolus in the farcical *A Funny Thing Happened on the Way to the Forum* (1962) on to the profoundly moving Tevye in *Fiddler on the Roof* (1964). And when Mostel attempted to revive the old habits during *Forum*'s run, changing lines and business to play to the gallery, he was not hailed but chided. Those habits were broken. Silvers, too, played Pseudolus, in the 1972 *Forum* revival—and Silvers played him straight.

This is why Silvers's and Mostel's predecessors were unique. They were *auteurs* in a broad sense, less players than improvisors, lending spontaneity to what might otherwise have been art made dull by its own good sense, believability, neatness. There is nothing wrong with intelligible storytelling—historians write as if nothing else mattered. Yet the preposterous is one of the American musical's salient qualities (or: it was), and these particular Babies supplied it. Without them, the musical might have been trapped in the groove cut by Gilbert and Sullivan and the Gaiety shows. The difference between *Florodora* and *The Wizard of Oz* lies not only in an ideology of narrative concentration, but also in a belief in the refreshing fantasy of the grotesque surprise. *Florodora* is measured, almost sensible, tame. *The Wizard* is wild. It was *Florodora* that set style, however, and in writing comedy organically, authors no longer depended on the jester's wit. We have lost some savor of the form in the process. We have gained grandeur, subtlety, polish, thematic idealism, musicality, and the Concept Production. We have lost the mad liberty of our gentlemen bums.

6

The Book

When a musical makes a hit, who gets the credit? The songwriters, the performers, the director, the choreographer, the designer, the producer, the orchestrator, the stage manager, even the audience—for its good taste. When a musical bombs, who gets the blame?

The author of the book.

It's an old joke, but a true one, and the reason for it relates to the helter-skelter nature of the early musical. A good musical comedy was hot numbers and sharp comedy. A good operetta was great singing. Books in themselves had a function but little quality. They were either serviceable or unhelpful.

George M. Cohan turned this around in his earliest musicals, which depended as much on spirited text as on songs and dances. Thereafter, there were glimmers, as in Blossom's text for *The Only Girl*. Historians favor the Princess shows, however, because they constituted the first conscious, serial experiment in integrating score and script into character stories on a scale small enough not only to define character but to stay with it.

The term "Princess show" derives from the Princess Theatre, a lovely little house on West Thirty-ninth Street. Built in 1912, it had had trouble finding suitable attractions for its 299-seat auditorium till in 1915 agent Elizabeth Marbury suggested to the owner, F. Ray Comstock, that he produce intimate musicals. No doubt she had the success of *The Only Girl* in mind, as it was still playing, only a few doors down from the Princess. But rather than commission a second small-scale show from the top-dollar Herbert and Blossom, they went to less expensive authors. Nor was there a tryout tour. After a chaotic public dress rehearsal, *Nobody Home* (1915) was rewritten, rerehearsed, and opened to moderate success.

The series was launched, but no history made. *Nobody Home*'s significance lies entirely in the fact that its main trio of collaborators—composer Jerome Kern, lyricist Schuyler Greene, and librettist Guy Bolton—would immediately go on to make the history in the second Princess musical, *Very Good Eddie* (1915). Their source, Philip Bartholomae's farce of 1911, *Over Night*, tells of two couples who accidentally switch partners on a honeymoon cruise. Rather than jazz up Bartholomae, Bolton tightened him, and Kern and Greene plucked song ideas out of Bolton. The result was honest and characterful, the numbers showing a story-needling verve at times heedless of Hit Tune procedures. As with *Nobody Home*, the small production budget kept the ensemble in contact with the public, where a big show brought forth a mob. (The chorus people were so few they could get character billing in the program, somewhat coyly, as Miss Gay Ann Giddy, Mr. Dyer Thurst, and such.) The budget also did away with any possibility of a star trip, with its caravan of specialty spots and play-yourself business. So not only did the authors write for story—Comstock staged for it.

Very Good Eddie has one of the most distinctive pair of leads of the day: a small, affable man and a nervous little doll of a woman, each married to a militant giant. Even the show's title is odd, a one-of-a-kind idea. In circus argot, ventriloquists' dummies were called "eddies," and the duller voice throwers used the line "very good, Eddie!" as punctuation in the act. Bartholomae called his diminutive hero Eddie because his efficient bride controls him as if she were pulling his strings—thus the famous lack of a comma in the title: not "Well done, Eddie!" but "Eddie is a dummy." However, as Princess shows liked to quote their snappy titles at the curtain, the piece closes with Eddie at last asserting himself and everyone cries, "Very good, Eddie!"

The show was a hit and the idea of a Princess genre established. We're not quite there yet: half of *Very Good Eddie* was anything but revolutionary. There were still the interpolative urges, the buttinsky other lyricists; the outlandish comic-cum-shtick in John E. Hazzard's nightclerk; the opening choruses, including one to Act Two, "On the Shore at Le Lei Wi," that has nothing to do with the script.

What was needed to bring the plan to culmination was P. G. Wodehouse. Joining the Princess team to work with Bolton on the books and handle the lyrics himself, Wodehouse brought something new to the scene: wit. Kern had spent time in England, Bolton was born there (of American parents), and Wodehouse was British, all this pointing to the secret derivation of the Princess musical: the Gaiety style. The Princess's lively bourgeois characters, sleek plots, and character scores are all essentials of Gaiety format. Bolton is cagey, Wodehouse droll—but Kern is *graceful*. No one before him had been. It was these three who made the Princess shows the major influence they were, though some Princess shows were written by entirely different teams and two Kern-Bolton-Wodehouse musicals in the Princess style never played that theatre. Their first collaboration, *Have a Heart* (1917), presents the trio's style still in emergence—yet, already, the Gaiety atmosphere is receding in favor of something American. The tale of a couple on the verge of divorce who decide to restimulate their bond by eloping, *Have a Heart* has no "I say!" or Continental tira-lira. Bolton's book makes dates, not rendezvous, admires an elevator boy more than a lord, and respects the personal ambition that shakes status quo. Wodehouse's lyrics follow through nicely, as in the elevator boy's "Napoleon," a portrait of the conqueror at war and in love. "He was sawn off short but one good sport," the boy crows, "and I take after Nap!" These are the years in which George Gershwin and Richard Rodgers heard Kern and were doomed to the stage in a thrill; and what they heard then, we still hear. Kern's *Have a Heart* tunes embody the changes Bolton and Wodehouse were making in the libretto with simplicity, verve, and a fresh look at the possibilities in heroes, heroines, comic intrigue, scene-setting, dance intervals. *Oh, Boy!* (1917) was the trio's all-basic Princess hit, but to my mind the most finished piece in the series is *Leave It to Jane* (1917), one of the earliest of the absolutely American musical comedies by master craftsmen, in the most American of genres, the college musical with its proms, townies, and big game. Jane is the daughter of the college president, her mission to flirt with an All-American halfback to keep him playing for the home team rather than the enemy, and her quandary her realization that she genuinely loves him. A secondary student couple and typical campus characters fill out the scene, all with little or no reliance on shtick or device. *Very Good Eddie* had its stick-out comic; *Have a Heart* partly characterized him; and *Leave it to Jane* at last did away with him altogether. All the characters share the fun equally. The closest thing to a comic in the show is the daughter of the proprietor of the local boardinghouse, eternally luckless in student love. But while the part is clearly there for pathetic fun, she too plays a person, not just for laughs.

The book itself, as narration, is a fine job, lean for the time. Most impressive is the natural way it gains and leads into each song. As most musicals were written in pieces, then fit together, the parts did not always tally. Princess style demanded a more organic collaboration—more forethought. Rather than lift the curtain on students—filed, ranked, and tuned—

Bolton and Wodehouse give the opening number to a small group of foot-ballers in sweaters. The other students drift in as they might prowl through the quad, chatting, strolling, thinking. And the song itself ("Youth is a dream that will not last . . .") is no "hey! let's go!" rouser but a senti-mental piece in the varsity manner. The first-act finale, too, is gentle, with a "Good Night, Ladies" feeling, as the students finish their dance and leave Jane and her athlete alone for a first kiss. Then she, too, leaves, and he is alone, reflecting on the delicate exultation of being a young lover. The whole show runs like that, all the lines right, with no pushed-in gags. Is it funny? Not really. But it's fun. Perhaps that was the great *aperçu* of Princess style: a good musical comedy need not strain for laughs if it tells its story clearly and with charm. This was the first step in the reintegration of the musical away from specialist comedy into more fully conceived writ-ing.

Bolton and Wodehouse were to have a wide influence, most immediately in an insurgence of smallish story musicals looking, vainly, for a Kern. Most like the Princess scripts were those of Otto Harbach, and least unlike Kern was Louis Hirsch, who acquired the Princess touch working with Bolton and Wodehouse on *Oh, My Dear* (1918) at the shrine itself. Hirsch was neither an innovator nor a melodist—his big hit from *Mary*, "The Love Nest," is so monotonous that Broadway wags liked to sing it through using only the first line ("Just a love nest, cozy and warm") over and over. Still, Hirsch sounded a lot like Kern, and he and Harbach (and James Montgomery) came up with one of the nicest of the non-Princess Princess shows, *Going Up* (1917). Not the best, not the most imaginative, but a spry adaptation of Princess style.

Going Up is musical comedy at its simplest: the author of a popular book on aviation is challenged to prove himself against a French ace. Prob-lem: our hero can't fly. The Princess shows were a little weak in casting—that budget again—but *Going Up* was a Cohan-Harris presentation, and grabbed the best, homespun Frank Craven as the vertiginous hero and *Irene*-sweet Edith Day as his inamorata. It's an interesting pairing. Craven, an actor-manager who was to became famous as the Stage Manager in the original *Our Town*, could not sing well, while Day was a sweetheart in song—yet they duet. Does it matter? Show biz says it should, but Princess style says play it as it lays. The heroine is a heroine, but the hero is a fake, an incompetent—maybe he *shouldn't* sing too well. This is Princess think-ing. Let the show be what it is—play for character.

On the other hand, Harbach could ready as loose a program as any. *Oh, Boy!* and *Leave it to Jane* are notable for their avoidance of genre songs, but *Going Up* at one point jives into that most impudent of conventions, the dance sensation. The 1910s were the decade in which America discovered ballroom dancing, solemnized in Irving Berlin's *Watch Your Step* (1914), with Vernon and Irene Castle, and even before that most musical comedies featured at least one dance numbo somewhere, somehow. It is typical of the Princess evolution that *Nobody Home* offered "The Chaplin Walk," *Very Good Eddie* dropped "I've Got To Dance" during its tryout, and *Leave It to Jane* did without altogether. But *Going Up* gave out with "The Tickle Toe", another of the countless songs which promise to teach the new step and then just enthuse about it. Day put it over. A verse sets it up—a "Mormon lassie with a Norman chassis" showed it to her in Salt Lake City. Now the chorus: "Everybody ought to know how to do the Tickle Toe." Yes, yes; but *how?* We never learn.

Harbach is not easily understood. At times he seems to show the stimulation of Princess thinking; at others he works in "well-made" farce. He came to Broadway in 1908, strictly for musical comedy, especially in tandem with Hoschna and Rudolf Friml. Suddenly, in the 1920s, he became a specialist in operetta. He favors certain composers, but will work with anyone. He writes words alone or with a collaborator, apparently without preferance. He has no trademark, no worldview. No one would place him at a hearing, as one might Lorenz Hart or E. Y. Harburg. His lyrics abound in archaic accidents and transposed word order. His rhymes may be clumsily reached. Yet Harbach was there when the art was made. With Jerome Kern he wrote one of the unique musicals of the 1930s, *The Cat and the Fiddle,* and it was Harbach who trained the young and unfledged Oscar Hammerstein II in the writing of librettos. Since Hammerstein went on to teach everyone else, this is a significant credit.

Harbach's career encapsulates the musical's time of growth in the pre-*Show Boat* years: before it took itself seriously. But the Princess shows taught that the book comes first, in a way: not as the most entertaining element, but as the element that gives all other elements their character. If Harbach was conservative—conventional, really—in *No, No Nanette* and *Sunny,* he could be revolutionary—better say ambitious—in *The Desert Song* (1926), another Hammerstein collaboration, the two aided by Frank Mandel. Here we catch up with the form crystallized by Victor Herbert in *Naughty Marietta.* A show about passion, disguise, loyalty, treachery set in the African desert with a Valentino-sheik atmosphere may seem an unlikely proposition for a libretto of audacity, but before any major changes in character and subject could be rung, librettists had to turn the book from a makeweight into a thing-in-itself. Harbach and Hammerstein had been fighting for greater sense and sensitivity in librettos, and in *The Desert Song,* to Romberg's music, they reached their goal.

Doubters will scoff. They know of *The Desert Song*'s overripe rhapsody and lurid villainy. The son of the Foreign Legion General leads a double life: in the fort, as Pierre, he is mild-mannered; out on the dunes he is The Red Shadow, chief of Arab insurgents. He loves Margot Bonvalet, but she wants a man of more spirit than Pierre: the Red Shadow. How can Pierre claim her without blowing his cover? The plot um, thickens when Azuri, a hot-blooded Arab maid, avenges a racist slight by pitting the General against the Red Shadow. Can a son kill his father?

Surely, the tale is too quaint to naturalize. And surely the business of sorting out the various relationships between the principals—all of which have been fixed before the show starts—will humiliate any attempt to fuse book and score. Curtain up, the Red Shadow's band are feasting in the hills, and no sooner has their chorus finished than they're carefully telling us who they are, what they want, who the hero is, who the heroine is, even who is the hero's rival for the heroine. It's as loud as a title card in a silent movie.

Yet *The Desert Song* is all of a piece, as neatly composed as a pane of glass, a libretto that extends so fully into the action that most of the numbers are a mixture of underscored dialogue and song. Romberg seemed to like working this way. Solos, ensembles, reprises, dances, recitative—whatever the action needs, Romberg supplies, making *The Desert Song* not unlike an opera with more dialogue than usual. He was unable to do much for the two comic characters, a cub reporter and his tagalong secretary who keep finding themselves in the wrong place at the right time. After all, operetta is not about comic scrapes but about romance. Other than the inevitable military numbers, every musical scene treats of love dreams, wooing games, flirtation, seduction, Western and Eastern views of women. Even the comics enter the dissertation, in "It," a burlesque variation. The emphasis on romance was of course habitual in this genre, but no operetta had gone quite this far before, not even *Algeria*. Since the score derives exclusively from the text—is nearly a component of it—*The Desert Song* becomes something like the greatest of operettas. The most fulfilled. The most self-willing.

To hear the regal opening theme, *maestoso* and ardent in its minor-key harmonies, is to plunge into a world that Herbert's operettas never quite encircled. To hear the enticing lines of the title song ("Blue heaven and you and I . . .") as the Red Shadow coaxes Margot to join him in his tent is to understand the musical's fascination for romance with a directness not practised by Herbert's lyricists. The very word "romance" has its title song here ("Romance, a playboy who is born each spring . . ."), set to a sweeping waltz tune; and, while Margot finds her romance torn in half by the hero's two identities, the hero's "One Alone (to be my own)" ends the flirtatious adventure in monogamy. This is no surprise; the happy ending to the love plot is the musical's most basic given. But few shows test that love so eagerly as *The Desert Song* does. For a while, in Act II, Margot honestly doesn't know whom she wants. The Red Shadow thrills but frightens her; Pierre reassures but bores her. What other musical has so thoroughly examined its priorities? Of course operetta heroines want, as Margot puts it, "a rough and ready man" who will "take me, shake me, break me." That's easy for her to sing. Push come to shove, she doesn't find being taken and broken all it's cracked up to be.

If the Princess shows developed tidy, sensible book writing and the Harbach-Hammerstein operettas worked on a blending of text and score, big brash urban musical comedy needed a specialist to rework its elements of satire and snazz. Integration of parts was all very well, but a tone of urbanity was a priority—something set apart from the *Sally*s and *Irene*s. The writer of books that framed scores by Rodgers and Hart or Cole Porter or the Gershwins wanted a savvy that Harry B. Smith and his contemporaries lacked. To an extent, Bolton filled in here, putting a swing into his Princess style in collaboration with Fred Thompson on such jazzy projects as *Lady, Be Good!* and *Tip-Toes,* both for the Gershwins. But Bolton could not accommodate the dear worldliness of Hart or Porter's sybarite's grin.

A younger writer was needed, one with no loyalties to Gaiety or Princess days, one who could deal with characters at once more suave and earthy than those known to Bolton's formative years—the man was born, after all, in 1884. Consider *The Sultan of Sulu, The Wizard of Oz, Little Johnny Jones, Miss Dolly Dollars, Sweethearts, Chin-Chin,* and *Very Good Eddie.* Now compare these new propositions for musical comedy: the son of the Grand Eunuch seeks to succeed to the high position while avoiding its salient perquisite; or: an American playboy in Paris bets he can woo and win an American girl without spending a cent of his own; or: the high and low life of Manhattan's demi-monde flirt and cheat; or: three forsaken wives take up with three servicemen to try love *à la mode.*

In other words: *Chee-Chee, Fifty Million Frenchmen, The New Yorkers,* and *Let's Face It*, all books by Herbert Fields, son of Weber's partner Lew and a revolutionary without ideology. Fields was quite willing to work in a conventional mode. However, the mode he favored didn't exist before he devised it. His scenes delight in sarcasm, teasing, impudence, ogling: the games of the city. And Fields's city is not Cohan's. It prefers polish to good intentions and has a flip rejoinder to all the gallant statements a Cohan might make about ambition, love, and country. Fields liked hip.

No wonder Fields did seven shows apiece with Porter and with Rodgers and Hart—these were lyrics for the city-dwelling hedonist who knows all the answers. Cohan's heroes want friends and fame; Hammerstein's want love and justice; Fields' heroes want a hot time. One of them goes some distance to get it, back to 528 A.D. in *A Connecticut Yankee* (1927). Conked on the head with a champagne bottle, William Gaxton dreams himself an alien in King Arthur's Camelot surrounded by hostile knights and suspicious ladies. But is he worried? Led in chains into the resplendant court, he cries out "Hollywood!" At party in Morgan LeFay's castle, he displays a concomitant of the Fieldsian hip, callousness. Her jazz band giving a less than scintillating performance, Le Fay reassures Gaxton, "They are really finished musicians." "They will be if they don't quit that," he replies. He orders them hanged, and they are dragged away. "Gosh," he concludes. "That's a system that should never have been abolished." Gaiety was dead.

Even books set in less sophisticated milieus and accompanying less sophisticated scores might adopt the Fields slant. B. G. De Sylva, who eventually teamed up with Fields, would texture the naïvely sexy scores he wrote with Ray Henderson and Lew Brown with somewhat less than naïve scripts. Their score for the college show *Good News!* (1927) is replete with ingenuous melody—"The Best Things in Life Are Free," "Happy Days," "Baby! What?," "Lucky in Love," "The Varsity Drag." And the plot tells of nothing more than how a coed coaches a football hero for an exam so he can play in the Big Game and she can win him over a chic rival. It's sweet as cake. But the text, by De Sylva and Laurence Schwab, carries a burlesque snazz.

They start with a risible chorus noise, "Students Are We of Dear Old Tait College," demolishing *Leave It to Jane*'s careful naturalism. Then they drop the exposition like a lump of lead as Babe, campus flirt, stalks in like a Greek messenger:

BABE: Say, kids, have you heard the news?
ALL: What news?
BABE: Our dear teacher, Professor Charles Kenyon, has flunked Tom
Marlowe in astronomy . . . He takes a special exam tomorrow.
But what good's that? He doesn't know a star from a chorus girl!

Babe is a favorite character in De Sylvaland, too earthy to play heroine but useful in gags. The boiling Beef Saunders thinks she's his girl, but she's playing not to get:

BEEF: (choking her) You little—
BABE: You can't win me with flattery.

Compared with Fields's debonair creeps, these *Good News!* kids are daisies in the glen. Yet they have the same timing as Fields's characters, the same takes and emphases. It is Babe who keeps the show moving, and Babe gets her tempo from Fields: picking up a milquetoast so Beef can threaten them; hiding under the bed in the milquetoast's room; and asking the boys to teach her to shoot craps and—of course—cleaning the floor. Much of this sticks out of the story as set pieces; nor do the authors finesse the song cues. When it's time for a dance numbo, on comes a singer:

> FLO: Oh, I'm sick of Latin and all the other courses at this stupid college.

The boys in the pit put down their racing forms as the students mull this over, and the conductor raises his baton to:

> FLO: Let 'em worry about their dusty old books. We'll make Tait famous for the Varsity Drag!

Well, who can argue?—they did make *Good News!* famous for it. The loose textual structuring allowed all the elements some easy play, and comedy was guaranteed with no freak specialist to worry about. The style is American musical comedy at its most familiar, laid out by Cohan and developed by Bolton but largely characterized by Fields. His career streams with hits—*Dearest Enemy, Peggy-Ann, Hit the Deck, A Connecticut Yankee, America's Sweetheart, DuBarry Was a Lady, Panama Hattie, Let's Face It, Something for the Boys, Mexican Hayride, Annie Get Your Gun.* Little of his work attracts the analyst, yet the man was very influential, not only in his putdown spoof, but in his strict division of text and score, his tempo for musical comedy. The script is the story. The score is how the people in the story feel. Operetta is play in music. Musical comedy is play with music.

Fields's plan, then, affirmed the division between operetta and musical comedy, the gulf separating idealism from naturalism, questing honesty from ribald solipsism, musicality from Hit Tunes. Yet the *composers* keep pulling the action into the center of the place, rooting the Fieldsian jests in a sense of personable sensibility. For all Porter's dry wit in the *Fifty Million Frenchmen* score, when he lets his feelings loose in "You Don't Know Paree," the whole show takes on an ambience Fields hadn't planned for. But then that's the wonderful flexibility of American musical comedy, and why in the end its putdowns don't irritate us. The book may tell a soulless story—but the score knows otherwise.

7
The New Style of Score

The history of American popular music is the history of its public. The history of the American theatre is the history of the actor. Who controls the product? Who gets the ideas? Who makes the major demands? Pop music was entirely constructed around the tastes and fancies of the public. It did nothing for art's sake. The theatre, however, took its marching orders from the leading actors, and many of these were oathed to art.

The American musical is in an important way a combination of pop music and theatre. Its history should be that of its public *and* its performers, right? It isn't. It is a history of its authors—mainly, its composers. They decided, they planned, they got the ideas. They dunned producers with notes due on imagination, adventure, a risk. And as producers were helpless to proceed without Hit Tunes, they had to give in. The irony is that, sooner or later, experimental shows succeeded as often as not— *Show Boat, Oklahoma!,* and *Sweeney Todd* were considered doubtful propositions when they were conceived.

"We all start as imitators of somebody," Irving Berlin has said: in the first titles written but not published, or in vaudeville or the grabbag revue, or interpolated numbers, or in college shows. But writing full-length shows on Broadway, the songwriters of the golden age were individual. Berlin himself had the novelty slant, the cliché poeticized, the contemporaneity: when he said, "Everybody's doing it now," everybody began to. Kern had the utter rightness of his line, pure in ballad, sweet in charm song, wacky in syncopation. The Gershwins stood out for their complicity in jazz, Rodgers and Hart for their mutual divergence. Rodgers was like a tidy Gershwin, a little prim; he didn't trust the blue notes, but knew where they lay. Hart was like Ira's crazy uncle, also clever—but wiser, with a whoopee cushion hidden in his valentine. And Porter wrote of the smart set in unprecedentedly chromatic tunes. Berlin was not as gifted as the others, the one who . . . but it's hard to say what he did. Kern is the man most analysts would call the most distinctive. But when someone asked Kern to place Berlin in American music, Kern snapped back, "Irving Berlin *is* American music."

Because these songwriters all came to real prominence in the generation that seemed to follow on Victor Herbert's greatest days; because they sounded so fresh compared with what had preceded them; because with the contemporaneous Friml, Romberg, Vincent Youmans, Arthur Schwartz and Howard Dietz, and De Sylva, Brown and Henderson added in, the aggregate made such a rich mix; and because no analogous profusion of talent followed them—because of all this, Kern, Berlin, the Gershwins, Rodgers and Hart, and Porter appear to lead a golden age of the musical, appearing around World War I to join an unflagging campaign of rethinking, rebuilding, reinventing.

It's not that neat. The timing, first of all, was not synchronized. Kern hit Broadway in 1905 and was famous by the late 1910s, while Rodgers and Hart were not established till the mid-1920s, and Porter made no stir till 1929. There are deeper complications. Berlin was more a Tin Pan Alley man than a show composer, as happy tossing off pop or movie tunes as writing for story—of his twenty-one stage shows, fourteen are revues. Then, too, there's a lot of Hollywood in these men's dossiers in the 1930s and '40s, and some of their best work was written for original film musicals.

As for the community of art revolutionaries, this was a community in no real sense, most of the inhabitants cordially disliking each other and strongly varying in ambition. Porter liked musical comedy packed with yoks and leg, and Kern, despite his astonishing forays with Harbach and Hammerstein, felt uncomfortable in the big forms, all his life preferring the light Gaiety style he had inculcated in his London youth, developed in the Princess shows, and seen die out in the 1920s. Rodgers, late in life, displayed a curious ambivalence about his work with Hart.

To group these men is to invoke the excitement of profuse originality; but it is wrong to think of it as one great experiment after another. There is a famous line, attributed to Rodgers, that the only formula was to have no formula. On the contrary, all these men dealt with formula books, characters, structure, some of them quite heavily—Berlin and Porter lapped up formula like babes to the end of their careers. What is revolutionary about these men is their songs.

Kern arrived on a scene fixed in all its parts: the Hit Tune, the star tailoring, the shtick, the interpolations, the prancing chorus, the musical comedy here and the comic opera there. Herbert was already mixing the two forms and showing a preference for leading women of operatic abilities, but Kern leaned toward musical comedy and the available larynx. His early songs show a remarkable consistency, the ballads all supply direct, the comic songs all ever so slightly eccentric, the dance numbers all shyly brisk. The melodies are infectious, yet tricky. After two or three hearings, you're ready to hum along—but you keep going off. Kern is deceptively simple: simple for him, distinctive to you.

The melody usually came first in those days, in genuflection to the god of Hits. This gave all initiative to the composer and a presumably salubrious structuring to the lyricist, so it is fair to credit the better composers with the decisive expertise that brought fresh character to canned tradition. When Kern builds "They Didn't Believe Me," in *The Girl from Utah* (1914), by responding to his main strain's linear drive rather than simply putting the strain through AABA-format paces, he is taking the Hit Tune into pioneer territory. When Kern and his collaborators plan songs about the irresistible appeal of syncopation, the Kern melodies for "I Want To Dance" or "Little Tune, Go Away" truly are irresistible, turning a convention into a virtue. Hacks and imitators, forced to present the *inspiration* of rhythm, turned out harangues; but Kern (and Berlin) used dance elementally. Moreover, with Kern we lose the sense of Hit Tune that all but Herbert sustained by their erratic melodism. Kern put out on every number, and his throwaway tunes can be exquisite. "Good Night Boat," for *The Night Boat* (1920) is typical. It's tiny, yet Kern sets it out in AABCAADA, uses a section of the verse in the chorus bridge, starts the chorus not in the expected tonic but on the dominant ninth, closes the bridge on a 6/3 chord, then reaches the tonic but with the melody on the seventh tone of the scale, and employs passing tones in his bass that would delight a harmony professor. Sit there and listen; it's simple charm. But analyze it, and it's a little stunner.

This is not to say that Kern never wrote humdrum. Working as often as he did (four shows in 1915) and in the highly variable collaborations of the stage, his talent was at time forced or compromised or humiliated. But this *is* to say that Kern was the first composer to influence both aspects of the musical, composition and production. If Herbert tamed the Performers' Rule, Kern virtually decimated what was left of it. From the affable youngster on call, Kern grew into a touchy expert seasoned by work with veteran pros, so sure of his authority that he switched from one lyricist to another throughout his career.

One might divide Kern's work into three periods. The first takes in the early musical-comedy Kern through the Princess revolution—the Gaiety Kern, in effect, working with librettos more or less derived from Gaiety shows. The second period might begin with *Sally,* a Gaiety show (the shopgirl on the rise was a Gaiety fixation) enlarged and Americanized; and *Show Boat* in 1927 would lead off the third period of Kern the master, gone beyond musical comedy for the rarer atmosphere of the musical play.

Let's take a reading of the first period in *Leave It to Jane* (1917), the college musical about the flirt and the halfback. The Princess budget allowed for no production numbos, and gala theme songs like "Alice Blue Gown" were barred by aesthetics: keep it light, conversational, articulate but unstudied. In this, no songwriting team was better balanced than Kern and Wodehouse, Kern so pointed, Wodehouse so melodious. They give the charm songs to the comic-romantic couple, Stub and Bessie. Their duets, "The Sun Shines Brighter" and "A Peach of a Life," have the Kern lilt, but because Bessie is an athlete, some of her lyrics refer to her prowess on court and green—this is theatre music, not Hit Tune City. The more comical figure, Flora, had an interestingly confessional solo in "Poor Prune," but this was dropped in tryouts in favor of the sprightly, biting "Cleopatterer." The Egyptian monarch was forever killing her sweethearts. "When out with Cleopatterer," Wodehouse informs us, "men always made their wills." And Kern responds with a goofy Oriental verse and a twee Arabian fanfare to usher in the chorus.

We don't get much collegiate rah-rah. There's a fight song and a rally scene, but Kern prefers a medley of established college songs to faking his own. To these authors the real work lies in bringing the students to life in character numbers. So Stub displays peppy positivism in "Just You Watch My Step," and he and two other boys plan their romantic futures in "I Am Going To Find a Girl." The big game of course promises manly pluck, but what of campus chivalry? It's dead, says Flora. Naturally: she's the townie the college boys throw over every spring. In a trio called "Sir Galahad," she, Stub, and another student recall the middle ages in a delightful soft shoe glide and a dollop of slang—"For them was the days when a lady was a lady and a gent was a perfect gent!"

Had the Princess shows been big, they would have had star parts; in this one, Jane would have filled in. But in this modified musical comedy the authors even out the personal elements, so Jane's numbers don't overwhelm the other songs. She does take the show's classic, "The Siren's Song," but while an off-Broadway revival in 1959 made it Jane's solo with a touch of chorus, it was written as a duet for Jane and Bessie, backed up by women imitating the plinks of the essential college instrument, the ukulele. In short, Kern and Wodehouse have overthrown traditional procedure. Solos and ensembles aren't mandated by who's performing, but by where the story stands at a given point. Nor is there any revving up at the start; the show doesn't want it, and the authors don't need it. Curiously, the 1959 revival juggled the order of songs and reassigned them to conform with well-made musical comedy. Over forty years after the premiere, *Leave It to Jane* was still an unusual proposition.

As of *Sally* in 1920, Kern enters his middle period, working with fewer partners (mostly Anne Caldwell) on bigger shows with some of Broadway's biggest headliners, like Marilyn Miller in *Sally* itself. He troubled to join Bolton and Wodehouse for an old revolutionaries' reunion in *Sitting Pretty* (1924), yet Kern had by then passed beyond the little things, *nolens volens*. This was a time not for adding to the experiments of the first period but for development of those experiments. However, Kern's contemporaries, challenged by his originality, his brevity in charm songs and expansion in ballads, altered their ideas about theatre scores. By 1925, Kern's influence was as paramount as Herbert's had been a generation earlier.

Kern's third period is a paradoxical one in which he draws further and further away from the amiable, subtly British Cinderella tales he trained in. Wodehouse and Bolton are out of the picture, and Anne Caldwell has retired. From *Show Boat* on, it's all Hammerstein and Harbach, as Kern increasingly broadens the architecture of his scores. *Show Boat* (1927) and *Sweet Adeline* (1929), both with Hammerstein, move partway between the spacious musical "scenes" of operetta and the simpler song chain of musical comedy. But *The Cat and the Fiddle* (1931) with Harbach and *Music in the Air* (1932) with Hammerstein again are built of such ample musical sections that they defy category.

Obviously, Kern's third period is, like his first, one of discovery and invention. It is not only because Kern has it in him, and it's pouring out: he is working with two of the finest librettists America ever produced, and they're in their prime. *The Cat and the Fiddle* was billed as "a musical love story," *Music in the Air* as "a musical adventure," and that's about as precise a generic description as one can make. Both are backstagers, *Cat* about the love affair of two composers in Brussels, she American pop, he Rumanian legit; and *Music* about a German village couple who get mixed up with theatre people in Munich. Nothing unusual there—though Hammerstein turns cliché around when he has the village girl do so badly in her theatre debut that a pro has to go on for her on opening night. Nor is the characterization unusual. It is all in the scores. *Cat* is about writing and performing music, and it's made of it almost exclusively. Lengthy sequences are enacted in a kind of ballet for words, dialogue and song interspersed as the tale wends its way from street to backstage to apartment to dream dance to onstage and back and around, encircling the character with images in sound of what is most on their minds: song and romance, which, to Kern and Hammerstein, are the same thing. Notice, too, that the old one-set-per-act plan is exploded for more fluent narration. Technology had caught up to Kern; the décor now floats along with the story. The music floats as well, not only through songs but through snatches of songs that wind in and out of the symphony, eternally renewable.

Those songs that do stand out make a medley on romance: the heroine's "She Didn't Say 'Yes' " and "Try To Forget," the choral "(I watch) The Love Parade (gaily going by)," the theatre piece "Poor Pierrot (loved his fair Pierrette)," the hero's "One Moment Alone" and "A New Love Is Old," and a street-singer's serenade, "The Night Was Made for Love" used commentatively throughout the evening. Romantic musicals—operettas—often emphasized love songs, but they were afraid to do so in a contemporary setting, as if their composers couldn't pull it off without a tantara of period costume to clear a path for them. But Kern and Harbach are contemporary—in mysterious Brussels, but *now*. They conjure up a magic in the everyday, in celesta cadenzas to suggest the wind dancing with a crystal chandelier; in a ferocious duel of pianos between the two leads, jazz versus fugue; in the *commedia dell'arte* masque of the play-within-the-play that reminds us what remote beauty is available just inside a theatre's doors. *The Cat and the Fiddle* is not musical comedy: the music works too hard. It's not an operetta: it's real. It's a *concerto grosso* in which the pit band of eighteen players is the *ripieno* and the cast is the *concertino*. No. It's "a musical love story."

Music in the Air is even more fully composed. Hammerstein set some of his dialogue to rhymes that loosely follow the orchestral activity, and Kern gave the four scenes of the first act and the seven of the second generic titles, as Berg did in his opera *Wozzeck*. Some of this is judicious. The opening, labeled Leit Motif, sets the plot into motion with, yes, a "leading motive," a bird call which the old village tunesmith works into the song that sends the young couple on to the Munich adventure: to sell the song to a publisher. (Kern himself borrowed the theme from a bird outside a window of his Bronxville home.) Flute and piccolo tease the string texture with the call for much of the scene, so Leit Motif it is. Scene Three, dubbed Pastoral, is just that, a potpourri of brook plashings, mill-wheel drippings, church bells, and rustic tunes as the two villagers rest on their way to the city. But the first scene of Act Two, in the city zoo, is hardly the Sonata Kern terms it, and the dressing room scene, Humoresque, is simply two songs reprised. However, Kern does make his finale, back in the village, a Rondo, as he says: the whole sequence, in which the alienated couple make

their amends, is set to a simple AABA song, "We Belong Together," the A
being the rondo theme and the B the counter-subject. This may sound pat,
but between them Kern and Hammerstein think of so many ways to frame
their tune that it keeps sounding different. A tavern piano introduces it,
little girls take it up, a boy whistles it on a woodpile, the hero raises it for
a full statement, other characters try it, a contralto hums it, the bassoon
gurgles it, woodwinds ripple about it, and at length, all well that ends well,
the full company takes it in block chords as bells chime out a coda. Kern
and Hammerstein have proved their thesis, from bird song to chorale: music is all around us.

Kern's music had grown remarkably from his Princess days. Compare
"Till the Clouds Roll By" and "Ka-lu-a" with "Smoke Gets in Your Eyes"
from *Roberta* (1933) or with "All the Things You Are" from *Very Warm
for May* (1939), his last show. These are weighty numbers, passionate where
a Princess tune was pert, enchanting where Princess music diverted. Some
say Kern had lost his swing—Kern, sometimes, among them. "She Didn't
Say 'Yes' " and "We Belong Together" prove them wrong. Kern had spent
his first two periods naturalizing flamboyant but personless musical comedy. In his third period, he reversed himself, joining Friml and Romberg's
partners Hammerstein and Harbach in reorchestrating romance. No matter what kind of show his successors wrote, then, Kern taught them how.
More important, he taught without reference to performing specialties.
Porter expounded upon Ethel Merman, Rodgers and Hart doted on a Helen
Ford or Vivienne Segal, the Gershwins put everything into Gertrude Lawrence or the Astaires. If a performer didn't like a song or couldn't do it
justice, the performer wasn't fired—the song was.

Not with Kern. He compromised with show biz opportunism when necessary, but seems to have been the first author who felt the work should
come first. (No wonder Oscar Hammerstein was the only lyricist who got
along with Kern: they shared this innovative credo.) There were no Kern
stylists of the Merman-Porter kind. On the contrary, Kern wrote outside
the traditions of vaudeville charisma and resented performers who were
better celebrities than they were singers. He was obliging to Fred Stone
because the star—one of the two or three biggest—was ready to forgo his
accustomed interpolations and sing Kern. He was respectful of Helen Morgan, who had the good taste to *become* famous singing Kern. However,
irked at having to build *Sally* around Marilyn Miller's growing reputation
(and iffy vocalism), Kern wrote tunes beyond Miller's range. They were
too right for *Sally* for Miller not to sing them; she got through them by
force of will. But they overextended her, and are probably why she had
no recording career.

If Irving Berlin is as well-known as Kern, as a theatre musician he is by comparison uninfluential. Yet no analyst would omit him from a masters' list. From the very start, Berlin is rich, his prodigious catalogue of the 1910s yielding affecting ballads, wacky comedy, irresistible rhythm numbers. "When I Lost You" touches everybody's story. "Lazy" sounds it, virtually meandering to its conclusion. "I Want To Go Back to Michigan" is as gently rural in tone as "He's a Rag Picker" is cranky and urban, "My Wife's Gone to the Country (Hoorah! Hoorah!)" sweeps one up in naïve mischief, and "Everybody's Doing It Now!" might have been the theme song of the whole dance movement in pop music. Typical that Berlin was the one who wrote it. He articulated what most people felt but couldn't say; couples claimed his love tunes for Their Song, and wags of the streets worked his satires into their patter. Berlin was prosaic yet original; he had a unique way of distilling the everyday into the ritzy. "Snookey Ookums," known to clear rooms with its insistent baby talk, tells of two sweethearts driving the neighbors berserk with their cooing. Grotesque exaggeration or pointed stylization?

Berlin was a primitive in composition. He could not even play piano, except in one key, by ear, quite badly. He had a conception of harmony, though not the knowledge: an assistant, working through Berlin's melody, would play chording possibilities till Berlin heard aloud what he had heard in his head when he wrote the song. Yet his craft is not to be denied, his instinct for voicing the thoughts of a nation—think of "God Bless America" and "White Christmas" alone.

Clearly, Berlin would fit into the film musical well, with its backstagers crammed with Hit Tunes. But where would Berlin place in on Broadway? In the revue, most easily. Yet he accommodated the book show as well. *The Cocoanuts* (1925), Berlin's twelfth score and first story show, to George S. Kaufman and Morrie Ryskind's book, was a satire on Florida land-grabbing with the Marx Brothers. In this age of *Whoopee* and *Sunny*, musical comedy did not stretch for character, and Berlin was not hard-pressed assembling the dance ("The Monkey Doodle-Doo"), the scene-setter ("Florida by the Sea"), the ballad ("A Little Bungalow"), a plot number ("When We're Running a Little Hotel of Our Own"), even a patter song for Groucho ("Five O'Clock Tea"). Knowing the Brothers would improvise from night to night, Kaufman and Ryskind wrote wide and open, giving Berlin the chance to plot in any likely Tune. In rehearsals, when dowager Margaret Dumont answered a question with a haughty "Yes, sir!," some wag chimed in with "That's my baby!." All present had a laugh, and someone suggested they add the business into the text. Better yet, Dumont would go on to say "No, sir!," the wag would cry, "Don't mean maybe!"—and Berlin, sensing a song cue, rushed to the piano to write "Minstrel Days," not that the dialogue or the song had anything to do with Florida land-grabbing.

How would Berlin do in the more precisely crafted thirties show? He did fine. *Face the Music* (1932), dealing with corruption among the sachems of New York City—names and all—had a book by Moss Hart and was directed by George S. Kaufman *and* Hassard Short. A heavyweight show. Yet Berlin's casual timelessness set him on the right course: Hart will skewer the topics of the day, and Berlin will baste the ethos of an era. Rich folk dining in an Automat sing "Let's Have Another Cup o' Coffee (and let's have another piece o' pie)." Couples coo to "Soft Lights and Sweet Music" and kick up their heels in "I Say It's Spinach (and the hell with it)." The increasingly New York-centered culture extrapolates its reinless tempo in "Manhattan Madness." *The Cocoanuts* score couldn't provide a hit; *Face the Music* was loaded. Historians offer Jay Gorney and E. Y. Harburg's eloquently tragic "Brother, Can You Spare a Dime?" as the anthem of the Depression, but more people were singing "Let's Have Another Cup o' Coffee." Part of being essential to pop culture is staying adaptable. In days of rag, the jazz age, and now in hard times, Berlin not only anticipated the general feeling but styled it attractively, gave advice that most people wanted to take.

Surely the forties musical would catch him up, through its fixations on artistry? It didn't. Rodgers and Hammerstein produced as well as wrote, and they asked Berlin to do the score for a property they had, based on the life of Annie Oakley. Berlin told them to do it themselves. But they had in mind something lighter in scheme than *Oklahoma!* and *Carousel*. Moreover, Ethel Merman was to be Annie, necessitating a star-vehicle approach they could enjoy as managers but not as authors. Berlin, despite his lack of musical training, is no high-rolling amateur. He had produced shows, built (with Sam Harris) his own theatre, worked with the expert Kaufman, Short, and Hart, seen Hollywood wrestle with the forms of the musical when it made the first talkies. He knows *Annie Oakley* will not be as simple as *The Cocoanuts* or *Face the Music*. Herbert and Dorothy Fields were writing the book; on the basis of their first act and a second-act outline, Berlin realized that he would have to come up with "hillbilly music." But Hammerstein pointed out that Broadway's idea of hillbilly comprised dropping the *g* in *-ing* words, a lazy pastiche. So Berlin decided to audition himself. He looked through the Fields script for some musical moments. He found one in Annie's speech on common sense being all the education her folks need and another in her fumbling first attempt to talk romance with the man she loves, sharpshooter Frank Butler. She knows nothing of love. She has heard about it. And so came, as effortlessly as usual for Berlin, "Doin' What Comes Natur'lly" and "They Say It's Wonderful."

Berlin went ahead and wrote the score for *Annie Get Your Gun* (1946), incidentally coming up with a workable hillbilly sound in "Doin' What Comes Natur'lly" and "You Can't Get a Man with a Gun." They aren't remotely in country style, yet their simplistic diction, melody, and harmony suggest folkish art. Most ingenious is "Moonshine Lullaby," a limber cradle song made of the beat, harmonies, and riffs of swing—even unto a back-up black trio. (The number occurs in a train scene; the men are porters.) Nothing could be more forties; the look and sound of it reminds one of countless moments in Fox and Universal musicals. Nothing could be less hillbilly, less aligned with *Annie*'s period setting. But, in context, the number not only works well but does truly affect a country flavor. Again, Berlin can be ecumenical and timely at once, heedless of pastiche yet in the precise groove.

By the time Berlin got to *Miss Liberty* (1949), on events attendant upon the erection of Bartholdi's statue in New York harbor, Berlin was even capable of operetta-like plot songs. The show's vocal arrangements favored the jiving choral scat originated by Hugh Martin and Kay Thompson, but Berlin's opening chorus, "Extra! Extra," takes us back to the early American musical. Newsboys for the warring *Herald* and *World* vie for custom, followed by separate statements from their respective readers: "I like the *Herald* filled with stock market news . . ." and "Couldn't eat a meal without the *World* . . ." Then Berlin charmingly runs the two refrains in counterpoint. This *quod libet* approach was long established; Gilbert and Sullivan used it regularly, and Herbert adopts it notably in *Naughty Marietta*'s opening, flower girls against street cleaners. But Berlin made it a specialty in the pop tune throughout his career, in "Simple Melody" (ragtime versus ballad), "Pack Up Your Sins and Go to the Devil," "You're Just in Love," or in his last song hit, a new number for the 1966 *Annie* revival, "An Old Fashioned Wedding."

Kern devised a new kind of theatre music working outwards from American pop; Berlin dwelled within pop from start to finish. George Gershwin followed Kern, starting in musical comedy tunes, working operetta forms into musical comedy, and closing with full-blown opera. Yet note as well a sign of the times in the dance-band sound, which Gershwin made his own: "jazz." At times, jazz meant any and all American band pop, carrying ragtime's syncopation over into more complexly harmonized melodies. Live or on records, bands made music that the home musician couldn't; and the home musician gave up. Music would be tricky now.

Gershwin is the first tricky composer. It was he who instituted "blue" harmony, who redoubled syncopation, who sported a piano technique beyond any player's challenge and set the style into his published songs. He is the first composer whose arrangements for performance are so much a part of the tunes that to ignore them is to go out of style. There is a jive in Gershwin that all his exponents must adopt, jive to carry them through ballads as well as rhythm numbers: because all Gershwin is jive.

"What moves a show along," he told Kay Swift, "is 2/4 rhythms." Energy, drive, pulse. Berlin's and Kern's dance songs beguiled or enthused; Gershwin's were a fascinating rhythm. His description of the *Rhapsody in Blue* as "a sort of musical kaleidoscope of America" might well apply to his slant on musical comedy, a scope of "our vast melting pot, of our unduplicated national pep, of our blues, our metropolitan madness."

This is a neat description of twenties jazz as well—and, when the self-proclaimed king of jazz, Paul Whiteman, gave a historic concert in 1924 to reveal the parts of jazz to an elite public, who, of them all, was the true king? Jazz is a paradox of ensemble and disputation: the band plays together, but individual instruments rise up to make their witness, tell the glory. *Who* is jazz? Whiteman's concert had not been going well till, in the "next-to-closing," Gershwin strode out to the Chickering to introduce this same *Rhapsody in Blue* and turn that kaleidoscope on American pep and blues and madness. Many could play hot piano; Gershwin alone wrote hot piano, hot ballads like "I'll Build a Stairway to Paradise" and "The Man I Love," hot charm songs like "Nobody But You" and "Innocent Ingenue Baby" and of course hot hot songs like "Nashville Nightingale" and "The Half of It, Dearie, Blues." Diverseness, pep, blues, madness: city music. Gershwin was city music. Gershwin was king of jazz.

The jazz style most generally was an expansion of the dance fad of the 1910s; more bands, more kinds of bands, more dance rhythms, more dance rhythms applied to more kinds of songs. A ballad written in 1910 stayed a ballad. A ballad written in 1925 would sooner or later be taken up by a band: jazzed. Never before or after in this nation's cultural history did its pop music have such homogeneity. Everything was jazz, or jazzed till it passed for jazz, and everything else vanished. Victor Herbert solemnized the revolution by dying shortly after the Whiteman concert, though according to legend it was not jazz but Florenz Ziegfeld that killed him. (Ziegfeld kept the composer waiting in his office while he auditioned a Girl in a hidden bedroom. Shocked and insulted, Herbert lost his temper and suffered a fatal stroke.) Still, the passing of the man who wrote the best American pop in the early 1900s and the rise of the man who wrote the autograph of the 1920s is not coincidental. Power changed hands.

In the year in which Herbert died, Gershwin found a new lyricist, his brother Ira. George is generally regarded as the most gifted composer of this generation—who else wrote an opera? But Ira has been somewhat taken for granted, like a pleasant relation tolerated in the family business. Wodehouse was Ira's idol, and it shows; Ira stands with the clever lyricists, playful, neat, alert. Joining his brother on *Lady, Be Good!* (1924), Ira wrote the kind of lyrics people like Fred and Adele Astaire could sing: as innocent as a brother-and-sister act. Not much happens in *Lady, Be Good!* The siblings hold chins high in adversity ("Hang On to Me"), the sister meets a guy ("So Am I"), society convenes ("A Wonderful Party"), and so on. It's *Florodora* in the city.

But Ira came alive for *Tip-Toes* (1925), about a girl and her vaudevillian uncles fortune-hunting in Florida. Another society background, another show with plot but no real story; very twenties. So the score is the show. George's mad pep and Ira's growing awareness go well together, like kids on the town. A Gershwin score is a sweet nature looking for a dance, Ira's naïveté riding on George's drive. *Tip-Toes* is conventional overall; its parts are unique. The chorus frames the action tritely in the scene-setting opening, "Waiting for the Train," and the near-closing heroine-salute in the title song. In between, however, is adventure and commentary. "These Charming People," Ira's first attempt at Wodehousian comedy, is truly funny, its slaps at the silly rich taking off of Michael Arlen's ironic phrase. "Sweet and Low Down" tells of cabaret—"Professor, start that beat!"—and "When Do We Dance?" urges on the riot. "Looking for a Boy" is pure as milk, "Nice Baby" (for a married couple) a touch wicked. And, behold, the first-act finale is five minutes' worth of plot in song. George and Ira are giving more than their pedestrian (if fast-moving) books would inspire in most writers. They seem to be flying on their own initiative.

Devoted to his younger, increasingly acclaimed brother, Ira deferred to him artistically. He could move along into any project as an equal, however, and the joy of *Of Thee I Sing* (1931) is how neatly Ira's wit suits George's ambition. George S. Kaufman and Morrie Ryskind wrote a fine book, nothing out of the norm in structure. It is the Gershwins who break ground. While serving the action, they stand outside it, dote upon it, tease it. When Kern musicalized musical comedy, he drove it toward operetta. When Gershwin musicalized musical comedy, he created a new kind of comic musical, a superspoof. The script, entirely given over to political satire, is funny—but the score, too, jokes. The *music* jokes, in George's pastiche, quotation, burlesque, and Savoyard pranking.

As early as in the overture, George pulls out a surprise: not a potpourri but a concise dramatization of the action. *Of Thee I Sing* follows its protagonist from candidate on a platform of love into the White House, where his First Lady helps him stave off a near-successful impeachment. Synoptically, this is a tale of love versus threatening outside forces—a restless public, corrupt pols, a difficult Congress. So Gershwin builds the overture out of opposition, the love songs on one hand and a theme used in the show both by reporters covering the party convention ("Because, Because") and, slightly modified, by the Vice-President when he calls the roll in the upper house ("The Senator from Minnesota"). So, after an electoral fanfare ("Wintergreen for President!"), Gershwin suddenly pulls out this antagonistic theme and builds the entire overture out of it, developing it symphonically, using it in counterpoint with one of the love songs ("Who Cares?"), and developing it climactically to lead into the title song. As Beethoven did in his four *Fidelio* overtures, Gershwin is announcing his subject impressionistically.

Of Thee I Sing's score follows this plan of commentative motion. *Tip-Toes*' "Waiting for the Train" dragged the curtain up on business as usual; *Of Thee I Sing* opens with Wintergreen's torchlight parade, less a chorus than an orchestral tapestry of oldtime rally tunes (from Sullivan and Sousa to "The Sidewalks of New York") interspersed with the mob's cries. There are other *hommages*. The intrusion of a French delegation is heralded by a quotation of Gershwin's tone poem *An American in Paris,* the First Lady's big solo, prompting a major turnabout in the plot ("I'm About To Be a Mother") is a breathless Viennese waltz, and solos by politicians of the regions call out a hornpipe, a cowboy strain, "The Farmer in the Dell," and, for the Dixiecrat, "Old Folks at Home."

Pastiche was a feature of musical comedy in its very origins as ballad opera. But the Gershwins' full-scale comic-opera ensembles are amazing. The first act finale presents Wintergreen's inauguration and wedding—his platform, remember, was love. George gets right into the pomp of the thing by introducing the Supreme Court to a rising and falling whole tone scale, then pulls the chorus in for a festive hip hip. Wintergreen appears to make an official's emptily pertinent remarks, and goes into one of the musical's favorite bits, the "So long, girls, I'm hitched" number, *Allegretto grazioso* ("A Kiss For Cinderella"). The bit is remade, however, for as Wintergreen goes into a repeat, the chorus sings another line above him ("He is toodleooing all his lady loves"), telling the audience—as Gilbert and Sullivan's characters so often did—what they can readily discern for themselves. But when the bride enters and reprises the song's last lines with new, feeling words, the whole game is overturned and the love plot reinforced. Without shifting gears, the Gershwins have encompassed satire and genuine sentiment.

Now the plot bestirs itself. In rushes the couple's prime antagonist, an unlikable southern belle who makes a legal claim to Wintergreen. After she tells her story in recitative ("I was the most beautiful blossom"), the ensuing argument is laid out in a volatile concatenation of tempos and textures, every line sung, but little of it in what the musical heretofore regarded as song. It's opera—but the sound is pop. Not to get solemn about it, the Gershwins gave the musical its most strategic new idea since Hammerstein and Harbach threaded *The Desert Song*'s libretto onto a musical spool.

This is an age of transformation. As Kern shifted the strengths of the musical with the reaching rightness of his melody and Berlin made the eternally youthful artlessness of his a tonic to cure the banal, the Gershwins infused the musical with wit, spoofing what Kern is styling and Berlin stating. The golden age is scarcely begun, and already the musical has been *flavored* as it had never been before. How different was Luders from Kerker? Harry B. Smith from Robert B. Smith? But how different is the Kern of "Wild Rose" and "Who?" from the Berlin of "Say It with Music" and "What'll I Do?"; and how different they from the Gershwins of "Dear Little Girl" and "Fascinating Rhythm." For the first time in the musical's history, one can tell who wrote a song on first hearing. The *song* tells you.

If the Gershwin brothers were beautifully matched as a team, Rodgers and Hart were not. Rodgers was dedicated, ambitious, and orderly, while Hart was capricious and undependable, amazingly fluent at the job when he buckled down but sometimes hard to find. The characterological discrepancy does not show in their work. On the contrary, no lyricist is more alert and inquiring than Hart; and Rodgers is mellow. In fact, their unlike natures make their work always fresh, Rodgers setting off the romance in Hart and Hart enriching Rodgers's sentiment with irony. As usual for the time, the music came first. But let Rodgers write an entrancing waltz, long-lined, upward-reaching, and carefree, and Hart would beautifully dispute it: "Falling in love with love is falling for make believe."

If Berlin specialized in revue and Kern and the Gershwins walked into operetta from musical comedy, Rodgers and Hart were sworn to musical comedy from start to finish. They preferred songs to musical scenes, casual vocalism to *operatique*, snappy doings to lavish dreams, here and now. Yet *Dearest Enemy* (1925) is very nearly a comic opera. The setting is the American revolution, the love motion Romeo-and-Juliet entanglements between our women and their soldiers, and the tension between the apparent comic opera figures (pompously randy officers, lacy ladies) and the authors' earthy characterization of them made the work something special. The ballads "Here in My Arms," "Bye and Bye," "Here's a Kiss," and the wonderfully conflicted "I'd Like To Hide It (I'd like to smother down the flame inside!"), all for youngsters, are attractive rather than revolutionary. But the comic songs have no precedent. The older characters, a Colonial dame and some British generals, offer such odd propositions as "(What do all) The Hermits (do in springtime?),", and "Full Blown Roses" and "Old Enough To Love," both paeans to the mature romancer. Naturally, Fields would throw in a few japes on the change in culture from the 1770s to the 1920s: General Tryon hopes to meet the "first families of the Bowery," and he finds New York refreshingly quiet after "the hustle and bustle of Philadelphia." This leads us to another Rodgers-Hart special, "Where the Hudson River Flows," listing the sylvan air of "a sweet, secluded Harlem glen," "the lovely Bronx," and Wall Street's moonlit wall: "Half a mile up Broadway you can hear the crickets call!"

With such an elastic sense of song topics, Rodgers and Hart could exhilarate otherwise routine musical comedies with Herbert Fields books. Even when they did unquestionably shatter formula, in *Peggy-Ann* (1926), the surprises in the book are not as striking as those in the songs. The heroine (Helen Ford, delectable in braids) spends most of the action in surrealistic exploits peopled by her associates from Glens Falls, New York— boy friend, mother, sister, rival, and friends. The show is famous for its lack of conventions, but it doesn't really lack them—it just stirs them around a little. It has no opening chorus, no number at all for the first ten minutes or so. But Herbert's *The Only Girl* had already tried this twelve years earlier. Anyway, once Peggy-Ann's friends troop on for "Hello" they are in effect delivering an opening chorus. It just got there a little late. Even the idea of the dream is not new: *Peggy-Ann* is a reworking of Marie Dressler's vehicle *Tillie's Nightmare*.

But the combination of Hart's insightful satire and Rodgers's feeling tunes, plus their unusual song projects, lend the feeling of tizzy, and the calm within the tizzy, that the dream and love plot need. Sally sings, "Look For the Silver Lining." Peggy-Ann sings, "Where's That Rainbow?," whose second line runs, "Where's that lining they cheer about?" Broadwayites, pirates, racetrack touts, guests and staff in an improvised wedding in a department store, and a Texas Guinan imitation all have their songs, the tizzy especially commanding in the Guinan's "Give This Little Girl a Hand," a salute to the prostitute, whose "great supply can never meet the great demand." This kind of number simply didn't exist in the Princess days. And naturally there are the tender passages, like "A Tree in the Park," without which we would have little reason to follow Peggy-Ann's adventure from metropolis to sea (in an open boat after a shipwreck—when a fish offers to tow them in, one of the group gets up and stalks offstage through the cutout waves) to Cuban resort and back to Glens Falls, where the love songs pay off. Peggy-Ann awakes, patches up her quarrel with boyfriend Guy, and gets engaged.

Just to list Hart's love lyrics is to celebrate his nuanced variety: the jaunty "Thou Swell," the sorrowful "I Still Believe in You," the pristine "My Romance," the confident "This Can't Be Love," the rhapsodic "With a Song in My Heart," the fanciful "Dancing on the Ceiling," the importunate "Can't You Do a Friend a Favor?," or the singular approaches implied in the titles of "My Funny Valentine," "I Could Write a Book," "The Shortest Day of the Year," "No Place But Home," "Everybody Loves You (when you're asleep)," "There's a Small Hotel," "Moon of My Delight," "Morning Is Midnight," and "Fool Meets Fool." Moreover, besides thinking up new possibilities for emotional engagement between characters and audience, Hart made his words work within each lyric to develop his themes, not simply restate them. Too many of his predecessors express no more in a whole song than they could fit into their first two lines. How perceptively Hart marks the bright and dull seasons of company-keeping among his fellow humans; even outside the context of the music and rhymes, single lines are eloquent—"My head is just a hat place," "A house in Iceland was my heart's domain," "The quick toboggan when you hit the heights," "An eyeful you'd die full of pleasure to meet," or "I admire the moon as a moon, just a moon."

In ballad, Hart and Rodgers make a right angle; in comic and charm songs they swing. Hart preceded E. Y. Harburg in the whimsical manipulation of English (as in "Sweetenheart") and joined with Porter in hailing sensuality and ribbing the celebs of the day. The tricky, mad rightness of Hart's rhymes would not suffer competition till 'Stephen Sondheim came along two generations later, as for example in the pairing of "hang around as bridesmaids" and "faithful fate that betides maids" in *Peggy-Ann*'s wedding scene. Perhaps more with Hart than with any other writer, we sense history being made by a unique personality rather than by an impersonal march of events. Hart is a Fred Stone, a Marilyn Miller of lyricists: a delightful thing *happens* when he comes on stage.

Rodgers and Hart never wrote without a story in mind—not that they couldn't. When Ziegfeld, irritated at the unpromising batch of plot and character songs they wrote for *Simple Simon*, demanded they supply a Hit Tune, they gave him a beaut, completely out of context, "Ten Cents a Dance," which went right from Ruth Etting's mouth to the nation's ears. Called to Hollywood, presumably for more of the same, they experimented, Gershwin-style, with the song quotient in musical comedy, writing the Jolson vehicle *Hallelujah, I'm a Bum* virtually as an opera. Strange, isn't it?, to find such antagonistic Babies in on the same stunt: the ambitiously authorial Rodgers and Hart and the inner-directed Jolson. This is the paradox of a transformational age: the parts of the art aren't all moving in the same direction at once. Indeed, Rodgers and Hart themselves were not to develop their Hollywood experiments. When they returned from the Coast—Rodgers in utter disgust and Hart somewhat wistfully, having enjoyed riding the Los Angeles demimonde circuit—they went back to writing straight songs.

Perhaps *Pal Joey* (1940) was the quintessential Rodgers-Hart show, the most potent arrangement of musical comedy practice by the team best suited to musical comedy. Some were shocked—a musical about people who sleep around, commit blackmail, and buy favors from the authorities? Yet it was a hit. Once again Rodgers and Hart had caught something between the fond and the factual, something not entirely likeable but certainly believable. The protagonist's "What Do I Care for a Dame?" and his wealthy *protégeuse*'s "What Is a Man?" and "Bewitched, Bothered and Bewildered" touched chords not sounded before. It can't be easy to be fresh in your twenty-seventh show, but *Pal Joey* disclosed musical comedy's properties so basically that it was not only fresh but ontological, defining the purpose of the form in its earthiness, its parodistic observation, its honesty. Kern and Hammerstein, if you will, offered to change the world; Rodgers and Hart described it. What they saw, in *Pal Joey*, was high and low lives on the make or the take. Much of the score laughs at the types—the many nightclub numbers spoof not only club numbers but the people who perform and applaud them. "Bewitched" is ironically *about* its singer as it expresses her irony—"the laugh's on me," she admits—and even the one apparently ingenuous ballad, "I Could Write a Book," is sung by a naïve sweetheart and the cad who is setting her up for a pass.

So Rodgers and Hart never felt limited by the song as their engine of expression, from the first shows in 1925 to the last, a revision of *A Connecticut Yankee*, in 1943. Seldom did they expand into the musical scene, as Kern and the Gershwins did. When Rodgers and Hart did try one, in *A Connecticut Yankee*'s eclipse scene, or in "He Had Twins," the highly expository opening to *The Boys from Syracuse*, the pieces sound nothing like *Of Thee I Sing*'s Savoyard numbers or *Show Boat*'s first-act finale, nothing like operetta. It's more like musical comedy with several songs going off at once.

But then Rodgers was at times so daring in his harmony that his songs could startle in themselves. Gershwin, of course, is famed for his testing of chromatic chording, as is Porter, and Kern varied his conservative simplicity with harmony of great adventurousness—his last song, "Nobody Else But Me," still waits for theatre music to catch up to it. Of the masters group, only Berlin was consistently old-fashioned in his harmony. It is perhaps Rodgers who led them all in advancing key relationships in the pop tune in *melody* as well as in underlying structure.

Cole Porter matches Gershwin in rhythmic ingenuity and Rodgers in harmonic dexterity. As lyricist, however, he was unique—the funniest and the slyest. Porter was odd man in this company, wealthy, urbane, born to midwestern sticks, raised to the northeastern prep school world, and Continentally established where the others were of poor or middle-class New York background and stayed within its touch when they got to Broadway. He was WASP; they were Jewish. He spent money; they worked for it. He had fancy, somewhat disreputable friends whom he celebrated in his patter songs; the others would have been ashamed to flaunt such things, to flaunt at all. What makes Porter the utter one is his disdain for the received values, the morality of a national culture. He didn't care, and he didn't care who knew it. Yet he was working in a medium most intent on preserving those values. It makes for an interesting set of internal contradictions. On one hand you have the boy-meets-girl, the Cinderella rise, the silver-lining optimism, the monogamy, the temperance, the innocence and idealism. On the other, you have "Let's Do It," "Find Me a Primitive Man," "Say It with Gin," "I'm a Gigolo," and "Why Marry Them?" Suddenly, musical comedy has become racy, and the communications authorities aren't sure how to handle it—"Love for Sale," from *The New Yorkers* (1930), was banned from radio play. Friml's tune by the same title and on the same theme, from *The Vagabond King*, had no such trouble. But then Clifford Grey's lyrics for Friml didn't offend the acceptable virtues. Grey's prostitute calls love "a sad, mad, fleet, sweet, bitter thing." Porter's cites "old love, new love, every love but true love." That's spit in the face.

Though he also wrote tender ballads, the characters and themes that attracted Porter tended strongly to a jaded sophistication. His charm is a candid, now-and-then campy glamor, his hobbies are relaxing and making love, his sport is to make lists, and his quirk is to put slang expressions into the mouths of the fabled great of the past. (For example, the line that kicks in the chorus of "Hey, Good-Looking": "and as Elizabeth Barrett Browning once said . . .") He was the first songwriter to make gay allusions, even calling it by name in "Farming" in 1941, in a jest about George Raft's cow's failure to throw a calf: "Georgie's bull is beautiful but he's gay."

These games seemed an inevitable concomitant of the peculiar milieu Porter both hymned in his work and enjoyed in life. His list songs, made wholly of nouns in simile, were a superb invention; his patter on the doings of the trivial elite were very taking. His songs called into play a new kind of show. No Gaiety, Princess, operetta, or Cinderella model could frame the images Porter sculpted. He and Herbert Fields were a great match (on seven shows), and Porter also went well with Howard Lindsay and Russel Crouse and Sam and Bella Spewack: all creators or developers of the post-*Sally* musical comedy that tolerated romance but really wanted sex.

Nymph Errant (1933) was right up Porter's alley, a picaresque about a British schoolgirl investigating the possibilities of sensuality from the French Riviera to Asia Minor. Based on a startling novel by a curator at the Victoria and Albert Museum and staged in London with Gertrude Lawrence, *Nymph Errant* could not possibly have been right for Kern, Berlin, or Youmans. The Gershwins would have made it too spunky; perhaps Rodgers and Hart? But Porter was most appropriate. He worked closely with librettist Romney Brent, filling out an episodic tale with a ton of characters who appear for a bit and vanish as the heroine dashes off to destiny. The plot's joke is that, try as she does, she cannot find an acceptable partner till, defeated and home again in North Oxford, she encounters her aunt's gardener—Eve and the apple, remember? But Porter has many jokes to spill from start to finish: a schoolmistress's exhortation to her students in "Experiment"; an aged harlot's lament, "The Cocotte"; a salute to the classic satyr, "Casanova"; a tourist's chorus, "Ruins"; a flirtatious duet sung in the desert, "Back to Nature with You"; a Parisian nightclub routine, "Si Vous Aimez les Poitrines"; the tale of a man with a distinctive marital problem, a thousand unfaithful wives, "Solomon"; and (the show's one familiar title) "The Physician," a list song about a doctor who adores his patient's anatomy but "never said he loved *me.*"

Nymph Errant was Porter's own nomination for Best Porter Score. Broadway's idea of a Porter show was *Anything Goes* (1934), with its quintet of hits in Porter's most popular style: "I Get a Kick Out of You" (the torcher), "You're the Top" (the ultimate list song), "Blow, Gabriel, Blow" (the rouser), "All Through the Night" (the love song), and "Anything Goes" (topical satire). Yet Porter's most characteristic show until *Kiss Me, Kate* was neither his favorite nor Broadway's. It was *Jubilee* (1935), one of the great events of its decade but considered so difficult to cast that it has not been revived full out in thirty-five years.

As with Brent, Porter collaborated carefully on this one, with Moss Hart, on a world cruise. Typical Porter: work is play. Too many Porter shows contain numbers that could slip in almost anywhere into any musical, but *Jubilee*'s sizable score has superb pieces right for it alone. Hart's tale of a royal family who steal away from political troubles on separate vacations hither and yon gave Porter, for once, a book that believes in the same things that Porter's songs do: spoofing the famous; letting go and having a hot time, ideally with primitive men; and knowing when to leave. The characters include tintypes of partygiver Elsa Maxwell, of MGM's Tarzan Johnny Weissmuller, and of Noël Coward (here called Eric Dare, which sounds more like the real thing than "Noël Coward" does). Naturally, most of the nobles take up romance on their adventures. The Prince dates an American dancer, the Princess dates Eric Dare, the Queen dates the Tarzan, here called Mowgli.

Photographs reveal a gorgeous show, one art deco nightclub set backed by bamboo blinds and dominated by a metal palm tree showing the very picture of an age. Hart's book is superb; Porter brought out the devil in him that his mentor George S. Kaufman suppressed. But it is Porter's score that most impresses, for imagination and pizzazz. The Princess's "Why Shouldn't I? (take a chance when romance passes by)" might be the motto theme of all Porter. "When Love Comes Your Way" restates the theme with a blunt sentimental beauty shocking in this context, revealing the little-known Porter who would have traded all the hot times for the real thing that he mocked and admired all his life. The "Entrance of Eric," the crowd's salute to "the idol of our matinees," is solid utilitarian theatre music, and Eric's ensuing narrative, "The Kling-Kling Bird on the Divi-Divi Tree," is the wry other-directed Porter, whose bird warns against entangling alliances—the heterosexual kind: "Oh, beware, beware of the ladies fair in the countries across the sea!" "When Me, Mowgli, Love" is unthinkable in any other show, a hilarious sendup of star egotism, moviegoer romance, and the native habitat. "Me and Marie" is a Porter surprise, a pastiche of the Hit Tune of the 1890s. But then there's "A Picture of Me Without You," the latest list song, and rather sedate for Porter till he pictures "poor Mr. Heinz, my dear, without a pickle!" And there were expectable Porter standards, "Just One of Those Things" and "Begin the Beguine," though for some reason they took years of recording and listening before they went over.

It must have been a heady experience to attend the theatre in those years, knowing that any given new work by these men might disclose not treasurable moments but a evening stuffed with gems. Even the less fabled teams are pleasurable—Arthur Schwartz and Howard Dietz, of the post-*Follies* revue; or B.G. De Sylva, Lew Brown, and Ray Henderson (respectively conceiver, lyricist, and composer) of the *Scandals* and comparably brash book shows like *Good News!* (1927). Schwartz and Dietz seem like Rodgers and Hart in their vitality; in revue, they made pop tunes into the cream of theatre songs. De Sylva, Brown, and Henderson were always simple and snazzy; they made theatre songs into the cream of pop tunes.

Count on them for dance sensations like "Black Bottom" or exploitations of fad like "Birth of the Blues," or the most artlessly hummable charm songs like "(This is my) Lucky Day," all from the *Scandals of 1926*. And when, in the *Scandals of 1931*, they* attempt a Cole Porter list song in "Ladies and Gentlemen, That's Love!," with its allusions to "What Is This Thing Called Love?" and "Love For Sale" and lines such as "When a toucan at the zoo does what only two can do," they are telling us of Porter's influence, of the spreading power of golden-age composition.

De Sylva, Brown, and Henderson are like Berlin in their reaching generality. It was they who wrote, for the *Scandals of 1928*, "(A real) American Tune," though they don't provide much of a recipe. Harry Richman introduced it, explaining to comic Willie Howard about jazz's conquest of the world. What is an American tune? Its parts are a "tear," a "lusty cheer," something "true" and "red, white and blue." And the *Scandals* offers samples—of what, though?—in Schubert, Wagner, and Victor Herbert.

Obviously, the *Scandals* had no firm idea of what is American in a tune. Just as obviously, Kern, Berlin, the Gershwins, Rodgers and Hart, and Porter did. Their styles, however different, agree on certain emphases in melody, harmony, rhythm, subject matter, and characterological attitude. Besides asserting creators' authority, these golden-age songwriters gave American performers and technicians something to dig into other than their tricks—and here at last vaudeville crumbled. Vaudeville's stylistic influence on the musical, from the Hit Tune to comic shtick, was strong when the character of composition was weak, derivative, miscellaneous. But Kern, Bolton, and Wodehouse held entertainment hostage to story. Berlin adapted vernacular ideologies into a working-class poetry. The Gershwins emphasized the drive and innocence of a once isolated, rural culture just coming into world power and city hip. Rodgers, Hart, and Fields sharpened the musical's satiric edge. Porter raised questions of class and sex. If Cohan's flagwaving and quickstep pacing were his way of instituting an American art in a medium too seldom American, these Babies, his heirs, could take their ethnicity for granted. And in turn they could collaborate with such definitively American performers as Marilyn Miller, Fred Stone, the Castles, and the Astaires, giving them the ultimate in American Tune. The question is not who can write one—they all could, by now. The question is: what, at their best, could they do with it?

---

* Brown and Henderson wrote the 1931 *Scandals* without De Sylva, who had taken up residence in Hollywood.

Kern and Hammerstein provide the answer in *Show Boat* (1927), for with this work everything changes. What Victor Herbert had auditioned, what Henry Blossom, Guy Bolton, and P. G. Wodehouse had discovered, what all the ambitions and lucky strikes had unveiled, this show gathered and developed. Significantly, *Show Boat* was neither musical comedy nor operetta. Ziegfeld billed it as "an all American musical comedy," but it is more like the "musical play" that Herbert revealed in *Algeria* and which Rodgers and Hammerstein would make the seminal alchemy of the 1940s: theatre with operetta's idealism and musical comedy's naturalism, operetta's musicality and musical comedy's energy, operetta's breadth and musical comedy's intimacy.

Show Boat is the musical's first epic. For a musical of the 1920s, it derives from a remarkably unlikely source, Edna Ferber's sprawling novel whose major feature—a floating theatre—would seem beyond the resources of the stage. Ferber calls into play the Mississippi, wide-open Chicago, the New York theatre, the south, the midwest, miscegenation, desertion, death, thespians, prostitutes, gamblers, blacks, the valorous, the flashy, and the seedy from the 1870s to the 1920s. Most musicals were by contrast mere days in the life of college sweethearts, bumbling bootleggers, or stout-hearted men. How could *Show Boat* possibly work as a musical, even a long one, even a huge one?

How? By planning and writing *Show Boat* as if it were the first musical, ignoring all the wisdoms on what was formally expedient. Kern and Hammerstein started in the 1880s and ended in 1927. They moved from a Natchez levee onto and around Captain Andy's *Cotton Blossom* (even into its auditorium for rehearsals and performance), back to the levee, progressed upriver to the Chicago World's Fair, down the mean streets to a music hall and back to the *Cotton Blossom* in Natchez. They included Ferber's principals and her variety of kind, softening the desertion and omitting the death but sharpening the miscegenation. They attacked the story straight on and told it securely and fully, letting song, dance, and comedy occur where the action called for it. Everything is characteristic; everything does something necessary, whether for story, for time, for place, for atmosphere. Going scene by scene, much of what they ended up with ran counter to prevailing Broadway craft, yet as a whole *Show Boat* feels like a retrospective of the musical from its beginnings to the 1920s, only newly ordered. It is, at one time, the conclusion of a half-century's art and the inception of the next half-century's art.

The problem of organizing and coordinating *Show Boat*'s parts might have defeated even Kern and Hammerstein had they not been so absorbed by the challenge of adapting the book. Ferber's people fascinated them, especially Captain Andy Hawks, who "thought only in terms of waterways . . . Towns and cities were to him mere sources of supplies and passengers, set along the river bank for the convenience of steamboats." Or his wife Parthenia Ann Hawks, whose life, but for her accident of union with Andy, "was meant to be made of crisp white dimity curtains at kitchen windows; of biweekly bread bakings; of Sunday morning service and Wednesday night prayer meeting; of small gossip rattled evilly under the tongue." The development of these two characters is central not to the love story of daughter Magnolia Hawks and the gambler Gaylord Ravenal, but to Ferber's view of human character as essentially dreamer or realist. (This follows through with the young lovers—Magnolia is the realist, who eventually takes over Parthy's role as absolute ruler of the show boat. Ravenal is the dreamer, a man of style, debts of honor, and nothing else, who vanishes partway through the novel without a look behind him.) Though they are thought of as supporting roles in the *Show Boat* musical, if Andy and Parthy are not perfectly cast much of Ferber's work, and Hammerstein and Kern's, is lost. Andy is not just a grizzled joker, but a splendid codger who personalizes the childlike enchantment of the theatre. Parthy is no mere grouch but a Cassandra, the only mortal who comprehends doom. Ziegfeld, wouldn't you know it, brought them utterly to life in Charles Winninger and Edna May Oliver. But since the 1950s these parts have been going to unsuitables—to superannuated hoofer Andys and "secretly" nice Parthys. It robs the structure of its foundation.

What is most taking in Ferber is her way of binding these people into the backstage of her setting: Andy and Parthy are producers, Magnolia and Ravenal are actors. Then, by expanding her theatrical subject to include music hall and the Broadway show, Ferber tells a parable of show biz, its cheap melodramas, story ballads, and Ziegfeldian spectacles all one. Kern and Hammerstein were not tackling another boy meets girl, but a legend about entertainment, about how the dreamers pass its enchantments on to each other through the generations despite the resistance or neglect of the realists.

But there were problems, first of all the Mississippi. The river and, by synecdoche, the show boat itself, rolling obsessively through the book— even in scenes placed far from water—must be central. These symbols are unwieldy, symbols within symbols, for while Captain Andy is like the show boat, full of charm and love and fun, Parthy is the river, unforgiving, righteous, destructive. How can all this be staged? It can't. It must be suggested. A theme song for the Cotton Blossom, a kind of motto figure, would work well, with a southern plunk in it for suggestive typing. But this was not enough, even when carried through in reprises. Hammerstein petitioned Kern for something on the Mississippi proper, and either he or Kern thought of modifying the motto theme to achieve it. Slowed to half tempo, its melody played in inversion, "Cotton Blossom" became "Ol' Man River," the former a frivolous view of river life, the latter the life of the river, folkishly simple, steady and strong and rising to an immense climax. Human life, symbolized in the *Cotton Blossom,* is quaint excitements that pass; natural life, symbolized in the river, is awesome and changeless.

There is more here. "Ol' Man River" is sung by the black deckhand, Joe, backed by a black men's chorus. Not precisely a song of social protest, it nevertheless enlarges the show's socialistic worldview, with its "tote that barge" and "lift that bale." Used as the theme song not just of the Mississippi but of *Show Boat* as a whole, it becomes bigger than itself, humanitarian and synoptic. More music for the black characters followed—solos for Joe's wife, Queenie, a chorus of foreboding called "Mis'ry's Comin' Aroun'," a dance number for pseudo-African villagers at the World's Fair, "In Dahomey." As the songs piled up, the tale grew in universality. Behind the main characters, all humankind watches, worries, waits. Yet the principals and the chorus are tied together, partly through Joe and Queenie, and partly through the miscegenation episode, which involves one of the *Cotton Blossom*'s players, Julie, exposed by a rejected suitor as a mulatto and ejected from the company in segregationist Mississippi.

Thus, the project grew in proportion while it kept its parts in alignment. Most tricky of all the challenges was not characterization, racialism, or the all-basic river, but the time span. Here is where Kern and Hammerstein pulled their greatest coup—yet showed themselves most traditional. They captured the sense of fifty years' passage by writing songs in styles ranging from ancient to current, progressing from the oldest to the latest as the action unfolds. But more: they raided the public domain, placing hoary strains, local allusions, and even a vaudeville story ballad into their score. *Show Boat*, after all, is a backstager—backstage at the melodrama, the nightclub, the Broadway star's party. So the years pass *as one listens,* from ragtime and vaudeville Hit up to theatre jazz, the whole tied together by the timeless pulse of "Ol' Man River."

Show Boat is three hours long; over two hours of it is music. Much of that is pastiche. Yet Kern supposedly didn't like faking style. When he and Hammerstein were talking about a musical based on a novel on the life of Marco Polo, Hammerstein said, "Here is a story laid in China about an

Italian and told by an Irishman. What kind of music are you going to write?" Kern replied, "It'll be good Jewish music." In other words, no rinkytink pentatonic shamming for color, just straight Broadway stuff. However, *Show Boat* is anything but straight Broadway circa 1927. "Cotton Blossom" might have been composed on a banjo in 1880. "Can't Help Lovin' Dat Man" revives the coon song. "Mis'ry's Comin' Aroun' " has a middle section suggestive of spiritual. A buck-and-wing leaps out of the 1890s into the first-act finale, the heroine's theme is dinky parlor piano, and other numbers carefully revert to Kern's earliest style. Even "Bill," rescued from *Oh, Lady! Lady!!*, is thought to have been composed in 1906—just two years before the time of the scene it appears in in the *Show Boat* chronology.

No musical had done this before; no librettist but Hammerstein could have conceived of a show that would have to, and no one but Kern could have brought it off. *Show Boat*'s singular feat is its evocation of fifty years of American life. *Show Boat*, novel and musical, contains the contradictions of Americana—the city versus country, the mobility versus holding to roots, the white versus black, the progress versus stability, the notion versus tradition. This is true epic.

Consider *Show Boat*'s score in diagram, counting the program heard on the Broadway premiere, the "Mis'ry" chorus (cut to a third because of time problems), and the songs which Kern and Hammerstein added for the first London production, the 1936 film, and the 1946 Broadway revival. Note the emphasis on love songs, the recurrence of the river theme, the use of pastiche and interpolation to carry the time scheme through, and the revision of music or lyrics as required to develop the juxtaposition of changing fashions ("human" time) against the consistency of universal values ("natural" time):

ACT ONE		
Overture	Love and tragedy presented together	Misery theme, quotation of "Can't Help Lovin' Dat Man" and the heroine's theme, development of the Misery theme,* full statement of "Why Do I Love You?"
Opening	The 1880s	Defining setting, era, and race. Quotation of "Can't Help Lovin' Dat Man," verse of "Ol' Man River," used in conjunction with "Cotton Blossom," 1st development of motto figure [C-C-A-G]. Pastiche: hornpipe
"Who Cares If My Boat Goes Upstream?"		Character song
"Make Believe"	Magnolia meets Ravenal	Character song
"Ol' Man River"	Natural time Introduced	Theme song, second development of motto figure
"Can't Help Lovin' Dat Man"		Pastiche: coon song
"Life On the Wicked Stage"		Antique character song
"Till Good Luck Comes My Way"		Antique character song
"Mis'ry's Comin' Aroun' "		Pastiche: spiritual, third development of motto figure
	Ravenal joins the Cotton Blossom	
"I Might Fall Back on You"		Antique character song
"C'mon Folks!"		Pastiche: cakewalk
"I Have the Room Above"		Character song
The Parson's Bride		Interpolations: "Hearts and Flowers" and oldtime "villain music"
"Gallivantin' Around"		Pastiche: coon song
"I Still Suits Me"		Pastiche: banjo-picker
"You Are Love"		Character song
Finale	Magnolia marries Ravenal	Plot number, with pastiche: cakewalk and reprise of "Can't Help Lovin' Dat Man"
ACT TWO		
Entr'acte	Love and natural time presented together	Statements of "Make Believe" and "Ol' Man River"
Opening	1893	Defining setting and era. Interpolation: Fatima's hoochy-koochy.
"Why Do I Love You?"		Character song, with quotations of "I Might Fall Back on You" and "Can't Help Lovin' Dat Man" in choral bridge
"In Dahomey"		Character song

---

* This includes a brief, wordless vocal solo, the first (and for decades the only) use of the human voice in a musical's overture.

	1904 Ravenal Deserts Magnolia	
"Bill"		Interpolation: Kern-Wodehouse trunk material Updated into ragtime
Reprise: "Can't Help Lovin' Dat Man" Trocadero music-hall show		Interpolations: Sousa, Offenbach, "Goodbye, My Lady Love," "At a Georgia Camp Meeting," "After the Ball"
	Magnolia returns to the <u>Cotton Blossom</u>	
Reprise: "Ol' Man River"	1927 Natural time set against human time	Updated in lyrics referring to World War I
"Hey, Fella!"		Character song, fourth development of motto figure
Reprise: "Cotton Blossom"	Human time reaffirmed	
alternates for same spot { "Dance Away The Night" "Nobody Else But Me"		Contemporary character songs
	Ravenal returns to Magnolia	
Finale: Reprise: "Ol' Man River"	Natural time ultimately reaffirmed	Theme song in original state, full cycle

This, then, is what a generation of master songwriters had been leading up to and would lead beyond from: the musical without set form, the protean musical, adherent of its own devices and no others. If there ever was an American Tune, it is "Ol' Man River." *Show Boat* is an American saga, told in the American idiom—all of its music, all the kinds. To collect so much in one outing, and at the same time to perceive so much in it, is to demonstrate for the first time the encompassing richness of this American Tune we call musical comedy. And *Show Boat* must be its supreme achievement: for nothing comparable to it was attempted for forty-four years.

8

The New Style of Heroine

In the 1920s, Americans acculturated the radio and the phonograph. They heard smooth baritones of the air, opera's sopranos on a visit to Herbert or Romberg, innocuous dance-band tenors of the sweet tones; and they began to wonder why such pleasant voices so seldom sang theatre music in the theatre. In the 1920s, the tradition that nourished Elsie Janis and Marilyn Miller was demolished. Now, *singing* heroines became essential.

As we have seen, the 1920s, age of Miller, had also widened character possibilities in the musical. This boded well, for some of the best singers were unsuitable for the hoyden heroines associated with Janis and Miller. Helen Morgan, for instance, fielded a fetching soprano unusual in her line of speakeasy torch singers, and she became the legendary member of the original *Show Boat* cast, lasting through the 1932 revival and—for sustaining appraisal—the 1936 film. Morgan would have been unthinkable as a heroine in the 1910s, with her sort of serio-comic look but a love singer's voice and a protagonist's sensualistic pathos. Her Julie Dozier is not *Show Boat*'s heroine; still she was more closely associated with the show than was Norma Terris, the Magnolia.

Worldliness was what the new heroine was acquiring. Most pertinent in this matter would be Gertrude Lawrence, for some the most appealing star that musical comedy produced. She was British, schooled in revue. Yet before she was through she had toured through every aspect of show biz from the West End to Broadway in Gershwin shows, experimental musicals, in farce, high comedy, and melodrama. Like her predecessors, she had a numbo. Morgan's was "Bill," a love song with a torch patina applied by the situation of the scene. Lawrence's was "Someone To Watch Over Me," a love song with jazz sweets. It picked up a vulnerability in Lawrence, as "Bill" did in Morgan. But Lawrence had far more than this to play, while Morgan peaked in plangency. And Morgan's reign was brief, while Lawrence went on and on till, literally, she dropped.

She could be hard to work with, not personally but technically. "She never does eight consecutive bars twice the same way," reported Agnes de Mille, choreographer of *Nymph Errant* (1933). "You expect Gertie downstage; she comes in center back—even with the curtain up and a paying audience. You expect her to play *grazioso* and gently; she is *allegro vivace* and sharp. You expect her in dark-green silk; she is in transparent gauze." Yet she was what show biz never has enough of, a spectacular individual. Noël Coward thought her "capable of anything and everything. She can be gay, sad, witty, tragic, funny, and touching." No one understood her better. He wrote *Private Lives* to play with her—and her alone: when she fell ill during the run, he closed the show till she recovered. Yet he, too, noted her instability: "She has every theatrical essential but one: critical faculty." When most performers open a show, they are finished with tryouts. When Lawrence opened a show, she *began*.

The New York critics, from her Broadway debut in 1924 in *André Charlot's Revue*, were wild about her; she was refreshingly earthy after all the Cinderella girls. Like Morgan, she brought something adult to the musical. Men didn't always have to court Lawrence; she could seduce them. In *Oh, Kay!* (1926), she meets her hero by fishing him out of the drink and makes her entrance sneaking into his house armed with a revolver. De Mille thought Lawrence had a problem meeting other women's eyes, but she could look straight at a man. Kay is a bootlegger, and might have to spend the night at her hero's house to evade the law. Won't she lose her reputation? "I'd sooner lose that," she cries, "than my freedom!"

Lawrence was especially apt in song. No star has been more attacked for faulty intonation, but her *Oh, Kay!* records tell otherwise. "Someone To Watch Over Me," sung to a rag doll, the dreamily optimistic "Maybe," and the energetic "Do, Do, Do" are vocally neither unstable nor secure. Rather, they reveal a woman who gave the utmost to an adoring public, almost by contract, and certainly without gauging intonation the way a well-schooled singer would. Lawrence was versatile? Lawrence was *spontaneous*. And adult. She is wistful, purposeful, wicked, perhaps more womanly than anyone before her, biologically complete. No wonder her only relatively successful soprano is more important for what it tells about her than what she can do with it. Sally looks for the silver lining. Evangeline in *Nymph Errant* wants to enjoy the perfect lay. Who else could have played the part?

One might say that of all Lawrence's roles. She was *the* principal in a number of *the* musicals—in *Oh, Kay!*, the high point of twenties farce; in *Nymph Errant* (1933), London's most eccentric statistic in musical comedy; in *Lady in the Dark* (1941), the most revolutionary musical after *Show Boat*; and in *The King and I* (1951), the last of Rodgers and Hammerstein's great musical plays. Kay, Evangeline, Liza Elliott, and Anna: four completely different parts, a bootlegger, a naïve sensualist, a businesswoman in psychological travail, and a Welsh schoolteacher fighting for democratic procedure in a barbarian land.* The woman made character into a personal enchantment, a life entirely made of theatre, like George M. Cohan's. Propose a vehicle and she was thrilled—but, oh wait! What about her dressing room, her flowers, her billing? What theatre had you in mind? Her agent must read the script, her astrologer must give consultation, her darling Noël will guide her, and what about the supporting cast?

Legends dim, especially now that the public seems to enjoy hearing grisly dish about the immortals. Years after Lawrence had died, of hepatitis, during the run of *The King and I*, Richard Rodgers churlishly denounced her performance of Anna for its flat notes. Perhaps he was bitter at having had to write around a star for the second time in a row (after *South Pacific*, for Mary Martin and Ezio Pinza), or perhaps the memory of the Lawrence contractual tizzy still gnawed at him. There were a lot of people Rodgers didn't like. But if there had been no Lawrence, would *Lady in the Dark* have taken the form it finally did? Others could have handled the part—Hart at one point threatened to go to Irene Dunne if Lawrence didn't end her shenanigans, and he meant it. But would Dunne, or anyone, have been able to cover all the edges in Liza Elliott, with her role games, her tantrums, her conflicted dream adventures of the woman who cannot believe in her own glamor yet presides over a demesne of the glamor world? Huxley wants to dedicate his book to her. Her likeness is to grace the next postage stamp. A Hollywood idol stands upon her orders. A fashion magazine awaits her executive decisions. Staff mutiny confronts her, nothing she can't deal with. But emotional turmoil under the businesslike façade is sending her into a crack-up, and when the play begins she is making her first reluctant visit to a psychiatrist.

It's an odd way to make a star entrance: "in her late thirties," the script tells us, "and plain to the point of austerity. She wears a severely-tailored

---

* Lawrence played a fifth book-musical part in New York, Ann Wainright in the Gershwins' *Treasure Girl* (1928). This, too, was different, a money-hungry heroine so grasping that the authors blamed the show's failure on the realistic delineation of the character. Lawrence, who had done her best, was devastated.

business suit, with her hat pulled low over her eyes. No single piece of jewelry graces her person and her face is free of makeup." Nor do the rest of Liza Elliott's comings and goings resemble at all the madcap Kay of the pistol and rag doll. Liza's lines are never funny, her associates are either magazine staff or men of the outside world she is virtually cut off from, and she does not fall in love with her psychiatrist. Where, then, is the Lawrence Broadway needed, the song-and-dance love heroine of "Someone To Watch Over Me"?

In dreams: three lengthy episodes in which the charms and terrors of Liza's private world come out in fantasy—the New York night of Liza Elliott, glamor girl; the wedding of Liza Elliott, interrupted by a jeering chorus; the trial of Liza Elliott, "the woman who cannot make up her mind." Her defense, "The Saga of Jenny," the woman who got into all kinds of trouble because "she *would* make up her mind," gave Lawrence her first chance in the show to cut loose in a numbo, and with the abandon of a burlesque queen. The song coincidentally reflects her own inability to commit herself—to offered parts, to stage directions, to costumer's designs, even at times to her oldest friends. And it is interesting that, like Marietta, Liza has a dream melody ("My Ship"), heard in fragments at first and only sung out in full near the end of the show; moreover, she has a dream man, it turns out, who can sing the song along with her. In the end, she can keep her sanity only by sharing her magazine with this man—and, we infer, her life.

This "happy ending" is unlike Lawrence, who turned down some impressive beaux because they wanted a wife and she wanted the stage. *The King and I*, then, seems more self-definitive, a romance between two people who cannot possibly marry. The show's attraction lies in the contrast between the two principals' inhibitions and the colorful abandon of the setting, most finely distilled in "Shall We Dance?," when Lawrence in her pink satin ball gown danced a polka with Yul Brynner in his full-dress pajamas. Actors habitually luck into and out of successes, passes, and flops, but they long for a smash to carry them through years of run, *Sally*-style. This was Lawrence's great smash. There was New York, London, tours, perhaps the film.

Suddenly, she died. They dimmed the lights along Broadway, the West End, and even in Hollywood (a real salute—she had not done well in the movies). "Her star quality," *The King and I*'s director John van Druten recalls, was "undefinable but intensely vivid." No one could say what she was.

While Broadway nurtured a livelier soubrette, a wordly woman, it still ran weak in leading men. At least they had changed character. In Donald

Brian's time they were stolid, military, and, where possible, dashing. Now Cohan's sassy dandy had taken over and, through the researches of Herbert Fields and B.G. De Sylva, had developed smarts and lost his morality. A lady dazzles; a man . . . what? Charms? They were short in charm too. True, some who might have served the musical in the Lawrence era went off to Hollywood—Fred Astaire in the 1930s, Gene Kelly in the 1940s. And what they left behind was William Gaxton.

Gaxton was musical comedy's sole enduring male headliner, first choice in casting Rodgers and Hart, Porter, Gershwin, and Berlin, introducer of "My Heart Stood Still," "Thou Swell," "Of Thee I Sing," "Who Cares," "Mine," "You're the Top," "All Through the Night." Historian Stanley Green describes him "slick-haired, chunky, nervously energetic . . . Hollywood's idea of what a press agent looked and talked like." In *Of Thee I Sing* (1931) and *Let 'Em Eat Cake* (1933) he was a crooked politician, in *Anything Goes* (1934) another brash playboy, in *Leave It to Me* (1938) a brash newspaperman, in *Louisiana Purchase* (1940) a crooked lawyer, in *Hollywood Pinafore* (1945) an agent (enough said), in *Nellie Bly* (1946) another brash newspaperman. Hardly a man to admire. And how similar all the characters are next to Lawrence's jumps in type. Nor was Gaxton remotely comparable to his leading women in allure, though the scripts keep telling us otherwise. In the title role in *A Connecticut Yankee* (1927), he catches the eye of Morgan Le Fay, who murmurs "Lovely" as she vamps him. But no, sorry, he just wasn't.

Not all musical comedy romantic leads were con men, of course, but to list other kinds of leads is to stray from stardom. The men who played conventionally respectable characters were more or less interchangeable, and while they might at length earn over-the-title billing, they were hardly box-office draws. Jack Whiting is the best known of these, a pleasant singer and an exceptional dancer, affably clean-cut. Whiting was seldom out of work, from the 1922 *Follies* to *The Golden Apple* in 1954, but what does a juvenile do about age? What can he grow into, William Gaxton? Ominously, Whiting did just that, playing Gaxton's role in *Anything Goes* in London. By the 1950s, in his last parts as sleazy city mayors, he was nothing but a dancing Gaxton.

Aging didn't always hurt heroes. Some matured into their prime. Alfred Drake began as one of the many youngsters in *Babes in Arms* (1937) and was still a little-known singer when he played the original Curly McClain in *Oklahoma!* (1943). Drake did so well as the cowboy who sings "Oh, What a Beautiful Mornin' " and "The Surrey with the Fringe on Top" that he went on to more native art in *Sing Out, Sweet Land* (1944), a review of American folk song. However, Drake was not cut out to be a juvenile, least of all an unassuming good-fellow. With his sturdy baritone and more-Shakespearean-than-thou ham spoof (or was it true ham?) he was ideal for the lead in *Kiss Me, Kate* (1948).

Big as *Oklahoma!* was, Drake could easily have faded away after it (as did his Laurey, Joan Roberts), for the star-making part in that show is Ado Annie. (Alumnae who went to big things directly after included Celeste Holm, Shelley Winters, and Barbara Cook.) But *Kiss Me, Kate*'s Fred Graham/Petruchio was a new character, a man with the fire of the Friml-Romberg hero and the earthy aplomb of a Fields-De Sylva wisecracker—in short, splitting the difference between operetta and musical comedy.

Drake originated only three more musical roles on Broadway, the beggar-poet in *Kismet* (1953), the actor-adventurer in *Kean* (1961), and the Chevalier role in the stage version of *Gigi* (1973), but his Hajj in *Kismet* was one of the outstanding star turns of the day. The part is close to Petruchio, but the show quite different from *Kiss Me, Kate,* a "musical Arabian night" filled with savagery and sensuality, its cast of fifty taking in opera singers, jazz dancers, whirling dervishes, and Steve Reeves.

Bagdad! "There's been nothing like it for a thousand years!" one of the characters exulted—and at the center of it was Drake, glibly extemporizing his art in "Rhymes Have I" and "Gesticulate," reflecting, to pounding tympani, on the irony of chance in "Fate," seeing fortune suddenly raise him from beggar to noble to Wazir's wizard, making love to the Wazir's steamy wife of wives, Lalume (Joan Diener, with the voice of Dalila, the poise of a Ziegfeld Girl, the comic precision of a top banana, and the physique of a French postcard), philosophizing on seizing the day in "The Olive Tree," and sternly tying up the plot by murdering the Wazir in full sight of his court, bringing his daughter and the handsome Caliph together, and assigning himself the job of doing penance in a fabulous oasis with Lalume. Lastly, alone, he reminded the public of the romantic musical's first principle: "Lovers come, lovers go, and all that there is to know, lovers know . . ." and the curtain slowly fell on one of Borodin's most lovely melodies, flute, harp, and celesta over muted strings—one of the first *pianissimo* endings in the musical's history.

We are already into the 1960s, still without a transcendant headline hero, an enduring musical comedy king who isn't a comic. Yet there were two queens, one reigning for forty years and the other for thirty. Both were singers for starters; both favored musical comedy over operetta; both worked with the best writers; and both became such big draws that every appearance promised a big event, no matter its subject or approach. The two are often compared—foolishly, for they are apple and orange. Yet, in the 1940s and '50s, as a pair they became something of a symbol of the

American musical, much as Cohan, Montgomery and Stone, and Miller had been before them. They were unique specialists whose specialties became norms for youngsters to aim for. And when, on June 15, 1953, these two women appeared in public for the first time as a pair, on television, in a marathon duet of old standards, such a furore arose that, for a moment, musical comedy seemed like the nation's most cherished art, the diversion it had first been and the stimulation it had become, at once. It was perhaps the last time that the country turned as a unit to the Broadway musical.

Ethel Merman and Mary Martin are therefore crucial in understanding the musical's character. Merman was nervy, candid. Martin was sweet, even coy; where Merman turned up as Nails Duquesne or Panama Hattie, Martin played the goddess of love, a long-suffering wife in a ceremonial Chinese show, and Peter Pan.

They could meet in a part—both played the title roles in *Annie Get Your Gun* and *Hello, Dolly!* But their contrast is spectacular: in professional technicalities such as Merman's distaste for touring and Martin's enthusiasm for it (she took *Hello, Dolly!* to South Vietnam in 1966); or Merman's strictly musical parts as opposed to Martin's stints in drama; in the very different voices, Merman's the classic belt limited in range but dynamite within it and Martin's a medley of possibilities from earthy songplugging to high coloratura; in Merman's drift toward Cole Porter and Martin's toward Rodgers and Hammerstein; or in their respective characterological origins, Merman's as a sidekick on hand for songs and yoks, Martin's as a cutie destined for traditional heroine parts. The force of their personalities made necessary certain changes in the musical's personal agenda, for Merman was too big not to carry a show, therefore had to become a romantic lead (and bring new information to romance) and Martin was too unusual to play traditional heroines.

Merman completes the arc begun in the rise of Fanny Brice, the seriocomic as heroine. A stenographer who, no one knows where, picked up the rudiments of belting,* startling breath control, and thorough diction, she went into the Gershwins' *Girl Crazy* (1930) in the kind of part Ruth Etting played in *Whoopee:* for song spots with as few lines as possible. In Act One, Merman did little more than check in; in Act Two, she had "Sam and Delilah," "I Got Rhythm," and "Boy! What Love Has Done to Me"— the only real singing in the show, what with Ginger Rogers, Allen Kearns,

---

*Belting means pushing the chest voice up into what would normally be the lower notes of the head voice. This yields a gutsy, vibrant sound with little beauty of tone and a sharply curtailed range. Merman had high notes—she displays a G in "Anything You Can Do" in *Annie Get Your Gun*. Still, she barely pecks out the note.

and Willie Howard as principals. "Sam and Delilah" is lazy blues, "I Got Rhythm" the rouser, "Boy!" the typical Gershwin song built on a stepwise ascending bass, with a repetitive figure dominating the melody (like "The Man I Love"). As Gershwiniana they were pleasantly in the groove. But who had been working this groove? Most recently, the Astaires, Oscar Shaw, Gertrude Lawrence, and Ruby Keeler, all better or worse practitioners of the light Broadway head voice. Merman's belt was ear-opening, her stamina a wow, her precise attack stunning, and her famous long-held note in "I Got Rhythm" utterly unlike anything a performer had ever done to suggest joyful confidence. Marilyn Miller or Adele Astaire might have danced it, of course, and Gertrude Lawrence could have glided about the stage in a wise smile. Merman just stood there and sent it over.

"You break all the rules of nature," Grace Moore told Merman. "Where do you breathe from?"

"Necessity," says Merman.

Cole Porter put it well in one song from *Something for the Boys,* calling her "the missing link between Lily Pons and Mae West." And she's tough, never dealing in euphemism or diplomacy when grouching or blazing will do. "If somebody needs telling off," she explains, "he'll get it with both barrels. A friend can doublecross me once—then, fing!" Her directness must have impressed the authors of her shows, for they wrote her parts around it. Even her songs were Mermanized. To match Miller's "Look for the Silver Lining" and Lawrence's "Someone To Watch Over Me," Merman had "Eadie Was a Lady" in *Take a Chance* (1932), a tribute to the hooker who had "class with a capital K." Setting a heavy march beat that rules the entire song, the verse introduces two blowzy daughters of the Tenderloin, Maud and Mabel, who recall Eadie Hayes, most deft of all the sisterhood, with her golden toothpick and her way of drinking brandy "with her finger sticking way out." Ultimately, we learn less about Eadie than about Merman, with her golden diction and no-nonsense pitch and her way of holding her ground, hand on hip, and telling you how it was. Her belt was the voice of the proletariat, of women who could sing of or even play a prostitute. She can sing it down and dirty or bright and gala— "loud, but honest," she has described it. If Lawrence was worldly, Merman was earthy. Thus was provisioned a new range for musical comedy character.

At first the character was a challenge to locate. Musical comedy folklore recalls Merman as the diva of *Anything Goes* (1934), because she is associated with most of the song hits and her character, the wisecracking Reno Sweeney, sounds like Merman in her archetypal fullness. On the contrary, Merman was in 1934 not yet integrated into musical comedy practice: she loved the hero, William Gaxton, but, as "I Get a Kick Out of You" tells us, she can't get him in competition with Bettina Hall, the technical heroine of *Anything Goes*. Moreover, while the book gave Merman plenty of role, it could do no better for her at the curtain than hand her over to a silly Brit of the Gaiety type, as if she were a mere gold-digging friend of the family.

Still, *Anything Goes* was crucial for Merman, her fourth show but the first that gave her a *role*. Her movie stints had not panned out well, so it looked as if she would have to count on Broadway. That meant finding something more to do than sing. Actually, Merman's part in the Bolton-Wodehouse *Anything Goes* script was minimal—but by chance the *Morro Castle* sinking took the fun out of their shipwreck plot, and Howard Lindsay and Russel Crouse were commissioned to revise the script. They must have viewed Merman as a godsend: build her up to replace the now useless shipwreck business. They were having lunch at the Algonquin when a tough-looking woman caught their eye. Interesting; who is she? They took her for an evangelist—this was the age of Aimee Semple McPherson. She turned out to be a nightclub hostess—this was also the age of Texas Guinan. Inspiration! Reno Sweeney is Guinan with a McPherson veneer! Blow, Gabriel, *blow:* for the Merman persona was born. And so it went through the thirties. By the time Merman faced off Bert Lahr in *DuBarry Was a Lady* (1939)—note the reference to her "Eadie" numbo—the persona was developed, patented, and a big seller. Now she got the guy and controlled the plot.

Take her *DuBarry* entrance. It's early in the show, two numbers down and the plot barely moving. Lahr has arranged for the night club employees to shower Merman as May Daly with roses—now that he has won the Irish sweepstakes, he's courting serious. "Here she comes!" the Girls scream. Remember comparable moments—Sally tripping in with the orphans, Sunny riding in on horseback, Kay's bootleg sneak with a gun she can scarcely hold, Lisa Elliott's cool entry into analysis. These women are stars for an era that glows; Merman says, Go on and *do* it. So she struts into *DuBarry Was a Lady*. The flowers fly. She stands there a moment. Then, fing!, she says, "*What the hell is this?*"

Nor will she flatter romance as the others did. She and The Girls talk of DuBarry:

> GIRL: She was a bad woman. Why, she only loved Louis for what he could give her.
> MAY: Now, baby, you wouldn't cheapen a beautiful thing like love by giving it away for nothing!
> GIRL: Money! There are lots of things in this world better than money!

MAY: Yes, but it takes money to buy 'em! It's funny. Men are women's foremost industry. We're put on earth to trim 'em, then along comes a pauper with a nice set of shoulders and we wind up washing his underwear!

That's the cue for May's first song, "When Love Beckoned (in Fifty-Second Street)," which everyone in the show thought was going to be *DuBarry*'s hit. It wasn't. Merman had better luck with "Friendship," a celebration of her platonic understanding with Lahr in the form of an eleven o'clock country swing that sent the customers home relishing the crazy big-apple turns to big-band blasts in the pit, the nonsense animal noises (Lahr very into his "woof, woof, woof"—"I like that," he says, trying it out a few more times), the encore foolery ("Ethel," Lahr avers, "you're solid, you're solid!"), and the closing "Good evening, friends!" Merman's other songs emphasized her cynicism about the gender war: "Come On In," a lubriciously funny (and sexist and racist) floor number; "Give Him the Oo-La-La," advice on how to get ahead (of men); and "Katie Went to Haiti," the saga of another Eadie.

With her next show, *Panama Hattie* (1940), Merman became the compleat headliner, her name alone above the titles. She was famed for her cool professionalism: once she finished the tryout tour, her parts were *frozen,* and you could measure the difference in her performances from night to night in calibrations so tiny they would have no name. A chorine once saw her standing in the wings, ready to go on, the picture of ready nonchalance. "Gee, Miss Merman," says the kid. "Aren't you nervous?"

"Why should I be nervous?" Merman asks her. "I know my lines." And she gets her cue and on she goes.

Merman credits *Annie Get Your Gun* (1946) as the show that renovated her persona, cut away the ribald big-city crust to reveal a more vulnerable heroine. And yes, in the end sharpshooter Annie Oakley throws a match in order to win back her prideful *vis-à-vis* Frank Butler. Yet the toughness followed her. It was hard to write a sweetheart part for Merman. When she first spotted Frank Butler, she locked her eyes with his and let everything in her body collapse, mouth wide as a goon's and legs gone cuckoo at the knees. When Chief Sitting Bull inducted her into his tribe, she wore her feathered headdress like a comic-strip warrior. When society turned out for her in lace and simpers, she taught them forthright manners. And when she and Butler met for the climactic shooting contest, Annie was as unyielding as DuBarry or Hattie, in "Anything You Can Do (I can do better)." Generally, *Annie* observed the vehicular structure New York had come to expect of Merman, with youngsters and dependables of secondary prominence in support, most of the songs reserved for the star, and many of her jokes relating to her impatience with fancy ways and euphemisms.

Nor did aging tame Reno Sweeney's informing elements of nightclub broad and evangelistic trumpet. *Call Me Madam* (1950) offered Merman as America's ambassador to imaginary Lichtenburg. The curtain rose on her taking the oath of office in a windy speech alien to her true lights. Something new in Merman: protocol. At last it's over, and she is asked when she'll arrive at her post. "I'm not sure," she replies, swivelling into her stuff as she asks Secretary of State Acheson, "Hey, Dean—where the hell is Lichtenburg?" That was the Merman New York loved—the only Broadway Baby who never had a flop.

But Hollywood couldn't get her: all but two of her roles went to others in screen versions. She continued to try the movies, always in her earliest incarnation as the serio-comic, little more than a band vocalist in costume. As late as 1938, Fox put her in *Alexander's Ragtime Band* just to sing Berlin standards and lose Tyrone Power to Alice Faye. "What do I have to do," she once asked, "to get hot?"

She could try something her shows never asked of her: acting. How exactly Merman derived the wherewithal to pull off Momma Rose in *Gypsy* (1959) is a mystery, for she went from a career of self-resembling caricatures drilled rigid into a performance of unreserved involvement literally during *Gypsy*'s rehearsals. Perhaps Jule Styne and Stephen Sondheim's score made the difference, or Arthur Laurents's book, or both, for *Gypsy* is a remarkably characterful piece, and there is almost nothing in it but Rose.

Certainly Rose is no Eadie-Katie, nor an Annie. Her shattering show biz ambition, blindly devouring every hazard in its path—including those she loves—is unlikeable, unreliable: something the earlier Merman never was, with her deadpan entrances and shrugs. In *Gypsy*, she charged up the aisle of the Broadway Theatre, sang about getting and taking, lured and teased a man who could manage her plans, turned from one daughter to another with ferocious commitment (to herself), and closed her story alone on stage with nothing in one of the most *unlike* eleven o'clock songs a star ever had. Not "Friendship" (anything but), not "You're Just in Love" (with whom? everyone's gone), but "Rose's Turn," fragments of *Gypsy*'s score spliced into an egomaniacal vaudeville turn, all for Rose. She announces herself, greets the orchestra, struts and sells it to brassy stripper music: "Play it, boys!" Honky tonk urges her on, a high violin note eerily dreaming, and she goes into a tune of five notes repeated over and over, protesting too much. "Momma's talkin' loud," she tells us, and "Momma's lettin' go—" No. That's just it. She can't let go. One daughter left her, her lover left her, the other daughter left her. The "Momma" bobbles horribly on her lips—was this *Merman?* She recovers, falters again, stutters. And at last she sees it: "Momma's gotta let go." That's the whole of it, the bitter message the play has been shouting to Rose all along. She can let go, perhaps, of her family, not of her obsession with stardom. Biting out a chunk of "Everything's Coming Up Roses," she pulls it all into a final cry for attention, *molto agitato,* all the decades of vaudeville specialties in musical comedy concentrated into the numbo of the headliner about the doom of the nobody. So, five times, she cries: "For *me!*"

In short, Merman proved to be a transitional figure twice over, first in the inculcation of her unusual type in heroine parts, later as the old-fashioned star who helped capitalize new-wave composition. This alone defeats any comparison with Mary Martin, for Martin came to Broadway most conventionally as the cutie with a song to sing and, presumably, a Hollywood contract to sign. The show was *Leave It to Me* (1938), the song of course was "My Heart Belongs to Daddy," a strip piquantly performed atop a trunk in icy Irkutsk, and Martin was quickly raised to the screen, unfortunately in a Paramount deal that put her in a batch of terrible films. Still, the glamor goddess approach made her a natural for *One Touch of Venus* (1943), her Broadway comeback (after an out-of-town disaster) as the goddess of love in Mainbocher gowns.

For some, the Venus Martin remains the most ingratiating one; her subtle cooing of "That's Him" alone far downstage on a chair is a bright memory yet. Never was she, or anyone, more unlike Merman than in that moment. Moreover, Venus was a role one could not easily imagine anyone else playing—Ava Gardner, in the film, cannot sing and Janet Blair, on television, was miscast. Martin's excellence may be the reason the show has never had a major revival. She was supple in "Speak Low," sensual in "I'm a Stranger Here Myself," gracefully wanton in "Foolish Heart." And at the tale's end, after turning New York upside down with her heathen enchantment, she reappeared as a suburban kid in a walk-on to tie up the love plot. "My name is—" but Kenny Baker stops her. "You don't have to tell me," he says. "I know."

Venus is not the role most people associate with Mary Martin. A rough-hewn quality uncovered in the national tour of *Annie Get Your Gun* made her perfect for Nellie Forbush in *South Pacific* (1949). Such songs as "I'm Going To Wash That Man Right Out of My Hair" and "Honey Bun" touch off a goofy verve, a rural gaucheness, not before encountered in a heroine. Martin is complex. Her hoyden and her coyness and her goddess are interconnected. "Some Enchanted Evening," remember, is sung to and about her: she inspires romance. "Daddy" in some ways identifies her, for it is worldly (in its lyrics), romantic (in its rumba beat), vicious (in its cynicism), and blithely unknowing (in Martin's performance—she apparently never got the double meanings in the lyrics) at once.

That makes Martin harder to write for than Merman. Merman's Reno

Sweeney cracks, the takes, the song subjects, the "What the hell is this?," the whole damn fing! are a cinch. But Martin? At her prime, she could turn up in a vehicle called *Jennie* (1963) that never quite came to grips with what Martin is about. Suggested by the early career of Laurette Taylor, *Jennie* hoped to be a period backstager about a woman let down by a vagabond husband who survives to become a stage legend. Okay. This could be Martin. But the score opted for the vaguest sort of genre songs— "Waitin' for the Evenin' Train" could have been written by the young Irving Berlin, "Born Again" by Rodgers and Hammerstein, "Lonely Nights" by—I have to say it—Silvio Hein; and "Before I Kiss the World Goodbye" is a numbo for a grande dame, not the soubrette Martin was supposed to be playing. The role was so off-center that one followed the story mainly through Irene Sharaff's costumes.

Martin considers *Peter Pan* (1954), a musical version of the ultimate trouser role, her greatest triumph, but the sappy *I Do! I Do!* (1966) may stand more vitally in the memory. Like it or not, here was a tour de force for Martin and Robert Preston (the entire cast) and Gower Champion, whose direction crowded the stage with event, including a duet of Martin on violin and Preston on saxophone—ragged, but authentic. Compositionally, *I Do! I Do!* was the least absorbing show Martin did, yet its marital sentimentality licked many a heart. Perhaps this is the greatest difference between Merman and Martin: excepting *Hello, Dolly!,* which both of them played, Merman ended by challenging her public and Martin ended by flattering hers, Merman as grasping marriageless mother and Martin as adorable lifelong bride. If nothing else, it displays the range of woman available to the musical in post-*Sally* years. Yet we still lack an inspiring group of leading men. Strange. Men run musical comedy, as producers and authors. What on earth are they thinking of?

Tough dames and trouser roles.

9

The Jazzmen

Jazz, on Broadway, carries two meanings. In the 1920s, jazz was the international buzz word for the generation of American pop music that replaced the story ballad, the hesitation waltz, the harmony quartet, and the coon song with the rhythms of new dance, ballads to the beat of a band. Jazz was fox trot, charleston, torch song, blues. *Sally*'s "Look For the Silver Lining" was a capstone of the old style; *Oh, Kay!*'s "Someone To Watch Over Me" was jazz.

The other jazz is the one we refer to today, the improvisational variations practised largely according to tenets developed by black musicians, starting in the ragtime era in dives and segregated clubs. As early as 1922 it infiltrated the mainline white musical, when George Gershwin made his first attempt to connect Broadway, opera, and jazz. Gershwin was still generally unknown and writing for George White's annual *Scandals,* and when B.G. De Sylva got the idea for a twenty-minute Harlem opera on a Frankie and Johnny theme, the composer leaped at it. Even White, a nononsense Baby, liked it. De Sylva called the piece "Blue Monday Blues," White staged it with white performers in blackface, and Gershwin's old friend Will Vodery, a black musician, did the scoring.

It bombed. Charles Darnton of the *World* called it "stupid and incredible." Noting that "a dusky soprano finally killed her gambling man," he went on, "she should have shot all her associates the moment they appeared and then turned the pistol on herself." White pulled it from the show, possibly realizing by hindsight that blackface was by rules of tradition appropriate only for comedy. If Darnton was outraged, the public was simply confused. They didn't know when they were supposed to laugh. Of course, they weren't supposed to at all, for what attracted Gershwin to black characters and black music was the pathos of an underclass, the private development of a culture within a culture.

Blue Monday's cliché situations brought out nothing from Gershwin but some pleasant piano noodlings, some dancey jive, and strangely unengaged recitative; the sad parts scarcely sound sad. But when he read DuBose Heyward's novel *Porgy* a few years later, he was certain he had the basis for the libretto he needed. He contacted Heyward, and they discussed the possibilities for a *Porgy* opera. Meanwhile, Al Jolson offered to play it in blackface in a musical by Kern and Hammerstein. This is preposterous history—the most undisciplined of stars working with the men who made the musical into art without stars? Luckily, their plans fell through and Gershwin, his brother, and Heyward collaborated on *Porgy and Bess* (1935). The question is not whether it's an opera—it is; so what?—but how successful Gershwin was in blending his institutions: that of the totally musical composition, the ethnic style, and Broadway production technique.

Take the opening of Act Two, the picnic on Kittiwah Island. We will see the citizens of Catfish Row on holiday, a rare moment of escape from their ghetto enclosed by white oppression, the lure of sin, and the condemnation of the pious. With the churchgoers elsewhere on some sedate relaxation, the less inhibited hold a jamboree. Gershwin prepares us for this scene in a remarkable prelude scored for two African drums in cross-meter and stabbed by wild brass in unison. Woodwind trills cue the curtain, which rises on a dance. Here Broadway assists—Rouben Mamoulian, *Porgy and Bess*'s director, could do what no opera director then and few now can to suggest the abandon of the scene, a sexless orgy of violent joy. "I ain' got no shame," the characters exult, the drums' startling meter now drawing in a wanton piano part. The thing rumbles and slithers at once, and, to the marking *Con brio e molto barbaro,* the singers now throw away words entirely to revel in meaningless syllables. At the climax, Gershwin spreads the voices into an open A chord without a third, bizarre over the stamping syncopation and cut short. Sporting Life, Catfish Row's semi-resident drug dealer and dude, now steps forward for a dubious Bible lesson, "It Ain't Necessarily So." Again, Broadway provides the best where an opera company would be unable to secure minimum competence: John W. Bubbles in the original, Avon Long in the triumphant 1942 revival, when critical recantations, general familiarity with the music, and the Gershwin cult resulting from his early death turned the opera's fate around.

Opera or not, *Porgy and Bess* does need something beyond opera for Sporting Life, and both Bubbles and Long were vaudevillians whose experience on stage and in life told them how the part should go, especially in this diabolical solo. The main strain, marked "happily, with humor," crawls obscenely around chromatic triplets in g minor; a middle section, "like a savage outburst," goes into a percussive one-step to cries of "Wa-doo" and "Scatty wah," closing in an unrestrained, only approximately notated whinny. Even granted that nothing like the primitivistic choral section had ever been heard in American music theatre before 1935, Sport-ing Life's song has been poked at as "Broadway" rather than "opera." But isn't that what Gershwin needed for the role, precisely that? Actually, *Porgy* belongs to opera in that only opera's voices can tackle it. Porgys, Besses, Serenas, Claras, and Crowns are the people who on other engagements sing Amonasro, Donna Anna, Santuzza, Pamina, Germont; of the princi-pals, only Sporting Life is open to "performers." But *Porgy* must be staged in a transcendantly theatrical arena, and in this it broke ground for the assimilation of the black vocal idiom on Broadway.

Gershwin's successor in this matter was Harold Arlen. As performer, Gershwin was a pianist. Arlen was a singer, a Jolsonesque "jazz singer" as a Jewish cantor's son who blended the talmudic wail with the blue moan of the black stylists he heard when he wrote for the Cotton Club revues in the early 1930s—and Arlen's jazz was so expert he could write specialties for Cab Calloway. When Arlen moved on to Broadway, he took this hybrid style along. Even *You Said It* (1931), a college musical with the likes of Mary Lawlor (heroine of *Good News*), Stanley Smith (hero of the *Good News* film), and comic Lou Holtz, could feature the Arlen touch in "Sweet and Hot," an attack on the highbrows "who arch their eye-brows" at jazz. Arlen says he got the idea for the sassy tune from a trum-peter's hot lick, revealing the Broadway jazzman's high regard for the spontaneity of the libertarian combo, and his eagerness to set it down for the record. Lyda Roberti, billed as "Broadway's preferred Polish blonde," sang the song as something like "swett ant chot" but the gist came through in the music, and went over so well that the show plugged it as a major asset, calling itself the "sweet and hot musical." At this time Arlen drew on the black style only for spot specials. *You Said It*'s other songs could have been written by anybody in imitation of anybody else—"If He Really Loves Me," "While You Are Young," "You'll Do," "What Do We Care."

Over the years, however, Arlen's affinities deepened. By 1943, when he and E. Y. Harburg wrote songs for MGM's film of *Cabin in the Sky*, Arlen had become Tin Pan Alley's ambassador to the court of black "rhythm." Returning to Broadway in 1944, he composed five book musicals in fifteen years, all either black shows or shows with black principals: *Bloomer Girl* (1944), *St. Louis Woman* (1946), *House of Flowers* (1954), *Jamaica* (1957),

and *Saratoga* (1959). He had logged plenty of hits in what is now reck-
oned as the "Arlen style" of mainline American pop liberated by jazz:
"Get Happy," "I Gotta Right To Sing the Blues," "I've Got the World on
a String," "It's Only a Paper Moon," "Stormy Weather." But now Arlen
comes into maturity with rich, savory music for projects so unusual that
despite Arlen's Hollywood connections no studio has ever made one of
them into a film.

Odd that they passed by *Bloomer Girl,* Harburg's feminist show, for its
1860s setting would have fit right in with *Birth of the Blues, Dixie, Atlantic City, Meet Me in St Louis,* and wartime's other nostalgic exercises in
Americana. Something bizarre, though, about *Bloomer Girl*'s score—as a
whole it sounds carefully dated, yet other than the inclusion of an unusual
number of waltzes, Arlen uses little pastiche. The black numbers leave
such a strong impression that one thinks of them first: an escaped slave's
amiable hymn to freedom, "The Eagle and Me," the crowing, bluesy "I
Got a Song," and a few little pieces for *Uncle Tom's Cabin.* Yet there are
no more than these in a very full score, in a play which is less concerned
with slavery than with Celeste Holm's romance with a southern aristocrat
and Holm's father's comical feud with his feminist sister-in-law. (The father manufactures hoop skirts; the aunt wants them abolished as sexist.)
In other words, if Arlen is writing of and for 1944 and within the conventions of musical comedy, why is his sound so . . . well, alien?

An answer may be found in the show's song hit, "Evelina." This marks
Holm's meeting with her southern beau, and as she knows he is courting
her for her money, and twits him with it, they can't sing the usual rhapsody. Harburg and Arlen concocted a duet whose curve would suit his
plangent suit as well as her sarcastic reply, making love and war at once.
The tune is fiddle-sprightly, covering a wide range and cut by facetious
riffs in the woodwinds, and the harmony is advanced. All this combines
to suggest the tonal style Gershwin devised for *Porgy and Bess;* and Harburg's lyrics, which spoof the old-fashioned spoon song, bring in the period. Thus all of *Bloomer Girl* extends to blackness; all of it touches upon
the antique. By the time the authors move to a jail setting, where appre-
hended slaves gather around a gifted minstrel who can sing on any subject
named, we are overwhelmed by the artistry not of re-creation but of suggestion. "I got 'em! I got 'em!" the man cries, urging on the requests, full
of the vigor of originality. "Gotta sing 'em while you're living," he explains, " 'cause you're dead so long." The Harburg touch.

If not *Bloomer Girl,* why didn't Hollywood grab *St. Louis Woman:*
Arlen tunes, Johnny Mercer lyrics, Pearl Bailey, and the high-stepping black
society of St. Louis in 1898, the racetrack, the bar, the balls? Here Arlen

gave rhythm and blues its head and dispensed entirely with period suggestion. Even "Cakewalk Your Lady," a choral number begging for ragtime,
gets none. Rouben Mamoulian again officiated, now styling not racial
tragedy but racial swank, the white world forgotten. White himself, Arlen
was in his element, letting out whole numbers according to aggressive
walking basses and devilish altered chords descending in stepwise forma-
tion. This, too, is Gershwinesque, but developed. Anyway, Arlen's importance lies not only in his technique, but in the novelty of his collaborations, the fresh ideas in character. *St. Louis Woman*'s principals are a
jockey, a free-floating woman, the taverner who is living with her, the
other woman who loves him. These are not exactly new ideas in the musical. But the songs for and about them are. "Since I been a little boy, I
been round the track" is the first line sung, launching a stable boy's tribute
to the jockey, "Li'l Augie Is a Natural Man." Or: "Free and easy, that's
my style," rolls the heroine into "Any Place I Hang My Hat Is Home."
And the big ballad begins, "I'm going to love you like nobody's loved
you": "Come Rain or Come Shine." Conversational lyrics. Free and easy,
that's Mercer's style. He wrote only seven shows, and seldom counts among
the Broadway masters. But his deceptively simple perceptions arouse a naturalistic poetry comparable to Lorenz Hart's. Mercer's comedy songs for
Pearl Bailey, "Legalize My Name" and "It's a Woman's Prerogative" are
spicy and true, and his solo for the castoff second woman, "I Wonder
What Became of Me," inspired one of Arlen's most depictive blues, a harmony lesson, Jazz 103, Advanced Progressions in Despair. Strange that it
took two Jewish composers, Gershwin and Arlen, to formulate the science
of the black sound on Broadway—but then Kern and Hammerstein wrote
Ol' Man River," didn't they?

Arlen went on feeding the pop mainstream, passing on the information.
Barbra Streisand helped him, some years later, in making "A Sleepin' Bee"
a standard. And it is likely that the gleaming blues wail in her style came
out of the songs Arlen wrote or inspired. Gershwin and Arlen didn't only
derive a jazz. They bestowed one. It is worth noting that Arlen's next
show, *Jamaica*, set aside the Broadway regulars he had been writing for in
hopes of starring Harry Belafonte in a folk tale. When Belafonte fell ill,
the show was revamped—to the horror of librettists Harburg and Saidy—
for Lena Horne, an acknowledged mistress of American pop from Kern to
Ellington in her sole foray into the book musical. Jazz is contagious.

Jazz became the term covering classical musicians' adoption of popular
forms in the 1920s and 1930s. Of them all, the composer who most cultivated the noise was Kurt Weill, a fixture in the Weimar Berlin obsessed
with American cinema, crime, heroism, and exhibitionism. Somehow, it all

found a one profile in jazz. Weill understood it so well he was spoofing it before he practised it pure, melding, for instance, the dance-band wacka-doo onto the Bridesmaids' Chorus from Weber's opera *Der Freischütz* in a moment of his and Brecht's *Rise and Fall of Mahagonny City,* infuriating his compatriots. *Der Freischütz* is an article of faith in Germany; to quote it lightly is blasphemy.

Ultimately, Weill had to flee Nazi Germany for more scandalous defi-ances of regime than this, and when he arrived in America in 1935, Dok-tor Jazz had the opportunity to test his medicine in the laboratory of its origin. But where Gershwin and Arlen moved progressively closer into it, into black shows and adaptations of rhythm and blues, Weill moved away from it, trying to place a pop style appropriate for his training, his theatre ambitions, and his adopted homeland. He had seen a generation of theatre composers in Europe pulling away from the public, experimenting on a level beyond that public's reception. If he had come to America to escape fascism, he had as well come to Broadway to help raise a popular music theatre, elevated in capability and penetration but above all accessible. In an interview published in the *New York World-Telegram* Weill expanded on the notion of jazz as food for the stage. "Rhythm and harmonic free-dom, simplicity of melodic material, directness—saying things as they are—these are the contributions of jazz." This is the loosest explanation yet of what jazz does. But Weill had a sharper one, too: "In all times, the dance has had an effect on music. It was so with Bach, Chopin, Beethoven, Schu-mann, and others. They took the popular dance music of their or other days and lifted it into the region of art."

In Germany, Weill worked with politicized writers, drew on classical and popular pastiche, experimented with the Brechtian *Verfremdung* ("alienation," i.e., commentary that stands outside the narration), and scored for shocking jazz band instruments. Weill had bite; he wielded the saxophone as a scalpel. Now, in America, he grew away from all this, spending the alienation and pastiche in his transitional *Johnny Johnson* and *Knickerbocker Holiday.* By his third musical, *Lady in the Dark* (1941), he was free to explore his new style—but he never lost his bite or his sense of adventure.

From *Lady in the Dark*'s first moment, one is aware of a new form in the making. One knew it was a musical, and with a little trouble one could see the orchestra sitting in the Alvin Theatre's pit. Yet there was no over-ture, not even a little *Vorhangspiel* to raise the curtain. Nor did the first scene suggest the taut upwinding of a musical's first moments, when the handbook insists on a number to set style and tone. No music, no upwind-ing, no tone: the star walks into a psychiatrist's office. They talk. At length, the doctor asks her to lie on a couch and tell him what comes into her mind. "You will get into your beard meanwhile, I trust," she says. But she goes along with it, and he intones the line that Moss Hart originally chose as his title: "I am listening." * What comes into her mind is a fragment of a song she knew as a child, a tune she hears when she's in turmoil or having "confused, fantastic dreams." These involve people she knows. "Yet they are not the people I know at all." She hums the fragment, the lights dim, the orchestra sneaks in to take up the tune. And the musical begins.

We see her dream: Park Avenue in early evening. Fans in evening clothes march on, the heroine's fans, to serenade her with "Oh, Fabulous One in Your Ivory Tower." Now her boudoir, where servants sing her praises. She floats in—*here* is our golden star—and opens a pile of telegrams. She is desired, implored, demanded. The great and the near-great need her to complete their sense of celebrity. "Oh, how thrilling," she observes, "to be the world's inamorata!"

Moss Hart's book is forgotten; Weill and lyricist Ira Gershwin have taken over. From scene to scene in this dream, everything is sung, from the heroine's soapbox oration in Columbus Circle, "One Life To Live," to a nightclub where she is hailed in "Girl of the Moment," then ridiculed as the motto fragment is heard and the dream becomes nightmare, "Girl of the Moment" churned out in bitter rumba, *furioso*. Weill has abandoned jazz for an eclectic style that never sounds like anyone but Weill. Anyway, Weill was never a jazzman, but an extrapolator of jazz, like Ives, Copland, Bernstein, and other Americans, an adaptor. "Jazz," or whatever it was, adds to him, never contains him. Jazz is only a piece of pop, or a euphemism for it, and Weill and Ira Gershwin distill all pop music in *Lady in the Dark*'s operatic dreams. In the Kaufman political satires, Ira and brother George were spoofing opera, or comic opera. In *Lady in the Dark,* singing is legitimate of itself.

Weill's next show, *One Touch of Venus* (1943), was conservative in format, but *Street Scene* (1947), behold, was opera. Based closely on Elmer Rice's melodrama set on the front stoop of a New York tenement, *Street Scene* emphasizes Weill's role as the foreigner measuring national styles in pop music—piano blues, jitterbug, school anthem (a real one), children's games, torch song, and blue-note lullaby sounding the urban microcosm. Yet it was *Love Life* (1948) that really brought out the American in Weill. (He was so insistent about his naturalization that he mastered a native W

---

* This eventually became *We Are Listening,* to emphasize the chorus' role as audience–antagonist in the dreams. Lawrence asked Hart to change it; somehow, a play without a title role took all the fun out of acting.

to pronounce his last name as "while.") *Love Life* is Alan Jay Lerner's examination of American marriage. We follow Sam and Susan Cooper from the 1790s to the present as they fight timely pressures and struggle to retain their youthful optimism. To hold it together, Weill and Lerner wrote the score in mini-*Show Boat* style, half character songs and half entertainment pastiche. As *Love Life*'s poster art proclaimed, the show was a vaudeville: acrobats and clowns, a minstrel quartet, a ventriloquist and dummy; the opening saw a magician hypnotizing Sam and sawing Susan in half and the finale found them trying to reach each other while balancing on the high wire.

Sam and Susan had numbers telling us how they felt—"Mr. Right," "Is It Him or Is It Me?," "Women's Club Blues," "I Remember It Well" (similar to the song Lerner later wrote with Frederick Loewe for *Gigi*). Interspersed with these, as the years pass and money worries, politics, career agony, infidelity, and modern neurosis each drives a wedge between the two, variety specialists would erupt with commentary. A male soft-shoe lineup told ironically of the virtues of "Progress." A black quartet cited the incompatibility of love and money in "Economics." A hobo's "Love Song" idealized closeness, gentleness, and purity in a world that has no use for them.

This is a preposterous, feckless, marvelous show, awkwardly deft, the kind only New Yorkers could love. There would be no movie sale, no revival, no tour; it would add neither praise nor blame to the résumés of its leads, Nanette Fabray and Ray Middleton, and its director, Elia Kazan; it would effortfully produce two standards of the secondary import in "Green-up Time" and "Here I'll Stay" but would generate no cast album. *Love Life* tantalizes in legend. And it bears out Weill's determination to develop what might be called a "theatre opera," American music drama that can call on any kind of talent from trained voices to vaudevillians and take any form, or even comprehend different forms. Jazz, to him, meant the *originality* of American popular art, a possibility without limits. By the time he rejoined Anderson on *Lost in the Stars* (1949), Weill was in his absolute prime, every project a problem with a unique solution and every score bearing out Gershwin's, Arlen's, and now Weill's belief that the musical needed a lot of music.

The three men all worked on black shows with Rouben Mamoulian, forging a link with the "other" jazz. However, their main concern as a group centers on jazz as the imaginative flexibility of American popular art. Gershwin in his introduction of opera mock and serious, Arlen in his vernacular profundity, and Weill in his continuation of Gershwin's opera, all had major impact on writers hoping to make more of the notion of a musical theatre than a *No, No, Nanette* or *Babes in Arms*. Such diverse works as *The Golden Apple, Fanny, Candide, The Most Happy Fella, Sweeney Todd,* and *Dreamgirls* point back to the jazzmen as the Babies of inspiration.

10

The Choreographers

Dance is ancient in the musical, from ballet to soft-shoe clog, but as late as in 1920 it remained unsorted, a function without a purpose. The dancing usually followed a song, not necessarily sensibly. Take a boy-girl duet. They share joy in song, then express it in dance; that's fair. But just as often, The Girls might come out after the vocal for a backup kickline, their sudden entrance defying the logic of story. Or the boy might saunter off-stage to let the girl dance with a male quartet, her joy running a little thin as she shared it with four total strangers. Worse yet, however amusing, were the "dance specialties," usually by dancers who might not even have legitimate parts in the script.

Performers with a unique dancing style, like Fred and Adele Astaire or Ann Pennington or Marilyn Miller, complied with system. But their unique styles brought in something revolutionary: dance as character. This was a tonic, for their great decade, the 1920s, was a high time of routine choreography. Bobby Connolly (*Funny Face, The New Moon*), Sammy Lee (*No, No, Nanette, Oh, Kay!*), and Busby Berkeley (*A Connecticut Yankee*) treated one show like another, operetta or musical comedy, Berkeley in particular making a fetish of having his dancers repeat some mechanical step over and over till the audience—in desperation, perhaps—gave them a hand. Because so many twenties musicals were shallow as art, their dancing too was trivial, a one-size-fits-all gaiety. However, when Miller as much danced as sang or acted Sally and Sunny (and Rosalie is almost entirely a dancing role); when Ann Pennington launched the "Black Bottom" with such flash that for once a New Dance Sensation actually made one; or when Fred and Adele Astaire helped style the *esprit* of the Gershwin shows by seeming to move to the way Gershwin played piano at parties, possibilities were opened for drawing dance into the musical as a full partner.

But Miller died, Pennington and Adele Astaire retired, and Fred went off to Hollywood. They had impact but no influence; too special. To get our bearings, let's consider the dance plots of two twenties shows, an operetta (*The Desert Song*) and a musical comedy (*Good News!*), both choreographed by Bobby Connolly.

Algerian romance, *The Desert Song* has one dancing principal, Azuri, and two comics, Benny and Susan, who hoof. An amiable economy allowed shows to cast separate choruses, one for singing and one for dancing; *The Desert Song* puts its all into singing, retaining only eight women as "native dancers." Already, one can see the way the land lies—Azuri will provide erotic stimulus, the comics will prance, the native dancer will lend color. There are no dance numbos. Connolly staged the "French Military Marching Song" in drilling patterns and put the heroine and the hero's rival through a ballroom fox trot in "I Want a Kiss." Otherwise, it is as we expect. Azuri has her big moment, but the bulk of the dancing is stock musical comedy. In "It," an elucidation of Elinor Glyn's recipe for charisma, Benny and Susan deal out a few verses, then go into their eccentric while the chorus women slip in grinning, neatly line up, and take the vocal. For oomph, Benny measures a few of them for It, making Susan jealous. This is nothing the musical hadn't offered countless times, as is another number in which a Spanish houri seduces Benny, "One Good Boy Gone Wrong," followed by their mock tango and closing two-step. Throughout the show, the dance music is not arranged or dramatized; the orchestra simply plays the preceding tune over in encore style.

Good News!, the college musical, is even more basic: song, dance, applause; comic duet, comic dance, applause; New Dance Sensation song, New Dance Sensation, with The Girls coming on in these cunning red coats, much applause. The dancing has nothing to do with student life. It has to do with show biz. "The Varsity Drag" advises one to "stay after school" in order to "learn how it goes" so when the professor calls for it, you'll be prepared and may thereby "pass many a class." Yet nothing in the number distinguishes it from comparable spots in other shows. It's "down on the heels, up on the toes." Marilyn Miller's or Fred Astaire's shows might include a number or two designed for them alone, to elate a public already familiar with their personae. In *Smiles,* Astaire's "Say, Young Man of Manhattan," the matrix of all his Hollywood top hat routines, and Miller's piquant cavorting with the characters of the comics page in *As Thousands Cheer*'s "The Funnies," are one-of-a-kind things for unique performers. However, most scores were written around less individual talents for standard-make characters. The breakthrough in choreography obviously depended on a breakthrough in composition, and once again, *Show Boat* makes the history for us, as Sammy Lee was so hemmed in by Kern and Hammerstein's conceptual planning that he had no choice but to help them tell the story. Ziegfeld or no Ziegfeld, there just wasn't any room in their piece for Girls in red coats.

As with the *Show Boat* score, the *Show Boat* dances deal separately with either character, racial depiction, or show biz pastiche. The character dances include spots after "Life on the Wicked Stage," "I Might Fall Back on You," and "Why Do I Love You?"—but these are not appendages. They are the direct sequellae of the singing: no one who is not in the song is allowed to join its dance. Comic soubrette Ellie sings "Wicked Stage" to a chorus of admiring town girls, so Ellie and the girls perform the dance. "I Might Fall Back on You" is Ellie and Frank's duet with the townies, so Ellie and Frank take the dance with a bit of perking and pranking from the girls. "Why Do I Love You?" is trickier. Magnolia and Ravenal sing it, the chorus takes it up, then Ravenal goes off to gamble, leaving Magnolia to take the dance herself, the tune altered from fox trot to waltz. Magnolia now exits, and the chorus sends the melody back into square meter so Captain Andy and Parthy can reflect on the love plot with a comic variant. Andy sings it alone (the original Parthy, Edna May Oliver, couldn't hack a note), but both tackle the ensuing dance. As Ferber made these two the yang and yin of her story, their partaking of Magnolia and Ravenal's love song is not an intrusion but a reminder of the two lovers' oppositional personalities. Parthy is the river, Andy the theatre, but their offspring Magnolia has both qualities, Parthy's strength and Andy's love. Staged properly, "Why Do I Love You?" can present this in terms of dance, building on what Hammerstein tells us in the book.

The black dances, scattered throughout, add to *Show Boat*'s chronological pulse, from the shuffling crowd in "Can't Help Lovin' Dat Man" and "Queenie's Ballyhoo" and the buck-and-wing in the first-act finale on to the more contemporary pre-*Blackbirds* jive of "In Dahomey," the show's sole big dance number. Similarly, the show biz dances takes us from the informal small-time of the show boat entertainment through Fatima's hoochy-koochy at the World's Fair midway and the Trocadero cakewalk to big Broadway. "Lookin' out to sea!" Captain Andy cries to the riverbank mob to caption the closing poses of Frank and Ellie's hornpipe. This is homey, antique, the simplistic variety of the backwoods stage. Three hours later, Lee's more detailed layouts for the finale pulled the time into the present, 1927. Magnolia's daughter Kim takes the eleven o'clock number, and as the original Magnolia/Kim, Norma Terris, plumed herself on her imitations, Lee had something less than a full-out number to work with. However, *Show Boat* is the great protean musical, subject to revision as long as Kern and Hammerstein were alive, and their last collaboration, "Nobody Else But Me" (for the 1946 revival), gave choreographer Helen Tamiris an opportunity to invoke the 1920s in a big number. It starts small, as a shy solo for Jan Clayton. But it builds, and at the close, as the bystanding ensemble moves in, Clayton tells of charleston and "hey! hey!" as the orchestra unbends, a clarinet solo recalling the salad days of jazz.

After *Show Boat,* choreographers began to delve, to describe, to inflect. In the 1930s, Hollywood's Astaire-Rogers series revealed how potent character dancing could be, and back on Broadway the better revues made interpretive or storytelling dance as focal as Clifton Webb's unassuming soft shoe or Tamara Geva's ballet glide. The kickline in the red coats didn't die out, never would. But ambitious musicals now despised such make-weights. The successors of Connolly, Lee, and Berkeley are great names in musical comedy—George Balanchine, Agnes de Mille, Jack Cole, Jerome Robbins, Michael Kidd—and their salient bequest was the reorganization of serious dance in the musical.

In the world of ballet, George Balanchine's is the most resonant name. Yet his influence in the musical is not that great. *On Your Toes* (1937), one of the earliest dance musicals, is a major credential, with its enduring "Slaughter on Tenth Avenue." Here, Balanchine had great impact. But *Keep Off the Grass* (1940), *The Lady Comes Across* (1942), *What's Up* (1943), and *Courtin' Time* (1951) do not count among the stimulating shows, and Balanchine ends up more a historical entry than a seminal stylist. No, in ballet it is surely Agnes de Mille who takes pride of place. She had choreographed musicals in London and New York in the 1930s, using both straight-on dances-after-songs and set piece ballets. But *Oklahoma!* (1943) placed her as the exponent of Americana in rich tableaus of romantic maidens and stalwart bucks out on the great youthful land for holiday revels. Her western ballet *Rodeo* got her the job on *Oklahoma!*. Though both she and director Rouben Mamoulian were hot-blooded collaborators jealous of working space, their attitude toward the show itself was as one.

Oklahoma! has a lot of dancing, some of it character material expanding lyrical ideas, but there is also a hoedown to open Act Two and the famous dream ballet that closes Act One, "Laurey Makes Up Her Mind."*

---

*This was by no means the first dream ballet in a musical. Albertina Rasch set a vague one into *The Cat and the Fiddle;* more narratively; Charles Weidman employed modern dance in *I'd Rather Be Right* to picture the blissful marriage of the two sweethearts, from wedding to senility, in "American Couple."

As the intermission nears, we know that Laurey is caught between two men, nice guy Curly and menacing Jud. Armed with a bottle of "elixir of Egypt" guaranteed to solve problems in a whiff, she prepares to settle the issue, her girlfriends hanging around with advices. Music has underscored the sniffing scene, and now it leads effortlessly into "Out of My Dreams," in which her friends urge Laurey to forget the smelling salts and follow her heart. As they drift away, Laurey takes up the waltz herself, Curly comes in and—because neither Joan Roberts nor Alfred Drake could handle what de Mille had in mind for their characters—their dancing counterparts Katharine Sergava and Marc Platt enter, stand by them, and become them through dovetailed pantomime. The two actors vanish, the orchestra sweeps into a rhapsodic restatement of "Out of My Dreams," and Curly and Laurey dance together. The dream has begun.

This artful blending of the musical's major elements—song, dance, and dialogue—is noteworthy in comparison with the proudly self-contained dances de Mille and others would soon be planning. But its most remarkable quality is its beautiful distillation of all that *Oklahoma!* is—the love story, the community of farmers and cowmen, the freedom and danger of life in a territory so green it isn't yet a state. Musically, it is a medley of the songs heard in the act, now arranged to narrate the dream—"The Surrey with the Fringe on Top" turns up as a wedding march. Jud intrudes on the wedding of Curly and Laurey, kills Curly, and carries Laurey off. The very use of a dream to reflect Laurey's confusion is exciting, but de Mille characterizes more than the principals. Their very environment dances, in the bow-legged romp of the cowboys or the dance-hall shimmy of the bimbos who accompany Jud, a personification of his postcard collection. The dream does not precisely close the act, but ends seconds before the curtain, when the actor-Jud shakes the actor-Laurey out of her reverie and leads her off to the hoedown as the actor-Curly looks on crestfallen. In one number, de Mille and the authors have moved from text into song and then dance, from real life into fantasy and back, to tell us what the characters themselves can't.

Conceptual ballet solidified de Mille's hold on theatregoers' imagination. The best musicals needed her as they had never needed Connolly or Lee. Put simply, she was the only one who did what she did. And she was versatile. In *One Touch of Venus* (1943), a fantasy set in Manhattan, she revved into city drive in "Forty Minutes for Lunch" and made make-believe in "Venus in Ozone Heights." Yet she could combine the two styles— "Forty Minutes" allows Venus to bring two workers together, romance in downtown, while "Ozone Heights" pictured the goddess of love making a go of suburbia. *Bloomer Girl* (1944) gave her a chance to simulate an old

Uncle Tom show, complete with its promotion parade down Main Street. *Carousel* (1945) returned her to *Oklahoma!*'s folkloric nostalgia and psychological elaboration. *Brigadoon* (1947), another fantasy, this one set in Scotland, called up native rites—market festival, bridegroom's bachelor party in the town square, bride's trousseau-packing shower, ceremonial sword dance, funeral piobrochead. Within the versatility, the stylistic individuality that had recommended her to *Oklahoma!*'s producers via *Rodeo* stayed in focus, and she assembled a corps of specialists in a way that no choreographer of the 1920s had had to. Any gypsy of that day could have taken the combinations from Connolly or Berkeley with no trouble: Connolly's were Berkeley's. With the emergence of de Mille (and her colleagues Jack Cole, Jerome Robbins, and Michael Kidd), dance came into its own with a purity and clarity not lightly undertaken. Bambi Linn was graduated from the *Oklahoma!* corps to a glorious stint as the daughter, Louise, in *Carousel,* winning an ovation for the big ballet in Act Two. Joan McCracken similarly stepped out of *Oklahoma!* into a featured part in *Bloomer Girl.* These artists began to share their styles, as when James Mitchell went on from Robbins's *Billion Dollar Baby* (1945) into de Mille's *Brigadoon* to become the envy of every gypsy for his feat with the swords in the wedding scene. Later, he went on to Gower Champion in *Carnival* and *Mack and Mabel.*

As technician, de Mille made her most splendid effect in tackling *Allegro* (1947), the third consecutive show for her, Rodgers and Hammerstein, and the Theatre Guild. But where *Oklahoma!* and *Carousel* were adaptations from plays, both in period folk style and essentially love stories, *Allegro* was original, contemporary, and more about making life decisions than a love match. It was, in a way and perhaps coincidentally, a show made to affirm the naïve glory of living upright and strong among one's people that the nation had gone to war to protect. Hammerstein was a sentimentalist, but even more a moralist. The two qualities come together here in a study, from birth to maturity, of Joseph Taylor, Jr., a doctor's son who weathers an awkward adolescence, deaths in the family, a bad marriage, and the materialism of the plutocrat's plush clinic to return to his hometown to take up his father's practice.

This is nothing like what de Mille had done before, but the *Our Town*-ish aspect of the show, with its omnipresent chorus and reappearances by characters who have died, suggests the rural Americana at the core of her art. Given the already unorthodox composition, it was decided to let de Mille stage the entire number on a bare floor, the essential dance space, with back-wall projections, using the huge cast as if *Allegro* were a ballet for actors. The authors had to spell her on the book scenes, for *Allegro* was too big for one person to control. Besides the constantly shifting chorus, informing the audience, advising the characters, and taking small parts, there were countless dances—for Taylor's schoolmates, for his first college dance, for his sweetheart on her European vacation, for newlywedded life, for the banal uproar of modern America. Every other moment there was music, and all the music called for motion. If *Allegro* is a problem show, weighed down by a mirthless, crackerbarrel book, it's also a show of insight and tenacity. It's doubtful that anyone but de Mille could have found the plastic equivalent of what Hammerstein wrote. Mamoulian might have, but he couldn't have planned the dances. Thus, the great choreographers of the 1940s were not only stylists of dance, but deputies of composition. They made certain kinds of musical possible that were previously unfeasible.

De Mille, Jack Cole, Jerome Robbins, Michael Kidd. The best thing about them as a group is that they all went after different things. Where de Mille would plan a "Civil War Ballet" for *Bloomer Girl* full of woman's anxiety and despair (even the progressive Harburg was unnerved enough to want to cut it), Cole would season *Kismet* with body English in an Oriental accent. Where Robbins would concoct an uproarious "Mack Sennett Ballet" for *High Button Shoes,* drawing on quick-cut absurdist Keystone farce to the strains of Offenbach and Liszt, Kidd would create for *Guys and Dolls* the atmosphere of Damon Runyon's Tenderloin, with tourists, guide, cop, sidewalk hustlers, bobby soxers, baby buggy, celebrity, autograph hounds, fancy Texan, and pickpocket.

Comparable to de Mille's achievement in *Allegro* is Robbins's in *On the Town* (1944), for, while George Abbott directed the show, Robbins proved that dance could treat nearly any situation a plot might run into—the selection and promotion of the New York subway's monthly Miss Turnstiles, or the loneliness of a sailor in a town brimming with couples, or the camp of a tawdry nightclub act. Robbins also came closest of this group to solving the problem of casting. How long could musicals go on ringing in dance counterparts for the principals, as de Mille had to in *Oklahoma!?* Robbins used a dancer surrogate for his hero, Gabey, in a dream ballet, but his Miss Turnstiles was a dancer, Sono Osato. However, the sword cuts two ways: Osato couldn't sing, and this left a hole in the program. (The hole gaped wider in the 1971 revival, staged by Ron Field, when Miss Turnstiles was Donna McKechnie, who *can* sing but—the role already written like so—didn't. One kept hoping she would.)

Cole and Kidd seemed most nimble in their ensemble routines, but Robbins went on looking for dancers who could carry a show, or performers who could fit into the dance. Perforce, some of this work went into straight-plain musical comedy, with singing principals, singing chorus, and dancing chorus, more or less deftly intertwined—*High Button Shoes* (1947), for instance, which let Phil Silvers and Joey Faye work the comedy, Nanette Fabray and Jack McCauley the songs, Lois Lee and Mark Dawson the sweetheart stuff, and which peaked in the Mack Sennett special. This was a set piece for the dancers, but the story was threaded into it in that con men Silvers and Faye are absconding with boodle during the number.

Similarly, *Call Me Madam* (1950) featured Ethel Merman, Paul Lukas, Russell Nype, and Galina Talva, none of them celebrated for *cabriole* or *plié*. Robbins worked around them. But Joan McCracken, locked into supporting roles in de Mille's shows, was graduated into heroine in Robbins's *Billion Dollar Baby* (1945), a twenties spoof now completely forgotten because of a score so dull even most buffs can't name a single song title. And in *Look Ma, I'm Dancin'!* (1948), Robbins had Harold Lang for his juvenile and Nancy Walker as the Milwaukee beer heiress who backs her own ballet company. Lang could dance as well as sing, and if Walker made a gruesome ballerina, so did her character.

Not till *West Side Story* (1957) was Robbins able to cast all the major characters—indeed, every character but the four grownups, little more than walk-ons—from a performer pool versatile enough to dance, sing, and act. Here, as not in Robbins's earlier shows, dance was so much a part of the narrative technique that *West Side Story* without the choreography would be unintelligible. There is dance as action: the lovers' meeting, the "rumble," the near-rape in Doc's drug store. There is dance as expression: the coiled-spring "Cool" or the desperately wishful "Somewhere" dream. There is even dance as sheer relief of tension in "Gee, Officer Krupke," which some buffs thought the most original number in the musical's history.

Obviously, dance was crucial to the Robbins era as it had not been to Connolly's. The difference lies not in the quality of choreography but in the quality of the shows themselves: in the rise of Authors' Rule. *West Side Story,* unarguably one of the great shows of its time, may be revived indefinitely with a merely talented cast. Everything it needs is written into it. The great shows of Connolly's era cannot easily be revived: *Sally* without Miller? *Whoopee* without Cantor? *Gay Divorce* without Astaire?

Our understanding of what constitutes a great show has changed. The separate revolutions in libretto, score, character development, thematic development, décor, stage direction, and, now, choreography began to come together in the 1940s. The result, so carefully integrated, stood so apart from tradition and habit that the terms "musical comedy" and "operetta" were no longer adequate. Rodgers and Hammerstein, the most significant proponents of the new art, wrote "musical plays."

II

The Musical Play

Lynn Riggs's *Green Grow the Lilacs* (1931) was a folk play, studying the mores and employing the vernacular of the American West and using folk songs for atmosphere. When Hammerstein transformed the play into the *Oklahoma!* libretto, he kept as close as possible to Riggs, lifting up whole scenes virtually as they were. His two sweethearts, Curly and Laurey, were already there, along with Laurey's Aunt Eller, the villain Jeeter (changed to Jud) Fry, and the neighbors. Hammerstein had only to enlarge Ado Annie and the Peddler, and invent Annie's boyfriend Will Parker to provide a subplot.

Hammerstein wrote his folk songs with Rodgers, but he took his cues from the text. For example, Riggs describes his curtain-up as "the kind of a morning which, enveloping the shapes of earth—men; cattle in a meadow; blades of the young corn; streams—makes them seem to exist now for the first time, their images giving off a visible golden emanation that is partly true and partly a trick of imagination focusing to keep alive a loveliness that may pass away." With only the public domain to count on, Riggs assigned "Git along, little dogies" to his hero for the scene. Rodgers and Hammerstein had their own talent, and so wrote "Oh, What a Beautiful Mornin' " to capture exactly the shimmering radiance Riggs invokes—"All the cattle are standing like statues," Hammerstein writes, and "The corn is as high as an elephant's eye." The introduction, before Curly sings, is keyed to the scene much more carefully than a musical's opening usually is, with bird calls on flute and oboe and a green-world rustling on the clarinet. Only Aunt Eller is onstage, churning butter and staring contentedly into the auditorium as if she could see across the plain clear to Kansas

City. Curly starts his song offstage—a cappella, as a cowboy sings on the range—before ambling on as the orchestra picks him up, just before the refrain. The effect dazzles today. In 1943, it must have been a sensation.

Whether one approaches this moment from the standpoint of the adaptation, the staging, the casting, or the song itself, it's revolutionary, as is all of *Oklahoma!*, for all these reasons. The very notion of turning a western folk play into a musical comedy is far fetched. The Girls in gingham? *Meadows* on your backdrop? And where do we get a swinging numbo? "No girls, no gags, no chance," runs the famous line, attributed to producer Michael Todd, who caught *Oklahoma!*'s premiere in New Haven (its first act, anyway). *Oklahoma!*'s success—flash, profound, and endless—changed a lot of minds about what was feasible in the musical, about what the musical had a *right* to treat. Even those who applauded its songful sophistication in the 1920s and its political awareness in the 1930s didn't relish the notion of a serious music theatre on Broadway, not if it were going to desolate the gags and dress The Girls. The brilliant, acerbic critic George Jean Nathan, who rated a musical by whether it had Bobby Clark or not and discussed The Girls' looks in terms that would have outraged a feminist-baiter, saw the Rodgers and Hammerstein years as the very collapse of what American musical comedy stood for. *Oklahoma!*, okay; he liked it, really. *Carousel,* too, he liked, though he saw signs of overweening ambition in "A little too much Agnès de Mille for comfort." But *Allegro* was pompous, "hokum mush" and—insult of insults—"another of the integrated species." The whole thing was out of control. If it wasn't de Mille it was Mamoulian. If it wasn't Rodgers and Hammerstein, it was *Bloomer Girl* or *Love Life*. It was a sudden determination to stimulate the audience, *address* it. It was, note Nathan's sneer, "integrated." They get these directors and choreographers who show how people feel. They turn their backs on the canons of casting and make musicals without established favorites, overturning one of the handbook's prime rules, to wit: major productions are built on stars. They deal with death, unemployment, war, sexism, and other dreary things. They write these integrated songs you wouldn't let into your kitchen. And they give you no Girls and no gags.

Not that *Oklahoma!* is the first integrated show. *Show Boat* precedes it by sixteen years. But the times were way behind *Show Boat*. They were ready when *Oklahoma!* came along; its dancing alone, we have seen, immediately began to give issue. Its way of dealing with songs as part of the overall layout, a Hammerstein specialty since *The Desert Song,* also bore fruit. *Show Boat* was an epic, and its method is epic: so what could it teach Broadway? Broadway is boy meets girl. *Oklahoma!* is tighter, more smoothly joined, its details open to inspection, as when "The Surrey with the Fringe on Top" pops out in strophes separated by sizable chunks of dialogue, changing its character as the conversation changes, or when Will Parker starts "All 'Er Nothin' " so colloquially, stating rather than singing his lines, that at first we don't realize that a number has begun.

Perhaps *Oklahoma!*'s most excellent instruction was not how to be revolutionary but how to revise the status quo for convention. Such standout shows as *The Cat and the Fiddle* and *Lady in the Dark* couldn't do more than *Show Boat* to change the musical because they, too, were one-of-a-kind shows. But *Oklahoma!*, under the folklore, is a commercial show: major sweethearts, comic sweethearts, ballads and charm songs, dance numbers, and boy gets girl. It even has a Dutch comic in the Peddler. *Oklahoma!* does not advise the musical to ditch convention, simply to treat it uniquely each time out. You can eat your cake and have it, too. You can even have Girls and gags: Hammerstein is *very* funny here (he wasn't always), and Jud Fry's "postcards" in the dream ballet are Girls to delight a Nathan.

The oddest thing about *Oklahoma!* is the sudden change in style it surprises in Rodgers. Gone are the syncopation and altered chords he used with Hart, the messing around. Now he sounds squared off, with a heavy-footed bass and a lot of strings. If Gershwin was the king of jazz, Rodgers is (starting over as) the king of hymns. Everything is white keys. There is almost—I say almost—nothing in Rodgers and Hart that prepares us for the Rodgers of Hammerstein. Granted that *Oklahoma!*'s ethnicity begged of Rodgers a style he had not had to wield in his slick city shows with Hart, still the turnabout is astonishing. Rodgers breaks with tradition in setting Hammerstein's lyrics rather than writing the tunes first, and fashions a pan-national sound that can "create" folk song ("The Farmer and the Cowman"), suggest it ("The Surrey with the Fringe on Top"), or steer clear of it yet still sound like nothing that has preceded it on Broadway (the vamp to "I Cain't Say No"). *Oklahoma!* has been hailed for many reasons. It has been called the first integrated musical, the first American folk musical; *Show Boat* got there first on both counts. It has been called the first great dance musical, but *The Lady of the Slipper, Gay Divorce, Jubilee, On Your Toes, I Married an Angel,* and *Cabin in the Sky* hold seniority. But *Oklahoma! was* the first American musical with an ethnic sound, words and music entirely in the folk idiom.

Nor did Rodgers and Hammerstein relinquish this style in later works, folk or otherwise. It might be argued that Rodgers's new sound was conducted to a great extent by Robert Russell Bennett, who orchestrated *Oklahoma!* and almost all the other R & H scores. Bennett, a dean of operetta or strongly musical scores, gave Rodgers a larger pit complement than most musicals make do with, with strong woodwind articulation of the famous Rodgers vamps, as in the seesawing $\frac{6-5}{2-1}$ fifths that run through "A Puzzlement." But Don Walker, not Bennett, scored *Carousel* (1945),* in most ways the essential R & H show. (It was Rodgers's personal favorite.) Moreover, Walker is one of the major progenitors of the musical comedy pit sound, not, like Bennett, an operetta man.

Obviously, the sound is Rodgers's. The relationship between *Oklahoma!*'s and *Carousel*'s songs is easy to spot—the folk approach in "Blow High, Blow Low," "This Was a Real Nice Clambake," and "June Is Bustin' Out All Over," and the more distilled folk slant of "Mister Snow" or "When the Children Are Asleep." The style is developing, too, reaching for a psalmlike transcendence in "If I Loved You" and "You'll Never Walk Alone" and expanding the musical-scene structure of "Surrey" in "If I Loved You" and the "Soliloquy." (Too, Hammerstein is again working in dialect; one song is called "Geraniums in the Winder.") In *Allegro*'s college dance, Rodgers brings in "Mountain Greenery" to recall the good old days and, incidentally, his own youth; the comparison between what he had written with Hart and what he was writing with Hammerstein is stunning. And when Rodgers does turn to punchy chromaticism in *Allegro*, toward the climax of the city sequence, in "Yatata Yatata Yatata" and the title song, he is using the jive he once lived on to suggest spiritual bankruptcy! The man had lost his jazz.

Actually, there are suggestions of the Hammersteinian Rodgers throughout the Hart years. In the 1930s, "I Believe in You," "Where or When," and "Mimi" have the melodic purity and diatonic chording of the later Rodgers, as does almost the entire score to *Pal Joey* (though it still has the swing that the later Rodgers lost), and the bridge of "The Colour of Her Eyes," from the British show *Ever Green*, directly points to the "A Puzzlement" vamp. One can even see the two Rodgers styles poised on the brink in the *Connecticut Yankee* revival, prepared after *Oklahoma!* had opened. Sitting in with the Rodgers and Hart of 1927 are the newly written "Can't You Do a Friend a Favor?," a courtship ballad right out of the old style, and "You Always Love the Same Girl," in the new Rodgers autograph complete with square-jawed vamp and a rather Hammersteinian lyric idea.

The term "musical play" concerns far more than Rodgers's revised style, the inclusion of de Mille theme ballets, or how carefully Hammerstein turns old plays into new musicals. Actually, the musical play is not so

---

*Prior commitments kept Bennett from *Carousel*, but he did score "The Carousel Waltz" and "Mister Snow." Walker returned to the firm for *Me and Juliet*, but Bennett handled everything else, including *Cinderella* on television.

much a form, a genre, as an aesthetic, a point of view. Before R & H, a truly artistic musical most likely had to be an operetta or something like: a show with a lot of good music but not much naturalism. No grip. R & H opened up a space between operetta and musical comedy that could count on good music and grip at once. Their space is strong in acting as well as singing, deals in theme as well as story, and makes such demands upon production technique as to be unstageable except in ideal, big-budget circumstances. These are not little shows in any sense.

Broadway's big shows, however, had always been Ziegfeldian turns, big in celebrity. The musical play drafts not performing whizzes but creative ones above all: the major performance is that of the authors and, to a degree, and following the demands of the text, the stagers. In a way, the musical play stands outside musical theatre history; it holds that total integration has already occurred, and all one need do is draw on integration's discoveries as the story invites. Each musical play is different from all other musicals: if each story is different. When, in *Carousel,* R & H dispensed with the usual overture and raised their curtain on a suite of waltzes suggestive of carousel piping, they were not making another entry in history's ledger. The story begins in an amusement park, with a carousel barker and the girl he fatefully meets on his job, so that's where you start the show. Nor were de Mille and Mamoulian, bickering over who got to stage the scene, worrying about the handbook. It was an artistic wrangle: is this a ballet or pantomime? (They collaborated, though there is no dancing in the sequence.) The musical play is the most significant of all developments in the American musical. *Show Boat* was the first musical play. Hammerstein designed *Show Boat.* So Hammerstein designed the musical play. That makes him the most significant figure in the musical's history.

It means also that the five shows Hammerstein wrote with Rodgers when their musical play was at its most influential—*Oklahoma!, Carousel, Allegro, South Pacific,* and *The King and I*—make a far more heterogeneous series than the Princess shows, or the Friml-Romberg operettas, or the Rodgers-Hart-Fields shows of the late 1920s. For, again, the musical play is not a genre. It is an approach that, at its best, produces a different result every time it is applied. Each of these five is different from the others, and not merely in such obvious ways as *Allegro*'s set-less look or *The King and I*'s Oriental dance and pantomime. Try to imagine *Carousel*'s "What's the Use of Wond'rin' " in *Oklahoma!,* or "People Will Say We're in Love" in *South Pacific.* Impossible. These songs are written so precisely that they work for one show and no other. Before the musical play, a song deleted from one show might easily slip into the next; George Gershwin put "The Man I Love" into and out of *Lady Be Good!, Strike Up the Band,* and

Rosalie before he gave up. But songs written by sound practitioners of the musical play had to work out that first time or never again. Not surprisingly, the many songs Kern and Hammerstein wrote for and finally didn't use in *Show Boat* were not heard from again. Indeed, it is the musical play's attraction that theme- or character-oriented composition gives the imaginative authors so many opportunities to make a unique show that they don't want to use trunk material: why press the caviar when you can fork it out fresh?

South Pacific (1949), the first R & H show they produced themselves, opened up yet another possibility in the musical play in that it was written for Mary Martin and Ezio Pinza. Star turns. "What on earth do you want," Martin asked them when they asked her, "two basses?" There were no microphones in theatres in those days, and she worried about how her Broadway voice would stack up against Pinza's operatic bravura. However, the difference in their characters—she a young American nurse and he a worldly French planter—needed just this difference in vocal quality. Anyway, they don't sing together that often. In their first scene, she delivers "A Cockeyed Optimist" about herself to him, he sings "Some Enchanted Evening" to and about her, and their one duet, "Twin Soliloquies," has them *taking turns* singing as he pours them glasses of cognac. As they drink and the number reaches its climax—just when we anticipate a duet—the *orchestra* seizes leadership, its roiling thunder telling us what the two are thinking. The musical play is such a big concept that it can incorporate stars without having to provide them with their "turns."

Another departure in *South Pacific:* no choreographer. Broadway kibitzers joked that this was so Rodgers wouldn't have to work with de Mille again. In fact, this relates to the musical play's fixation on production planning. Given World War II for a subject, dance might have trivialized the work. Also, Hammerstein had no direct experience in the service. So Joshua Logan, who had the experience, collaborated with him on the book and directed the show, including the numbers, to give it the appropriate itchy camaraderie. Jo Mielziner, who had done so well designing and lighting *Allegro*'s tricky stage, helped Logan create a fluid scene plot for *South Pacific* that allowed the action to move through coterminous scenes. As one ended, the other was already beginning. As with Weber and Fields in their burlesque of the quick-change artist coming and going at once, a new set of characters was pushing in as others were exiting—or shorter scenes "in one" dissolved as bigger scenes broke into view behind them through a transparent curtain. There was some dancing—the restless pacing of the woman-hungry Seabees in "There Is Nothing Like a Dame" or Martin's talent-show drag bit with Myron McCormick, "Honey Bun." These, too,

were for Logan: not de Millian art revelations but naturalistic construc-
tions, happenings. Each story is different.

The King and I (1951) was most different of all, the authors' struggles
to get Anna's and the King's songs right enduring past rehearsals into
tryouts. Their four preceding shows were in trim when they reached the
stage. *Oklahoma!* lost "Boys and Girls Like You and Me" in favor of a
reprise of "People Will Say We're in Love," *Carousel*'s heaven sequence
was reworked, *Allegro* virtually went on as written, and *South Pacific* lost
two songs. But *The King and I* lost and gained important numbers because
the authors had caught the ceremonial gravity of the Siamese too well.
The score came off as ponderous.

Anna's relationship with the King turns on her principles versus his autocracy, and on their first meeting this broke into song in "Waiting." She
wants the terms of their agreement honored, he wants His Majesty flat-
tered, and neither will give way. It's good musical play thinking. But the
song is heavy, with the "Puzzlement" vamp clocking through it like a met-
ronome. Anna does take on her duties, but a number of points have not
been resolved, and near the end of Act One she is ready to leave Siam. In
any other show, this is the boy loses girl; *The King and I*'s equivalent was
a suite of songs for Anna, Lady Thiang, and the Kralahome. Anna's "Shall
I Tell You What I Think of You?" is first-rate, free in form like *Carousel*'s
"Soliloquy." But Lady Thiang's "Now You Leave" and the Kralahome's
"Who Would Refuse?" were two versions of the same message: we need
you, and the King especially needs you. Worse yet, while "Now You Leave"
was lovely, "Who Would Refuse?" is a dull death march.

How to keep the show light without losing the identifying gravity of the
two Hammersteinian ideologues—the authoritarian King who needs tol-
erance and the mercurial liberal who needs structure? "Waiting" and the
Kralahome's solo were dropped, "Something Wonderful" put in for Lady
Thiang in place of "Now You Leave"—still heavy, but stronger, urgent.
And "Getting To Know You" was added early in the act for Anna. Now
the show flowed more enjoyably, and with greater point. Still, it is the
heaviest of the R & H shows, as dark as *Carousel* on a bigger idea.

It may be that the musical play is too demanding to sustain its authors'
careers. It stimulates the imagination; perhaps drains it as well. For after
these five glorious adventures R & H went into musical comedy, not great
ones at that. Theatregoers weren't sure what to make of *Me and Juliet*
(1953), an amiable backstager with a lot of principals, a lot of Broadway
hoofing, a lot of "let's do a little something while the story takes a rest."
It was the kind of thing George Abbott did; sure enough, Abbott did this
one. There was some curious lampoon of the "modern" musical—the play-

within-the-play, also called *Me and Juliet,* turned out to be a symbolistic, tendentious piece with a commentative chorus. What was Hammerstein's burlesque supposed to be burlesquing? The only symbolistic, tendentious piece with a commentative chorus that anyone could remember seeing was *Allegro.* Where was the humanism, the musical scene, the ethnic ballet? After the great five, a show whose only innovation lay in its having two overtures was a letdown.

Was it possible that the musical play simply couldn't encompass musical comedy? Was it a limited form, huge and strange and incapable of growth? But R & H did write a superb musical comedy, *Cinderella* (1957). Unfortunately, they wrote it for television in the days before videotape was in use; it was seen once, live and true. A year later it was staged in London as a Christmas pantomime, with interpolations (from *Me and Juliet,* mostly), in defiance of the musical play's aesthetic, and in 1965, after Hammerstein's death, Rodgers grimly superintended a revision that turned a deft comic romance into a soggy mess about as deft as *Me and Juliet*'s asbestos curtain. This is the *Cinderella* that is shown today.

That first *Cinderella* was beautifully cast. Julie Andrews, still in *My Fair Lady,* was the heroine, Edie Adams the Fairy Godmother, Ilka Chase the Stepmother, Kaye Ballard and Alice Ghostly the sisters, Howard Lindsay and Dorothy Stickney the King and Queen, Jon Cypher the Prince. Setting the story without modern interpretation as a neverland fairy tale, the authors trod lightly, accepting the magic (but not doting on it), fulfilling the love story (but not hoking it), and spending plenty of comedy. There were no surprises; yet everything was new minted. The Godmother doesn't believe in miracles ("Impossible!" she sings—but she performs them), the town crier has his mouth full spitting out the royal family's many given names ("Sidney?" the townsfolk repeat, dubious; "Sidney!" he bellows), and the two sisters are divertingly earthy ("He is more than a prince," they recall the morning after the ball, "he's an ace!"). The raucous Ballard and the fussy Ghostley were a treat, Andrews perfect, and the approach so vital and uncloying that even the limited staging area available to the home screen and Cypher's two lyric flubs in "Do I Love You Because You're Beautiful?" do not detract. The whole ninety minutes (less times out for the five commercials, so tactful that it's hard to tell just what the sponsor is selling) is poised precisely between romance and spoof. This is a feat in an essentially romantic tale, and proves the adaptability of the musical play. It certainly explains why it engrossed the musical in the decades that followed that first sweeping cavalcade of R & H in the 1940s. Old hands despaired of keeping up or labored to outdo themselves, as Cole Porter did on *Kiss Me, Kate* (1948). Some newcomers wrote shows that R & H might have written, and in their style—Lerner and Loewe's *Brigadoon* (1947) or *Paint Your Wagon* (1951), for instance. This is not imitation. R & H had revealed the destiny of the musical. Different stories provision different shows.

Betty Smith's novel *A Tree Grows in Brooklyn* offers a case in point, an episodic and tragic tale of growing up Irish in Williamsburgh at the turn of the century—but it *might* work if done right. Smith wrote the book with George Abbott and Arthur Schwartz and Dorothy Fields handled the score, all attempting to infuse the show with a spirited nostalgia without losing hold on the love plot between hard-working Katie and ne'er-do-well Johnny, developed through courtship, marriage, and the raising of their grave adolescent Francie. The R & H classics all touched on death, even that of a sympathetic principal, and *A Tree Grows in Brooklyn* (1951) suffered the passing of Johnny Nolan:

> HILDY: He collapsed while he was working. They took him to Bellevue.
> KATIE: I'll go.
> HILDY: Katie . . . he died there.
> KATIE: (*After a moment*) You lie, Hildy Moran! You lie! You always hated me because Johnny wanted me instead of you. All these years you've been trying to get back at me. And you found out Johnny's been gone a few days. So you come here . . . (*Beginning to break down*) Women have to go through so much, you'd think they'd stick together instead of always being so mean to each other. (*Pleading without hope*) Say you lied, Hildy. Say you lied! I won't hold it against you. (*The quiet tears come.*)
> HILDY: (*Taking Katie in her arms*) Katie . . . Katie . . .
> KATIE: (*Clinging to her friend*) Oh, Hildy, what am I going to tell Francie?

A strong scene, unthinkable in musicals before *Carousel*. However, *A Tree Grows in Brooklyn* included one element R & H did without, the star comic. As Katie's sister Cissie, Shirley Booth expanded her dramatic triumph in William Inge's *Come Back, Little Sheba* to become a prize find for musical comedy with her daffy line readings and singular vocals. But it was difficult for the audience to shift from the Nolans' hopes and despairs to Booth's sitcom bits, set into *A Tree Grows in Brooklyn* as if in revue: Cissie fakes childbirth, Cissie has rendezvous with old flame, Cissie repossesses strayed husband. In the context of the musical play, Cissie is a throwback to *The Desert Song*'s Benny and Susan and other hired jesters. She doesn't even have all that much to do with the Nolans' story—yet she holds the center of the play far more than they. This adaptable the musical play is not. It works on an all-or-nothing plan. By its nature, its greed for integration, it coopts all talents, all the entertainment. It would have been interesting to see what Hammerstein would have done with Smith's novel, especially considering how seldom he pulled off a truly funny lyric, which

Fields did with ease here. Funny situations Hammerstein had in plenty—funny lines, no.

By the 1950s, the musical play was so influential and carried such swank that everyone not sworn to out-and-out musical comedy was writing musical plays. Irving Berlin, of all masters least able in this kind of theatre, plotted for years with Joshua Logan to adapt James Michener's novel *Sayonara*. Even Harold Rome, heretofore limited to ditties on the culture of New York's Jewish working class, turned, quite successfully, to the musical play in *Fanny* (1954), typically a tricky adaptation, a ballet-rich production with a distinctive nautical flavor, and a score of operatic breadth.

This in itself reveals the problem. Adaptation, dance, concept, opera. What of the original, heedless, satiric *and political* show, musical comedy in its purest and most irreverent state? Could it observe Hammerstein's integrated composition? E. Y. Harburg proved that it could—provided that one set one's tale in fantasy. The musical play presented the truth of the world; so musical comedy must recapture the dream. Harburg was whimsical, idealistic, and leftist; he saw Hammerstein's plan as a chance to reconcile the fun of the musical with the tetchy honesty of theme. In Harburg, an elated faerie of magic formulas can save or end mankind, pots of gold yield three wishes, and the Other World makes mischief and gives advice.

Oddly, when Harburg got started he was a realist—one of his first notable lyrics was that to "Brother, Can You Spare a Dime?" But in the raising of a socialist Americana—an R & H plus politics—Harburg ranged the commentary within an escapist format. His social prescriptions were so generalized and his satire so imaginative that he came off more as an absurdist than a social commentator. When Harburg used the musical for a parable about a pacifist who stymies the war-mongers—as Paul Green and Kurt Weill did in the somber *Johnny Johnson*—the result was slam-bang bizarre musical comedy at its incorrigible best: *Hooray for What* (1937), with Ed Wynn as a horticulturalist who stumbles upon a formula for a gas that could destroy humankind. The comparison between *Johnny Johnson* and *Hooray for What* tells us much about the difference between the kind of political musical that defies public apathy and the kind that instructs it. *Johnny Johnson* was staged by a perennially impoverished acting company (the Group Theatre) of great socioprofessional resolve; *Hooray for What* was a star-comic vehicle produced by the Shuberts. *Johnny Johnson*'s score took the audience out of the story to comment upon it; *Hooray for What* had Arlen tunes for Harburg's panacea—torch songs mock ("Down with Love") and true (Moanin' in the Mornin' "), love songs ("I've Gone Romantic on You"), patriotic self-congratulation ("God's Country"), good for what ails you. *Johnny Johnson* ultimately told us that there are too few good men to keep the world whole—the curtain falls on the protagonist, now a toymaker, wandering through the empty days, unknown, harmless, unheeded. *Hooray for What* told us that an idiot can lose the doomsday formula and the world won't shatter because the bad guys will espy the formula backwards and manufacture not death gas but love gas and all nations will join in brotherhood.

There is no question that Harburg had the talent to bring his worldview to life with originality and spirit. He built on Lorenz Hart's games with language and Porter's allusion to the famous, adding in a pronounced susceptibility to the sillier forms of fun—taking walks, riding roller coasters, fooling around, singing and dancing for joy. Even taking stands against racism and sexism can be fun when Harburg shows one how. *Bloomer Girl* (1944) dealt with both in a Civil War setting, and *Finian's Rainbow* (1947) strengthened the discussion on race relations, adding in digs at capitalist consumerism.

Bloomer Girl's period dress and historical details set it apart from the very modern-day *Finian's Rainbow*. Still, the pair are equally funny, loving musical comedies with a strong will toward timeliness, *Bloomer Girl*'s war theme obviously of moment in 1944 and *Finian*'s *charge it!* mania a reflection of life in these United States in the booming postwar days. The scores are classics, Burton Lane's *Finian*'s tunes so appealing that virtually every melody caught on with the public. Harburg was feeling strongly Popular Front at the time—his hero, a freedom-riding, guitar-slinging populist, is named Woody after Woody Guthrie, and Harburg originally wanted him to sing folk songs or something like. He got the idea that Lane would collaborate with Earl Robinson, oathed to folk-leftist theatre and the composer (to Latouche's words) of the extremely innocent but nonetheless controversial "Ballad for Americans," introduced in *Sing for Your Supper* and later a vehicle for Paul Robeson and various choruses. Lane didn't want to share the job, and Harburg gave in, all to the good, as Robinson's style was too serious for Harburg's brand of musical theatre.

Unlike *Hooray for What,* these two forties musicals deal in earnest and very specific social critique. At times they are shockingly realistic, as in the murderous rage that steals in under the julepy drawl of *Finian*'s racist senator and his henchmen. A twinge of earthiness, too, shocks, for *Finian* featured an impish David Wayne as the leprechaun Og, who has followed Finian from Ireland to reclaim the pot of gold Finian stole. To his horror, Og is growing mortal in America:

> OG: Look at me—it's crept up past me ankles already. (He shows Finian Exhibit A: socks and golf shoes) . . . I've got a peculiar *human* feelin' in me thighs lately.
> FINIAN: Your thighs! Don't let it go any further, man!

It does, though. "I don't want to be a mortal!" Og squeals. "I want to go back to Fairyland!" But his first kiss changes his mind. "Fairyland was never like this!" he then booms, his voice dropping to a virile bass. And he takes on what Harburg assures us is the essential human quality, libidinous promiscuity, celebrating with "When I'm Not Near the Girl I Love (I love the girl I'm near)."

Og is Harburg's most typical creation, his pixie whimsey calling up all sorts of pranks and neologisms, as in the rhymes for "Something Sort of Grandish": "sugar candish" and "hand-in-handish," or "mouseish" and "Eisenhowsish." But Harburg's most typical and distinctive musical, unfortunately, is one of those wonderful pieces that somehow doesn't click on its premiere and never quite recovers, surviving only as a record album treasured by a cult. This is *Flahooley* (1951). Who but Harburg would have been willing to come into town with a show with such a crazy title? Who but Harburg would have started with the premise that, in a world where children's dolls cry, a laughing doll would spread an epidemic of joy to terrify the Corporation and threaten to throw the business world off its pins? Who but Harburg would have gone on from there to add in marionettes, a genie in a lamp, a Christmas carol called "Sing the Merry" that ironically cited the names of stores and products and begged Americans to "give Christmas back to Christ," and Yma Sumac, singing what sounds like Mayan rites in her slightly less than ten-octave range?

Flahooley is the most Harburgian of musicals, more timely, more pixilated, more evangelical, more comprehensively satiric than the others put together. As with *Bloomer Girl* and *Finian's Rainbow*, Harburg wrote the book (with Fred Saidy) along with the lyrics, but this time he also staged the piece, and bravely registered one of the few attacks on McCarthyism to be heard on the American stage. In its Philadelphia tryout, when *Flahooley*'s producers decided to drop the reference to Christ at the close of "Sing the Merry," the show was a huge success, and word filtered back to Broadway that Harburg had the hit of his life. Insiders joked that any show with dolls, puppets, and a genie in it was bound to go over in a place like Philadelphia. Sure enough, the show didn't take in New York. All the magic, all the sharp satire, all the lovely music (by Sammy Fain), and even the remarkable (to say the least) Yma Sumac went down the drain in a few weeks.

Yet the show drills home a message of note that politicized Babies have been alluding to or promulgating through the century: wealth and power will devour the human spirit if they aren't checked. Perhaps this is why *Flahooley* did not succeed. The message urges the public to a kind of war; in 1951 everyone was sick of war, any kind. It's doubtful that *Strike Up the Band*'s laugh at militarism or *Pins and Needles*'s trade-union rally would have done well at this time—a fine revival of *Of Thee I Sing* failed just a year later. Still, Harburg thought his message feasible precisely because it lacked the solemnity and musical organization of R & H—puppets, no less. Their wisdom is Harburg to the core: "The World Is Your Balloon." Even *Flahooley*'s toy executives—The Corporation!—act like children, exulting over their domain of playtime "where everything is candy 'stead of canned!" The musical play told of timeless truth. Musical comedy, as Harburg restructured it, is of today: "Get your utopia now!" he urged in *Bloomer Girl*. No wonder he kept turning to fairyland for sustenance. The musical's original mandate was to describe a haven where boy meets girl and money doesn't matter, a worldview which peaked in *Sally*. Even such very post-*Sally* and political works as *I'd Rather Be Right* reaffirmed that haven. So the budget isn't balanced? So you can't afford the necessities? So what? Marry and be well! Harburg's plan was to realign a more sophisticated art along those original lines. He succeeded because his talent and his simplistic solutions were both highly appealing.

But what happened when authors lacked Hammerstein's unified composition and Harburg's contemporaneous perceptions? Less fully conceived shows could not satisfy tastes whetted by the one or the other. In particular, any musical dealing with a serious theme or characters of dimension could no longer work the conventions, and those that tried to failed. Take *Saratoga* (1959).

Here's a show that, in planning, looked *very* sound. The source, Edna Ferber's novel *Saratoga Trunk*, is far more adaptable than her *Show Boat*—tidier, nearly intimate—yet turns on the same conflict of pragmatism and idealism that the American adventure myth delights in. (*Gone with the Wind* is perhaps its classic entry.) In the 1880s, the beautiful, brilliant offspring of a lavish Creole demimondaine comes to New Orleans to blackmail her late mother's enemies, falls in with a handsome Texan, and goes with him to Saratoga to scandalize society and make her fortune in marriage while he makes some trouble for the railroad capitalists who devour the land. There is satire, farce, violence, suspense, high chivalry. And, Ferber being Ferber, the fortune hunter ends up in the Texan's arms.

Already, shape and tone are implicit: society versus upstarts, established robber barons versus unknown adventurers, colorful New Orleans and staid Saratoga, her scheming and his bravado. Producer Robert Fryer assembled some telling collaborators—Harold Arlen and Johnny Mercer for the score, Cecil Beaton for the décor, Carol Lawrence (fresh from *West Side Story*) for Clio Dulaine, and Howard Keel (not fresh; but what can you do?) for

Clint Maroon. To direct, Fryer hired Morton da Costa, on top of the lists
for his supervision of *Auntie Mame* and *The Music Man*. Obviously, the
show is going to be a musical play. Ferber's characters are too large for
cut-and-paste musical comedy, and the epic clash of the railroad money
bosses and the lone-wolf paladins calls for some thematic margin. Besides,
there are tricky subsidiary characters to bring to life in Clio's retinue of
black voodoo duenna, dwarf groom, and (expanded from the novel) worldly
Creole aunt. Here casting was very strong—contralto Carol Brice, posses-
sor of one of the greatest instruments in the concert world, the agile dwarf
Tun Tun, and operetta veteran Odette Myrtil. These are the fixings for a
fine musical: *if* it can produce Clio's recklessness and Clint's murderous
strength; *if* it can play on the tensions of personality, history, locale, fortune; *if* Clio's bizarre suite can express themselves in song pitched to their
odd culture; *if*, similarly, the society and railroad crowds represent what
they are, money and power, instead of coming off as merry villagers in
top hats; and *if* all concerned agree from the start on what *Saratoga* is
about so every piece of the final product can tell us.

Disaster. Da Costa wrote his own book, limply and vaguely. Beaton's
ravishing sets and costumes bore no relation to the way the cast carried
itself; they might have been day-trippers in a theme park. Ferber's New
Orleans is lazy and sensuous; in *Saratoga* it was loud. Ferber's Saratoga is
conspiratorial and repressed; in *Saratoga* it was loud. Most disappointing
was the score, empty tunes that reduced the characters to diagrams.* The
heroine's chaperones' duet, "Getting a Man," was funny, and gave Brice
and Myrtil a main chance. But it is completely wrong for the taciturn Kaka
and the unfocused Aunt Belle. "Petticoat High" had Clio wildly kicking
up a shindy in the New Orleans market scene—no! The woman is careful,
precise, only decorously sensational. Sure, Lawrence needs a dance specialty. But Clio does not. Anyway, the song itself is gauche. Arlen had no
trouble setting up the scene, in a jazzy strut for the lights-up as the vendors
indolently cried their wares. But once the song proper began, all sense of
character went flying with Lawrence's crinolines. A chorus to open Act
Two, "The Cure," had the Saratoga fashionables bleating like Shubert
prisoners at last released from a *Blossom Time* tour; and the robber barons sang "The Men Who Run the Country" with a jaunty verve: only
they're supposed to be somnolent monsters who rock on a porch while
their minions loot the nation. At least Brice had a fine solo in "Goose

---

* Out-of-town plague laid Arlen so low that he went home, and Mercer, a sometime and
very rudimentary composer, is said to have written some of the music.

Never Be a Peacock" in Arlen's trustworthy black style. But the show's only moment of originality was "The Railroad Fight," a bloody battle staged by Ralph Beaumont in slow motion, and its one affidavit of style was Beaton's sumptuous design for the poster. Hammerstein and Harburg made Broadway dangerous for the routine.

12

A Newer Style of Heroine

First they were charmers, then singers turning into acting singers. By the 1950s, the musical play had made character the essence of performing, yet the concomitant explosion of narrative choreography made dancers more crucial, even in lead parts. Ideally, a fifties heroine might be equipped to handle any element in musical comedy production.

Nanette Fabray seemed a likely candidate for stardom as this new era dawned, though a series of sweetheart roles in the early 1940s told little of her talent. Replacing Celeste Holm in *Bloomer Girl*, she revealed her gumption, leading the women in "It Was Good Enough for Grandma (but it ain't good enough for us)" with a verve that gave feminist rebellion a kick, a charm. Thereafter, she originated roles, as the mother in *High Button Shoes* (1947), young for the part but game; the wife in *Love Life* (1948); and the not always efficient woman-who-would-be-a-soldier in *Arms and the Girl* (1948). Set during the American Revolution, this was the first show in which Fabray dominated the action, capturing a Hessian mercenary (Georges Guetary) who deserted the British side, protecting an escaped slave (Pearl Bailey), playing a mock vamp scene and trying colonial "bundling" with a soldier (John Conte) she believes to be a spy, blowing up bridges (ours, alas), and at last receiving the compliments of General Washington, who, albeit, advises her to "stay the hell out of this Revolution!" There was a lot for Fabray to play here—comedy, patriotism, Deanna Durbinesque scheming, romance, and derring-do. This was a departure in heroines, a warrior Sally who doesn't look for but seizes the silver lining—Fabray could even whistle through her teeth, and too often did. There was resistance, particularly to Fabray's athletic side. George

Jean Nathan called for a moratorium on "these arbitrary clowns who rightly belong in circuses" and a return to "the gentler and more conformable heroines."

Helen Gallagher, small and lithe in Colleen Moore bangs, fit in better than Fabray because she danced as well as sang and played no bold heroines to scare reactionary men. Starting in the line in the mid-1940s in such shows as *Seven Lively Arts, Mr. Strauss Goes to Boston, Billion Dollar Baby,* and *Brigadoon,* she acquired training no school could grant: with Balanchine, Robbins, and de Mille. But her first roles, like Poupette in *Make a Wish,* mired her in convention, and her first lead, in *Hazel Flagg* (1953), somehow did not take her anywhere. It was an all-out star role, in an adaptation of *Nothing Sacred,* the Carole Lombard-Fredric March satire on PR about the New England girl supposedly dying of radium poisoning, who is treated to a last spree on the town. There was Gallagher's likeness on the poster, there her name first above the title, and the Jule Styne-Bob Hilliard score gave her a ballad ("The World Is Beautiful Today"), the typical Styne take-it-easy tune ("I Feel Like I'm Gonna Live Forever"), eleven o'clocker ("Laura de Maupassant"), and plenty of chances to step. A big part, this: funny, vulnerable, pushy, bewildered, romantic. Indeed, it was a big show, with lots of would-be numbos and a big chorus to field Hugh Martin's crazy vocal arrangements, a sort of singing complement to jitterbug. Gallagher made the most of it, at her best in the scene in which her fellow citizens see her off to New York at the train station, the music swollen with sympathy, local pride, and railroad onomatopoeia. Hazel is unbowed, eager to start the last vacation of her life. "There's only one thing that I want," she tells them, "and that's to git *outta* Vermont!"

What she got *to* was fast flops, replacement stints, and, in 1971, secondary-couple position again, opposite Bobby Van in the *No, No, Nanette* revival. Neither she nor Fabray became a star in the Marilyn Miller sense, yet in Fabray's comedienne and Gallagher's little belter-dancer dynamo they each established a character. Broadwayites spoke of "Fabray" or "Gallagher" types, even while passing up the originals to hire less gifted samples of the types they had coined.

Even a heroine who got the breaks didn't necessarily stay with it. Julie Andrews, still in her teens, dazzled the town in *The Boy Friend* (1954), fulfilled her promise in *My Fair Lady* (1956), and emerged the prima donna in *Camelot* (1960), all British shows by origin or adaptation. Quite lacking Fabray's buffonery and Gallagher's dancing jive, Andrews was mainly a singer, mainly elegant, mainly precise, and winning in that precision. Some of her resources were not tapped till she joined Carol Burnett for a revue televised from Carnegie Hall in 1960, spoofing and crazing with panache.

But then Andrews seems to have been brought over to retrieve the musical's lost grace. Like the heroines of Herbert's day she was a soprano rather than a belter or a "theatre" singer, and could not whistle through her teeth. At any rate, she didn't. But she did top "I Could Have Danced All Night" with a competent top G; and it is notable that while her performance of the song reflected the wound-up intensity invoked by the lyrics, her singing was serenity itself. Andrews was staidly vital, lively pure—and a very hard act to follow. Eliza Doolittle shouldn't be difficult. Indeed, Andrews made it look easy, comprehending (in her transformation from Cockney into lady) Shaw's premise that language is social class. But if the role is so easy, why is it so hard to find good Elizas? Rex Harrison coopted Higgins both in the film version and the 1981 revival, perennial in his Big Role like a veteran of Mrs. Fiske's day. Yet Ian Richardson in 1976 bettered him completely: there is more than one Higgins. When Andrews abandoned her role after her London run, however, she was not even to be equaled.

Broadway didn't serve Andrews well. After *My Fair Lady* she had a right to something meaty, like a revival of *Lady in the Dark*. *Camelot* was not the thing. Faced with the task of assimilating T. H. White's Arthurian epic of satire, mysticism, and misanthropic philosophy, *The Once and Future King,* into a stately musical play, Alan Jay Lerner shaved everyone down from characters to jobs. Arthur (Richard Burton) has to establish democracy. Lancelot (Robert Goulet) has to be First Knight, not least to Arthur's First Lady. Pellinore (Robert Coote) has to repeat the lovable old Brit he had played in *My Fair Lady.* Mordred (Roddy McDowall) has to foment mutiny. And the Andrews Guinevere? She had so little in sheer role that she could find herself only in the songs: romantic in "The Simple Joys of Maidenhood," supportive in a reprise of "Camelot," roguish in "The Lusty Month of May," petty in "Then You May Take Me to the Fair," tender in "Before I Gaze at You Again," dejected in "What Do the Simple Folk Do?," crushed in "I Loved You Once in Silence." Okay; character development in song is what the musical play is for. And Andrews does stately better than anyone, to the relief of those alienated by Nathan's "arbitrary clowns." Still, it can't be said that *Camelot* was an advance over *My Fair Lady* for Julie Andrews. Even *Cinderella,* from a much less fertile source than *Camelot,* showed Andrews in fuller bloom.

What was the fifties and sixties heroine? Hammerstein's shows tended to strong-willed women who survived their men, like Julie Jordan, Anna, and, in a way, Magnolia. Katie Nolan in *A Tree Grows in Brooklyn* and Fanny fell into this line. But this was an era devoted to musical comedy, to comedienne dancer-singers. Perhaps Liza Minnelli would prove symptomatic. One among many principals in the 1963 off-Broadway revival of *Best Foot Forward,* the teenaged Minnelli stood out as Ethel Hofflinger, her big-eyed energy and avid belt already notable in the opening number, "Wish I May." "Listen, Ethel," one girl cries, "you keep your hands off of Clayton!" She pulls her boyfriend out of reach. "All right, all right," says Liza with a shrug; she'll get him later. This was a dandy showcase for Minnelli, the authors presenting her with an eleven o'clock song not in the original and mother Judy Garland thoughtfully coming on the second night so as not to spoil the debutante's glory on the first.

A good commencement, then—and even better continuation in *Flora, the Red Menace* (1965), a buoyant, satiric Depression-era *Bildungsspiel* with a fetching score by John Kander and Fred Ebb and only one voice to do it justice. Hers. Minnelli's three solos—"A Quiet Thing," "Dear Love," and "Sing Happy"—are the wonderful personality pieces that become theme songs, one hushed, one a tautly swinging waltz, the other a crescendo of manic jubilee. (If there's one thing that Minnelli can do without rival it's build a number. On a scale of 1 to 10 she can start at three, climb each digit like a Victorian general flying up his colors, and where she finishes does not show up on the chart.) The way she sailed her voice out over the tune in "All I Need (Is One Good Break)" was indescribable joy to hear— all the real-life star-is-born legend that Minnelli carries by information of genes working through into a part *about* making it, getting born.

What man, in Minnelli's day, has been able to run a show on magnetism alone? Robert Preston, a surprise song-and-dance king as of the surprise success of *The Music Man* (1957), came to grief in *We Take the Town* (1962), on the adventures of Pancho Villa with a score by the authors of *Happy Hunting,* Dubey and Karr. *We Take the Town* couldn't even take Philadelphia, and never came in. *Mack and Mabel* (1974) did, after protracted tryout revisions, but *The Prince of Grand Street* (1978) didn't. This is a terrible record for a performer whose professionalism, charm, and capability went down like tonic in 1957.

A movie actor unschooled in the musical's conventions, Preston made them bracing. Harold Hill, the music man, was one of those daredevil catalogue parts musicals seldom allot to a man—he runs the plot, leads the score (in rhythmic patter as well as song), unfreezes the librarian, makes the evening's major character leap from swindler to lover, and locates the show's Iowa-stubborn atmosphere by the contrast of his agile personality. The show opened on a railroad car filled with traveling salesmen arguing the music man's abilities, piquing a poker player who till then had been hidden by the stage picture. "Gentlemen," he suddenly said, "you intrigue me. I think I'll have to give Iowa a try." He rose, suitcase in hand: Preston.

And as the halves of the train glided into the wings with the shocked salesmen, he stepped into the middle of the midwest.

This was a neat way to announce the hero's opposition to intransigent midwestern skepticism: improvisation, wit, fearlessness. A Hollywood hero. But the American musical seldom confronted that kind of man except in operetta, where he was usually played by baritones with the swank of a curate and the nerve of Cracker Jack. The musical really prefers boy-friends, kiddos, or unreformable hustlers; the prospect of a solid man throws it off its foundation. The musical is a woman's medium, largely, where Sally is an orphan and Eadie was a lady.

Even Richard Kiley's bravura stint as both Cervantes and Don Quixote in *Man of La Mancha* (1965) could be seen as a frame for Joan Diener's voluptuous Aldonza, at first contemptuous of, then converted to (and re-deemed by) Quixote's utopian quest, known to every ear in the country—there was no escaping it—as "The Impossible Dream." Yet Kiley faced down a kangaroo court of cutthroats in the Inquisition's prisons, turned into Quixote in a flash, fought his windmills, loved his Dulcinea, nurtured his vision, died (felled by mirrors, by mean truth), and, Cervantes again, made ready to face the Inquisition as an awesome stairway was lowered into the dungeon and the cast urged him on with a last chorus of "The Impossible Dream," numbo of numbos.

Surely this is one of the musical's biggest roles, and, yes, Kiley did be-come a star in it, as Preston did in *The Music Man*. However, it's interest-ing that the show's long run, foreign productions, and tours never had trouble finding decent Quixotes. It's Aldonzas who are hard to cast. It seems that all sorts of men can fill in as the knight—operetta baritones, Shakespeareans, even semi-singers, who try to whisper their way through "The Impossible Dream" as if in a trance. But Aldonza is more distinctly drawn, and makes heavy demands on the voice. In London, the versatile Keith Michell played the hero, and Aldonza was . . . Joan Diener. In Paris, Jacques Brel played the hero, and Aldonza was . . . Joan Diener. Was she trying to tell us something?

Not only were successfully show-carrying heroes in short supply—mu-sical comedy developed the apocalypse of the heroine in the Big Lady Show: big ladies, big shows. The trend-setter was *Hello, Dolly!* (1964), based on Thornton Wilder's *The Matchmaker*. Michael Stewart adapted the script, Jerry Herman wrote the score, Oliver Smith and Freddy Wittop designed it, and Gower Champion staged it. Out of town in Detroit, the show was in what Broadway calls Big Trouble, and altercations between Champion and producer David Merrick only ended when Champion told Merrick to leave town and let him tinker in peace. The show came in a smash, ran over six years, and has become a staple in the musical comedy cupboard. It's easy to enjoy, very funny and dancey; but it's also a grand, gorgeous excuse for a large cartoon of a woman to come pushing in and out with the bass of Chaliapin, the warmth of Fort Ticonderoga, and enough wigs to outfit a drag ball. The numbo, of course, is the title song, Dolly's return to the high life she departed some years before. As designed and staged, the moment takes her down a stairway into a corps of fawning waiters who join her in a buck-and-wing, hands-behind-the-back cakewalk, kick-step-with-finger-snap, duck waddle, and the like, using a runway built around the rim of the pit. The number didn't just work; it brought the house down. But there's a lie in it. If Dolly has no real generosity, no giving ease, no *humanity*, then what on earth is the celebration about?

Hello, Dolly! came into Broadway as a star vehicle. Yet the show is Bigger than its Lady. It changed tone as various stars assumed the lead. After Channing's lifeless brawn, Ginger Rogers was haughty, Martha Raye fun but wrong, Betty Grable too nice. (When the stage manager introduced her to the company with reverential punctilio, she giggled, "Oh, please.") Pearl Bailey lazily led an all-black cast, Phyllis Diller was stoogey, Ethel Merman animated a plaster image of herself. The best of them was their standby, Bibi Osterwald, and her only rival was Mary Martin, of the national tour and London. Osterwald understood the part and played it as it lays; Martin backed away somewhat from Dolly's aggressive heft but liked her coy candor. "Horace Vandergelder," Dolly declares, "you go your way and I'll go mine." She points the ways: they're the same way. She eats a chicken. She rebones surgical corsets, pierces ears, teaches guitar and mandolin, reduces varicose veins, matches up your maiden aunts, puts her hand in. She meddles. But, no matter how many feathers she's got flying out of that numbo wig, no matter how testy her full-figure bodice or kicky her fringed flounces, if she isn't real, you have a fake show. And some Big Ladies aren't real.

Lorelei (1974), a second Big Lady vehicle for Channing, was like television with a curtain. Similar intentions devised *Applause* (1970), with Lauren Bacall in Bette Davis's old role in *All About Eve*. It was a busy musical—Big Lady shows are as a rule—but Bacall seemed to be forever standing still while the cast ran rings around her: presiding over, rather than taking part in, her vehicle. *Lorelei* and *Applause* are shows for stars who don't have to do anything to get famous, stars in whom celebrity itself is the essential credential. Strangely, some Big Lady shows depended on women of talent and charm. *Mame* (1966), like *Hello, Dolly!*, had a Herman score and a promising source, Jerome Lawrence and Robert E. Lee's comedy about Patrick Dennis's iconoclastic aunt. It also had Angela

Lansbury as Mame. Lansbury's singing is odd but telling, her dancing capable, her geniality invigorating, her acting excellent. Dolly as written is eccentric and determined, Mame is eccentric and generous. Of all famous Dollys, none but Betty Grable was known for personal *give*—and Grable was not a correct Dolly. It would be interesting to see what Lansbury would do with the role; or would the character's sensory underload defeat her?

The Big Lady aesthetic doesn't tally on talent as much as on guts, on a self-willing celebrity—*famous* guts—that virtually forces the public to applaud one's entrance, one's numbers, even one's lines; and of course a standing ovation at the close is now considered formal ceremony. It's good show biz, but bad musical comedy, to build an evening around the glamor of guts. It's working backwards. Anyway, the two standout long-term heroines of the 1950s and 1960s thrived because they were at their best in a good show, whether musical comedy, musical play, or novelty. Barbara Cook was a singer, Gwen Verdon a dancer, but both proved to be formidable actresses, and even in Cook's several superflops and Verdon's successful but empty vehicles, their fullness as performers kept the evening hot.

Cook was the Atlanta kid with the bright and rangy soprano who came to New York's Blue Angel in 1950 to explore her taste for what she terms "late-night songs"—the cabaret literature of Rodgers and Hart, Gershwin, and such. Hard times followed *Flahooley*, but stints as Ado Annie on tour and Carrie Pipperidge at the New York City Center led to her first hit, *Plain and Fancy* (1955). This was the kind of musical comedy Broadway used to take for granted: standard two-couple love plots, tuneful score, funny book, and novel setting. Two New Yorkers visit Pennsylvania Dutch country; a parish outcast loves the girl his oafish brother will marry; a burned barn is rebuilt before your eyes in the opening of Act Two; the New York woman suffers culture shock among the isolated Amish; the outcast brother protects the oafish brother on a drunken spree in the sinful metropolis (Lancaster); the nation hums the hit, "Young and Foolish"; and everyone works for fourteen months. There were no stars, but plenty of principals, and Cook's Hilda Miller proclaimed her gifts for standard-make musical comedy in its post-R & H maturity. However, her next job took her to a one-of-a-kind piece for which Broadway gave no training, cast as a bizarrely inconsistent Continental noblewoman with a vocal range that would discourage a Lakmé. Cook made her history as Cunegonde in *Candide* (1956), perhaps the greatest of cult musicals.

"I had no life," she recalled twenty years after. "None. I was like an athlete, because of the demands. If it had run longer, I don't know if I could have done it eight times a week. But then I didn't know it was impossible." It's a startling credit for a Broadway performer because of the vocal hurdles; but it would be hard to name an opera soprano of the time who would have tolerated the rigorously theatrical ambience of Tyrone Guthrie's production. Those who need to categorize had a hard time placing Cook when she ripped into "Glitter and Be Gay," a spoof of coloratura showpieces with pensive, plaintive, showy, and demented coursing upon each other, the whole thing roiling with cadenza and peaking on a high E Flat.

The Gay Life (1961), another cult show, put Cook's name above the title for the first time, between those of Walter Chiari and Jules Munshin. Chiari was an Italian film star imported for reasons his work in *The Gay Life* never made clear, and Munshin was an irrelevant comic. It was left to Cook to center the show. The score, marking the reunion of Arthur Schwartz and Howard Dietz, was a dream; the book, a mess. They were still trying to fix the show after it opened, still fixing it when it closed, are perhaps fixing it now in Cain's Warehouse. Chiari is a womanizer, Cook the simple maiden who longs for and wins him. She cannot match the womanizer's many flames; they are another sort of woman, Eadies, and Cook is a lady. "Is she waiting there for you?" she sings to Chiari, the snow falling on them in the street. "Listening on the stair for you?" They are free women; she is the heroine we loved in Edith Day and Marilyn Miller. At the close, Cook joyfully gave herself to Chiari—on the morning of their wedding.

Through her committed singing, Cook revitalized the ingenue, lent the musical play's determination and individuality to musical comedy. Even in a perfectly miserable score, like that for *Something More!* (1964), Cook has such musicality and verve that one rushes out to buy the song sheets, only to realize that the material is empty without her.

Moreover, as an actress Cook makes the corniest situations persuasively natural. Put her, say, in a smallish show about life in a boutique where she bickers with the manager, meanwhile carrying on a lonelyhearts correspondence with a stranger who turns out to be—yes! This was *She Loves Me* (1963), perhaps Cook's best-known credit and a third cult show, not least because of Cook's trio of numbos of highly telling rhapsody, vulnerable ("Will He Like Me?"), crushed ("Dear Friend"), and recovering ("Ice Cream"). The first two are wide in appeal, catching the insecurity of dressing for a blind date and the disappointment at being stood up. The last is a gem of one-time-only musical comedy precision: writing to "dear friend" about the aborted meeting while one's mind is distracted by a visit from the manager and his present of a carton of ice cream. Laid out in the form of a letter with free-associative interpolations, "Ice Cream" is ingenious, excitingly observed, and capped by a B Flat so closely identified with the timbre of Cook's voice that no one else dares attempt the song.

By the mid-1960s, Cook had become the kind of performer you hire for a gala revival of some classic, her individuality good for the action and her seniority in class acts like *Candide* and reputable charm pieces like *She Loves Me* making her something other than a star, an insider's signet, perhaps, a symbol for the cultivated musical comedy buff. Richard Rodgers accordingly cast her as Magnolia when his Lincoln Center Musical Theatre Series got around to *Show Boat* in 1966. Magnolia is a tricky part, too young for most actresses in the first scenes and too old in the last. Cook is right for it, but this abysmal staging seemed literally to have no director. No one in the show appeared to have given any thought to the story, to the relationships. When Magnolia and Ravenal are reunited after decades of separation, we should be blown away. In this production, everyone came out with gray in his wig and posed, Magnolia glancing up at the husband she hadn't seen in decades as if he were her chauffeur, right on time with the car. It was Cook's first poor performance, in a role she above all others was equipped to do—tenacity is Magnolia's salient quality, and it is what gave Cook's heroines their unusual appeal as people.

Perhaps *Show Boat* is one reason why Cook began to withdraw from the musical, taking non-singing parts and eventually returning to the concert stage she had started on. There was also *The Grass Harp* (1971), another of those flops with a great score; how many cult musicals can one woman do? Cook was the ideal singing heroine of the years that assimilated the R & H musical play (she made a young yet excellent Anna at the City Center in 1960), but had been feeling anything but liberated by characterization. She wanted to sing as herself, cabaret-style. *She Loves Me*'s audiences admired her moving crying jag in the "Ice Cream" scene, but later Cook complained that the portrayal had become so rote-learned that after a while she had only to look at the bedspread for the tears to flow. So, taking her three *She Loves Me* numbos, other show tunes which she would never have sung in context, and some new pieces, she repaired to bistros and then, at Carnegie Hall in 1975, at last became a star. Ironically, it was not as Cunegonde, Marian the Librarian, or Amalia Balash, but as Barbara Cook. It seems she needed Broadway less than Broadway needed her.

Gwen Verdon offers a different case, as a dancer rather than a singer and, quickly enough, a star on the Merman order who could run a lackluster show for a year, hot ticket. Where Cook began as the trim, bright-eyed young woman typical of the singing heroine, Verdon had the dancer's lean body tone and a topping of very red hair, altogether distinctive. Her voice was hoarse, improbable in song, yet it worked. Anyway, in the days when she began in the line as Jack Cole's protégée, dancers didn't have to sing. Even in a featured role in *Can-Can* (1953), as Claudine the "laundress," she could pass nicely in her one vocal, "If You Loved Me Truly," and breeze through the rest of it on terpsichore. Lilo, the show's star and a latter-day Marie Cahill, fumed; but Verdon got the notices.

Poor Lilo: she never did get the hang of the American musical. In Paris, where she reigned, musicals run so loose that divas who don't care for book scenes can omit them entirely and simply make numerous entrances in superb gowns, the most superb, by tradition's command, being the last, in the curtain call: Performers' Rule. Occasionally, they sing. One thing no French star suffers is competition from the line. Who was this Gwen Verdon? One minute she's in the chorus of can-can girls, upstage of Lilo (where they belong) while la star puts over "Never Give Anything Away." Next minute, Verdon is playing Eve in Michael Kidd's "Garden of Eden" ballet at the end of Act One and the stupid audience is clapping its head off! The crowning blow was director Burrows's refusal to let Lilo hold up the curtain calls while she changed into her most superb gown.

Lilo was not prepared for the jazz of musical comedy, the inventions and switch-hitting, but Verdon was. From dance specialties she went on to a full singing-dancing role as the Devil's ageless vamp Lola in *Damn Yankees* (1955), thence to a musical play based on O'Neill's *Anna Christie, New Girl in Town* (1957). Verdon had hooked up with Bob Fosse on *Damn Yankees,* and he devised her formative numbo, "Whatever Lola Wants (Lola gets)," the striptease seduction of a ball player (right in the locker room) and a startling comparison with "Look for the Silver Lining," "Someone To Watch Over Me," or the gala waltz that Barbara Cook was singing in *Plain and Fancy* that year, "This Is All Very New to Me." Lola was not exactly a star part. There was no Entrance—just lights up, rather late in the first act, on Verdon on a bench, filing her nails. Nor was Verdon in the show's best dance number, "Shoeless Joe from Hannibal, Mo," a hoedown on the diamond. All the same, Verdon's Lola held the show from root to tip—her photograph served as the show's logo, first covered up in baseball uniform and then, when ticket buyers feared to tread, in her striptease tights. The customers rushed in.

New Girl in Town was planned to let Verdon come into her own as an actress; the part of a bitter prostitute doesn't seem to call for dance, anyway. But Verdon had built up a following on her dancing, and in tryouts the show began to turn into a musical comedy, with a joyful production number at a ball to close Act One and a sordid dream ballet representing

Anna's former life in Act Two. The ball was nifty, with a gleeful softshoe for Anna and two boys in that very, very precise nonchalance that Fosse is famous for. But the bordello ballet made a number of people uncomfortable, including Abbott and the producers. Verdon and Fosse loved the dance and resisted its suppression, Fosse pointing out that people had thrown fruit at Stravinsky. As Abbott dryly comments in his memoirs, "the act of throwing fruit at a project [is] not in the strictest logic an absolute proof of its high art." Fosse revamped the ballet somewhat, but it was put there to tell why Anna's revulsion toward sex is affecting her belief in romance, and even revamped it still looked . . . well, striking.

New Girl in Town was more notable for Verdon's acting than her dancing. In looks and tone she was perfect, scarlet and brazen and sour; in her romantic reformation she was reluctantly vulnerable; and Abbott even retained O'Neill's ambiguous ending, with a happy feeling but no clear denouement. Most surprising was the score by Bob Merrill. Author of "How Much Is That Doggie in the Window?" and a composer who taps out his melodies on a toy xylophone, he rose to the Hammersteinian challenge. Anna's songs really told dramatically, her first, "On the Farm," defining her worldview with devastating bite. If *New Girl in Town* was Verdon's vehicle—clearly, it was—it was no Big Lady Show, but a dare to be taken by going all the way. As for letting Verdon dance—frankly, the show needed the lift.

Redhead (1959), another Fosse show, this one set in Victorian London, was nothing but a vehicle. Its murder mystery plot was unusual, also its trick of showing us the crime first thing, even before the overture, so we could thrill to the stalking of Verdon by the man who appeared to be the murderer. This time out, Verdon was definitely slated to dance, all to the good, as the plot was silly, the score (by Albert Hague and Dorothy Fields) silly, and most of the cast silly. Verdon's numbo was a dream ballet, laid out in pastiche variations on her song "Merely Marvelous": entrée, first variation with xylophone, can-can, pas de deux, gypsy dance, and military march, a show in itself. Amid the silliness, Verdon was still better served than Joan McCracken had been in *Billion Dollar Baby* or Helen Gallagher in *Hazel Flagg*—or is it just that Verdon's personality spread her out more? She was unique as a dancing star in her ability to play more than musical comedy roles, and she brought that edge to her roles in musical comedy.

But the days of celebrity guts and superproduction were to sweep her away, perhaps to exhaust her. By 1975, when she and estranged husband Fosse (he can't have been that estranged, come to think of it) put on *Chicago*, Verdon alone could not keep it running—this is where Liza Minnelli came in. Nor could Verdon hold down the whole show herself; Chita Rivera was an equal partner as Velma Kelly to Verdon's Roxie Hart. Both played murderesses scheming to get off on PR, and both were at their brilliant best, as strangers, as rivals for the public's heart, and at last as a vaudeville duo.

These dancing women are really something. From the line busting out to center stage, in good parts and bad, they have provided much of the energy on which postwar musical comedy has run. When, in *Chicago,* Verdon climbed onto an upright piano to take on the ancient torch ritual in "Funny Honey"; when she sat to the side to watch Rivera's one-woman sister act, "I Can't Do It Alone," Rivera stripping off her housecoat to reveal the stomach of a weightlifter; when Verdon went into "Roxie" with a snapping-finger, side-shuffling, exquisitely selfish speech on her hunger for fame; or when the two joined in the final vaudeville strut to Peter Howard's fast-rag version of "Funny Honey," two murderesses freed on grounds of celebrity, "poetry in motion," the orchestra playing and playing and playing one figure till an incited public clapped one last time for the irreplaceable, for the guts of *talent,* the Forty-sixth Street Theatre was not unlike a museum on reserve, holding the last of Broadway's performers whom later generations will wish they had seen. We of today wonder what *Anything Goes, I'd Rather Be Right, DuBarry Was a Lady, Lady in the Dark, St. Louis Woman* were like. What shows after *Chicago* have this resonance? *Annie? Barnum? Dreamgirls?* Are these propositions for legend?

We have perhaps come to an end of talent stardom to a time of survivor-guts stardom, when being haughty and available is its own reward. For it would seem that the opportunities for talent are limited. When investors only want to back musicals with the likes of Lauren Bacall, who can neither sing, dance, nor act, and when critics rave and the public, ordered to attend, administers its office with the solemn festivity of cranks, and the theatre community, panicked by the collapse of their industry, vote Tonys for this shlock, neither material nor performance matters. This is what *Chicago* was about: fame is the first virtue.

"Just to see me goin' through it," Rivera sang in *Chicago,* "you would think there's nothin' to it." There was plenty to it, but little left of it, as Rivera discovered when she enlisted in *Bring Back Birdie* (1981), the abysmal sequel to *Bye Bye Birdie,* Rivera's first break after *West Side Story.* In *Bring Back Birdie* her big number was "I Love My Life." Maybe. But now, when the compositional integrity of the musical play should have freed character to the utmost, there's less character than ever. What there is is superproduction, the musical as one big numbo. In such endeavors, character is puppets.

13

The Superdirectors

From Julian Mitchell to John Murray Anderson to Hassard Short to Rouben Mamoulian, there have been directors of such stature that at times they are larger than the shows they stage. As conceivers of composition, as editors, as unifiers of the performing ensemble, as enlightened pictorialists or dance-oriented tricksters, they have affected musicals noble and trivial. Yet they were exceptional in their profession and not renowned outside it. A much older tradition regarded stage direction as the rite of the practised thespian, often an actor or a playwright. Direction was competence, no more. If the public thought of directors at all, it thought of these competent directors, governing the entrances and exits, administering shtick, dispensing lore, and measuring volume. They were not thought of as wizards of image and motion.

A typical director of musicals, then, would be George Abbott, an actor and playwright whose bent for sensible organization, no-nonsense technique, and fleet Cohanesque pacing sent him into directing. (He also became his own producer, after losing patience with the lying and idiocies of the managing fraternity.) Abbott's forte was conventional musical comedy; he helped fix the conventions. He perfected the "in-one" crossover, a quick moment downstage during a major set change that pulled the plot along or threw in a cute bit, with the actors moving across the stage from wing to wing. He cast with a gift, as happy to work with unknowns as with pros, and often choosing leads from an "open" (non-union) call. *Best Foot Forward*, for instance, tapped Nancy Walker and June Allyson. If they lacked seasoning, at least they were fresh; anyway, Abbott would season them. "Are you trying to be funny?" he asked Russell Nype during rehearsals for *Call Me Madam.* Nype had been; his line was a joke, and he was hoping to help it along. "Just deliver it," Abbott told him. "If it's funny, they'll laugh." He was direct, fair, open, and too experienced to suffer a fool through more than one dumb suggestion. What was the Abbott touch? "I make them say their final syllables."

Obviously, there is more in it than that. But the master himself, analyzing his touch in his memoirs, had nothing to say. Perhaps it's because he staged a diverse lot of shows—college musicals, period trips, dance shows, star vehicles, farces, a costume operetta, and even a few musical plays. This blocks the trail to an essence of Abbott. His most notable achievement was the creation of a foundation elastic enough to give full play to the most cunning scores. It was an Abbott show, *On the Town* (1944), that proclaimed the dance musical with great dance music, and Abbott (with *Town*ers Bernstein, Comden, and Green) who in *Wonderful Town* (1953) revealed the conventional musical with unconventional songs. With a thirties Greenwich Village setting, *Wonderful Town* would have period pastiche. But, as it turns out, the opening number ("Christopher Street"), the first-act finale ("Conga!"), the jazz number ("Swing"), and the eleven o'clocker ("The Wrong Note Rag") all pull sly tricks, such as the laborious vamp that opens "Christopher Street," a piano cliché scored for orchestra to catch the sham bravado of the typical tour guide as he herds his lambs through bohemia. The Abbott shape can take us anywhere—on campaign with Congressional candidate La Guardia through New York's ethnic neighborhoods in *Fiorello!* (1959), from law office to smoke-filled room, to Washington, D. C., to the mayor's chair; and all along the route the crossovers catch us up on a bit of character or plot. Abbott is still telling story during the curtain calls, when La Guardia is seen taking the oath of office after he regains his mayoralty.

A problem with Abbott is the shallow acting of his casts, a bane in the musical from day one. Not till R & H instituted the musical play was there any *regular* need for acting performers (which is a major reason why Gertrude Lawrence stood out among her peers). Abbott's shaping makes a show intelligible as a whole, but his actors are delivering lines, not portraying characters. A peculiar Abbott problem is the slightness of his second acts; he gets so much done in Act One that after the intermission he has too little story to deal with and tends to irrelevant episodes or a spate of numbos. *Fiorello!*'s "Gentleman Jimmy" is one such, a charleston number that the show doesn't really need.

The *Fiorello!* people must have liked Abbott's mysterious touch, for they all immediately went on to *Tenderloin* (1960), another period show about a reform campaign in New York. Now it was a crusading minister versus the vested interests, a star Shakespearean (Maurice Evans) as the minister, a slightly older New York with a *Police Gazette* look, and an adaptation, from Samuel Hopkins Adams's novel. Abbott and Jerome Weidman did not write as interesting a book as they had written for *Fiorello!*, but Bock and Harnick outdid themselves; and again the structure of the production allowed their talent a free range. From the "fourth wall" un-naturalism of the thirties musical, Abbott had come to a more flexible plan. So *Tenderloin* can open, after a dizzy comic-opera overture, with a dramatically contrapuntal view of the show's two opposing sides in the coming war of purity. Out of the darkness, spokesmen for the Tenderloin appear—an opportunist without profession, a hooker, a bought cop. All invoke America as the "land of opportunity." Immediately, they vanish and a church choir appears, singing of the same land but of a different opportunity. Now the Reverend himself appears, thundering a sermon on "the monument to harlotry" he is determined to close down. He fades into the darkness as the Tenderloin assembles, prowling and grouching into "Little Old New York." And suddenly the lights are up, the Tenderloin is in full swing, drunks, swells, thieves, cops, prostitutes, and their strenuous madam crowing and juking in their checks and stripes and feathers. The show is on, its premise defined in a picture.

Famed as Abbott was, few gave him ultimate credit for the shows he guided. Had not *On Your Toes, The Boys from Syracuse, Too Many Girls,* and *Pal Joey* scores by Rodgers and Hart? Had not *On the Town, Billion Dollar Baby, High Button Shoes,* and *Look Ma, I'm Dancin'!* Robbins choreography? *Call Me Madam* was a Merman show, *Damn Yankees* Gwen Verdon's showcase; *Once Upon a Mattress* introduced Carol Burnett and *Fade Out-Fade In* emblazoned her. Anyway, de Mille's nearly single-handed staging of *Allegro* argued a case for the *choreographer* as director, and some people must have been wondering what *On the Town* would have been like if Robbins had staged all of it himself.

They got the chance to see a Robbins show in the Mary Martin *Peter Pan* (1954). Filled with faerie of every sort, including pantomime animals, Neverland foliage that bloomed as one watched, a manic Tiger Lily in sneakers, and of course the traditional counterweight flying on wires, Robbins's *Peter Pan* proved the wisdom of expanding choreography into direction—which, of course, simultaneously expanded the notion of what direction might do. Theatre people had been worrying about the time element, about who would work with the actors while the dancers, in a separate room, were learning the combinations. But it was a matter of style, not of time: by putting the dancers and the actors together, under one hand, a musical could try for a unity it too seldom had in the past, in which everyone on stage would do everything as if in one feint, one profile. *Peter Pan* had this unity, and Michael Kidd's *Li'l Abner* (1956) production scored a greater success and suggested that a new era was in the making.

Some theatre people were still jittery: choreographers don't care about the book and can't hear the music; they put too much movement in; everyone's sick of ballet; and dancers are weird. Nevertheless, Robbins and Kidd caught the essence of their respective properties and brought them forth. What is *Peter Pan?*: a fantasy about staying young and having adventures. That's what Robbins's *Peter Pan* was about, moment to moment, that daring and comaraderie and wistful wonder. What is *Li'l Abner?*: a comic strip in which colorful bumpkins rout the menaces of the outside world. That's what Kidd's *Li'l Abner* presented, in gaudy crazes and foot-stamping hoedown, every character outlined in bold and the action racy and dangerous, forever hanging over a cliff. From the barnyard fiddle that ignited the overture, and the show curtain picturing a fence covered with Dogpatch graffiti, right through to the wedding of Abner and Daisy Mae—interrupted at the last second by Marrying Sam's compulsive homage to the town's sacred cow, Jubilation T. Cornpone—the show buzzed with a screwy drive that made it, like *Peter Pan,* a special case. Like *Allegro*, these shows had a unity of performance techniques that made one think that no hypothetical revival was going to work as well. And notice how well the director-choreographer approach works in different casting strategies. *Allegro* by its quasi-allegorical nature called for somewhat undistinctive singing actors, performers who would seem to be ordinary people. *Peter Pan* was a star vehicle with a lot of kids, a Captain Hook (Cyril Ritchard) out of the British pantomime heritage, and a vaudeville Smee (Joe E. Marks) left over from the 1950 production with Jean Arthur, staged by British traditionalists: a gallimaufry. *Li'l Abner* gathered in an ensemble of Kidd veterans for the dances, the lead roles taken by singers who bore a likeness to Al Capp's originals (except Charlotte Rae, amusingly disfigured in a ton of greasepaint as Mammy Yokum; Marks got into this one, too, as Pappy).

It began to look like the thing: director-choreographers got billing larger than directors had. Even without choreographer's credentials, Morton da Costa could claim, on the posters of *The Music Man* (1957), an "entire production staged by" credit. A star dancer's vehicle was another likely proposition for a choreographer turning director, and Bob Fosse took charge of *Redhead* (1959) for Gwen Verdon. But there were more choreographers than star dancers, so the directing choreographer was never limited to "dancing" shows. In this era, most musicals had a lot of dancing, anyway. Once Gower Champion brought in *Bye Bye Birdie* (1960), no limitations could be placed on a dance man turned big chief. For *Bye*

Bye Birdie was the sort of show they call a "sleeper": no big names, no advance, and the smart money says it will flop. *Birdie* was a hit. If its simple generation-gap satire did not call for the organizing eye that oversaw *Peter Pan* and *Li'l Abner,* it was at least pleasantly brought off.

Champion's second major* job of superdirection, on *Carnival* (1961), gave him more to do on a show of a different color, somewhat dour and open to countless director's choices. One of Champion's was historically notable: the introduction of the unit set. The curtain was up when the public came in, on an empty field. No overture. Pierre Olaf wandered on, began to play a tuneful waltz on an accordion, the orchestra took up the tune, and other brightly-garbed people appeared, hauling on ropes, fitting pieces together, riding in on wagons. Presto!, up rose B. F. Schlegel's Grand Imperial Cirque de Paris. Schlegel himself now entered, with pompous pizzazz, to urge the company to parade into town and sing their own praises. Led by Kaye Ballard, they ripped into "Direct from Vienna" as yet more circus materialized—a dancing harem girl, a trained dog, a stiltwalker, a dwarf with a trumpet.

The rest of the show followed upon that approach, suffused with a carnival atmosphere. The roustabouts shifted the set furniture; the love plot between waif Anna Maria Alberghetti and bitter cripple Jerry Orbach was carried on through the puppets he uses to factor his personality; a magic act pulled volunteers up out of the audience so magician James Mitchell could pull a goldfish out of a woman's hat and rip the shirt off a man's back in a facile sweep. At the end, the circus was dismantled as it had been raised, the stage again empty. A Concept show.

Carnival as written is interesting. It offers one of the musical's rare *acting* parts in Orbach's puppeteer, ravaged by self-hatred and redeemed by the innocent girl who falls in love with his little dolls. Michael Stewart's book (from the movie *Lili*) sets the man's anger off well, while Bob Merrill's score reveals the feelings beneath. Nor did Merrill fail to come through with a song to match *Lili*'s "Hi-Lili, Hi-Lo," naïve and sweet, like the heroine herself: "Love Makes the World Go 'Round," the waltz Olaf used to open the show.

Indeed, *Carnival*'s score is suprisingly good, considering Merrill's compositional limitations, its lyrics particularly touching a strange, simple, extreme poetry. The girl is wild, the man is sad, the puppets are dear and dotty. This comes through all at once in "Beautiful Candy," sung after Lili has joined the dying puppet show, revived it, and become a sensation. To

---

*Champion had staged and choreographed *Lend an Ear* (1948) just after de Mille and somewhat before Robbins and Kidd inaugurated the era of superproduction, but *Lend an Ear* was a small revue, logistically easy to control and without a Concept.

the puppets' horror, Lili suggests throwing some money away on a good time. "The sun today will be scrambled for my soufflé" and "Treat yourself to some dreams from the upper shelf" are appealingly nutty; they sound right coming from a girl whose best friends are four hand puppets. The dolls themselves are her spiritual kin, types of the comic-romantic personality that the American musical approves of as characterization for a lover. Lili comes by it naturally—she's so young that she's still enchanted by magic acts and puppet shows. Her reluctant suitor must acquire it: so he can love himself and thus love Lili.

So "Beautiful Candy" is an important number, a turning point in which, for the first time, we see these two lovers (and of course the puppets) utterly relaxed and free with each other in a charm song, an "I've Got Five Dollars" or "It's a Lovely Day Today." Merrill wrote a breezy waltz with a calliope vamp and doodle-doo refrains for the puppets, and Champion staged it as a high point, an irresistible jubilation swelling out from the little puppet stage to take over the whole circus. As candy and novelty vendors punctuate the waltz rhythm with their cries and the corps dances in, the swaying puppets and the ebullient Lili capture the exhilaration of catching on big as a midway act. And, of course, at the same time, we get to experience her first date, more or less, with her sweetheart. This is fine showmanship and great storytelling.

Carnival was well cast, too, Alberghetti exactly right, Orbach very convincing as the puppeteer, Ballard grand as the husky Rosalie, and James Mitchell apt as the slithery magician, Marco the Magnificent (though the songs strung him out a little). And, as a David Merrick show, *Carnival* had enterprising PR, in a feud that Alberghetti was supposedly having with Merrick. (She probably was; it's easy to do.) Still, Champion was clearly the major collaborator, his single set astonishingly versatile and his direction literally that: aiming the story and firing it at the nexus points.

There is a problem in all this. A first-rate composition has its production plan more or less written into it; did not Rodgers and Hammerstein have a strong idea of how their shows must look as they were writing them? However, a show that needs extravaganza plonked onto it is a second-rate show, and the notion of a director not serving but *saving* a show, with gimmicks, suggests a tendency to start with second-rate texts (or worse) and hope for the best. Some began to feel that the director-choreographer was becoming too useful to Broadway, to the detriment of the literature (though when they were in trouble out of town, they put in their call to Robbins or Champion quickly enough). Some thought the idea a vanity. Sage Abbott points out that "entire production conceived and staged by John Doe" is like saying "entire part of Mother played by Lizzy Flop."

Yet comparable credit was becoming the mark of the reputable musical by the 1970s—or not reputable: say "preferred." With the passing of Tin Pan Alley (the "name" of the time when theatre music was pop music) and the decline of the performing star, celebrity in the musical devolved upon the superdirector, and the styles of Bob Fosse and Michael Bennett have become the most recognizable on the musical stage. They are the Marilyn Miller, the Eddie Cantor, the Ziegfeld, the Gershwin, the Wode-house of their day, the people you think of when you remember the best times you had at a show. The trouble is, with only dancing and production Concept to run on, the musical is going to be weak in characterological substance, the one thing that, to Hammerstein, was indispensable and the very reason one wrote musicals in the first place.

Bob Fosse's sloe-eyed, splayed-leg, foot-dragging shuffle was already known from his movie work when he set it into one of his classic numbers, "Steam Heat," for Carol Haney, Buzz Miller, and Peter Gennaro, all in tuxedos and derbies, in *The Pajama Game* (1954). We're talking Abbott second act, so there's no real story engagement and no character. The number is excused as entertainment at a union rally, but basically it's there for the fun of it, and Fosse can go wherever he likes: funny mouth noises for the boiler, games with the derbies, crawling, creeping, and the ultimate Fosse strut of the long grin and waving arms.

Outspoken sensuality was also part of his kit, as the bordello dream in *New Girl in Town* (1957) revealed, and he could handle comedy, as when Eddie Foy, Jr., in *The Pajama Game* visualized what married life with Haney might be like—lovers hiding in every crevice of the bedroom. All of this was distinctive. But Fosse's gift for the *grande geste* with the full ensemble is what pointed the way to his organizational coups in *Pippin* and *Chicago*.

New Girl in Town's ball scene is a case in point, a last grand holiday for Anna before an offended blabbermouth reveals Anna's past to her beau and sends her back into the man-hating despair she was trying to escape. This musical was dark and constricted, so the ball must be flashy and roomy. It began with a crossover, "At the Check Apron Ball," staged for the chorus moving rhythmically from left to right, boy after girl after boy, on their uppers in their duds, sounding the refrain and bouncing counter-point off it, always moving, always in high style, on and on through the number without running out of bodies till the audience realized that as each one exited he or she would race behind the traveller curtain to get back on line and reenter. A cute idea—and it does convey the picture of crowds of people happy for a good time. When the curtain rose on the ball itself, everyone, from stage to house, was in the mood. Fosse also

thought of a novelty to bridge the intermission, closing Act One on a superb can-can line strung out across the very edge of the stage, Anna flustered and shining at the center of it. As the curtain rose on Act Two, the
can-can was still going. Neat fun—but also good storytelling, to emphasize
the height of her rise so, later, we can appreciate her fall.

Sweet Charity (1966), again with Verdon and the third show Fosse directed, ushered in a new era for Fosse in choreography almost entirely
related to his personal dreamworld of debonair ghouls, from frugging
Manhattan fast-trackers to dance-hall "hostesses," junk at the barre in
"Big Spender." *Pippin* (1972) was his almost entirely, a huge hit widely
believed to be a triumph of production over material. Its composer-lyricist
Stephen Schwartz, author of *Godspell,* felt that Fosse had perverted and
aggrandized his little piece on life-choices offered Charlemagne's son. But
Fosse's jiving *commedia dell'arte* treatment was arresting, opening with
gloved hands in smoky darkness and open to all sorts of stimulating and
meditative pleasures as the episodic plot unraveled. The show would have
been hopeless without Schwartz's score, which was not well characterized—nor was the show—but melodic and contemporary without feeling
trendy. "Corner of the Sky," Pippin's theme song, came off through sonic
electronics as an available rhythm and blues Hit Tune. But, stripping away
the mike fuzz, one finds an extraordinary Bachian toccata in the piano
part that could, on an empty stage with a decent voice, thrill the ears.

Ultimately, *Pippin* did seem empty, if only because the hero himself never
came to life; it could have used a male Verdon. (It had a female Verdon,
in a smallish part, Leland Palmer, who not only resembled Verdon but
played her in Fosse's film *All That Jazz.*) *Chicago* (1975) had Verdon, not
to mention a substantial chunk of the *Pippin* corps—auditions were uncomfortable because Fosse was trying to be open but clearly wanted to
retain his initiates, as de Mille and Kidd habitually did. *Chicago* could not
be perversion or aggrandizement: Fosse was colibrettist (with Fred Ebb)
and the maximum leader of the project, his style even carrying over into
Tony Walton's spectacular design for the show curtain (used on the poster),
seven women in languorous Fosse poses.

Perhaps something should be said here about the change in the look of
the gypsy in this era. Heretofore a somewhat motley group whose unifying
feature was a manic smile, the gypsy now came into his and her own—
Pippin's ensemble numbered twelve, small enough for one to get to know
them under the clown white Fosse scrubbed over their features. Small
enough, even, for them all to earn billing on the *carta.* Economics dictated
the small corps, but so did the director-choreographer, who feels at greatest ease working with dancers exclusively. After all, he and they speak the

same language; actors are often mystical, with their insatiable need for "motivation." Champion, who introduced the small all-dancer corps in *Carnival,* drew on what was there, but Fosse's line stood out for its spectacular women. In a sense, Fosse's Girls are the last in their line of lookers whom the "butter and egg" man supposedly came to see, the descendants of Lydia Thompson and her British Blondes and Ziegfeld's subjects of glorification, though of course today's line works much harder than Ziegfeld's did. While *Woman of the Year* could stage its ballet number, "Happy in the Morning," with the Boys (for once) way downstage wearing nothing or less and the hapless Girls gayly relegated to the background, Fosse uses his small group deftly. In *Chicago,* they played reporters, criminals, collegiate preppies, citizens, and a circus (during the trial scene), making more of a contribution in all than the more populous but more limited chorus of the Gershwin years could.

Fosse's line has spawned lead performers: Ann Reinking, who went from *Pippin*'s corps into *Goodtime Charley,* succeeded Verdon in *Chicago* and Donna McKechnie in *A Chorus Line,* and went on to the films *All That Jazz* and *Annie;* or Pamela Sousa, who also played, some say definitively, McKechnie's role in *A Chorus Line.* Fosse's corps is electric with The Gift.

Fosse's stars are, too; Verdon was so good that he married her. *Chicago,* her last hurrah, was based on Maurine Watkins's twenties satire on twenties style, on the beginnings of today's grab-the-loot, no-fault morality. Kander and Ebb, dynamite when their shows give them something to write into, had dealt with such larger-than-musical topics as Nazi Germany in *Cabaret* and the life force in *Zorbá,* but here they wrote their best score, punishing the tenets of the Hit Tune with revelations about the cultural hypocrisy that created them. A money-grubbing lawyer sings "All I Care About Is Love," a corrupt prison madam sings "When You're Good to Mama (Mama's good to you)" in ode to the payoff, Roxie sings "Funny Honey" about a husband she detests, a gullible reporter sings the Sally-esque "A Little Bit of Good" (an almost point-for-point replica of "Look for the Silver Lining"), Roxie sings the Canforesque "Me and My Baby" about the pregnancy she has faked to gain public sympathy, and so on, all lies.

Chicago was the greatest of the superproductions. Everything in it was going, everyone on, something doing each second—colored lights spelling out the title, elevators, feather fans, megaphones, weirdo clown costumes, a speakeasy handkerchief for the prison matron's center spot, one man playing all twelve of the jury—razzle dazzle 'em, as one of the songs advises. Razzle dazzle is what the show exposes; ironic that it so dazzled while exposing it. But then there is a lie in show biz, which few musicals have been able to confront: it wants to please and share, but it's made of narcissistic exhibitionism.

Sammy Lee wouldn't have recognized this chorus. Nor would he have felt comfortable with Tony Walton's abstract unit set. The presentation was hard, bright, and mean—like its subject. It was fashionable to knock Fosse that season, so praise was muted. But this was, in overall conception, in composition, in design, in orchestration, in casting, and in the minute editing that ran right through the New York previews, one of the most stupendous shows Broadway has even seen, the hand of dance at work from start to finish, the motion of it wild and bitter. It's one of the few musicals not by Oscar Hammerstein or E. Y. Harburg with a moral foundation supporting the performing fun. You jerks! the murderesses virtually tell us at the close. We got off because of our presentation, which in this man's system has nothing to do with guilt or innocence. They throw flowers at the audience, but the irony stings, and that may well be why *Chicago* couldn't compete with *A Chorus Line*.

You wonder why the musical's authors go early gray and get a little crazy and end up writing things like *Rex* and *Saratoga?* It's because making a show perfect means losing so much that is vital but isn't in the right place at the right time. *Chicago* got to New York with two actors playing versions of the same part, David Rounds's agent and Mary McCarthy's matron. Two hustlers of the percentage deal: better conflate the two and split the difference. But while McCarthy was indispensable in the many prison scenes, Rounds in his straw boater and cane had one of the show's best numbers, "Ten Percent," flawless twenties reconstruction in a whining tap numbo that galvanized the audience nightly at that crucial moment early in Act One when you get hit tension or flop coma. Rounds also served as an interlocutor, introducing the characters, announcing the songs, calling out real names for curtain calls. *Chicago* was a "vaudeville," so he was the agent, neat.

But Kander and Ebb could write "When You're Good to Mama" for McCarthy to replace "Ten Percent" and the corps—plus conductor Stanley Lebowsky—could handle the introductions. Rounds was dropped. True, the show ended up tighter, more sensible.* But how would you like to be the author of a great number that gets killed? How would you like to be the actor who loses his part? How would you like to be the director who arranges it all, plugs it into the current of talent, and takes the praise or

---

* One flaw: as a talent agent, Rounds made the strategic connection between criminal notoriety and show biz PR that the show's theme feeds on. With him gone, it's not clear why the murderesses are planning vaudeville careers, or where they are in the (vaudeville) finale.

blame for hit or flop? *Chicago* was a hit, and Fosse took blame anyway. Twenty years from now, they'll die to see it—but, like *The Wizard of Oz*, *Chicago* will be a wild card already played. It won't even be in the discard pile. It's over.

Gower Champion's plastique is less identifiable than Fosse's, less individualistic—his gypsies always look conventionally attractive and are pleasantly attired; in the Beyond, Sammy Lee smiles when Champion's team goes to work. Champion more than anyone laid down rules for building a production numbo; eventually, the reputation dogged him, so he tried to live it down by building *Mack and Mabel*'s big number, "When Mabel Comes in the Room," with less energy than usual, to only half-pitch, as if he feared applause. Something new in the musical: a guilty numbo. But in his last work, *42nd Street* (1980), he went back to the big musical with lots of sets, conventionally attractive decor, cartoon acting, and plenty of dance numbers.

Like Jerome Robbins, Champion became known as a doctor of shows ailing in tryouts. His famous coup was the saving of the *Irene* revival of 1973, which on its Toronto opening was in terrible trouble, mainly through director John Gielgud's unfamiliarity with musical theatre. New York heard tales of a musical comedy paced like *Cymbeline* and about as much fun, of street clothes filling in for costumes, of script revisions that sounded like frantic improvisations, and of one night when Debbie Reynolds was too disheartened to appear and Gielgud went on for her (No! *Yes!*), when Reynolds suddenly showed up in costume but stood at the side of the stage, enduring it but not in it. New York readied itself for a delicious bomb.

Reynolds called Champion in, and Champion repaired it. He cut the book, speeded the scene-to-scene transitions, expanded the title song from a duet into a production numbo, and, basically, made Reynolds look good. He was not *Irene*'s choreographer—Peter Gennaro had already designed the dances. Champion was *Irene*'s dresser. By the time the show finished its extended tryout tour, it was ready to go over, and did—but of course this was not the *Irene* that Edith Day had played in 1919. Gone was the little-show naïveté, the tenement fire escape, and the sedate society parody. This *Irene* was a Big Lady show, in a lurid tabernacle of a theatre whose sacrament would be the star's entrance and whose moment of absolution the star curtain call. Not much happened in between. And "Alice Blue Gown," the song that helped fix the Cinderella trope for a decade of heroines, came off as a wily Hit Tune. Reynolds just doesn't strike one as the kind who once had a gown which was "almost new." The role needs an unknown.

Champion did much better by Reynolds in *Annie Get Your Gun* in Los Angeles in 1977, with Harve Presnell. "Restructured by Gower Champion," the bills cried; and so it was, for the differences in the 1946 *Annie* and modern showmanship prove how much formal integration had been developed in the interim. *Annie,* of course, did not have to be "saved." It's already solid. Still, its seams showed, when Champion approached it, with blatant song cues and no chance for an organizing choreographer to tailor a dance to a theme.

Champion had long been a stickler on integrating songs, on slipping into them through a staging situation. Here is where a superdirector affects composition, revising text in rehearsals; tryouts, or, as here, revival. In *Mack and Mabel,* Mack sings "I Won't Send Roses" to Mabel on a train heading west for the new cinema of Hollywood they will help to invent. This is what is on Mack's mind, and always will be, not romance. So, realizing that he and Mabel have reached a certain verge, he blurts out this apology. But please—not with the fake tension of an orchestral lead-in, descriptive, sensitive, dramatic, and a tired wheeze after two decades of overuse. The lead-in is like the musical play: serious. The musical comedy vamp is silly, but it's adaptable—that's the bite of jazz, the fun of it.

Meanwhile, how to get "I Won't Send Roses" going? Champion was devious. He furnished Mack's railroad car with a record player, a wind-up model as they all were then. As Mack reaches the Moment, a record is scratching out a vamp—the vamp, it turns out, to "I Won't Send Roses." No conductor raises a baton, no strings steal in. Mack opens his mouth and sings to the recording. Once the number is under way, *then* the orchestra can join in.

When he got to *Annie Get Your Gun,* Champion was less than enthusiastic about its song cues. In 1946, someone delivered a line, an instrument sounded a "bell tone" to set key, and Merman hit it. In Champion's *Annie,* the songs just happened, or chimed in, or elaborately prepared their way—anything but that dead-giveaway bell tone. Staging "Doin' What Comes Natur'lly," Champion hummed an approximate vamp—just standing there, putting on the show. After it was scored, Champion placed it under the dialogue preceding the song. The vamp starts, then stops. Starts, stops. The audience knows it's getting a song—it might even know which one—but it doesn't know when. The spontaneous new cue vastly improves upon the contrived fing! of the old cue—and in "My Defenses Are Down" Champion started off with the song's *climax,* bouncing off a kiss between Reynolds and Presnell. He has been resisting; now he's in love. So, after the kiss, instead of slogging through Berlin's verse, he rips into *"But . . . I must confess that I like it."*

Unfortunately, Champion dropped two of *Annie*'s best songs, "Moonshine Lullaby" and "I'm an Indian Too." But he added a splendid theme ballet on "There's No Business Like Show Business." In 1946 this was one song among many, often reprised but never given much staging. However, over the years it has become something of a show biz anthem, and as *Annie* is partly about making it in show biz, Champion made it the numbo of his production, a surrealistic masque on a bare stage against a cyclorama in which the cast, made up as freak versions of themselves, welcomed Reynolds into the fraternity of the theatre, and she too emerged in *commedia dell'arte* makeup. The number—the whole show—was a sensation: a post-Hammerstein version of a Hammerstein-era show. Jack Lee, *Irene*'s and *Annie*'s music director, thinks the musical will be in trouble when this generation of director-choreographers passes, and it virtually has passed, with Champion dead and the others in a sort of retirement. Actually, the day when the musical realizes that it cannot fall back on dressers and editors might prove stimulating to composition. That day might not come, for younger superdirectors have bowed in, some with great success.

Michael Bennett started, like Fosse and Champion, as a dancer, first gaining prominence as choreographer of *Promises, Promises* (1968), a highly contemporary show that seemed to sweep everything—cast, wily Burt Bachrach cross-rhythms, office chrome and West-Side walkup clutter—into a realistic valentine to who knew what. Somewhat later, after cast replacements and long-run blues slowed the show down, only the dances held up. Bennett was on to something, in the coy glitter of *Company*'s New Yorkers reveling in a set like a steel trap, or in the solipsistic reverie of the ghost showgirl who opened *Follies* alone, suspended in an endless moment downstage center, then seen to be traversing the stage with a terrible, almost motionless grandeur. *Seesaw* (1973), which Bennett choreographed, directed, and, 'twas said, rewrote during troubled tryouts, placed him in the high ranks, for what little of *Seesaw* most people liked was Bennett's work—its color, its jive, its picture of Manhattan as a heartless place inhabited by people with heart.

Unlike Fosse and Champion, Bennett gravitated to the New York show, glorying in its contradictions of fellowship/megalomania and rough edges/diamond centers. These contradictions inspired *A Chorus Line* (1975), set at an audition call: where everyone is most ruthlessly scrutinized yet where a benevolent director-choreographer plays father-confessor to friendly strangers. *A Chorus Line*'s staggering money success was big enough; its critical acclaim and cultural clout made it yet bigger. There had been nothing like it before, but what made it and Bennett unique was its lengthy gestation in workshop. As it is performed, so was it written: a potential cast talked openly about themselves, providing the basis for book and score. The show's most telling contradiction is that some of its characters become very sympathetic to us in the course of the evening as principals, yet they are there only to gain the miscellaneous dancing line. How alive they seem—the girl who had the hard time in her first and very phoney acting class and who felt nothing when she heard that the creepy teacher had died; the star-on-the-rise whose failing career has sent her back to the line (and to the director, her former lover); or the tough wisecracker offended by the unusual audition procedure. By the end of the show, we want to see them win, get the part—but there are no parts. All they can get is into the ensemble, where Bennett, in an opulent finale, puts them.

Life respected the show's premise and made no stars of the original cast. And the score, by Marvin Hamlisch and Edward Kleban, has not been given its due, possibly because, in musical-play fashion, it works too well in the theatre to travel outside unless you have seen the show. Most of the credit went to Bennett: for the idea, the nurturing of it (what other big hit musical was improvised into being?), the presentation.

It was a shock, then, when Bennett's *Ballroom* (1979) died so suddenly, for tawdry as its plot scenes and songs were, its many dance numbers were electrifying. But then they were not unlike twenties dances in their lack of character content: we're in a dance hall, so people dance. Audiences raised on Rodgers and Hammerstein weren't sure how to take it.

They knew how to take *Dreamgirls* (1981), though, once the *New York Times* gave it a historical rave notice, a review of reviews. Warned of incalculable greatness, not to mention the three-million-dollar budget, the public virtually entered the Imperial Theatre already applauding, and certainly the show looked great, Robin Wagner's traveling towers, sequined curtains, and catwalks gliding up and away giving the first Motown opera the atmosphere it needs, hot, painted, slick. And, no question, Bennett had pulled off another directorial coup, translating his New York savvy into a black equivalent for a study of a vocal trio beset by turmoil among the personnel and controversies on black style in a white business. Some of Bennett's cast, notably Cleavant Derricks, Ben Harney, and Sheryl Lee Ralph, were exceptional; Bennett clearly can talk to actors as well as dancers. Derricks was so from life in his portrayal of a Harlem shouter who hates the black-tie marketing of big-dollars rock that one wonders if he knows what he's playing; maybe he just is. But *Dreamgirls* is almost all score, and this score is a poor one. Henry Krieger's music is about as adaptable as this kind of rock can be, and he rises to the challenge of writing songs that represent the group's hit singles. But Tom Eyen's libretto is the most illiterate nonsense since . . . one has to go back to Glen

MacDonough for a reference, and at that MacDonough seems a Shake-speare by comparison. The very idea for *Dreamgirls* was Eyen's; it was he who brought in Krieger and Bennett. Yet his contribution is not compa-rable to theirs. With no understanding of what the word "rhyme" entails, the psychology of a comic-strip artist, and the charm of a sycophant, Eyen created a pointless charade whose time had come: the *Times* declared Jen-nifer Holliday the overwhelming debutante on the basis of no acting talent whatsoever and the willingness to wreck herself nightly in the first-act fi-nale torch song mad scene, "And I Am Telling You I'm Not Going." Ben-nett had produced the first Big Lady Show whose star was scenery.

Tommy Tune, younger than Bennett and a Bennett beneficiary from his stint in *Seesaw* (Tune had the numbo, "It's Not Where You Start, It's Where You Finish," with balloons and stairs), is about to rival Bennett on the basis of a number of off-Broadway successes and two big Broadway hits, *The Best Little Whorehouse in Texas* (1978) and *Nine* (1982). Two shows could not be less alike. *Whorehouse* is an affable musical comedy in the old anti-repressive politics of Kaufman and Harburg (opportunistic bluenoses close the bordello down), placed in a hideous unit set and graced only by Carol Hall's tuneful country score and Tune's staging of the num-bers. *Whorehouse* went awry in its book; even Hall fell apart in a burst of musical-play characterization in "Doatsy Mae," a revealing soliloquy for a waitress who promptly disappeared from the show. Why write a char-acter song for a walk-on?

Nevertheless, *Whorehouse* was a popular hit, and Tune went on to take full status as the guide of *Nine,* though ultimate credit must go to Maury Yeston's dazzling score in one of the outstanding debuts of new authorial talent in Broadway history. Arthur Kopit's book was called vacuous and inconclusive, but so is his source, Fellini's film *8½,* about an Italian film director with the world's eye on him, a contract to fulfill, and no project in mind. Given the limitations of the action—there is no story qua se, just episodes on the way to no movie—actually much is learned about Guido Contini's rather broad world. Many of the movie's famous sequences fell victim, inevitably, to the change of medium, though the dance of the whore Saraghina on the beach before the schoolboys, one of Fellini's most reso-nant autobiographical reconstructions, was smartly translated into "Be Italian," a robust pastiche number staged with Saraghina and the kids playing tambourines to the beaming witness of the twenty women in Gui-do's life.

Nine's most Felliniesque correspondence was drawn not from *8½* but from *The City of Women:* all his self-defining soliloquy, self-enlarging art-istry, and self-disguising pranks are made in relationship to women, from his mother and the nun who turns into Saraghina to the actress he admires and the starlet he exploits. It was richly, even daringly, cast—Karen Akers as Guido's wife was a cabaret singer without acting experience and Liliane Montevecchi something like a dancing Lilo in a part bigger than dance; and a show with four little boys in it, one of them a principal, is asking for trouble. But Akers was superb, Montevecchi a startling bijou, and the kids ingratiating. Lawrence Miller's white set and William Ivey Long's black- and white-coded costumes gave the show a visual punch that left *Whorehouse*'s big empty nowhere space and cowboy kits way at the bottom of Tune's résumé. Superdirector status depends not just on staging genius but on a unique appearance, and the unit set is prestigious, personal. (The director presumably doesn't design his shows, but for some reason he gets the credit for his show's physical state.) Champion's carnival fairground, Fosse's *Chicago* drum, and, now, Tune's Venetian gallery and runway are the sites of an era, the places where the campaign was waged and the enemy, convention, met.

Superdirection may be its own convention, however. It was certainly one in *Dreamgirls,* a show in which nothing happened but the stage—the stage!—kept reacting as if the show were crowded with event. Superdirectors have tricks, but they'd better be true ones, and Tune's are. At the end of Act One, he closes with Young Guido on the near side of the fallen curtain, and has the little actor cut around a corner of the auditorium to return backstage. Then, in Act Two, when Guido's wife leaves him after a brutal solo, "Be on Your Own," Tune had Akers march straight on *through* the auditorium to its very back, building on little Guido's ruse to make this exit that much more final. Some of the standees were so impressed that they followed Akers's progress down the theatre's main stairs into the lobby, as if concerned that she might have walked out on the play.

The superdirector has evolved considerably from his counterpart in the 1950s. In *Li'l Abner, Redhead,* or *Bye Bye Birdie,* they were choreographers staging conventional musical comedies with an emphasis on dance. Now they deal in shows beyond genre and don't necessarily design the dances—Bennett collaborated with Michael Peters on *Dreamgirls* and Tune left *Nine*'s dancing to Thommie Walsh. Most important, directors were not thought ultimately crucial in the 1950s, except perhaps Robbins, at that mainly for *West Side Story* (1957), admittedly a solid property as written. *Gypsy* (1959) boasted Robbins's name in giant letters, after "entire production directed and choreographed by," though *Gypsy* needed no superdirector by virtue of its powerful character structure; its dances, in any case, offer no main chance. But it was Robbins who most famously affirmed the benefits of superdirection, in *Fiddler on the Roof* (1964). That show may mark the turning point: before it, the best choreographers might also direct. After it, the best directors were (except Hal Prince) choreographers.

Yet, for the present, strong production is Broadway's first priority. Once, one could tell the big shows by who wrote the songs or who played the lead. *DuBarry Was a Lady,* by Porter and with Lahr and Merman, was as big as they came; who then or now could name its director?* Still, there was a show-biz fascism in much of Broadway that placed emphasis on performance—Merman in *Happy Hunting,* without Porter or anyone comparable, was even so a big show. The musical play made composition a formidable factor, and in its wake the librettist came into something like repute for the first time in the musical's history. Yet at the same time the rise of the superdirector, *also* a product of the musical play in that unique composition needed unique staging, shoved authors to the side once again. The big difference now is that when a superproduction flops, the director takes more blame than the librettist. Serves them right, say some. As Tom Thumb sang in *Barnum,* an empty frolic made to work through Joe Layton's circus panorama, "Bigger Isn't Better." Physician, heal thyself.

* Edgar MacGregor.

14
The State of The Art

We all start as imitators of somebody. Jerry Bock and Sheldon Harnick's first score together, for *The Body Beautiful* (1958), on the boxing world, was limp. It imitates no one, and everything. But they stripped the gears for *Fiorello!* (1959) and *Tenderloin* (1960), reaffirmed the small show in *She Loves Me* (1963), and *Fiddler on the Roof* (1964) has amazed the West, reprising the jazz that Gershwin and Weill sought, not in ethnicity (though *Fiddler* surely has it) but in originality.

Some operas only Broadway can pull off. *Fiddler* is a musical play, the kind of simple-looking, secretly impossible project only Broadway's Babies have the perseverance and imagination to maneuver. And it's so damn moving and human and true that it confounds those who make definitions on the forms of music theatre. Musical? Operetta? The semantic ambiguity testifies to the musical's unlimited range, and the contributions to the original *Fiddler,* from Jerome Robbins, top banana Zero Mostel, and Hammersteinians Bock and Harnick (and librettist Joseph Stein) proved how terraced a collaboration it is. Which Baby won the pull for power? The work.

What international sensation could be more parochial? Drawn from Shalom Aleichem, *Fiddler* tells of man and wife, father and daughters, daughters and suitors, rabbi and flock, an entire place of being, complete even unto the Cossack outsiders who encircle the village of Anatevka. Bock used profuse pastiche—with orchestrator Don Walker—in all the township numbers, from "Tradition" to "Anatevka," letting the love songs go their own way. "If I Were a Rich Man" crows with hasidic melisma; "Sabbath Prayer" is gently modal, undulating with ageless ritual; and "Sunrise, Sunset," a minor-key waltz of great sentiment, has become the numbo of Jewish weddings from San Diego across the long way to Canberra. Perhaps the greatest achievement was "Tevye's Dream," a fabulous pooling of everything that the musical has which no other theatre form can duplicate. Opera isn't this nimble. Drama lacks the music. Ballet isn't specific. Broadway can fuse Hammerstein's musical flow with Harburg's satire—Herbert's sweep with Cohan's punch—to capture this pseudo-nightmare of superstitious pageantry with a mischievous horror. It's a wedding of ghosts and cranks—musicians out of Chagall pop up behind Tevye's bed, a dead grandmother warns against a betrothal, guests chant "Mazel tov" with a Savoyard zest, a seven-foot goblin puts a curse on the proposed match, and through it all Tevye confers with his wife (to whom he is telling the dream) even as his dream unfolds.

What was *Fiddler?* What is the modern musical? A superproduction, a star vehicle, or a bid to claim the attentions of Broadway's Jewish theatregoers? *Fiddler* was none of these: a great composition superbly realized. As *Anatevka,* without Mostel, in stagings not even modeled on Robbins's, for European audiences historically not in sympathy with Aleichem's characters, *Fiddler* has triumphed. It is fully thought out, rich in atmosphere, never approximate or quaint when it must be exact or brutal. And of course it is very inspiring at the end, not only because of the sorrowful forced dispersal of the villagers and the thrilling last view of Tevye and his family pushing their pitiful cart off to the promising life that we know awaits them in America, but because the whole play has extrapolated the *aperçu* outlined in "Tradition"—that a hard life can be endured, even enjoyed, by a folk who live on sacrament and community. With the interest in adapting challenging theatre pieces, someone was surely going to do *Our Town* as a musical play. Now no one has to; *Fiddler on the Roof* supersedes any conceivable *Our Town* musical, for *Fiddler*'s alien culture is so fully presented that it expands into the universal, on the subject, How Humans Live.*

Fiddler's opening "Tradition," phrasing the scheme of the entertainment in sound and sight, is essential in the post-Hammerstein musical play's absorption of the superproduction. Where once the first number was a greasy dither, now it was the very foundation of a show, like the "Carousel Waltz" a key turned into its theme and its production concept. It was the mark of the important musical. It was certainly the mark of the Hal Prince musical. When he first became a producer, as Robert E. Grif-

---

* There was a sort of *Our Town* musical on television in the 1950s, badly conceived with Frank Sinatra as the Stage Manager. A Hit Tune survives, "Love and Marriage"—what could be less appropriate for Wilder's solemn microcosm?

fith's partner, his shows had solid but hardly innovative productions directed by George Abbott, and the openings were useful, no more. *The Pajama Game* (1954) opened "in one," with Eddie Foy, Jr., singing a snatch, telling who he was, and taking us into the pajama factory in full swing for "Racing with the Clock." We get the message: the workers are intent on getting a raise of seven-and-a-half-cents an hour, and labor trouble brews. *Damn Yankees* (1955) was less pointed: "Six Months Out of Every Year" gave us the husbands and wives of America separated by the fanatic viewing of televised baseball games, an amusing idea when the women sing their complaint against the men's cries of "Slide!" and "You're blind, ump!," but the merest introduction to the show. However, *Tenderloin* (1960) strikingly announces its feelings in the aforementioned opening of the pious versus the profane, and *A Funny Thing Happened on the Way to the Forum* (1962) is famous for its inappropriately charming "Love Is in the Air," replaced out of town by the expediently unseemly "Comedy Tonight," perhaps the most practical prelude an American musical comedy has ever had. It tells what musical comedy is—unruly, democratic, sexy, and crazy—and then shows how it works in pranks and surprises, the whole cast trooping on for a display of the archetypes, "lovers, liars, and clowns."

All Abbott shows. In the early 1960s Prince began to direct himself, first little shows like *A Family Affair* (1962) and *She Loves Me* (1963), then big ones, big in structure, in theme, in the freewheeling probity of the Concept production. A meticulous planner who pulls his technical cohort in for considerable discussion before they all move as one, Prince revealed a typical example of the unique musical in *Cabaret* (1966). The unique cannot typify, of course. But, in joining *Fiddler on the Roof* in the promulgation of fine shows written to be finely produced, it suggested that a new era was gathering around the musical play. Based on Christopher Isherwood's tales of decadent Berlin, with a book by Joe Masteroff and a Kander and Ebb score, *Cabaret*, like *Fiddler*, *West Side Story*, and *Allegro*, felt inseparable from its production. Again, the opening number was crucial *in extenso*, its huge mirror establishing a "see yourself" understanding with the audience, its interlocutory Nazi harlequin emcee presenting himself as a commentator who will direct the cabaret numbers to address and elaborate on the story, and the cabaret itself—girls, waiters, all-woman band—gradually collecting as if conjured out of nightmare. "Life is a cabaret," one song tells us; and the cabaret is life, raised up at the start and dismantled at the close. But if all the world's a stage, what role are *you* playing in the show?

The most influential shows in the American musical at present are the series Stephen Sondheim has written for Prince production. Sondheim is Hammerstein's certified heir, by personal tutelage, for he grew up in Pennsylvania a few country miles from the Hammersteins and became Oscar's protégé. Where Kern got his practice writing interpolations and Rodgers and Hart wrote college shows, Sondheim won a splendid apprenticeship at the fount, writing four musicals in informal course with the master— one workable adaptation from the stage, one unworkable adaptation from the stage, one adaptation from a non-theatrical source, and an original. Yet Sondheim was not to travel Hammerstein's road indefinitely; at a certain point he began to break away from the kind of show Hammerstein had created while using what he needed of Hammerstein's methods.

Sondheim hadn't planned to come to Broadway as lyricist to other men's music. His first score, for *Saturday Night,* was all his. But the producer's sudden death killed the project, and there came offers, for lyrics only, that were too promising to turn down—*West Side Story* and *Gypsy.* With *A Funny Thing Happened on the Way to the Forum* (1962), Sondheim claimed status as composer-lyricist, especially beguiling in the way his main strains lead, verbally and melodically, onto the releases. In these songs, the AABA form falls away to a kind of AAAA, each A an incarnation, each section a revision of set material, each song swept away by its own spontaneity. There have been four supreme melodists in the American musical, four who not only never run out of distinctive melody but who also develop those melodies with effortless rightness, compressing or expanding as feeling demands: Victor Herbert, Jerome Kern, Richard Rodgers, and Stephen Sondheim. This is elite company.

Forum's overture gave warning that the ancient trio was about to be made a quartet. The piece doesn't start; it *pops,* into a quotation of the jittery, "wrong"-note "Free," then opening up into a full statement of the regaling "Love, I Hear"—decorated by the sneaky "Free." There was so much music in this score, it had to be sent out in lots. Curtain up, the words added, the ear swelled. A young Roman noble came forward to tell us of his unique malady: a crush on the girl next door. Well, that was to be expected of a classic farce—and the same actor, Brian Davies, had enjoyed a not dissimilar spot in *The Sound of Music,* singing "Sixteen Going on Seventeen." What was unusual was the brio of the plaint:

> I pine, I blush, I squeak, I squawk,
> Today I woke too weak to walk.

topped, in the second chorus, by a sudden swerve in thought:

> I'm dazed, I'm pale, I'm sick, I'm sore,
> I've never felt so well before!

It was an unusual score altogether, evading Hammersteinian integration to provide atmosphere for the love plot and punctuation for the farce, quite ready to halt the proceedings for a vaudeville turn in "Everybody Ought To Have a Maid." The song walks in on a pretext—that's the fun of it—and Mostel enjoys it so much he invites the other men to help him through a few encores. *Forum,* then, marked a gala return to the old comedy musical of Montgomery and Stone or of Lahr—but with discipline and a score geared to the comedy, loony tunes themselves.

Anyone Can Whistle (1964) was downright mad, a social satire with a book by Arthur Laurents completely out of the musical play pattern he had observed in *West Side Story* and *Gypsy.* Here the score directly confronts the wildness of the story and characters; where *Forum*'s songs were treats and embellishments, *Anyone Can Whistle*'s further the initiations made in the text. You don't have to care about *Forum* to enjoy its songs. If you don't like *Anyone Can Whistle*'s characters, you can't like their numbers. *Forum* was daffy and tasty, *Anyone Can Whistle* taut and renegade, an almost vicious show set in a ruined town where a fake miracle revives commerce and a fake psychiatrist shatters received ideas on sanity. Angela Lansbury played a silly mayoress, Lee Remick a nurse, Harry Guardino the affable faker, among them outlining the play's points of vantage: corruption, romanticism, cynicism. As the corruption was quite genuine and powerfully stated; as the romantic nurse found it more congenial to idealize than to actuate the ideal; and as the cynic hid a romantic core, the show had a lot to cover. This is always a problem in the musical—for Broadway's theatregoers, unfortunately—and the authors' Swiftian bite also put people off.

Perhaps, too, the public had grown too used to the straitly proportioned naturalism of the integrated musical, in which even the ditsiest, most trivial tales could gauge their lineage in terms of Hammerstein, Harburg, de Mille, Porter. *Anyone Can Whistle* was fantasy-naturalism, independent and querulous. The crucial first minutes found the townspeople doing strange dance breaks; Lansbury interrupted a scene change—literally halted machinery and orchestra—to get a glove on, humming all the while; Act One ended with Guardino telling the audience "You are all mad," followed by the sight of the cast sitting in theatre seats, clapping and laughing. It was perhaps as far as the musical could go from Hammerstein.

With the Prince series, the breakaway is complete: *Company* (1970), *Follies* (1971), *A Little Night Music* (1973), *Pacific Overtures* (1976),

Sweeney Todd (1979), *Merrily We Roll Along* (1981). Back in the R & H era, the musical play had a strong linear narrative, essentially admirable characters, and a solid sense of social wholeness, of community. "The farmer and the cowman should be friends," Hammerstein observes in one show; "You will shake the hands of men whose hands are strong," he urges in another, drawing an errant soul back to his people; and "You'll Never Walk Alone" and "Climb Every Mountain" are best sung to families or at least people with close relations. In Hammerstein, one always has a belonging place, a safe one. When the community is overrun by Nazis, one walks into Switzerland.

Sondheim's musicals don't necessarily have linear narratives. *Company* is episodes, a cross-section. *Follies* recounts the first half of its story in flashback while the second half is in progress. *Merrily We Roll Along* runs backwards. Admirable characters? Sondheim sculpts rather in human character, let the chips fall. So *Follies'* principals are not admirable as much as interesting, Sweeney Todd is a barber who indiscriminately cuts his customers' throats, and *Merrily* spends the evening trying to learn why its protagonist became such a creep.

In social background Sondheim's projects are most advanced from Hammerstein's. *Company* refers to community, but a limited one of Manhattan couples who love, distrust, idolize, patronize, importune, and neglect bachelor Robert. In *Follies,* the community takes in, by synechdoche, the American nation; and it has broken down on dreams that couldn't come true, symbolized in the show's poster logo of a monumental Ziegfeldian Girl cracking right through. And while *A Little Night Music* and *Sweeney Todd* both treat strongly of social system, it is not through brotherhood but in stratified classes. Much of what happens in *Night Music* is inconceivable out of the context of caste, from the pompous count and the courtesan in profound retirement to the lawyer and the actress downward to the servants. Even the commentative quintet that flit in and out at will are dressed, we notice, to allow them enough leeway to be as appropriate at the theatre as on the lawn of a suburban villa. And all of *Sweeney Todd*'s action is the result of the exploitation of the proletariat by the bosses. Sondheim believes in free will as much as Hammerstein did, but his view of the individual's access to it is socially much more sophisticated.

Production technique, too, has advanced from R & H days into the free-form (at times, vaudevillian) neo-naturalism associated with such super-productions as *Cabaret* and *Chicago*. In *Oklahoma!, South Pacific,* and *The King and I*—even in *Carousel*'s sequence set in heaven—scenes comprise exchanges among people in direct contact. Only in *Allegro* did the stage hold more people than were physically "present," in the psychologically articulate chorus. Generally, the musical play did not go beyond that except in ballet. In *Cabaret,* however, the emcee is not only the compère of the Kit Kat Club but of the show itself, and *Chicago* flows ceaselessly with the intrusions and assistance of hosts and kibitzers. This is the musical's neo-naturalism, using Hammerstein's communicative honesty in non-realistic spaces.

Company, then, happens all over town in one chrome-girt space of elevator and balconies. *Follies* holds a nightlong party in a ruined theatre, but the gathering includes ghostly younger versions of the guests. *Night Music*'s characters wander at their ease from house to house, through a forest, or into a formal dining hall simply by turning around, and *Pacific Overtures* borrows the rituals of the Kabuki theatre. It took the musical about a century to refine its realism to a persuasive validity; twenty years later, this realism was shattered for a more artful approach.

Company was a shock. Neo-naturalism had previously been most apt in colorful jaunts into the past or in satire. Here was a show for here and now, mainly about feelings—the true ones, as inconsistent as they are passionate. People feel strongly in *Company,* but they feel many things at once—"sorry-grateful," as one song phrases it. The show's premise alone was unique, the study of a single man through somewhat climactic encounters with his married friends. But the score especially had impact, as the first contemporary sound in theatre music that had beat but still worked as theatre music is supposed to, as scene, dialogue, reflection, choral celebration. An old-fashioned trim made "Side by Side" easy to love; a progressive harmonic reach made "Being Alive" a haunting statement of approach-avoidance nearing the approach. A small cast did everything: act, sing, dance. It was convincing, therefore hard to take, for the musical was not supposed to challenge its public's self-perceptions. Lines like "children you destroy together" and "everybody dies" are not what popular theatre was raised on, not in the musical's mandate. *Company*'s boy did not even get girl: the complexly derived conclusion, following up a complex emotional development, confused audiences eager for a clear button, *ta-da!* Then too, it was Sondheim's songs rather than George Furth's text that defined the hero; in the book scenes, his many friends came across more clearly than he did.

If *Company*'s ending was tricky, its beginning and middle also had their tricky moments. Michael Bennett staged "Side by Side" with the whole cast of couples and their bachelor lined up straight on, each couple taking a quick dance break together, partner to partner. Then the bachelor did a little something and beckoned to his partner . . . nobody. In that moment, the battle lines were drawn. Those stimulated by theatre were invigorated;

those who just want to relax were puzzled, and they had a feeling that if they understood it, they wouldn't like it. Worse yet, the growing enthusiasm of the stimulated angered the relaxers, seemed to tease them about a great party they couldn't get into. Slow ears required a second hearing to catch Sondheim's sound; it was sophisticated and didn't plug itself in reprises. However, the television culture doesn't believe in second hearings of anything. Today, everything is a money-sucking bonanza or a bankrupt curio.

"Children you destroy together." Really, what happened to the goodtime musical? I'll tell you: its promises couldn't be kept. The silver lining doesn't fly by because you waited for it, and few Irenes ever left Tenth Avenue for real. *Follies* reclaimed the sound and sights of the goodtime musical—the performers' vehicle—to explain just why it was finished. Here the Prince production reached its gala in a knot of collaborators—Boris Aronson on sets, Florence Klotz on costumes, Jonathan Tunick on orchestration, Michael Bennett for dance and co-direction with Prince. James Goldman's book offered a reunion of old Ziegfeldians in an old theatre, two of them, with their husbands, having unfinished business to complete. Ben enjoyed Sally but married Phyllis; Sally married Buddy but has treasured a dream of Ben ever since; and Phyllis knows it. As the deputies of old ideals of beauty gather, the four principals group and regroup, single, pair, triangle, quartet, to confront these ideals on a more personal level. To the extent that they can.

Follies is a rare case in the musical: there are two versions of it. The first, *The Girls Upstairs,* is more naturalistic, jumping from one part of the theatre to another and enduring the principals' strange reversions to the past as if people in extreme situations could reenact their history. The score, too, was naturalistic, almost all character songs. But on the way to *Follies* the text was rewritten to include a second cast of the characters' younger selves. Now the past is not recalled; it actually happens along with the present, a one-way street with two-way traffic. Michael Bennett suggested they show up in black and white, Boris Aronson designed a Ziegfeldian spectacle to make the sense of the past relived more experiential, and Sondheim filled out the score with allusions to the musical's history, taking form back as he takes the characters back—to Irving Berlin's Girl anthems, the torch song, the Friml-Romberg bittersweet waltz, the gimmicky dance numbo, the top-hat-and-tails rouser, and so on.

The piece expanded. As with *Show Boat,* pastiche became a metaphor for America, its beliefs falling out of the song literature that modern America grew up on. Some of *The Girls Upstairs*'s character songs were replaced by more tightly personalized numbers, and the juxtaposition of past and present was carried through in the entire production. Everyone has a ghost. Even a numbo has a ghost, "Who's That Woman?," the Mirror Number, performed by two troupes simultaneously, the black and white spectres of a time when a Mirror Number seemed respectable, and their present-day counterparts, slower, heavier, off pitch.

As *The Girls Upstairs* turned into *Follies,* the theme and characters of an unusual but regular-sized musical grew outward to take on a symbolistic grandeur. Its character songs were the most advanced Sondheim had done; yet his pastiche culled the past. This is not contradiction. It is taking tradition on into the next era. The dark picture of a theatre on the eve of its destruction (in *The Girls Upstairs,* the party is broken up by the arrival of the wrecking crew) populated only by aged retirees or the stupid young catering staff was colored in by the explosive materialization of an old *Follies,* the goodtime stage in which everyone is fresh and eager and bright. The cast was not just playing veterans: they *were* veterans—Mary McCarty, Michael Bartlett, Ethel Shutta, Fifi D'Orsay, Arnold Moss, Ethel Barrymore Colt, Helon Blount, Yvonne de Carlo, Alexis Smith, Gene Nelson, Dorothy Collins. It was *A Chorus Line* of old showbiz; even a founding member of the musical play, Jan Clayton, turned up as Collins's replacement. As the fictional theatre of *Follies* was alive with memories, so was the Winter Garden, where *Follies* played, and as the highly concentrated book pressed the characters through their revelatory admissions, some lying, some slipping around the truth, some direly honest; and as the confrontation of what we planned to become and who we are went crash into the falling of the Urbanesque tapestries and the gliding forth of the radiant Girls into Loveland, "where everybody lives to love" and "loves to live," the forty-four years between *Show Boat* and *Follies* were swallowed up in a testament bearing witness to the past as it reflected it back through the present. *Follies* was the newest kind of show about outdated forms of self-perception, huge in detail, most wide when most close, and able to invoke an epoch in a slashing stroke. It was an incomparably rich evening, a musical about the good time but not a goodtime musical: like Sally Plummer, we must let go of unfeasible dreams. Many of those who saw it regard it as the greatest of all musicals.

It is certainly one of the most influential, not least in its overthrow of the traditional balance between dialogue and score. *Follies* is mostly score, virtually opera, and just as Hammerstein's colleagues began to follow his lead in writing for character, so have Sondheim's coevals begun to regard this operatic elaboration as a happy medium. Like Hammerstein, Sondheim is mainly interested in character development; and when you can put so much character into a song, why stint? Bob Merrill wrote nearly two full scores for his adaptation in 1966 of Truman Capote's *Breakfast at Tiffany's* because the out-of-town finagling drastically reshaped Abe Burrows' Philadelphia yokfest book into Edward Albee's dreary Boston one. However, all Merrill found in the piece were musical comedy ditties or hopeless Hit Tunes sung by minor characters. But bring *The Girls Upstairs* and *Follies* together and one has quite some trove of portraiture.

Sondheim's heavy use of pastiche in *Follies* is not only essential to the way the show works—it's essential to the musical in general, part of the commentative burlesque that musical comedy grew up on and retained even in operetta and musical comedy. There couldn't have been an American musical without it, from Victor Herbert's ragtime and gypsy fiddles right up to *Fiddler on the Roof*'s shtetl coloring and *Chicago*'s historical reconstructions. Pastiche is a first tenet of the jazz—or how is one to suggest the Ziegfeldian beauty anthem, for instance, one of the great tropes of American show biz? A musical about the past, filled with references to Kern, Friml-Romberg, and the like, recomposed in contemporary reflection, can elate the initiate and the unpretentious tyro at once. The former will parse the panorama, the latter sense it generally. This is, after all, our cultural heritage, and is perhaps why *Follies* struck such a strong response in so many theatregoers: while telling its story, it used the allusive references to extend that story by implication to the culture that had seen its gods crack like the Girl on *Follies'* poster. Its certain moments of showman's lightning are still talked of—the opening promenade of dead Broadway people to a gorgeous, just descernibly crippled waltz; the Mirror Number; the dazzling chain of star turns in the closing *Follies*-within-*Follies;* the woeful farewell at the curtain as the four ghosts watched their older selves go, Young Buddy still reaching for his dream of a golden girl who was never there. "Sally?" he asks wistfully; ghosts cannot die. *Follies* lives in the memory. Aficionados returned to it repeatedly to watch it like cameras. *Follies* is a ghost. "It's like a movie in my head that plays and plays," one line runs. And it is not just the moments that we remember. It's the whole show.

Follies ran over a year, but its running cost, despite emergency economies, left it a financial failure. *A Little Night Music* (1973) ran longer to bigger houses and made money. It also produced one of Broadway's few recent standards in "Send in the Clowns." Still, hit or flop, there was feeling by this time among theatre buffs that Sondheim was not being given his due. In truth, he was the first major talent in the musical who got more resentment than support from the critics. And as the Sondheim-Prince ventures were the only ones that were fresh and stimulating as a rule, it looked as though the musical was not going to be *permitted* to pursue its history.

It may be that Kern, Gershwin, Hammerstein, and Harburg made it easy for the slow to catch up to them by alternating their experiments with less bold entries. Sondheim's problem is that he cannot rest on a find but must tackle the next one.

A Little Night·Music, from Ingmar Bergman's film *Smiles of a Summer Night,* actually got good reviews, even raves, though it was romantically lyrical and therefore, in this cynical age, less approachable. In its fine cast (Len Cariou, Glynis Johns, Hermione Gingold, and Laurence Guittard, among others) its sumptuous decor, its astonishing blend of neo-naturalism and realism, and its ironical idealism that knows people aren't admirable yet wants and allows its three pairs of lovers to couple with an ecstatic sense of release, *Night Music* suggested a turn in the musical's fortunes: an uncompromising show makes a hit. Those who weren't up to careful listening could sit back and be entranced, the typical Broadway sensibility. Those who heard noted with conspiratorial rapport the elegant symmetry of the characterization within theme, outlined near the close in a servant's disquisition—outsiders see more clearly, most fully.

Originally, the number was "Silly People," for a manservant, a postcoital rumination to a dark chromatic heartbeat in the bass. The endless summer night of the northern sky smiles three times in Hugh Wheeler's text: at the young, "who know nothing," at the fools, "who know too little," and at the old, "who know too much." "Silly People" retrieves the thought in a rising, insistent line building to a climax:

> When now it smiles it smiles for lovers.
> When next it smiles it smiles for fools.
> The last it smiles it smiles for them,
> The others, the rememberers,
> The truly silly people.
> Them and us and all.

This is the oblivious darkness of love: the shyness of romance confronting sex, or the exhibitionism of sex insulting romance, or the wilted memory of the romancer who knew only sexual liaison, the three archetypes of silly people the show has presented. Unfortunately, the song was dropped in Boston. But its replacement, "The Miller's Son," for a maidservant, offers another perspective on the theme. In folklike strophes she styles the show's three male principals, the miller's son (=the juvenile), the businessman (=the lawyer), and the Prince of Wales (=the hussar), now not darkly but lightly, almost unfeelingly using them to frame her own image of romantic fulfillment.

Pacific Overtures was arguably the best of the Sondheim-Prince shows, even bigger than *Follies* and more subtle, a clunk of history cut, ordered, explained, characterized. Commercial America visits isolated Japan, opens it to the West, and commercializes it. A Brechtian narrator oversees the events, and two men symbolize the warring forces of culture and era, one progressive, the other conservative. Devoted friends at the start, they come to a fatal duel at the end, yet neither cause can win: they have been swallowed up by the pressure of history.

As in all these shows, superproduction was brought into play, in adoption of the Kabuki style. But again it is the score that turns each key of comprehension: songs to state the *ipso facto* of historical flow, to comprehend the two symbolic principals, to sense the alien environment, to engage the conflicting drives to hold Japan pure or ransom it to industrial expansion.

It was the most theatrical of theatre pieces, its Japanese theatre model following upon a Japanese approach in composition: in John Weidman's text, in Sondheim's melodic contours and his use of spare haiku-like imagism, in Tunick's orchestration. The staging is not a conceit; it is part of the composition. Just as the two opposing cultures are brought together in symbiotic alliance in the action, so are they in the work itself, so congruently that it is difficult to decide where the forms of the American musical end and those of the Kabuki stage begin.

At times, the Kabuki predominates. "There Is No Other Way" presents the parting of a husband and wife in pantomime, the wife protrayed by a man in elaborate costume (as Kabuki demands), the song itself handled by two "observers" kneeling at the sides, one describing the scene and the other telling what the woman thinks, their lines dovetailed in austere poetry. Austere, too, is the scoring, recorder over the beat of a small drum. As the melody emerges in the vocal line, harp and strings take it up, and at length the separate lines fit together in achingly beautiful concord.

Other moments favored the American style, the musical's characteristic burlesque very forward. In the opening of Act Two, "Please Hello," deputies of America, Britain, the Netherlands, Russia, and France vie for most-favored-nation trading rights in gunboat diplomacy. Each is an admiral, in outlandish native costume singing native pastiche. The American parades to a Sousaesque march:

> Emperor read our letter? If no,
> Commodore Perry very sad.
> Emperor like our letter? If so,
> Commodore Perry very merry,
> President Fillmore still more glad.

The deals are so layered, so interconnected and internationally competitive, that years pass not between but *during* the numbers:

> Treaty meet approval? If no,
> Commodore Perry very fierce.
> Disregard confusion below:
> President Fillmore now name Pierce.

The British deal in Savoyard patter (note the interior rhymes in each line):

> Hello, I come with letters from Her Majesty Victoria
> Who, learning how you're trading now, sang "Hallelujah, Gloria!"
> And sent me to convey to you her positive euphoria
> As well as little gifts from Britain's various emporia.

The Dutch section is a breezy waltz clog, the Russian a frosty moan from the steppes, and the French wrap it up, to popping champagne corks, with an Offenbachian galop and one of the Western musical's oldest tricks, a topical jest. "It's détente! Oui, détente!," the Frenchman sings, "Zat's ze only thing we want!"

A show this full—and complexly so, an epic distilled rather than epic plain—is going to have troubles winning a public that *Show Boat* never had to consider. This is the ultimate theatre piece, too good live on stage to travel out in neat PR excerpts. Typically, it was the British revue *Side by Side by Sondheim* (1977) that had the easy success: all its numbers were out of context, pre-packaged as excerpts. The revue was nothing but Sondheim, three singers, two pianos, and an insufferably precious narrator. Still, it marked a change in air in that some of the very numbers that had stumped the critics on first hearing now thrilled them. Raves wafted out to village and farm, and the old saw that Sondheim's lyrics were tops but his music "unmelodic" broke apart. On the contrary, it is the music that stands out, for while there have been a few very gifted lyricists, no one, not even Kern, wrote music this good.

There has sprung up a schism between what the musical was historically heading for and what it is pressed into being. It was heading for a glorious integrity of project—but what wins is PR, tricked up in superproduction. It was heading for an integrity of composition, as practised by Gershwin, Weill, Bernstein. But inferior musicians take precedence. To hear that *Hello, Dolly!*'s dance arranger Peter Howard thought up the jazz-waltz embellishment that gives "Dancing" its flight, that Howard arranged the "Waiters' Gallop" (from a song discarded during the tryout panic) that gave the central scene so much of its zing, that a number of songwriters are said to have made anonymous interpolations into the score, and that the title song brought litigation from Mack David over its resemblance to his "You Are My Sunflower" is, in all, to learn that smart business is going to do better than genius.

How hard Sondheim's predecessors had worked to make the history, when history-making shows were the hits. Now the musical's artistic advance runs counter to its economic safety. But what is permitted teaches us nothing. Oddly, most of Sondheim's shows deal with the present challenging the unfulfilled promises of the past, and this is the musical's position at present, turning around to find revivals acceptable but modern developments of what the original shows pointed to hunted from the scene. To think of *Show Boat, Finian's Rainbow, Love Life, The Golden Apple,* and to find today's opinion makers drooling over *Woman of the Year*—they didn't like *Chicago,* either—is to realize what a roll of dice Broadway is. It's arbitrary; love ya, baby, nothing personal.

Yet Sondheim outmaneuvered them on *Sweeney Todd;* word of mouth from the lengthy previews warned the Grub Street gang that to jump this one would be cultural suicide. As with *Porgy and Bess,* those who attack it imperil their standing. Weill's jazz still operates despite it all, and Broadway remains the place where an American opera will be made. If Prince's industrial-strength production seemed more than was needed, his casting of Angela Lansbury and Len Cariou was very, very successful. Sweeney comes from doom, with drastic prescription; Mrs. Lovett wants to keep house, set out flowers, and do the, uh, cooking. They meet at the center: he'll murder any who cross his path, and she'll grind the corpses into meat pies, dog eat dog. "It's so hard to be good," Glenda Farrell said in *Gold Diggers of 1937,* "under the capitalistic system." But there's nothing like running your own business. Theatregoing initiative can't be moribund if a piece this challenging stunned the nation and made money. It also redeemed Broadway of its atrocious Big Lady Shows in that Lansbury, who might well have invested her time in some empty vehicle, threw in her lot with Sondheim-Prince and gave what may be the greatest single performance in the musical, one to compare to . . . well, what's like it? Miller was an elf, Lawrence a love, Merman the liberating dame, Cook and Verdon the heroines of some rich parts, real people. But Lansbury is the devastator, woman out of mind. In *Anyone Can Whistle* she was a burlesque totem—and fought perilously with the authors over characterization. "I don't know what you want!" she screamed. "Tell me, and I'll try to do it!" Mame was easy. Lansbury knew what to do: Mother Goose. A little earthy and a lot chaste. But her Mrs. Lovett is one for the books: because no one, *no one,* can do what Lansbury did in this role, a bizarre music-hall intrusion into a romantic opera, realistic complement to Sweeney's dreaming obsession of a revenge plot. Here is a Malibran of the musical, someone Kurt Weill never thought he'd have to discover, the singing actor who can effectuate Weill's Broadway opera. "I don't know what you want!" Sometimes they want too much. There are as many competent Mrs. Lovetts as there are competent Normas. This is writing beyond Broadway, beyond critics and producers, beyond history. This is being too good for your good. Yet they got it on, they paralyzed critical resentment of art, they cast it, they replaced the cast, they toured it. They won.

So they paid for it on *Merrily We Roll Along,* from Kaufman and Hart's strangely unfunny comedy. Actually Sondheim paid for it. George Furth, who wrote an unintelligible book, and Prince, who cast grotesque amateurs and called for a unit set of high-school lockers and part-encoded tank tops that couldn't be read past the tenth row, got off with beneficent reprimands. Sondheim was smashed, though he was the collaborator who had done his job—following the score was the only way one could tell what was going on. But the solipsistic Manhattan rage is always crazing against its own icons. As the days go by, those who listen to the cast album are going to wonder what gets into the people who write theatre reviews. It's a fine score, plotted to the script's reverse-time arc to pare away and clean, to diminish, almost, rather than develop, though we reach a climax in "Our Time," a spacious chorale caught right on the brink of coming into one's youthful power and ambition. The show unwisely held its tryouts in New York, catering to the *Schadenfreude* set, who dine out on doom. They spread the bad word. Though the book was trimmed and made sensible and the most incompetent kids de-emphasized, an atmosphere of failure had been communicated, and was duly passed on by the critics.

It's a strange note to end on perhaps; but it's inevitably notable that Broadway's most gifted Baby has to work in an environment seething with hostility. What makes Sondheim's shows so exciting to the rest of us is their sense of tradition and innovation spliced together. It is why they have provided a kind of structure for the musical's last fifteen years. They draw richly on a unique native heritage while they develop it, showing its future, how to spend the jazz, how to deal out wild cards in every hand. And is this not what Herbert, Brice, Wodehouse, Kern, Gershwin, Hart, Lahr, Champion, have done? The problem is we don't roll along merrily anymore. "One must accommodate the times," *Pacific Overtures* warns, "as one lives them." That's easy to say in a boom, when R & H unveiled the musical play and found themselves holding the mortgage on the American musical. Still, it moves; we sneak in the jazz. Listen for it.

A Selective Discography

Researching the American musical theatre through recordings brings one to exultation and despair. What an invention the original cast recording was, the performers of the premiere capturing the style, breath, and life of a production, with what immediacy, with such truth! But why did American companies take so long to start making these recordings? The 78 rpm disc was on sale before 1900, the year the British made the first London cast album, of *Florodora*. The British were, furthermore, to catch a few American shows in their West End runs. But the first Broadway cast album was not made till 1938 (of *The Cradle Will Rock*) and the second—the first with chorus and orchestra—not till five years later. By 1949, when the long-playing record finalized the acculturation of the Broadway cast album, shows were recorded as a rule, and virtually every major show is in the can. (This even takes in a few that were never commercially released, such as *Bonanza Bound*. But think of what treasures we might have had! What would *The Wizard of Oz* have sounded like with Montgomery and Stone? Or *Naughty Marietta* with Trentini? Imagine hearing legendary titles as they were first heard—*Little Johnny Jones*, the Princess shows, *Irene*, *Sally*, *The Desert Song*, *Show Boat*! True, pieces were saved here and there. Edith Day made an *Irene* album with the London cast, and various participants in *Show Boat* companies and revivals have put in their share, including Helen Morgan of the original cast. But the losses far outweigh the gains.

Nowadays, we regard the cast album as an accessory to stage production; technology has spoiled us. Back when the record was new, it was accessory to nothing, its noisy surfaces, unobliging phonogenics, and untheatrical singers bearing no relation to what was heard on Broadway. For the first quarter of the twentieth century, all recording was treated "acoustically"—from real life through a horn onto disc or cylinder, warts and all. This did not make for verisimilitude; on the contrary, it disabled extremes at the top and bottom of the sound range. Sopranos and basses lost a lot of their color and a cymbal crash came off as an ogre diving into a huge pie. Moreover, because recordings and playing apparatus were so expensive, few expected them to carry any weight in the culture. So most theatre stars made no or few recordings. Anyway, why should the record companies hire those temperamental, inflexible Broadway names when they could assemble a house troupe to master recording technique and turn out a batch of discs by the week, solos, ensemble, opera, pop, you name it? Caruso sold recordings, yes; Farrar, Galli-Curci, Scotti, yes. But would Montgomery and Stone? Would Lulu Glaser? Elsie Janis? These headliners had huge followings—but would these followings buy a disc that cost nearly as much as a good seat at their shows? Opera singers had swank; the upwardly mobile had cause to buy their records. Musical comedy people were comics and dollies.

Still, it is worth meeting the artifacts, for many shows were documented in one form or another. Hit Tunes were often singled out. There were also the "light opera company" medleys, a quick tour through the refrains of from four to seven songs from a given show, lasting about five minutes. Victor pioneered the medley on single-sided twelve-inch discs, later releasing them on double-faces, two shows to a disc. Columbia and Brunswick picked up the habit; these are scarcer.

There are drawbacks to these medleys, though they are the mediums through which many famous shows received their only "full-scale" recording. The acoustic sound is so boxed in that anyone who doesn't already know the words cannot make them out when more than one person is singing, and, while aspects of the original pit scoring were honored, in all the performances don't attempt to re-create a theatre style. Again, these were recording people, not actors, technicians of *recording* aiming at repeated hearings for home use. With a few exceptions, such as Victor's delightfully acid-voiced Billy Murray, these are circumspect, even drab artists.

Those I haven't daunted are in for a treasure hunt, for many shows were given the medley treatment, some on two sides, unfinished symphonies of naïve ambition. Victor thought so much of DeKoven's *Robin Hood* that it not only brought out two sides' worth of medley but recorded the show again—in exactly the same arrangement—when the "electric" method of recording (through a microphone) superseded the acoustic in 1925.* *Robin Hood* had earned classic status by then: Brunswick also issued a two-sider, one of the few medleys to feature intense singing and dynamic conducting in the true spirit of comic opera. There are also the occasional historical pleasantries, as when Victor Herbert conducts orchestral medleys of his shows or when Victor's *Rio Rita* medley takes in J. Harold Murray, the original Captain Jim.

An entirely different type of show recording is the "hit tune" approach of the dance band on ten-inch discs, the staple of the 1920s and '30s. Everyone from Paul Whiteman's boys to five-and-dime pickup combos joined in, in arrangements usually allowing for a vocal chorus by a band singer but mainly featuring the players. Some of the arrangements are beguiling, some brilliant; countless hours of listening fun await. But is this *theatre music?* It was the major medium of communication for theatre songs, but it changed them around entirely to suit requirements for dance tempo, midcult taste, and scoring strategy. At the time of *Sitting Pretty*, in 1924, Jerome Kern spoke out against the dance band—"jazz," as it was known— in refusing to allow the score to be recorded: "None of our music now reaches the

---

* Trivium question for experts: what was the first American electric recording? Answer: selections from a University of Pennsylvania *Mask and Wig* show, *Joan of Arkansas*. *Mask and Wig* is still vital at Penn; the shows haven't improved much, however.

public as we wrote it except in the theatre. It is so distorted by jazz orchestras as to be almost unrecognizable . . .The trouble with current popular musical rendition is that it runs everything into the same mold."

However, scattered through the 78 era are souvenirs of theatre performances, as the ensuing pages will reveal. The utopian album, involving the performers, orchestra, and conductor of the premiere, versed in their business from rehearsals and tryouts, was only gradually arrived at in America. Brunswick brought out a *Show Boat* set at the time of the 1932 revival, eight twelve-inch sides complete with opening and closing orchestral medleys. But only two of the singers were associated with the show, and only the six standards recorded on the vocal sides. Victor tackled *Porgy and Bess* with the original orchestra, chorus, and conductor, under Gershwin's supervision, but with Met singers Lawrence Tibbett and Helen Jepson in place of the true cast. The Musicraft *Cradle Will Rock* set no example, but there were portents of the cast album in the very early 1940s. Liberty Music Shop put out show sets in miniature, Ethel Merman *sola* in numbers from *Stars in Your Eyes* and *Panama Hattie*, Mary Jane Walsh in *Let's Face It* led by the show's conductor Max Meth (with, for good measure, two sides of dance-band medley). Liberty's *Cabin in the Sky* discs had not only Ethel Waters but the overture used in the theatre.

This was closer and closer, and at last Decca turned the trick in 1943 with twelve ten-inch sides of *Oklahoma!* made by the original cast and crew, with a grand photograph of the show's finale on the cover, photos of each song's staging on the inside, and a booklet of notes and lyrics. The album's very feeling was theatre, and history was made, for virtually every American who bought records bought this set. The project proved so successful that Decca later filled it out with an appendix of the three *Oklahoma!* numbers it hadn't caught, making the show the first American score caught in its theatrical entirety (save dance music and reprises) from overture to finale.

Most of the hit shows that followed *Oklahoma!* in the 1940s got a cast album. Decca led the way, but Columbia got *Finian's Rainbow, Street Scene, Miss Liberty,* and *Kiss Me, Kate,* Victor took *Allegro, Brigadoon,* and *High Button Shoes,* and Capitol nabbed *St. Louis Woman.* There were odd gaps here and there. But the introduction of the unbreakable, lightweight, long playing record at the end of the decade revolutionized the practice of original-cast documentation.

The LP might have been invented for the cast album. Symphonies, operas, and chamber works come in all lengths, and pop recitals are cut to order. But the roughly one-hour playing time that the LP afforded caught most of a musical. A bonus was the habit, in the 1950s, of including some of the spoken cues to effect a theatre atmosphere, and further possibilities were opened by Goddard Lieberson's recording of *The Most Happy Fella* complete on three discs and, recently, CBS's issuing of an eighty-five-minute cassette of *Nine,* twenty minutes longer than the disc. There was no rule about how "good" a show had to be or how long it had to run to qualify; almost everything was recorded. Revues were neglected— television was making them unnecessary, and Schwartz and Dietz had no successors. But Broadway's book shows were basic to American popular music then, and—hard as it may be to believe now—the public stormed the stores when a *My Fair Lady* or a *Music Man* came out, invariably within a few days of the opening. In the 1955–56 season, only one book show missed out on recording; in 1956–57 only two; in 1958–59 everything was recorded, including a Menotti opera, *Maria*

Golovin. Show albums did such good business that alternate editions came out along with the cast albums, renditions by pop balladeers or easy-listening or jazz treatments. The rise of rock forced theatre composition off to the side, leaving smaller companies to record the shows that the big deals ignore. At the same time, a renewed interest in the moribund Broadway tradition has inspired several series of compilations from 78s, new recordings of old numbers standard and obscure, and reissues of older albums.

There is, then, a mass of material to assimilate. I do not propose to cover it all. Nor do I find it makes for pleasant reading to fill the eyes with matrix numbers, reissue coding, and the like. These have meaning only for elite collectors, anyway. I propose simply to navigate this territory following the chapter structure of the present book, pointing out recordings of historical stimulation. With so much documentation put down, it is not enough to read about personal style. They saved the music for us: we are posterity, and must hear for ourselves.

Retrospectives and Compilations

Ella Fitzgerald put out two-disc sets for Verve Records on Irving Berlin, Cole Porter, and Rodgers and Hart, plus single LPs on others and a five-record Gershwin festival. Style is a major consideration here. Much of this material was written in the percussive 1920s or the swinging 1930s, almost none of it in the 1950s when the easy-listening arrangement was popular, when verses were omitted and singers virtually mandated to make everything sound alike. Ballads were smooth, not intent, rhythm numbers eased down. Those in search of the authentic ring that Merman brought to Porter or the Astaires brought to the Gershwins will be disconcerted. Those too secure in style to need it on every single gothrough will find these Verve records a trove. Fitzgerald rejoiced in one of the great instruments in pop music, employed a superb "scat" (the wordless jazz vocal variation), and, in phrasing, never made a wrong choice. Comparing Fitzgerald's "I Got Rhythm" to Merman's (from 1947) and Garland's (at the time of her *Girl Crazy* film in 1943) gives us a fix on style. Merman, the woman who made belt Broadway's choice in heroine song, and Garland, comparable in film, go for drive; they got *rhythm*. Fitzgerald is almost pensive in the verse, less lively than bright in the chorus; she got *music*. But she knows what Gershwin is saying, and translates it for us in a scat finale.

Joan Morris dwells in another world altogether. She comes out of the 1970s, a time of archaeological reconstruction. Authenticity is absolute. Moreover, she is married to the outstanding accompanist in the repertory, William Bolcom. That Bolcom is, under another hat, one of most imaginative of avant-garde composers has not hurt his love for this old and so very tonal repertory. On the contrary, he sounds like an enthusiast of the day. Morris has the voice many Broadway shows were written for but not sung by, a light mezzosoprano with precise intonation and endless "sympathy." Versatile, extremely musical, and nifty, Morris is one of the queens of Broadway song.

Bobby Short, upholder of the line of gala cabaret that has been diminishing since the 1950s, plays his own piano in his own style. Where Bolcom re-creates the atmosphere in which these songs were introduced, Short reintroduces them to a latter day in modern arrangements (with bass and drums) of an authentic tang. Morris's repertory takes her back as far as the nineteenth century; Short empha-

sizes the golden age of Porter, Gershwin, Rodgers and Hart, and of all others today
he seems to me to be the most acute. In Porter, his turn of a phrase such as "Miss
Peggy Joyce" in "Why Shouldn't I?" captures the composer's wistful hedonism in
its essence; in Gershwin, his "Innocent Ingenue Baby" and "Do What You Do"
feature the chiding amiability of the brothers to a T. Short's three recitals, all two-
disc albums for Atlantic (there is one on Noel Coward as well) mix the familiar
and neglected. Some of Short's earliest takes, from 1957, including a few orchestral
tracks, were published as *Nobody Else But Me* in 1970, and this collection is all
unusual, what might be called obscure hits. You may have heard the titles, but not
the songs: the jaunty "Nobody Else But Me," last of the *Show Boat* additions;
Rodgers and Hart's "Where's That Rainbow?" (from *Peggy-Ann*) and "Over and
Over Again" (from *Jumbo*); even a portion of *Of Thee I Sing*'s first-act finale,
Short supplying both Wintergreen's "Kiss for Cinderella" solo and the choral commentary that contrapuntally accompanies it, though he doesn't ask technology to
play them back to him simultaneously. Film, British, and cabaret songs fill out the
disc; after hearing it, you'll understand why Short has referred to himself as "a
kind of singing Smithsonian."

The Smithsonian itself entered the field in the 1970s with a series of "archival
reconstructions" of shows from the 1920s and '30s. The aim is to gather not any
or all 78s made from a single score, but only those of some relevance to the original productions. This can limit the fun, as when the *Oh, Kay!* album includes
mere snippets of the Columbia and Brunswick medleys to avoid cuts made by
studio vocalists. Yet the aim is not consistently observed: *At Home Abroad* includes cuts of recent vintage to pull in songs otherwise unavailable.

That quibble aside, these are highly impressive records. Expert liner notes, sump-
tuously illustrated, detail the historical background and the entertainment itself,
and the sound is all one could wish, clear and correct. *Whoopee* and *The Band
Wagon* are spectacular, and *Oh, Kay!*, with its Gershwin piano cuts and the one,
true Gertrude Lawrence, will stun the ear. Lately, the Smithsonian has expanded
into recording its own productions, and Victor Herbert fans should also note the
three-disc collection cited a few pages hence.

Back in the 1930s, Liberty Music Shops troubled to record performers and works
neglected by the commercial labels. Now, Music Masters of New York is doing
similar work in rescuing forgotten 78s; unlike the Smithsonian albums, these issues
do not disdain dance-band recordings if it means adding in a title. Quite some
variety here—albums on Kern, Porter, and Rodgers and Hart separately taking in
films and shows, compilations on Merman and Lahr, collections of ancient Kern
and Herbert medleys. and a series called *The Music of Broadway* that collects
material by year. The 1930 album, for instance, takes in such classics as *Strike Up
the Band* and *Girl Crazy* as well as arresting but less well known titles by Rodgers
and Hart (*Simple Simon*), Sigmund Romberg (*Nina Rosa*), and Cole Porter (*The
New Yorkers*) and includes a number of cuts by the original performers.

Least easy to describe is Ben Bagley's *Revisited* series, launched in 1964 and now
totaling upwards of thirty titles. Bagley is unquestionably dedicated. He has, against
all commercial prospects, set about reviving lost portions of our great American
heritage of show music, songs not heard for decades—some scarcely heard at all:
written for but not used in shows. There is a cheap truism to the effect that songs
are deleted from productions or ignored by the public for good reasons. Bagley
proves otherwise. Few of these rediscoveries are duds, and many dazzle.

But Bagley's approach is questionable. The savage putdown humor of his liner notes carries over into the arrangements. Rather than retrieve the original sound styles of Porter, Gershwin, Berlin, or Youmans, Bagley goes out of his way to inflame them with incorrect bizarrerie—forties Hollywood raveups, fifties cabaret torchorama, lubricious new lyrics, crazy-gang medleys, and performers who too often are spectacularly inadequate. Some numbers Bagley treasures; some others he ridicules. To compare Kurt Weill's song "Youkali" in versions made by Teresa Stratas, authentic to the note, and the Bagley gang, tuneless and camping, is to realize how far off the mark much of the series is. Bagley seems to respect Rodgers and Hart in particular, for three of their four *Revisited* albums are the best in the series, clean of gimmicks. And Porter, I imagine, would be more amused than shocked at the way Bagley extends the author's ironies into great looney binges of carnal self-knowledge. But the Coward and Weill discs are loathsome and the Gershwin discs out of style. I think it important to note that Bagley's arrangers Norman Paris and Dennis Deal are highly gifted; they are limited by their employer's caprices. In brief, enjoy the repertory but listen forewarned. These are not reflections of the past but comments upon it, by someone full of the dickens.

Preceding Bagley in the *Revisited* form—and strictly in style—was a series put out by Walden Records in the early 1950s. Walden was main line: Kern, Rodgers and Hart, Schwartz and Dietz, the Gershwins, and such, featuring little-known singers backed up by John Morris's small combos. The very Broadwayesque Hirschfeld cartoons used as cover art typify Walden's devotion to style; the Arlen set counted Arlen among the singers. Walden's program included standards among the rarities, making it less useful than Bagley for nitty-gritty rediscovery. Also, the records have become very scarce. However, they are gradually coming back into the catalogue—Citadel has reissued fourteen takes from three Walden discs as *Gershwin Rarities,* and the cast includes one unknown who Made It, Kaye Ballard. And lo, the Hirschfeld cartoon of the brothers at work adorns the jacket.

Around 1950, Columbia's Goddard Lieberson and conductor Lehman Engel made a series of recordings of great scores that had preceded the cast album era. Their plan took in wide variety with the first (nearly) complete *Porgy and Bess, The Desert Song* and *The Student Prince, Girl Crazy* and *On Your Toes,* and it lasted into stereo years with *On the Town* and *Lady in the Dark.* A laudable project. But were these truly show albums? Casting sometimes favored an alluring name over theatricality, as when Mary Martin takes over the *Babes in Arms* hits in "personality orchestrations" regardless of their stage context, or when she tackles *Anything Goes* almost singlehanded. With no fellows to address (especially in the collaborative "You're the Top"), she might well have billed the disc as "entire production played by Mary Martin." Then, too, Lieberson didn't like dialogue and deleted spoken lines—even from operettas with Hammerstein's extremely crucial musical scenes. Thus, Columbia unmade history while it honored history.

Still, the best of Lieberson and Engel is very fine. Their *Porgy and Bess* contributed heavily to the acculturation of this masterpiece and is highly theatrical, spoken lines, sound effects, and all. Their *On the Town* (Engel prepared it but Bernstein stepped in to conduct the taping) nearly is an original cast album, with four of the premiere's five singing leads. Their *Pal Joey* sparked the 1952 revival; their series as a whole may have inspired the postwar interest in restaging classic shows. I append this discography because so much of the musical's history is made of performers' stylistics, but also because recordings have to a great extent shaped our perception of the past. A score recorded is a vital entry in the annals: a score unrecorded is a statistic.

Introduction. Broadway, 1900

Start with vaudeville, which fed the story stage with material and performers. The first two of several indispensable Joan Morris discs recommend themselves here, both big sellers on Nonesuch, *After the Ball: A Treasury of Turn-of-the-Century Songs* and *Vaudeville: Songs of the Great Ladies of the Musical Stage.* The first gives us numbers associated with Lillian Russell in her Weberfields years, Marie Cahill, Blanche Ring, and others, incidentally proving the durability of these oldies in that some of them reappeared in *Show Boat,* the MGM film *Meet Me in St. Louis,* and *Reds.* The second recalls the likes of Nora Bayes, Bessie McCoy, May Irwin, Anna Held, and Eva Tanguay. Like these, her glorious predecessors, Morris doesn't just sing a number; she Puts It Over.

Vaudeville was not pure; any compilation includes a lot of musical comedy. Audio Rarities' *They Stopped the Show,* from 1969, gathers up as many stars of the story stage as of variety, the whole narrated by Chamberlain Brown in a charmingly raspy voice but without savvy—he insistently says "Ziegfield" and seems unaware that George M. pronounced his name Co-en, no "h." Some of these acts are classics, but Lillian Russell's "Come Down, Ma Evenin' Star" is worn of voice, Eva Tanguay's "I Don't Care" manically arch, George M. scratchy in "I Want To Hear a Yankee Doodle Tune." Bert Williams, Nora Bayes ("Over There"), and Weber and Fields come through.

Early musical comedy has not been covered well, but New World makes an excellent survey in *I Wants To Be A Actor Lady,* newly recorded selections from shows from *The Black Crook* to Herbert, Cohan, and first Kern. The performances are ingenuous, the arrangements authentic, and the liner notes extensive. Otherwise, the pickings are lean unless you have access to 78s and a "Victrola," the old general-use term for a record player. Actually, the Victrola was only one make— Victor's, obviously—along with Brunswick's Panatrope and Columbia's Grafonola.

Those who track down the few LP transcriptions can revel in the medley. Ivan Caryll, Gustav Luders, Gustave Kerker, and other tantalizing statistics are here, some titles in competitive versions. Luders's *The Prince of Pilsen* proves its popularity in three different medleys; *The Merry Widow,* supreme for that touch of elegance within the foolery, copped at least six. *The Sultan of Sulu* squeaks by on Victor, but *Florodora,* queen of Gaiety, is exceptional with its various medleys, one-shot titles, and twelve sides' worth of original (London) cast album recorded by the phonographic pioneer Emile Berliner. He must have thought the show historically essential, for to Berliner sound was a museum to be opened. He caught statesmen, actors, proselytes of various sects (including atheism), even Teddy Roosevelt's San Juan Hill trumpeter. Those in search of the Gaiety style, so seminal in American musical comedy from the Princess shows to *Sunny, Oh, Kay!,* and *Funny Face,* should acquire the World Records LP transcription of selections from four Gaiety shows—*Our Miss Gibbs, Houp-La, The Quaker Girl,* and *Bric-a-Brac*—all with London favorite Gertie Millar. The sound is dim—*Our Miss Gibbs* dates from 1909. Yet the spirit comes through. Millar married one of the Gaiety composers, Lionel Monckton, and he lavished his best on her, though it was generally agreed that she wasn't a great singer. Her coos of delight in the dance section of "Houp-la" are Gaiety to the life, and Americans will aprove the interpolation of Blanche Ring's signature "Yip-I-Addy-I-Ay" into *Our Miss Gibbs* and of "Pretty Baby" into *Houp-La*. Readers of Hugo H. Munro, celebrated as Saki, will at last get to hear "Bertie the Bounder," which plays a convulsive part in "The Open Window."

1. *The Score*

The Smithsonian's irresistible three-disc album, *Music of Victor Herbert,* offers an introduction to his six best-loved scores, plus the two operas and some concert selections. All the cuts were made during Herbert's lifetime, some under his super-vision, so authenticity is assured. However, these are mainly studio renditions. There is no Fritzi Scheff in *Mlle. Modiste,* no Montgomery and Stone in *The Red Mill,* no Emma Trentini in *Naughty Marietta.* There never was, except live on stage. However, some of the studio people are excellent, and we do get four Ber-liner tracks of Alice Nielsen's troupe in *The Fortune Teller* and Christie Mac-Donald in three numbers from *Sweethearts.* Opera buffs may prize Frances Alda's "A Perfect Day," from *Madeleine,* Herbert's experimental opera composed in the flowing recitative Debussy introduced in *Pelléas and Mélisande.* The Met had com-missioned the one-act *Madeleine* specifically for Alda, but when she saw the score she made a commission of her own—for an aria. Interpolations, interpolations. Herbert gave her "A Perfect Day," and audiences were glad. Also on hand, in *Natoma,* are Alma Gluck and John McCormack; I think the Smithsonian might have included Earl Cartwright's superior version of "Vaquero's Song" rather than Cecil Fanning's. The set's best feature is Herbert's own conducting. Sample his "March of the Toys," his *Naughty Marietta* Intermezzo, his *Sweethearts* selection to hear how the music sounded when lilt and sweep had give-and-take. Those curious about the 78 medley can hear the Victor Light Opera Company racing through *The Fortune Teller, Mlle. Modiste, Naughty Marietta,* and *Sweethearts,* quite creditably.

Victor issued a comparable album in the 1930s, two volumes of five twelve-inch 78s each, all newly recorded and covering more territory than the Smithsonian does. *Babette, The Only Girl, Eileen, Algeria,* and *The Princess "Pat"* join the familiar titles and concert bits, under Nathaniel Shilkret. (His conducting of "Pan Americana," tango framed in ragtime, is smashing.) The late-middle electric sound is fine, so all the words come through. But remember that the variety of the exper-imental scores is lost in this potpourri Hit Tune treatment. *The Only Girl* gets only two ballads; on such evidence it might be any old operetta instead of an unusual play-with-songs. And *Algeria* is utterly turned around: the heroine's two great so-los, "Rose of the World" and "Twilight in Barakeesh," are assigned to a tenor! True, out of context they sound more appropriate on a man. But they were written to display Abadie's fiery heart, her finesse—this characterization is elemental in the development of American operetta.

Beverly Sills offers yet another *Music of Victor Herbert,* on Angel conducted by Andre Kostelanetz. I have reservations: no chorus, no middle section on the "Ital-ian Street Song," and the pop version of "Kiss Me Again" is used. In *Mlle. Mod-iste,* the number, "If I Were on the Stage," puts the heroine through an audition's paces as a gavotting country girl and a prima donna before she reaches the waltz ballad itself. For concert emergencies Herbert provided a verse to introduce the ballad alone, and this short weight is all Sills gives us. I have stronger objections to the overproduced orchestrations, a curse on Herbert since the MacDonald-Eddy years; Kostelanetz's two ersatz sinfoniettas are a blight. Otherwise it is gold, Sills at her best in eight of Herbert's best-liked songs, plus Sills's encore specialty, "Art Is Calling for Me," the opera singer spoof from *The Enchantress.*

Show by show, one finds no full-length recordings in Herbert's own day (no London casts, either—Herbert did not go over abroad), a few in the 1940s, after his sound style had become corrupted, and the most complete recordings in the 1970s, when Herbert stagings are rare. Decca recorded eight cuts from *Babes in Toyland* in 1946 with a theatre feeling; Walt Disney made a *Babes* film, but the soundtrack album reveals a debauchery, the tunes noodled into soup with new lyrics that might have come out of an aerosol can. *Mlle. Modiste* claims only a Victor EP* of the four hits. *The Red Mill,* however, is well covered. Victor released an album in conjunction with the 1945 revival but used none of the Broadway cast. The kit was elaborately produced with notes, pictures, and an explanation of changes made in the script. But the four discs offer fiendishly untheatrical arrangements, unenlightened singers, and far too much orchestral scene-setting by Al Goodman. Decca riposted with a sensible album—Wilbur Evans, Eileen Farrell, Felix Knight, and six songs in a theatre atmosphere. The young Farrell sounds great, and Evans delivers "Ev'ry Day Is Ladies' Day with Me" as if he had coached it with the composer, despite a tiny blemish as he struts into the second chorus— he and conductor Blackton aren't together on tempo for about two seconds. As part of its operetta series featuring Gordon MacRae and various sopranos, Capitol put out a *Red Mill* in fifties orchestrations but containing, as the series habitually did, a few neglected numbers. Turnabout brought out the first full-length LP in 1980, but the singers, apparently chorus people, have no sense of how this repertory plays.

We come to the only note-complete recording of a Herbert score, the Smithsonian's *Naughty Marietta,* based on their 1980 revival. Given that the original production skimmed the cream of a world-class opera company, one hoped for a more exciting performance, but it *is* the *Naughty Marietta* that Herbert wrote, orchestrations and all. James Morris conducts a competent if stiff reading, *senza rubato,* and Judith Blazer delivers what the Italians would call a "correct" Marietta; perhaps better. She has the accent, the notes, the arch insinuation—but the vivacity? Perhaps Morris' stolidity limited her. Capitol's MacRae *Marietta* touches all the major bases (twelve numbers), including the mysteriously neglected waltz quartet "Live for Today," which producer Hammerstein thought would be the hit of the show. MGM's MacDonald-Eddy *Naughty Marietta,* the off-style arrangements accepted, is grand listening—five numbers in trim, three others reworked, and among the Herbert cetera is his concert piece "Punchinello," a gem recut to a Gus Kahn lyrics as "Chansonette."

Turnabout followed up its *Red Mill* with a more listenable *Sweethearts*—but what of *Eileen,* the composer's favorite? He led cast numbers in two singles, but

---

*Short for "extended play," Victor's answer to Columbia's LP. It ran as long as the old twelve-inch 78s but was light, relatively unbreakable, and turned at 45 rpm on a thick spindle that seldom worked properly or on individual adaptors that kept getting lost. By the late 1950s, the EP was retired, to general relief.

his two-sided Victor medley is most notable. This is solemn work, tune after tune unfurling Gaelic pageantry till the listener yearns to see this remarkable piece in full true on a stage.

Herbert is rightly and wrongly regarded as operetta's founder (rightly, I think—but too often for the wrong reasons). So we might follow the progress of the form in the work of Rudolf Friml and Sigmund Romberg. As with Herbert, Victor issued a Friml medley-and-concert album in the 1930s under Shilkret; it's the best chance to hear the hits from *You're in Love, High Jinks, The Firefly,* and *Katinka,* all samples of early Friml in musical comedy (1912–17). Of the operetta Friml we get only three titles in full. *Rose-Marie* fares well. The 1925 London cast made eight cuts, giving us not only Edith Day and D'Oyly Carter Derek Oldham in the grander numbers but also the comics, Hard-Boiled Herman and Lady Jane, to remind us of the struggles operetta underwent trying to integrate fun into the romance. The MGM style gushes forth in MacDonald and Eddy's cuts of the hits—five of the "Indian Love Call" alone. If you like these two, this is the key cut, their numbo. Till the Smithsonian releases its complete *Rose-Marie,* the choice traversal is Victor's LP starring Julie Andrews, just then flush with her New York and London success as Eliza Doolittle. Andrews is miscast. Rose-Marie is a heavily-accented French-Canadian with an edge, while Andrews is an English lady. Still, she sings it well. The absurd Jewish inflection in the Hard-Boiled Herman, Meier Tzelniker, is authentic—the role is one of the last of the Dutch comic turns till Irving Jacobson's Sancho in *Man of La Mancha.* A curiosity: *Rose-Marie* is very popular in France, and there are several French recordings. As a rule, "Le Terrible Herman" forgoes the Jewish accent.

The Vagabond King claims a few souvenirs from both New York and London productions; only Dennis King's "Song of the Vagabonds" is worth hearing. The most complete LP is Victor's, with Mario Lanza and Judith Raskin, but the filmland scoring is a bane. I prefer Decca's ten-inch LP with Alfred Drake, Mimi Benzell, and Frances Bible, something of a theatre cast. Strangely, for all his fame, Friml is nearly over at this point: an LP preserves the six cuts made by the London cast of *The Three Musketeers,* his last major work. Dennis King (who created D'Artagnan in New York) is in almost every number, in top form.

Romberg makes a better showing, but then Romberg stayed with it longer. A great introduction: Victor's LP reissue (on Camden) of its medleys, including *Maytime, Blossom Time,* and *My Maryland* as well as the big titles. These are spirited performances, *Blossom Time* the ace curiosity for its legendary durability as a Shubert Brothers touring hit. No cast was too lurid, no production too cheesy to discourage the regional public. Suddenly, in the early 1950s, it utterly vanished. Made of the "life" and music of Franz Schubert, *Blossom Time* was in fact the third version of an international hit. The first, *Das Dreimäderlhaus,* is pure Schubert plus lyrics. The second, London's *Lilac Time,* has a fuller score but terrible words. Romberg's is easily the best. It's hard to miss with Schubert's tunes, but Romberg developed them with great theatricality and added in some fine Romberg as well. Al Goodman's 78 Victor set makes a good case for the piece, with a superb cast.

The Student Prince is an unusual item in the canon of twenties operetta in that its score attempts to fake a style almost throughout, that of the German university with its student glees and may waltzes. In *Blossom Time* Romberg worked with Schubert's naturally Viennese melodies; here he must instruct the sound himself.

Decca's ten-inch LP with Lauritz Melchior seems the best choice—the Wagnerian tenor has the glee and the waltz down cold. Like Decca's *Vagabond King,* the disc has a nice fifties-theatre scoring. Note the orchestral statement of "Golden Days" that follows the vocal—this was the sound of the scene-change in post-R & H shows.

I confess to a nostalgic fondness for Decca's 78 *Desert Song* with Kitty Carlisle and Wilbur Evans, the set I grew up with. It's gutsy and musical, exactly what the cast album might have been like if *The Desert Song* had been written in the 1940s. There's a lot of lead-in dialogue, much of it not by the authors. Is it road-tour tradition that prompts Carlisle to murmur "I can't kill you" before she soars into "I love you!" as she tosses her revolver away and throws herself into the Red Shadow's arms? This isn't in the score. It's typical of the abandon Carlisle brings to the role—but why does she pull the tempo around so much? Angel's *Desert Song,* annoyingly reorchestrated, has the gorgeous June Bronhill and some of the comic songs.

The British rescue *The New Moon* from studio editions, for Evelyn Laye, Ben Williams, Howett Worster, and Drury Lane personnel of 1929 survive on LP. This is syllabus listening, a document of style. Americans had taken up the cast album themselves in time to catch up with the later Romberg, but *Up in Central Park* (1945) didn't get one. It didn't *not* get one, exactly: Decca grabbed Wilbur Evans and Betty Bruce from the show, added in Eileen Farrell (for voice) and Celeste Holm (for show smarts) and used the theatre chorus, orchestra, and conductor, Max Meth. Eight cuts. This is a spryer Romberg than most know—Evans gets downright giddy in "When You Walk in the Room." But then, working with Herbert and Dorothy Fields, Romberg was not likely to turn out pure operetta. Victor took down six cuts with Jeanette MacDonald and the very young Robert Merrill. Decca's cast is better, but the arrangements are largely the same on both, and of course MacDonald is worth hearing. Operetta buffs should think back to her Lubitsch period with Maurice Chevalier: there's more to MacDonald than the "Indian Love Call." Exhibit A: "The Fireman's Bride."

Romberg ended his career as he began it, in musical comedy, with *The Girl in Pink Tights* (1954), an amusing sample of mid-fifties musicals. The subject is of note to buffs: the making of *The Black Crook,* that begetter of musical comedy histories if not of musical comedy. The cast is characteristically diverse: Jeanmaire and comic Charles Goldner from Europe, baritone hero David Atkinson, opera belter Brenda Lewis for I'm not sure what, and, from the Paris Opera ballet, Alexandre Kalioujny to partner Jeanmaire. In all, it's a treat—more than can be said for the soundtrack album to MGM's Romberg unbio, *Deep in My Heart.* The program includes gems known and obscure, but the scoring is glop and the many singers enthusiastically deficient in style. When Wagnerian soprano Helen Traubel plays a Bowery café owner and dances ragtime and is still the best thing in sight, you're at a horror show.

2. *The Urban Ethnic Emergence*

New World's *Don't Give the Name a Bad Place: Types and Stereotypes in American Musical Theater, 1870–1900* captures the rise of non-WASP subjects in popular music, some of it from shows. Max Morath leads a fine little group in five numbers from the Harrigan-Hart *Mulligan Guard* series, and Danny Barker handles the black tunes (a very moving "Stay in Your Own Backyard"). However, the "Dutch" material isn't very Dutch (i.e., Jewish). Better let Weber and Fields fill in here, on a number of sketches they recorded in the early 78 era, really little more than exchanges. These have not, to my knowledge, made it onto LP in quantity.

George M. Cohan's hold on recordings is shaky, unless one counts the soundtrack of *Yankee Doodly Dandy* or the cast album of *George M!*. While Cohan laid down a few tracks himself, he was one of those performers you get live or not at all. Both the film and the show biographies are worth hearing, though of course the style is anachronistically souped up. In the film, Cagney offers a genuine Cohan, having learned his hoofing and song-selling in New York when Cohan was still a living presence and coached the part with Cohan associate Johnny Boyle. *George M!* features a great choice of songs, rare ones as well as the hits which the film plugs.

Bert Williams was a prolific and expert recording artist; there's a good selection on Folkways. Al Jolson was another ghetto buster, so big a recording star that Columbia issued his cuts one to a disc, with flip sides by house staff. Thus Jolson sold twice as many "units" (as they now call them) as he might have done. Don't hope to reconstruct the Jolson musical from his show tunes, for his numbers were invariably vaudeville specials having nothing to do with the action—as, indeed, Jolson was himself. Columbia has preserved three LP's worth of prime cuts from 1914 to 1932, Jolson's heyday, in *The Legendary Al Jolson.* Jolson soundtracks are essential, and a good bet is Take Two's *The Singing Fool,* including all the sound sequences (this was a part-talkie): seven songs, dialogue, reprises, title and closing music, and annotations.

To fill out the ethnic excursion, sample the remarkable Sophie Tucker. She did only three book shows, far more a vaudeville than a Broadway star. But in her feminist persona she counted heavily in pop music. When Jolson sang a song, it became a national hit; Tucker's seldom became popular. But she herself did. Westwood's *Some of These Days* collects fourteen choice cuts—Dixie tunes, torch ballads, charm songs, and comic novelties. "Hollywood Will Never Be the Same," Tucker's report on her adventure in the early talkie, *Honky Tonk,* is as startlingly risqué as it is startlingly personal, Sophie as Sophie. "I Ain't Takin' Orders from No One" is a war cry, "He Hadn't up till Yesterday (but he will tonight)" an act of aggression. The woman is stupendous—forthright, lavish, and a great singer. When she at last reaches her theme song, "Some of These Days," with its wild, high, angry swing, you realize how necessary Tucker was in the creation of the post-Marilyn Miller heroine.

3. *The Great Glorifier*

Pelican's *Stars of the Ziegfeld Follies* offers Van and Schenck, beauty-anthem tenor John Steel, Eddie Cantor, Nat Wills, Bert Williams ("Nobody," in the sonically preferable 1913 remake), Nora Bayes, Marilyn Miller (the opening number from her third and last film, *Her Majesty Love,* taken off the track), and a wild two-sided 78 medley of the 1927 *Follies,* with Berlin songs and Franklyn Baur, the Brox Sisters, and pianists Fairchild and Rainger, all from the cast. Moreover, the Smithsonian has assembled a partial original cast album of the 1919 *Follies,* with

Steel, Cantor, Williams, and Van and Schenck. No Miller: she never released a commercial recording.

MGM made *The Great Ziegfeld,* using some of his staff for accuracy, so the soundtrack album is useful in a vague way. The story is rot in its details but reportorial in overall effect; and the tempestuous Lillian Lorraine is not scanted (Virginia Bruce plays her as "Audrey"). That isn't Cantor as himself, though it's a good imitation—but Fanny Brice plays Fanny Brice. The album includes her dressing-room sketch in which she mistakes Ziegfeld (William Powell) for a peddler and buys Bruce's mink coat right out of his hands. If Brice is the basic Ziegfeld star, the retrospective of her 78s on Audio Fidelity the basic Brice disc: "My Man," "I'd Rather Be Blue," "Second Hand Rose," "Cooking Breakfast for the One I Love," "I'm an Indian," four others, and a sketch, "Mrs. Cohen at the Beach." (A curiosity: in the early 1950s, Kaye Ballard recorded most of the same numbers in *The Fanny Brice Story in Song* on MGM, carefully observing Brice's inflections and business.) To hear Brice in setting with other great woman singers of the day, try Take Two's *The Original Torch Singers,* veritably a Ziegfeld sampler with Etting and Helen Morgan (also Libby Holman) as well as Brice. Listen to the swinging ease Brice lends to the uptempo version of "My Man." The song is moving too fast to make sense, yet she pulls it off with musical heft. The slow version, also here, is a knockout, the *bel canto* of torch. I mean it.

To catch up on the post-Ziegfeld revue, consider Arthur Schwartz and Howard Dietz. Their songs for *The Little Show, The Second Little Show, Three's a Crowd, The Band Wagon, Flying Colors,* and *At Home Abroad* follow the progression of high-smart variety from intimate to sizable, from young producers (Tom Weatherly, Max Gordon) to old hands (the Shuberts), from 1929 to 1935. Evergreen offers a fine sampling on two discs in bright modern performances. For the sound of the era, the Smithsonian counters with *The Band Wagon* and *At Home Abroad.* The *Band Wagon* disc is a historical sensation in that most of it comes from an early Victor LP experiment—featuring some of the ballet music and with the two Astaires on five cuts! Clifton Webb typed revue's debonair singing hoofer but Astaire idealized the trope in story musicals; hear him here in mid-campaign, in his last job with Adele before he broke out on his own against the predictions of some Broadway sages who thought him her accessory. A few songs Victor missed can be heard on Columbia's *Band Wagon,* with Mary Martin and a chorus.

4. *The Heroine*

Tracking down the sound of the American musical in the first decades of this century is difficult, for few of the original performers recorded, whether they fielded vocal cream or *Sprechstimme.* In the 1910s and 1920s London casts made albums, yet the British don't really fill a gap. The operettas can be impressive, but the musical comedy casts are vocally quite poor, the heroines more charming than musical and the men acidly toneless in "silly ass" personae, a theatre filled with Jack Buchanans.

Major names are missing. Lillian Russell, Eleanor Painter, and Elsie Janis left remote mementoes. We do have Edith Day, for her extensive London career gave her access to the recording studio on *Irene, Rose-Marie, The Desert Song, Show Boat, Rio Rita,* and, three decades later at the end of her career, Noël Coward's

Sail Away. World offers a sampling of Day in the 1920s, throwing into relief her musical comedy tang and operetta savor. The two *Irene* cuts, unlike those she made in New York, sound theatrical, complete with the spoken portion of "Alice Blue Gown" and the jig that runs contrapuntally with the title tune. This is Day, sweetheart of the slums. The big Drury Lane operettas reveal a doer rather than a trembler. Like Evelyn Laye, Day lacked the last word in high notes but has commitment. Of special note is a 1934 medley of Day specials. Wonderfully hushed in "Romance," unnervingly coy in "Alice Blue Gown," and full of fox trot in "Why Do I Love You?," Day covers the heroine spectrum in four minutes.

As for Miller, only on *Rosalie* did she attempt a recording, and her test pressings were not released. The curious may hear her via soundtrack on Take Two's *Legends of the Musical Stage:* two cuts from Warner Brothers' *Sally* film, "Look for the Silver Lining" and (new for the film, not by Kern) "If I'm Dreaming." Miller's partner is Alexander Gray, a Broadway baritone drafted for talkie work, so their duets make a kind of translated Broadway. The album also takes in Jolson, Cantor, Tucker, Brice, and Merman, all in rare film cuts, so it's a fine investment all around.

As for the British *Sally* album (eight numbers plus Herbert's "Butterfly Ballet"), the singing of Dorothy Dickson and Gregory Stroud bears out my report on West End vocalism. Dickson, incidentally, was an American who nabbed her fame in London productions of American musical comedy (as Day did in operetta): *Tip-Toes, Peggy-Ann,* and *Hold Everything,* after *Sally,* her first big one. *Sally* was revived in London in 1942 as *Wild Rose,* this time with Jessie Matthews, who celebrated with a few cuts. Matthews is the only Sally who makes something of the music.

5. *The Top Banana*

You realize what little contact the star comic had with the music in his shows when trying to track down his records. Each made a cut here and there, but of oeuvre there is no show—nothing like a recital of Brice standards or a Merman cast album. Bert Lahr lasted long enough to catch *Two on the Aisle* with his colleagues, but the songs are weak, and a private label released a *Foxy* taped in the theatre in unlistenable sound.

Of this generation only Cantor can be encountered in style, partly because he was a good recording artist but mainly because he instituted the comedy film musical in his series for Samuel Goldwyn in the early 1930s, including an authentic souvenir of the stage *Whoopee.* A double bill of *Kid Millions* and *Roman Scandals* preserves typical Cantor numbers—the cheer-up rouser (to fight Depression), the minstrel special (to fight Jolson), the ribald comic ditty (to fight a culture that admires big men). The Smithsonian's *Whoopee* is the nearest thing to a Cantor cast album, albeit in dance band and studio cuts.

Phil Silvers and Zero Mostel, of a later age, were preserved on film and recordings in full. Mostel's *Fiddler on the Roof* album solemnizes the integration of the comic into art, the last of burlesque's tutees in one of the most self-intent of shows. But Silvers's *Top Banana* preserves one of the last of the chaotic comedy musicals—as does the film, made in the theatre with the stage cast. *Do Re Mi* is a little dull, even with Nancy Walker opposite Silvers.

Failing a compilation of musical comics, try Living Era's *Hollywood Sings,* which takes in Cantor, Groucho Marx, and Clayton, Jackson, and Durante—mainly Durante, in a song he often used on stage, "Can Broadway Do Without Me?," which popularized the now widespread mispronunciation of the Great Glorifier as "Ziegfield." No one—not even Gershwin or Porter—could write for Durante the way Durante could. Other cuts feature Jolson, Astaire, Bill Robinson, Helen Morgan, and Charles King, a serviceable leading man in late Cohan and early Rodgers and Hart. For a record of film personalities, this disc contains a lot of stage trainees, some still observing a stage sound. Note, for instance, Groucho's Savoyard delivery of "Hooray for Captain Spaulding," taken over from the Brothers' Broadway vehicle *Animal Crackers.*

6 and 7. *The Book and the Score*

First, Jerome Kern. As his last show appeared in 1939, fresh Kern is all 78s, medleys and singles—no cast albums except of London productions or American revivals. Folkways has transcribed solos and medleys in *The Theatre Lyrics of P. G. Wodehouse,* virtually a tour through Kern's Princess shows. There are also full-length sets of the 1976 Goodspeed revival of *Very Good Eddie,* the 1918 London *Oh, Boy!* (retitled *Oh Joy!*), and the 1959 off-Broadway *Leave It to Jane.* DRG's *Eddie* is a treat. Numerous deletions and interpolations defeat the researcher, but the style is sure and every number a gem. (For the record as the album is mum: "Good Night Boat" and "Left All Alone Again Blues" are from *The Night Boat,* "Hot Dog!" was deleted from *The Bunch and Judy,* "Honeymoon Inn" is from *Have a Heart,* "Moon of Love" from *Hitchy-Koo of 1920,* "Katy-Did" from *Oh, I Say!,* and "Bungalow in Quogue" and "If You're a Friend of Mine" are themselves odd interpolations, the latter with the same tune as the hit from *The Stepping Stones,* "In Love with Love.")

Oh, Boy! has never impressed me. Kern's biographer Gerald Bordman thinks it one of Kern's best scores, so buffs should browse. The London cast includes Beatrice Lillie, but the twelve cuts neglect my nomination for best *Oh, Boy!* tune, "Flubby-Dub the Caveman." Strand's *Leave It to Jane* is superb, very stylish and spirited, with lead-in dialogue for that touch of theatre. "A Peach of a Life" and "What I'm Longing To Say" are missing, but "Poor Prune" is reinstated. Note George Segal in a minor part.

Of Kern's second period, a London *Sunny* comes back across the Atlantic with Binnie Hale, Elsie Randolph, and Jack Buchanan. But of such wonderful scores as *Good Morning, Dearie* (1921) and *The Stepping Stones* (1923) there is little—not even a medley. To fill out the canon, try Bagley's *Revisited* disc, one of his earliest and most faithful disinterments, led by Barbara Cook and Bobby Short at their best, and World's British 78 compilations. The first includes *Oh, Joy!, Sally,* and a number of spot rarities and the second treats the senior Kern of *The Cat and the Fiddle, Music in the Air,* and two shows seen only in England, *Blue Eyes* and *The Three Sisters.*

The third period brings us to *Show Boat.* First off, Paul Whiteman issued a two-sided 78 medley of the six hits, furiously paced, with Paul Robeson utterly defeated by the dance tempo in "Ol' Man River." The 1928 London cast made some cuts (including "In Dahomey," not recorded elsewhere) and Brunswick's album (now on a Columbia LP), timed to Ziegfeld's 1932 revival, pulled in Morgan and Robeson. Still, while *Show Boat* holds a record as the only musical to produce six absolute standards, its score has a great deal more than these six—"Life on the Wicked Stage," for instance, or the fastidiously breezy "Till Good Luck Comes My Way," or "Queenie's Ballyhoo," an adjunct to the banjo-plucking suggestions in "Cotton Blossom" and "Ol' Man River."

Show Boat is adaptable. Tommy Dorsey put out an album in forties dance-band approach; Victor tried it with opera singers (Robert Merrill, Patrice Munsel, and Risë Stevens). Both are amusing. But *Show Boat* needs a *cast* album, rehearsed and performed. In this, the 1946 revival on Columbia holds several aces. Hammerstein coached it, the casting is first rate, and the atmosphere is that of the theatre. Ten twelve-inch 78 sides give full measure (unfortunately to only nine songs and a new overture). A *Show Boat* buff I know, miffed at the cuts Hammerstein made at the expense of the comic elements, calls the 1946 *Show Boat* "the *Carousel* version." It does seem a little heavy in ballads.

In 1962 Columbia put out a not very theatrical LP with Barbara Cook, John Raitt, Anita Darian, and William Warfield, conducted by Franz Allers. Everyone's in good voice, Cook much better here than in the 1966 Lincoln Center try (on Victor), and it's a treat to hear Fay de Witt, the super-belt chorus leader of *Flahooley,* in "Life on the Wicked Stage." But the conducting is dainty, the chorus sounding like people who have never seen a musical, let alone been in one. Moreover, the LP doesn't try to get in much of the score. (It does include the buck-and-wing dance in the first-act finale, another rarity.)

How to assemble a complete *Show Boat?* Only "Hey Feller" has never been recorded. Start with Morgan and Robeson on Brunswick, add in Tess Gardella's "Ballyhoo" with the original conductor and a theatre orchestra and chorus (on Music Masters' *Music of Broadway: 1927*) and the London cast's "In Dahomey." This provides a nucleus of Ziegfeldian authenticity. Then combine a few LPs to pick up the odd items like "I Might Fall Back on You" and "Till Good Luck Comes My Way" that turn up rarely. Did no one think to try a two-disc *Show Boat* with all the songs? EMI says it did. When it recorded the 1971 London revival, it put out a single disc crammed with material and a two-disc special claiming to contain the whole score in all versions. It doesn't. The revival itself was a lively affair, with handsome lovers and amusing comics, but the modern orchestrations shock purists and Cleo Laine's Julie throws the time setting off with her jazzy renditions. Angel Records promises a total Show Boat for 1988.

There are two soundtracks, from 1936 to 1951, the first on a private label and infinitely preferable for its stage-trained cast of Irene Dunne (from the tour), Allan Jones (from a summer shot), Helen Morgan, Paul Robeson, Charles Winninger (all three from Broadway), and Hattie McDaniel (from a west coast shot). The authors strengthened the theatre motif in 1936, giving Magnolia a coon song for the show boat olio and taking the camera into a Broadway house to catch daughter Kim's debut. A new song, "Gallivantin' Around," supplies both scenes, and here's your one chance to hear it—worth the trouble, as it's flawless period pastiche. Note the business with the "moon effect," a lit candle carried across the backdrop from behind to the crowd's simple thrill. Note Winninger's own prideful thrill—his naïve love of the theatre turns the key into *Show Boat*'s theme.

Another curiosity is the *Show Boat* tone poem Kern constructed at Artur Rodzinski's commission for the Cleveland Orchestra, no medley but a development of the melodies in conformation to the story line. Rodzinski recorded it, but Andre Kostelanetz's reading with the Philadelphia Pops on Columbia is more exciting. These "symphonic scenarios," as they were called, were popular in the 1940s and early 1950s; Robert Russell Bennett arranged *South Pacific* and *Kiss Me, Kate* in this form. These two are little better than potpourris. Kern's plan is more incisive, though it disappoints when the "Dahomey" prelude tapers off just when we expect the barbaric "Dahomey" chorus to come crashing into glory.

Later Kern is best heard on the Music Masters two-disc volume of Kern soundtracks, of *Sweet Adeline, Music in the Air,* and *Roberta* (plus two screen originals, *High, Wide and Handsome* and *Joy of Living*). Irene Dunne seems to be in nearly everything, and she's a fine Kern stylist (even if Kern didn't think so). *Roberta* has Astaire, Rogers, "I Won't Dance," and "Lovely To Look At," all added for the film version. Sadly, single albums of these shows haven't gone well, and *The Cat and the Fiddle,* which demands the full-time LP treatment, claims only an EP of four cuts and a side of an Epic LP, backed by *Hit the Deck.*

Of retrospectives, Walden's two-disc set features a delightful rediscovery in the early "Go, Little Boat." A long forgotten disc by Marion Marlowe on Design, entitled *Dearly Beloved,* offers a stunning soprano in ten classics. Camp collectors may know of her, for Design was one of those bizarre fifties labels found in supermarkets (sample another Design title: *Golden Hits of Italy by the Botti-Endor Quartet*), and Marlowe appears on the cover yawning *en negligée* before a petite *table à toilette*. But the singing is terrific, and so are the arrangements, their fifties beat aside. Touches like the use of a bit of *Porgy and Bess* as a riff in "Can't Help Lovin' Dat Man," blues on blues, so to speak, suggest an imagination at work. Purists will prefer the venerable Irene Dunne 78 set. A few great non-cast album Kern cuts: "Left All Alone Again Blues": Marion Harris; "Who": Harry Archer and his Orchestra (for dancing); "Smoke Gets in Your Eyes": Gladys Swarthout; "The Blue Danube Blues": Barbara Cook and Bobby Short; "You Never Knew About Me": Joan Morris and Max Morath.

Now, Irving Berlin. A good way to test Berlin's cultural-chronological reach is to compare Ella Fitzgerald's set with World's compilation of the earliest Berlin 78s, all quirky, shrill, parodistic vaudevilliana with percussive oompah. To encompass the utterly astonishing Lew Hearn and Bonita on "Snookey Ookums" in 1913 as well as mellow Ella in the 1950s is to have the whole world in one's hands. And note that while Berlin's first Broadway score, *Watch Your Step,* dates to 1914, he survived to see five shows get the cast album treatment, the last as late as in 1962. *Annie Get Your Gun* has had a number of them—original cast, 1966 revival, a second Merman remake, Mary Martin and John Raitt in the 1957 television "spectacular," Doris Day and Robert Goulet, even a German cast, *Annie Schiess Los!*. You're wondering how "There's No Business Like Show Business" translates into German: "Schauspieler sind Schauspieler" (Show people are show people). The desert island Berlin disc is Joan Morris's *The Girl on the Magazine Cover,* early and middle Berlin in gala style. Listen for the typical Berlin contrapuntal effect in "Pack Up Your Sins"—Morris does both parts with a double track. A few great Berlin cuts: "It's a Lovely Day Tomorrow": Binnie Hale; also Gladys Swarthout; "Tell Me, Little Gypsy": Paul Whiteman's woodwinds (a jazz classic); "They Say It's Wonderful": Jo Stafford; "How's Chances": Ella Fitzgerald; "Harlem on My Mind": Bobby Short.

George and Ira Gershwin: the rise of jazz. George, before Ira joined him, shows no individuality on *Primrose,* a London show—the only Gershwin score preserved with its debut cast. Thereafter, it's George and Ira in trim. *Lady, Be Good!* and *Funny Face* are available in the London casts with the Astaires, but the West End *Tip Toes* is choice, Ira's lyrics just beginning to witicize, so to say, and George's rhythm charging up. This score has fewer hits but more information about the style. *Oh, Kay!* is the best score yet, and offers alternatives: Engel's Columbia try, complete with piano duo in the pit, the 1960 off-Broadway revival (with interpolations), and a Smithsonian reconstruction with the original duo-pianists, Arden and Ohman. This piano emphasis is essential to Gershwin's style; each of the three Smithsonian discs features George at the keyboard. Piano tricks are composed into Gershwin's songs. He himself tells of adopting Mike Bernard's "habit of playing the melody in the left hand while he wove a filigree of counterpoint with the right." *Girl Crazy,* in 1930, becomes the most Gershwinesque of scores, not a note in it possibly sounding like anything but our piano-tricking Gershwin. Engel again made the first LP, with Mary Martin all over the place but no suggestion of Willie Howard's cab driver. *Of Thee I Sing* comes off best of all, in the 1952 revival, a theatre performance to the life with Jack Carson, Betty Oakes, and Lenore Lonergan. Victor Moore was to have come out of retirement to play Throttlebottom again, but he pulled out at the last minute, fearing that he had been jinxed in the theatre; Paul Hartman replaced him. Beware the 1972 television production, with Carroll O'Connor, Cloris Leachman, and Michele Lee.

In recitals, Fitzgerald is paramount; here jazz connects to jazz across the years. However, Bobby Short's set comes full up to the palm. In standards ("Embraceable You"), rediscovery ("Do What You Do"), and piano medley (from *Porgy and Bess*), Short dazzles. Morris's Nonesuch disc is tasty. Bagley's disc holds largely to the early Gershwin of the *Scandals* but neglects the piano basis in the arrangements. Still, he has an apt cast, with Short (no doubling *vis-à-vis* his recital), Barbara Cook and Anthony Perkins delightful in "Under a One Man Top," and Elaine Stritch forceful in "Virginia (don't go too far)." Stritch, of course, goes too far; that's her joy. Bagley also put out an Ira Gershwin disc, one of his worst. Michael Tilson Thomas and Columbia bring out six overtures in *Gershwin on Broadway,* implausibly reorchestrated from the sleek pit tone to fit the Buffalo Philharmonic like a colossal baggie. It sounds like the Bremen Town Musicians to me, but Gershwin set great store by his overtures, and some of them are quite symphonic, so perhaps it's allowable. Or perhaps not: when we hear John McGlinn's authentic recollections of the pit band on Angel's *Gershwin Overtures,* a more adventurous program than Thomas's in the sound of the day. *Primrose* reprieves itself, as modern sonics let the avid jive at last burst through.

A few great Gershwin cuts: "Summertime": Ethel Waters; also Eleanor Steber; "Nashville Nightingale": Marion Harris; also Bobby Short; "Sam and Delilah": Scrappy Lambert, Duke Ellington Orchestra; "I Got Rhythm": Valaida Snow, vocal and trumpet (a scat classic); "But Not for Me": Polly Bergen; "Hang On to Me": Joan Morris and Max Morath; "The Lorelei": Ella Fitzgerald; also Morris; "Oh, So Nice": Fitzgerald; "K-ra-zy for You": Short.

Rodgers and Hart. Surprise: *Dearest Enemy* has been recorded complete on a little British label, Beginners Productions, just for the fun of it. A few musicians and a lively cast have caught Rodgers and Hart at their start, with the forms of older masters tugging them one way and their own lights leading them onward in another. This is a great score, no duds—and notice how nicely the outline of the story comes through in the lyrics. Thereafter we pass a decade with no complete documents save Music Masters' transcriptions of soundtracks to *Love Me Tonight* and such. Most of the famous later shows have been recorded; these are virtually current properties, still good for a revival in stock or showcase. Of *Chee-Chee, The Girl Friend,* or *America's Sweetheart,* we have only a few dance band cuts, but *On Your Toes* has been done twice (Columbia studio cast and Decca revival), *Babes in Arms* claims a Mary Martin-Jack Cassidy Columbia LP, Bagley has a neat *Too Many Girls,* and *The Boys From Syracuse* and *Pal Joey* count three LPs each (Columbia, revival, and London casts). *Pal Joey* has an odd disc history. Neither Vivienne Segal nor Gene Kelly made singles in 1940. Segal joined Harold Lang for the Engel LP, and both went on to the 1952 revival—but Capitol's revival cast rings in Jane Frohman and Dick Beavers, both a little smooth for this gritty entry. The 1980 London revival is grand. Sian Phillips is the ultimate in cynical suave, and while Denis Lawson is cavalier about notes and rhythm and overdoes the accent, he does recreate O'Hara's sexy heel. The scaled-down orchestrations respect the originals, and the similarly smallish women's chorus is a delight. Atmospheric, a must—and a fascinating comparison with the next and last Rodgers-Hart score, *By Jupiter,* as whimsical and sweet as *Pal Joey* is captious. Victor caught a fine off-Broadway revival.

There is one original cast Rodgers and Hart album, from overture to finale, Decca's, of the 1943 revival of *A Connecticut Yankee* with Vivienne Segal as Morgan le Fay. Segal had started as a conventional operetta heroine—Margot in the original *Desert Song,* for instance—but longed to show her comic abilities. Rodgers and Hart obliged in *I Married an Angel* and *Pal Joey;* now they beefed up le Fay for her, adding in "To Keep My Love Alive." Segal does all the verses of the song (as few do), but does them all exactly the same way. The album gives one a chance to hear what Vera-Ellen's singing voice is like—she was dubbed in her Hollywood musicals. To fill in on some other Rodgers and Hart shows, try the Music Masters two-disc set of 78 transcriptions—a lot of *Too Many Girls;* a few cuts by original performers in *Jumbo, I Married an Angel, Higher and Higher,* and *Heads Up;* Helen Morgan in two ballads from *Peggy-Ann;* Rodgers himself in a medley from the Bing Crosby film *Mississippi.* (Warning: the title song for *I'd Rather Be Right* is not the one used in the show.)

On recitals, Ronny Whyte and Travis Hudson deliver finds and standards in *It's Smooth, It's Smart, It's Rodgers and Hart,* to Whyte's ample piano (and kazoos on "What's the Use of Talking?"). A long-lost Barbara Cook LP on Urania is a treasure; apply to fanatics for tapes. Bagley has four *Revisited*s on this team. The first—his debut in the series—is sensational, free of bizarrerie and pointed in ballad or novelty. Volume Two is repulsive; in "A Lady Must Live" he has Blossom Dearie asking Bibi Osterwald, "Do the duke and duchess?" Bibi replies, "Oh, *honey!*" But Volumes III and IV are excellent, keen arranging, keen performances, keen rediscoveries. Keen researching, too: Arthur Siegel proves how impossible it was to write for Jimmy Durante in a number from *Jumbo,* Anthony Perkins, Lynn Redgrave, and Blossom Dearie disinter more ballads dropped from *By Jupiter,* Johnny Desmond delivers the correct title song from *I'd Rather Be Right,* and Redgrave gives the complete version of "I've Got To Get Back to New York," a rouser heard only in fragment in the Jolson film, *Hallelujah, I'm a Bum.*

A few great Rodgers and Hart cuts: "You Took Advantage of Me": Morris and Morath; also Crosby, Beiderbecke, Trumbauer, and Whiteman; "It Never Entered My Mind": Leontyne Price; "Wait Till You See Her": Barbara Cook; "I've Got Five Dollars": Short; also Fitzgerald; "Why Can't I?": Charlotte Rae; "Where's That Rainbow?": Barbra Streisand; "My Heart Stood Still": Gladys Swarthout (despite a lyric flub in the verse); "This Is My Night To Howl": Travis Hudson; "Fool Meets Fool': Lynn Redgrave; *By Jupiter* piano medley: Peter Mintun.

Cole Porter. Sadly, his very characteristic early scores have not been recorded except for the few standards. Fred Astaire, Erik Rhodes, and Eric Blore from the stage *Gay Divorce* all made the film, *The Gay Divorcee,* but the EMI soundtrack is no help, as only "Night and Day" was retained. Not till *Nymph Errant* do we get a kind of album, Lawrence in five songs and Elizabeth Welch singing her numbo, "Solomon." Welch, a New York social worker, was one of the original Blackbirds in 1928 and settled in London at the time of *Nymph Errant,* in which she played a harem girl who speaks a few lines and then pops into "Solomon." She made a great effect in the part, and became (like fellow Americans Edith Day and Dorothy Dickson) a major contributor to performing tradition in the British musical, right up to the old-survivor role of Berthe in *Pippin.* She recorded her one *Pippin* song for World.

The Porter scene widens as of *Anything Goes.* Ethel Merman recorded her four big tunes at various times; Jack Whiting, Jeanne Aubert, and others from the 1935 London run left six songs, Aubert in an impenetrable French accent but lots of whizz. The show's first full album derives from the 1962 off-Broadway version, with Hal Linden, Eileen Rodgers, Barbara Lang, and Porter interpolations. (This revision is now in general use.) The 1969 London staging of this version failed, and Decca decided not to release the disc, though it had been recorded and packaged. A very few copies glided out of the warehouse, making this *Anything Goes* the rarest of LP cast albums, till TE released it in 1984.

Jubilee was passed by except for Paul Whiteman's brilliant two-sided medley. Even Artie Shaw's Bluebird disc of "Begin the Beguine," which made both the song and Shaw hits for the first time, came out in 1938, three years after the show opened. An astonishing document is preserved on Columbia's *Cole:* Porter's own renditions of nine of the songs, made to assist the cast in mastering the style. Porter's was a nasal, unsteady voice and his piano style nothing to leave home for, but his sure rhythm and unabashed *esprit* is what his style most needs, so the performances are fascinating. Columbia filled out the flip side with classic Porter, two songs each from Mary Martin (*Leave It To Me*), Danny Kaye (*Let's Face It*) and Ethel Merman (*Anything Goes*), who may have learned them off just such a medley as this one from *Jubilee.* A festival of style, with lots of photos and notes.

With *Mexican Hayride* we enter cast album territory, though Decca did not enlist Bobby Clark; the show's baritone Wilbur Evans takes Clark's numbo, "Girls," perhaps the most typical thing Clark ever did. *Kiss Me, Kate* has had two original cast albums, exceptionally, as the original stars and conductor went back to the studio for a stereo duplicate eleven years after their first go, using exactly the same text as before, note for note: still using the entr'acte instead of the overture (which doesn't end but runs right into the show for a *coup de théâtre*) and still omitting "We Sing of Love." The Columbia original remains a classic in catching a show on disc, and the Capitol remake finds everyone in trim in better sound.

Porter's successive scores and casts are less fetching. *Out of This World* does have Charlotte Greenwood, a regional favorite decades before for her *Letty Peppers* musicals, but George Gaynes's basso spreads over the place like Sargasso weed, and generally this score feels smutty rather than wicked. (A last good list song, however, in "Cherry Pies Ought To Be You." For a twist, Greenwood and David Burns deliver a complementary "hate" version, a kind of "You're the Bottom.") *Can-Can* is fun, but why does Lilo keep putting an "m" on the ends of lines ending in vowels (e.g., "Try to remember, ma bellem")?

Silk Stockings was fast and funny, but its score is dull and Victor's halfhearted album duller. Porter's final score, for television and dullest yet, was *Aladdin*, though Barbra Streisand revived "Come to the Supermarket (in old Peking)" with success. The British staged it as a Christmas pantomime, filled out with more Porter; reissued on Stet.

On the retrospective, Music Masters has two albums. One record collects Decca's *Mexican Hayride*, some cuts from *Seven Lively Arts* and *Around the World*, and some tapes of Merman, Lahr, and Bob Hope live onstage. A two-disc set presents Porter himself, the Whiteman *Jubilee* medley, another medley for *Red, Hot and Blue!*, Merman's Liberty *Panama Hattie* quartet, a wartime broadcast of *Something for the Boys* hits with William Johnson, Mary Jane Walsh's Liberty *Let's Face It* cuts, and other treats. From the cynical "Gigolo" to the sentimental "Only Another Boy and Girl," from the list song to the intent ballad, from celebrity plugola to the rhythm numbo, this is Porter in all his parts, sung by supreme stylists. One lack: not a single song on these two records really needs a theatre context to go over. It's all Hit Tunes.

Great singers like Porter for that reason: a whole show in a song, nothing missing. Ella's two-disc set may be her best issue, and Bobby Short's is one of the most impressive pop recitals of any kind. Hubbell Pierce is not in their company on sheer voice, but he has a wry way with these lyrics; and heavyweights wrote the liner notes for his privately issued disc—Julius Monk of the cabaret revue and Rogers E. M. Whitaker of *The New Yorker* Jazzmen, too, love Porter, for his chromatic provocations and devious rhythm. Trombonist Wilbur de Paris, on Atlantic, runs the standards through a Dixieland groove. Even the elite *concertiste* craves her Porter: mezzo Jan de Gaetani, on Columbia's *Classic Cole*. An expert in Schoenbergian modernism, de Gaetani treats the songs with great respect, straight on, and her accompanist Leo Smit plays for the most part right off the song sheets as if they were Schubert. (Smit also writes intriguing liner notes.) Some Porter buffs dislike de Gaetani's expertise; they want the hip *Schlamperei* of the theatre. But I suggest that this music has never sounded better; and de Gaetani gives full measure in nineteen songs on one disc, verses and all. Taking sheet music as documentary art has the drawback that few composers write out piano parts. But Porter worked closely with Chappell's editor Albert Sirmay, so Porter's sheets, at least, are authentic. Nay, they're better: when you hear Smit strike up the vamp to "At Long Last Love," it *does* sound like Schubert. A great recording.

Bagley has a lot of Porter, an original cast of a Porter revue and four volumes of *Revisited*s. The revue, led by Kaye Ballard and Harold Lang, is the best, impish but not ghouly. Volume I has a fine choice of songs plus Ballard and Short; Volume II overdoes Porter's camp side; Volume III is erratic but contains the best cuts in Lynn Redgrave's "A Lady Needs a Rest" and "I Want To Be Raided By You," Helen Gallagher's "Make a Date with a Great Psychoanalyst," and a lubricious delight dropped from *Can-Can,* "Her Heart Was in Her Work"; Volume IV is not good, though it does allow Dolores Gray to sing her number from *Seven Lively Arts,* "Is It the Girl (or is it the gown)?" Perhaps the best "revisited" album is Victor's *Cole,* a London revue that runs through Porter's work chronologically. Because the text is recorded along with the songs, the two discs end up as a bio, a beautifully stylish one. If Bagley listened, would he mend his ways?

These giants were the top of Broadway. Some might add Vincent Youmans to the list, in which case Evergreen's two-disc *Through the Years* is a useful survey and *No, No, Nanette* the indicated full-score LP. Take Columbia's album of the 1971 Broadway revival with EMI's studio cast to assemble the whole score—each disc has cuts the other lacks. Both were reorchestrated, Columbia's especially. But to go back to the 78s made by the cast of the London premiere (which opened before the Broadway one) yields a West End flavor quite unlike that of Broadway. Shows with a Gaiety base, however much buried, like *Lady, Be Good!,* weren't all that different in the two cities, especially as the Astaires led both productions. But *No, No, Nanette* derives from the tradition of the American bumble farce, with rustic performers like Charles Winninger for whom there were no British equivalents. In London, *No, No, Nanette* featured a performer like George Grossmith, son of a founding member of the Gilbert and Sullivan style and the very essence of Gaiety la-di-da.

What of more conventional fare? De Sylva, Brown, and Henderson represent the best of the devoutly unambitious, and their *Good News* has been released on two records by Wayne Bryan, Bobby in the 1974 revival, on the proceeds of his winning streak on a television game show. Bryan put together one disc's worth of straight performance (from theatre sound systems, presumably) with a second disc of addenda to catch most of the original score, other songs by the authors that were toyed with on the revival's lengthy tryouts, and a taste of rehearsals. It was not a great production; too much of 1927 was lost in a mess of humdrum 1974, and the presence of Alice Faye and John Payne further skewed the timeplace with their echoes of Fox threesome musicals of the 1930s and 1940s. The last word in *Good News* recordings is sounded, *un peu rudement,* in an obscure private recording of the Queens Community Theatre production of 1971, with the complete original score, including the idiotic opening chorus of mis-accented words, Babe's "Flaming Youth," and the secondary couple's comic duets, "Baby! What?" and "In the Meantime," not recorded elsewhere. The women leads, belt, soprano, and comedienne, are dynamite.

8. *The New Style of Heroine*

Helen Morgan's legend has dwindled into the picture of a woman sitting on a piano holding a handkerchief belting out torch songs. Morgan sat on pianos in her various speakeasies, another one opened directly the last one was padlocked, but she was all head-voice soprano. Indeed, her high wail was what made her torch songs singularly affecting. Polly Bergen played her on television and registered an LP of Morgan hits, vocally inaccurate but interesting. Better sample Morgan herself on Audio Rarities' collection of fourteen standards.

Gertrude Lawrence didn't record much, but her four most famous roles are on disc in whole or part. *Oh, Kay!* is the skimpiest, just three cuts. All are prime; the

Smithsonian album includes both London and New York versions, London's in theatre atmosphere and New York's slicker, for the studio. In seeking out the *Nymph Errant* 78s, auditioners who sing "The Physician" should note how Lawrence spins through the list lines strictly in rhythm, saving her *Luftpausen* for the release. Nothing ruins a Porter list song more than the amateur's laughter-spaces.

Lawrence typically dawdled on the matter of the *Lady in the Dark* album for Victor, and was furious when radio singer Hildegarde scooped her on Decca. Both albums are worth hearing, Hildegarde giving a fuller "Jenny" and Lawrence's team catching more of the score. Those who question just how irreplaceable Lawrence was can sample two complete LP versions of *Lady in the Dark*. Risë Stevens, on Columbia, is sluggish and prim; she sounds as if she's preparing to play a dull Anna in *The King and I*, which she duly did, at Lincoln Center. The Victor *Lady in the Dark* dates from a 1954 TV version with Ann Sothern, very right for the part. But even Sothern lacks Lawrence's urgency, her quizzical aplomb. Lawrence lived long enough to make an original cast album: *The King and I*. A classic performance.

William Gaxton and Jack Whiting—and the numerous others who played roles like theirs—may have been crucial to the musical but not to show biz as music. They have left few telling souvenirs from their prime, Whiting's London *Anything Goes* cuts being the best of them and at that he's miscast. Whiting also lasted out into the cast-album era in *The Golden Apple* and *Hazel Flagg;* these are great numbers, but they have nothing to do with who Whiting had been. Alfred Drake, of a later vintage and a more solid sound, can be heard to advantage on *Kiss Me, Kate, Kismet,* and *Kean.* Perhaps *Kismet* is the best for its stupendous orchestrations by Arthur Kay. Columbia's cast album re-creates the spaciousness of the show; it's also a chance to hear Richard Kiley as a juvenile; Brooklyn's own Doretta Morrow, one of the last of the pure operetta soubrettes, the original Tuptim in *The King and I;* and the amazing Joan Diener of the uncategorizable voice, deep, wide, and high. The Lincoln Center revival, also with Drake, on Victor, is in clearer sound but somehow misses the original's barbaric glitter (also its marvelous overture). One new song, for Anne Jeffries, "Bored," written for MGM's *Kismet* film. *Kismet* without Drake makes one appreciate him more. 1964 saw two new *Kismet*s. Capitol's has Gordon MacRae and Dorothy Kirsten merrily singing their way through the score as if it were *I Do! I Do!* London's has a full cast and conductor Mantovani respects Kay's scoring. But while it is fun to hear Regina Resnik as Lalume gaming with her heavy Met mezzo, Robert Merrill's Hajj is a fiasco.

Ethel Merman was a great recording artist, yet her discography is small, taking her through not enough cast albums and too many remakes of some fifteen or so songs closely associated with her. In brief: first there are her thirties singles for Victor and Brunswick, and her soundtracks (only recently issued). Later in the decade and slipping into the 1940s are her mini-albums for Liberty of *Red, Hot and Blue!, Stars in Your Eyes,* and *Panama Hattie.* As of 1946 and *Annie Get Your Gun* the original cast albums begin to come. In the 1950s there are LP recitals, including the two-disc *A Musical Autobiography,* mainly reissues of Decca file material with Merman delivering a running commentary to organ noodling. Stereo brings more recitals. Lastly there was a disco album, the warhorses trotted out yet again and ground out to the idiot beat.

It sounds like a lot. But the constant repetition of the standards and the heavy recording schedule after the voice had lost its bloom (if a belt can be said to have bloom at all) reduce the pickings. Then, too, there is the Merman precision, which turns out each song *exactly* the same way each time, even over the course of forty years. Listen to *Merman Sings Merman,* her London LP of 1972 (with atrocious arrangements), including "I Get a Kick Out of You," "Eadie Was a Lady," and others such. Compare these cuts with the earlier versions. There's literally no difference in Merman.

Columbia has transferred the Brunswicks onto LP (Mae West and Lyda Roberti take the flip); this is heavy Merman, with two cuts of *Anything Goes,* a complete "Eadie Was a Lady" (the 78 original covered both sides), and some piquant novelties. The aforementioned Music Masters Porter sets bring in *Panama Hattie* and *Something for the Boys,* and two live cuts from the late 1930s for those who want to test out the Merman belt in the theatre in its prime. Jump then to *Annie Get Your Gun,* in Decca's original cast setting, for Merman at her senior best, comic, lovelorn, competitive. *Call Me Madam* gave her less to work with. As with *Annie,* she dominates the score, doesn't just center the show but spreads out through it through the songs. But while Victor made the cast album, Decca held Merman by contract and made its own *Call Me Madam* in a studio rendition. Victor has the theatre atmosphere (and Dinah Shore, miscast), but Decca has Merman and, thus, the show.

Happy Hunting, on Victor, is prized by collectors for its gauche fun. Some of the worst songs ever written for a musical are here,* but Merman rises above it, actually enjoying herself on "Mutual Admiration Society" and "A New-Fangled Tango." She does sound a little stumped by "The Game of Love," but she is at her best in a numbo, "Gee, But It's Good To Be Here." *Gypsy,* alas, is the last of Merman on stage. After Channing, Bailey, and Martin (not to mention Tatjana Iwanow in German and Annie Cordy in French) had all made LPs of *Hello, Dolly!,* there seemed little commerce left in a Merman fourth. Ironically, the show was written for her. She did produce her own 45 of two of the songs, a curio in that they were dropped when Channing was hired and only reinstated for Merman. They do not represent Jerry Herman's best work.

Merman came in fully formed, Eadie is a lady; Mary Martin's ambiguous image clouds her early 78 set of Cole Porter songs for Decca, the album emblazoned with glamor-girl photos and featuring rather uninflected renditions, even of her numbo, "My Heart Belongs to Daddy." Martin's role cast her as a sexpot; she is anything but. Sophie Tucker, who was nothing but, gave Martin instructions, famous in showbiz legend, to look toward heaven on the sexy lines. It sounds right, but it seems unlikely that Martin knew which lines were sexy, even such giveaways as "to dine on my fine Finnan haddie" and "I never dream of making the team."

One Touch of Venus has a provisional cast album—ten cuts with Kenny Baker and the theatre pit without the rest of the cast—but that same capable, impersonal singing style, brightened only when Weill's jazz finally gets to her on "I'm a Stranger Here Myself." She is even more lost as Madame Salvador in *Pacific 1860,* Noël Coward's operetta produced in London, though it provided her first all-out cast album. But Annie Oakley found her and Nellie Forbush owns her; Capitol caught Martin's *Annie* (with John Raitt) and Columbia has *South Pacific.* But what if

---

* *The* worst, "For Love or Money," didn't make it on to the record: it marked one of the last views of an unreconstructed Ziegfeldian Girl number.

Peter Pan is the most Martin of parts, wherein she cavorts and crows most freely (and revives her coloratura soprano)? Interesting to compare "Doin' What Comes Natur'lly" with "A Wonderful Guy" with "I've Gotta Crow." Which comes closest to the magic core? Another comparison: Jean Arthur's more Barriesque hero, on Columbia (with a few songs by Leonard Bernstein), set against Martin's version, on Victor. Julie Andrews buffs regard Martin's Maria von Trapp in *The Sound of Music* as interloping, but, after all, the authors wanted Martin first off, and she certainly answers the demands of the part, even unto the yodeling in "The Lonely Goatherd."

Vocally, *Jennie* is Martin's most expansive role, and *I Do! I Do!* true tedium. *Hello, Dolly!* capitalizes on her whimsical grit, and the London cast album is a treat. If Martin and Merman both played fine and very different Annies, Martin was the superior Dolly, almost human in the part against heavy odds. For years, there had been suspicions of a feud between Merman and Martin, fired by Merman's oft-quoted remark, on Martin, "All she's got is talent." Merman never said it; some journalist did. Anyway, they dovetail nicely on Decca's ten-inch LP of the Ford anniversary television show, one side devoted to their marathon medley duet of old standards, "I" songs, and numbos. Who got first billing? The album came out with the same "cover" on both sides. On one side, Merman stood on the left in the photograph and her name came first. On the other side, Decca flopped the picture and put Martin's name first. There's no business like show business.

9. The Jazzmen

Turnabout has recorded *Blue Monday Blues,* but this is merest projection next to *Porgy and Bess.* For years, the only recording was Victor's 78 highlights set, made under Gershwin's supervision. Helen Jepson is not only white but pale; Lawrence Tibbett, however, is grand and Alexander Smallens the best *Porgy* conductor of all. Decca released two sets of highlights using the original cast (Anne Brown, the first Bess, does all three soprano leads) under Smallens, less exciting here, and Leo Reisman put out a set of eight dance-band cuts with *Porgy* veterans Avon Long and Helen Dowdy. Decca's albums, stuffed onto one LP, proved the most enduring, though Engel's three-LP set of 1951 with Lawrence Winters and Camilla Williams affirmed the work's integrity for a post-Gershwin generation. Exciting in its spontaneity and beautifully sung, Engel's reading might easily have been the cast album of a major revival—sure enough, the famous four-year tour that brought *Porgy* to La Scala and the Bolshoi followed hard upon it. Victor superseded the Decca disc in 1963 with highlights with Leontyne Price, William Warfield, John W. Bubbles, stereo sound, and a cover photo of Price and Warfield in action that no curio collector could pass up. It's a gala performance (under Skitch Henderson), maybe a little Broadway; maybe *Porgy and Bess* should be. Price and Warfield had been in the tour and Bubbles was the original Sporting Life, so the disc has history as well as art.

A number of black singers have put out their own *Porgy* recitals in a non-theatre context, among them Sammy Davis, Jr., and, together, Lena Horne and Harry Belafonte. My choice is Diahann Carroll, backed by the André Previn Trio, on United Artists. Some of the ten cuts hold relatively close to the original settings; others are expansive jazz impressions. Carroll is a stunner in this music, and it's interesting to hear her in songs usually reserved for men and in two of the rarer items, "Oh, I Can't Sit Down" and "There's Somebody Knockin' at the Door."

The mid-1970s saw the issue of two three-disc, note-complete sets. Both feature young American singers of reputation, but London's, under Lorin Maazel, suffers from a "conservatory" approach with a classic's Solemnity. Victor's, from the Houston Grand Opera production under John de Main, has bite. It is a *cast* album: not of singers collected in a studio, but of singers who have sweated out performances. The Houston revival itself needed Mamoulian. But these discs sound as if from the theatre all the way.

With Harold Arlen we come to the only Broadway master who was also a distinctive vocalist; naturally, his own recordings make a central study, with their black-Jewish plaint sitting right into the melody. Some composers work at the piano; Arlen wrote on the voice—his. He has left a number of recordings on various labels. I like the two-disc Walden set; it sets him off nicely with younger singers.

Arlen composed nine theatre scores, the last five given cast album treatment. Arlen drilled *Bloomer Girl*'s singers carefully, spending hours with Richard Huey to get down the nuances in "I Got a Song" and appearing on the album himself in "Man for Sale." Decca gave *Bloomer Girl* the treatment, getting down everything but the overture and the dance music (the overture is on Engel's Columbia disc cited below, the ballet on DRG in a piano rendering). The LP reissue deleted half of "Sunday in Cicero Falls." Hearing Mabel Taliaferro leading the operetta-like "Welcome Hinges" side by side with Huey's boogie blues and the bawdy carol of five drummers, "The Farmer's Daughter," brings home the richness of the forties musical, caught midway between tradition and the instigations of the jazz.

House of Flowers, on Columbia, offers a case of the album making more of an impact than the show. Bailey emphasizes this in an ad lib at the end of "One Man Ain't Quite Enough," when she speaks of being "so busy at the theatre." She means the Alvin Theatre, and by separating record performance from stage performance suggests that the show album is no longer an adjunct, but might be a significant presentation on its own. United Artists covered the 1968 off-Broadway revival, but without that great original cast and Ted Royal's orchestrations, it doesn't really play (though it does reinstate material left off the first disc or dropped from the show before the opening).

Fewer singers than one might expect have made Arlen recitals. Perhaps company executives were deterred by his lack of household-word fame, a long-standing joke in Alley circles. Let the essential Arlen disc be Capitol's original cast reading of *St. Louis Woman,* most basic in its all-black cast and ethnic cut of melody. Here, as not in *Bloomer Girl,* one can imagine Arlen singing every number himself. The operatic expansion of *St. Louis Woman, Free and Easy,* written in the wake of the cultural coming out of *Porgy and Bess,* has not been recorded. But, at Andre Kostelanetz' urging, Arlen outlined and Samuel Matlowsky arranged a suite called *Blues-Opera,* drawn from the work, and Kostelanetz recorded it on Columbia. A wonderful piece.

Not till *Street Scene* was Kurt Weill to experience an original cast recording in full, about an hour's worth of the show in an experiential rendering. The album, a hefty pile of 78s, was famous in its day, for the coeval *Finian's Rainbow* and *Brigadoon* were recorded at about the same time with nowhere near the care that Columbia took with the much less commercial *Street Scene. Love Life* was not set down, but one can assemble much of it on Bagley's Lerner and Weill *Revisited*s. Decca's *Lost in the Stars* cast album was wrought to give the stay-at-home the sense of how the show felt, though the dynamic, bitter opening of Act Two, "The Wild Justice," wasn't included. Todd Duncan, the original Porgy, does not impress as the protagonist, a South African village minister whose son stands trial for the murder of a white social reformer. Duncan has voice but little intensity. "I wasn't trying to reproduce the native music of Africa," Weill told the *Times*, "anymore than Maxwell Anderson was trying to provide with words a local-color picture of life there." He made one concession to American jazz pastiche, "Who'll Buy?," a blues on a walking bass.

There are two Weills (among others), one of the savage German shows, the other (from *Knickerbocker Holiday* on) an Americanized and Broadwayized composer, though Broadway was in its turn Weillized. To place the first Weill, hear Teresa Stratas's recital of Weill arcana on Nonesuch, already regarded as one of the classic recitals on LP. Felicia Sanders made a fine disc of the American Weill on Mainstream, with a full orchestra, veering from Weillish arrangements to questionable pop settings. Bagley's *Revisited*s are almost completely out of style. However, he does review interesting material, such as the grotesque "Dr. Crippen," from *One Touch of Venus,* so out of sync with the comic-romantic style of the show that some *Venus* fanatics have been pretending that it never existed. Chita Rivera does a nice job on it.

Consider also Leonard Bernstein's *On the Town*. Here's a work with no apparent ties to Gershwin's opera, to Weill's *Verfremdung* songs, to Arlen's Great American Cotton Club. But there's another jazz—the city music that seemed to distill the aggressive hustle of the American style as it began to coalesce in the 1920s, a vast Chicago-taxis-girders-subways-cranks-and-commercials syncopation of Walt Whitman and Krazy Kat. This is what Bernstein and Robbins caught in music and dance. "Cripes, what I would give to see a good old hoofing chorus," one critic complained. But Victor affirmed ballet's arrival by putting out an *On the Town* album with as much dance music on it as songs. Decca put out an *On the Town* set entirely taken up with songs, some by cast members Walker, Comden, and Green and some by Mary Martin. Columbia's 1960 LP of *On the Town,* with Walker, Comden, Green, John Reardon, and Bernstein, is filled with jazz. Has anyone caught that American city music so exuberantly as Bernstein: here, for innocence; in *Wonderful Town,* for satire; in *West Side Story,* for romantic naturalism? When Bernstein raises *On the Town*'s curtain on sounds evocative on an immense, still space (the Brooklyn Navy Yard just before six a.m., in fact) and slowly awakens the sleeping city through the bluesy yawn of "I Feel Like I'm Not Out of Bed Yet," this is jazz. When Walker rips into "I Can Cook Too," filled with risqué puns and set to a strutting swing boogie, this is jazz. And the naïve cosmopolitanism of the brassy, cross-metered Times Square jive dance is also jazz. Columbia republished this great performance in 1971 with a restored cut, the music students' number, "Do-do-re-do." The 1963 London cast, on CBS, is fine—but who can compete with the unique originals? As for the Bagley Bernstein, the best is too good not to hear.

On the black musical, the classic followup to *Porgy and Bess, Cabin in the Sky,* was recorded in its 1964 off-Broadway revival, a faithful one. In his liner notes, Vernon Duke declares himself pleased with the cast, but they are such terrible singers that the album isn't even a mixed blessing. Too bad—it's the only full-length disc of a first-rate score by the gifted Duke. Bette Davis, in Duke's *Two's Company*, helps see the old headliner revue to its doom, while Bagley's *Littlest Revue* discoveries suggest the exuberance of getting ready to make it. (Tammy Grimes, Charlotte Rae, and Joel Grey even did so.)

Carmen Jones (on Decca) is basically Oscar Hammerstein's translation of Bizet's opera in an American setting for a black cast and an early approach to the super-production in Hassard Short's masterminding of a distinctive look and style. Muriel Smith, who played Bloody Mary and Lady Thiang for Hammerstein in London, leads a game cast, vocally a little uncertain but dramatically persuasive. For a completely different idea, try *Mr. Wonderful* (on Decca), not a black show but a white musical comedy subsuming a black love plot. *Mr. Wonderful* was a vehicle for Sammy Davis, Jr., so much so that it made room for his nightclub act as an eleven o'clock number. The ingenue was the winning Olga James, the comic secondary couple Jack Carter and Pat Marshall, and Chita Rivera was graduated to solo status after her neat job in the trio of streetwalkers in *Seventh Heaven* the year before, 1955.

The classic musical "of color" (as Harlem pride preferred to term them at the time) was 1921's *Shuffle Along*, like the Williams and Walker musicals a revuish book show. Noble Sissle and Eubie Blake wrote the score, Sissle played a part and Blake the pit piano, and New World has collected some of the records they made together of the songs. Perhaps the best of the black shows of this era was *Blackbirds of 1928,* written and produced by whites but presenting a very high grade of black talent. Columbia assembled the relevant singles on LP; and one would do well to follow onto the career of Ethel Waters, the most distinctive talent black show biz threw off. As "Sweet Mama Stringbean" young Waters rivaled even Bessie Smith (to Smith's irritation), singing racy songs of Harlem and Dixie. After *Blackbirds*, she became Broadway's choice black singer, then actress. Somewhere along the way, she repented of her jazzbo irreverences, and restyled her image along nearly graven lines. Yet the dynamic "Heat Wave" and casual "Thief in the Night," with its spoken putdown section ("And don't go bragging 'round Harlem you had an affair with me! . . . You call that little thing an *affair?*") are the songs by which she is recalled. Two Columbia albums recommend themselves, both 78 collections, *Ethel Waters' Greatest Years* (two discs) and *Ethel Waters on Stage and Screen*, which takes in black revues, *As Thousands Cheer, At Home Abroad*, and *Cabin in the Sky:* untouchable stuff.

10. *The Choreographers*

Of course Bernstein had to write the dance music as well as the tunes, not only because he is a finished musician, but because his very urban musicals need the panorama only he can paint. Still, this runs counter to practice. The dances are usually worked out in the choreographer's rehearsals, laboriously; this would drain the composer's time. Most musicals have "dance arrangements," elaborated by an expert out of the score (or his own ideas) to the choreographer's express requirements.

Bernstein was not the first to break with tradition. Victor Herbert wrote his own ballet music, even wrote the big set piece for Kern's *Sally*, the "Butterfly Ballet," a suite in Continental style which the curious can hear on the West End cast records. Before the dance revolution of the 1930s and 1940s, dances scarcely needed to be arranged; the orchestra started the song over again after the vocal and the hoofing began. An early break in the tradition may be heard in "Slaughter on Tenth Avenue," from *On Your Toes*. Rodgers wrote it himself; Hans Spialek scored it; Ray Bolger (the *World-Telegram* called him "a jazz Nijinsky"), Tamara Geva, and George Church led the dancing; and it finished the show on a dazzling note of anticipation of what could follow it in future shows. It has been much recorded, including by the New York Philharmonic with Rodgers conducting (on Columbia). The readings in the *On the Toes* albums are better. Kurt Weill was another composer who wrote his own dance music; Decca included two ballets in the *One Touch of Venus* set.

With dance prominent, cast albums began to include the more notable pieces— A *Tree Grows in Brooklyn*'s "Hallowe'en Ballet," say, or *Seventh Heaven*'s "Gold and Silver" dream, one of the strongest things in the score. Sometimes one has to fuss around a bit to find these cuts. The impudent "Mardi Gras" from *House of Flowers* and "The Embassy Waltz" from *My Fair Lady* did not turn up on the cast albums—but Percy Faith included them on his easy-listening instrumental alternates. (Arlen also recorded "Mardi Gras," piano solo, on Walden, and "The Embassy Waltz" slipped onto the 1976 revival cast.)

Some cast albums capture dance flowing through the score, especially those from the 1950s, when dance of all kinds had been fully assimilated. Let's take one satiric and one romantic show, both set in Manhattan and both by Bernstein: *Wonderful Town* and *West Side Story*. Decca got *Wonderful Town*'s original cast, but Columbia's, drawn from the 1958 television showing, is better, with Rosalind Russell leading the original players, their equals (Jacquelyn McKeever for Edie Adams), or improvements (Sydney Chaplin for the ponderous George Gaynes). Here is a musical where dance is almost all part of the action. The opening "Christopher Street" is punctuated with screwy music for pantomime renditions of Village life—cranks, modern dancers, hepcats, a violent al fresco art show. Later, in "Pass That Football," an athlete waiting out the off-season leads the neighbors in a pass-and-tackle prance, and the first-act finale, "Conga!," starts as a dance lesson, develops into a conga line, and ends in riot. Eileen is thrown in jail for assaulting a cop, but wins the hearts of the precinct boys, prompting Bernstein to turn some Irish pastiche in "My Darlin' Eileen," staged as a group jig. Only one dance number is self-contained, "Ballet at the Village Vortex," and even this is very useful in recalling the anomie of the pioneers in beat.

West Side Story is more thoroughly choreographed. Its Prologue of street gang collisions, "Dance at the Gym" (with a cha-cha setting of "Maria" when the two lovers first meet), "America" (marked *Tempo di Huapango* and showing the same metrical caprices as the Czech *furiant* that Dvořák made famous), "Cool," "The Rumble," and the "Somewhere Ballet" are all on the record; you could scarcely make one without them. Some listeners prefer the *West Side Story* soundtrack, sentimentally (because the film at last put the work over as a popular masterpiece) or because they enjoy the beefier orchestration. Much of the singing is dubbed. Bernstein made a suite of the ballet music, *Symphonic Dances*. His recording is on Columbia; Seiji Ozawa has a competitive one on Deutsche Grammophon.

In the late 1950s, Lehman Engel made a Victor LP of Broadway ballet music— at that, dances never before recorded. Apparently the disc was not released; Bagley issued it on his label as *Ballet on Broadway*. Engel's selection avoided the musical play to capture the more devilish musical comedy approach, featured the great choreographers (Robbins, Cole, de Mille, Kidd), and put the spotlight on the two best arrangers in the business, Genevieve Pitot and Trude Rittman. However, the results are disappointing. The "Bathing Beauty" spoof of *High Button Shoes* is here, as is *Li'l Abner*'s "Sadie Hawkins" chase, but they don't represent the best of the line, and the other pieces are even less worthy. *Can-Can*'s "Garden of Eden," moreover, is a shred of the piece published in the score. Why didn't Engel record *Bloomer Girl*'s "Civil War" ballet, or *Paint Your Wagon*'s "Lonely Men," or *Carousel*'s "Hornpipe," all excellent and at the time unrecorded? These might be "serious," but they're worth hearing. And, as for musical comedy exuberance, one comes closer to the source in "Essie's Vision," the dream dance Roger Adams composed for *Redhead*—storyless, even pointless, but the absolute center of flash vitality. It's on Victor's cast album.

11. *The Musical Play*

Decca's *Oklahoma!*, DA 359, the 78 album that implanted the original cast recording as a staple of the American phonograph, holds up well, sound and all—and *Time-Life* has put that first set together with the little-known appendix of "Lonely Room," "It's a Scandal, It's an Outrage!," and "The Farmer and the Cowman" (two sides), which yields a complete song program. Growing up with the original casts of R & H tends to infix their performances as the only acceptable ones, so that basically unstupendous singers like Joan Roberts, Lee Dixon, Christine Darling, Eric Mattson, and Larry Douglas became the ne plus ultra in style. And certainly the early LP attempts to supersede the originals, such as Columbia's *Oklahoma!* with Nelson Eddy or Victor's *Carousel* with Patrice Munsel, Florence Henderson, and Robert Merrill, do not remotely challenge Decca's authority. Eddy is a tedious Curly, Merrill a clumsy Billy. Even the expansion of stereo did not at first bring any important additions to the R & H canon, though producers were ingenious in devising "effects" to induce the public to cross over from trusty mono to stereo Equipment.

The 1979 *Oklahoma!* revival finally brought in a cast album superior to the original—conducted, ironically, by the original conductor, Jay Blackton. Victor's Thomas Z. Shepard produced a disc that captures the show to the life, a full score from dialogue lead-ins through reprises. The cast itself is not surpassing; only Christine Andreas as Laurey and Martin Vidnovic as Jud possess truly fine instruments. Yet the excitement of the show is there in every cut; its originality comes through as never before. Thirty-six years after it opened, *Oklahoma!* sounds like a new show, all pep and sly wisdom. The London revival of the following year was recorded live in the theatre, yet Shephard's studio rendering has more tension and immediacy.

This survey touches only a few flashes of history; the whole account takes in not only original but revival casts, British and foreign-language casts, television casts, studio makes, jazz interpretations, instrumental versions, creator LPs like Noël Coward's recording of *Sail Away* or Cy Coleman's of *Barnum,* or bizarre concoctions along the lines of *Two Hundred Banjos Play No Strings,** medleys, singles,

---

* Odd as it seems, many people like show music but not show albums. Whether because the words distract, the slashing theatre style unnerves, or because they don't like the full-scale runthrough with its pushy plot songs, these record buyers would buy the alternate choral

soundtracks—*Oklahoma!* has, by my count, twelve full-length LP recordings, *The King and I* fourteen. Are they all that different? I wouldn't praise Shepard's disc so if they weren't. There are theatre "performers," theatre singers, opera singers, pop singers, in all combinations. Does *Show Boat* need "real" voices or "real" actors? There are variations in text—as we've noted in the shifting selection of numbers on the *Show Boat* records. There is the very thrust of the performance. Easy-listening? Theatre feeling? Theatre intensity? There is simply the matter of how one initiates the experience. The start of the overture on Columbia's *Gypsy,* with its spectacular fanfare of the "I Had a Dream" motive, brass players shooting up and down the scales, and a whistle breaking space for "Everything's Coming Up Roses," sets up a vastly different atmosphere from Victor's *110 in the Shade,* which omits the arousing overture to open on the still, bad heat of the opening number, "Gonna Be Another Hot Day."

The R & H shows don't vary as much as some from production to production. Their London stagings were literal duplications of the Broadway originals, often with Americans in the leads. There would be no localizations, no assimilating. Musical plays were inviolable. True, Betty Jane Watson throws in a nervy high D at the end of "People Will Say We're in Love" in the London cast (on World), sounding an odd note in the roughhewn atmosphere, but in general the ministrations of the R & H London office initiated the precise transfer of production that became the rule in the 1960s and broke the tradition that London stagings of American musicals produced, osmotically, British musicals. As producers of *Annie Get Your Gun,* R & H didn't just mail it over. They entrusted it to Helen Tamiris, with Dolores Gray and Bill Johnson in the leads; the recording (on World with *Oklahoma!* and *Carousel*) testifies to the fidelity of the lend lease. Gray is softer than Merman, Johnson livelier than Middleton, but it's the same show right down to the porters who harmonize on "Moonshine Lullaby."

It's fair that an R & H show kicked off the cast album habit, for R & H were careful producers, deserving careful reproduction on disc. Decca's *Carousel* remains the great one, beating out the abbreviated London cast, a surprisingly lively Command performance with Alfred Drake and Roberta Peters, and Victor's Lincoln Center revival. The last two are more complete than Decca. Only on Victor can you hear the musical scene built around "If I Love You," nearly ten minutes of underscored dialogue, snatches of song, meditations, and confessions during which two strangers become lovers. Yet no other set approaches the Decca. Perhaps there is an excitement in hearing what *Carousel* sounded like before anyone knew that R & H were changing the musical's history. *Oklahoma!* had to work; its self-belief was too infectious not to conquer. But *Carousel* kills off its hero, ends its love plot sadly, and deals with poverty and class snobbery rather darkly just at the end of the show. Decca's album came out when the American musical

versions, dance versions, string-heavy symphonic versions, or even the jazz improvs. Because these were less of a production than cast albums and could be released before a show opened, to cut a little PR edge, the company with the rights to the cast album would market the alternates almost as a rule, as many as six or seven to a show. Capitol and Victor were the most enthusiastic, Columbia a little squeamish. The records themselves vary greatly in quality. Some of them provide the characterless background tapes that stroke us in supermarkets; others are striking—a jazz treatment of *West Side Story,* say, which is somewhat jazz as it is. My own favorite of the alternates sounds a little nutty: a *Carnival* on Capitol "featuring zither stylings by Ruth Welcome." It's charming.

was just becoming proud of itself, just beginning to see that it had a past of one kind and a future of another. To gaze upon Decca's cover photograph of the "Carousel Waltz," with Raitt grinning at Clayton from his perch above the crowded midway, is almost to travel back in time to a Broadway of richer promise than today's, a Broadway where Harburg, Arlen, Porter, Weill, Rodgers, and Hammerstein flourished.

In singles, Fritz Reiner and the Pittsburgh Symphony made the best "Carousel Waltz" of all, complete on two Columbia 78 sides, a little fast but terribly exciting. Columbia also released Frank Sinatra's two-sided "Soliloquy," a revealing study in how the musical play enforced stronger acting parts than the musical was used to: Sinatra is hopelessly overparted, a voice without a character. Strangely, he signed on for the part in the *Carousel* film; wisely, he pulled out before shooting began. One odd textual note: Sinatra, like Raitt, includes a brief transitional sequence ("When I have a daughter . . .") just before the big "My little girl" tune. Yet no one else has sung this since then—not even Raitt at Lincoln Center—and the section isn't in the published score.

Victor didn't exert itself on *Allegro*. Their five ten-inch 78s give no taste of the show and, while no major songs are omitted, it feels as if no major ones were included, either. Perhaps the singers are a little sluggish; perhaps more of the choral commentary or one of the ballets should have been included; perhaps the heavy Rodgers tread burdens the score just where it needs to fly, in "Money Isn't Everything" or "So Far." The results were so disappointing that Victor didn't bother to transfer the show onto LP in 1949–50, when half the nation was tossing out its 78s and all the companies were frantically turning their backlist into new ware in LP transcription. Victor finally reissued *Allegro* (in fake stereo) in the 1960s, deleted it, and gave it another shot in the mid-1970s, in its true mono. Not till that third release did *Allegro* sport a "logo" cover (copying the poster) as show albums customarily do.

South Pacific claims only two decent recordings, the original cast and the Lincoln Center revival with Florence Henderson and Giorgio Tozzi. Even the fine London cast made only half an album, omitting Martin's solos because Columbia sent over its Broadway disc. But *The King and I* has done well, not least because Bennett's scoring does so much to keep the Siamese setting in hearing. The London cast, headed by Valerie Hobson and Herbert Lom, is impressive, and has been reissued on Stet.* In 1964, Thomas Shepard produced the best recording till then for Columbia, filling in two songs the cast albums didn't get to, submitting the whole to a new orchestration by Philip J. Lang, even securing excellent liner notes to take one through the work by number. The cast is terrific: Barbara Cook, Theodore Bikel, Jeanette Scovotti, Anita Darian, under Lehman Engel. Cook is the most intent actress of all Annas, giving the verse to "Getting To Know You" the feeling of a classroom lecture; Bikel, too, points his lines, relishing the wordless octave leaps in "A Puzzlement" as no other does. The same year, 1964, Rodgers launched his summer Music Theater of Lincoln Center (after an incongruous *Merry Widow*) with a *King and I* with Risë Stevens and Darren McGavin. Victor's recording gives no character insights, but Lee Venora and Frank Poretta make a fine set of lovers,

---

* Stet's final band, "Shall We Dance?," seems to be drawn from another disc with Lois Hunt, perhaps because of a damaged master. Stet's London *Wish You Were Here* similarly closes with the American cast.

the disc is studded with welcome bits of dialogue, and at last "The Small House of Uncle Thomas" was recorded. Victor went this one better on the 1977 Brynner revival with Constance Towers, recording virtually everything in the score, even the opening music (so we can hear the Kralahome's guards' chant lead into "I Whistle a Happy Tune") and the two kids' reprise of "A Puzzlement." There wasn't room for the ballet, obviously, but by acquiring these two Victors one would have a rare chance to study a musical play's entire score from curtain rise to curtain fall.

The rest of R & H seems less like R & H than like a team influenced by R & H. *Pipe Dream* is a lovely score, but one hears the shadow of Steinbeck lurking at the edges rather than holding the center. *Flower Drum Song* contains perhaps the only atrocious song R & H ever wrote, "Chop Suey," on American diversity. Columbia caught *Cinderella* in both television versions: the Andrews is vastly preferable. And *The Sound of Music?* When the film is better than the show, you're in trouble; still, the cast albums, New York and London both, have the two cynical numbers that the film dropped, "How Can Love Survive?" and "No Way To Stop It." Coming from Hammerstein, they sound almost violently bitter, but then this is the show in which he spoke of "a lark who is learning to pray." Epic's disc of the 1981 London revival with Petula Clark is decorated with what look like movie stills and follows the layout of the film's songs. Surprisingly, it's good theatre. The old Australian cast, with June Bronhill, is embarrassingly semi-amateur, but Bronhill is utterly amazing. If she, not Martin, had created the part, every Maria would have been a voice-rich soprano, not a "theatre" singer. Bronhill was graduated to the Mother Abbess in the Clark revival, but her Australian Maria remains one of the most vocally fulfilled parts in the epic of the American musical.

Is there life after Hammerstein? Rodgers's *No Strings* songs are of interest, and it's fun to hear the Rodgers vamps scaled down for Ralph Burns's small wind combo. Burns also made his own *No Strings* album, without vocals. *Do I Hear a Waltz?* is less vital Rodgers but has Sondheim lyrics. "Here comes Godzilla," the gypsies would mutter whenever Rodgers walked in, and insiders' dish has it that Rodgers threw out the ironic lyrics Sondheim originally wrote for "We're Gonna Be All Right" as one smashes an unflattering mirror. Maybe not; they make a brilliant marital satire in any case. Hear the painted-over Broadway lyrics on Columbia's cast album, then cut over to Warner Brothers' Sondheim Salute or Victor's Sondheim revue to hear the original. Columbia's *Two by Two* preserves Danny Kaye's stint as Noah but not his contemptible out-of-character antics nor the time he screamed abuse at Walter Willison on stage in front of the audience. They got their money's worth that day. Victor sold so few copies of *Rex* that it virtually went into release in remainder bins. *I Remember Mama* claims a studio cast (TE); still, the TV commercial would make a nice single.

It's easy to trace the R & H influence. Lerner and Loewe's *Brigadoon* and *Paint Your Wagon,* both on Victor, had de Mille ballets, threats of violence (even murder), and a fluid song-dialogue ratio; *Paint Your Wagon* also cut off another strip of Americana in its gold-rush setting. Loewe deals heavily in pastiche. *Brigadoon*'s prelude sounds like a bagpipe dance, and *Paint Your Wagon* has "folk songs" in the *Oklahoma!* vein, not to mention a prominent banjo on the knee. When stereo came in, Columbia brought out a more complete *Brigadoon* with Shirley Jones and Jack Cassidy; the great Susan Johnson snaps out the comedy numbers with an entrancing belt.

Victor's *Fanny* affirms that score's trusty character orientation. Character is action: you can follow *Fanny*'s action just by harking to the four principals. The singing is grand, Pinza still robust at the end of his career, Slezak witty, Henderson raw and vivid, and Tabbert thrilling when his bright baritone soars up above the staff. In a way, *Fanny* is the forerunner of *The Most Happy Fella* (with a not dissimilar story), musical comedy so expanded by the tactics of the musical play that much of what might have been script turns into song. This is perhaps less noticeable in *A Tree Grows in Brooklyn*, but Columbia's cast album contains thirteen songs, an overture, a ballet, and one of those potpourri finales put together for the record that recall the old 78 medleys. This is a lot of music, even if Schwartz and Fields are dealing strictly in verse-chorus songs.

Frank Loesser shows some R & H effect in *Guys and Dolls*, pointedly using reprises and musical scenes, even operatic recitative. He didn't think much of Jo Swerling's book, but, oddly, went ahead, intertwined his score with that book, and then demanded the book be rewritten—around his score. Decca's thorough cast album is another classic, though the cast wasn't all that good, weak particularly in Robert Alda's gambler and Isabel Bigley's "mission doll." Bigley made Loesser so angry at one rehearsal that he socked her. I can't imagine how anyone who sounds so dull could figure in a backstage geschrei anecdote; Bigley's duet album with Stephen Douglass on Design of R & H favorites is so boring it put Lilo to sleep. In 1982, England's National Theatre mounted a *Guys and Dolls* that has proved one of their biggest hits. Chrysalis recorded it, American accents and all (not a single slip), with brassy orchestrations respectful of the originals. It's a more complete reading, and this team is far superior to the home squad, especially the Adelaide, Julia McKenzie. Still, we have our local nostalgia—and Stubby Kaye's "Sit Down, You're Rockin' the Boat" remains untouchable. It's a rouser, but he doesn't rouse it: just lets it out, with lots of voice.

Loesser didn't reach the musical play proper till *The Most Happy Fella*, and he went so far over that it's virtually opera, "a musical with music," he called it. I'll say: it became the first Broadway show that had to be done complete, immediately—*Porgy and Bess* waited twenty-five years for Engel's three-disc set, cut at that. Some of *The Most Happy Fella* is musical comedy—"Standin' on the Corner" is sheer Hit Tune, "Big D" an excuse for a dance number, "Fresno Beauties" a scenic curtain raiser using the characteristic Latino brasses. But "Joey, Joey" is a remarkable ballad, casual and sexy and remote at once, "Mamma, Mamma" a soliloquy of detail, and much of the rest is similarly rich. Moreover, the overture is no medley but a tight statement of themes developed and climaxed. The London cast, all American leads except Inia Te Wiata as Tony, wins the prize for Helena Scott's lovely Amy, Libi Staiger's formidable Cleo, and Jack de Lon's Herman, *molto tenore*. It's too bad Houston's 1980 revival wasn't recorded. The staging was poor, but the text was garnished with music cut in 1956. One odd point: everyone thinks of *The Most Happy Fella* as a modern-dress show. It takes place in 1927.

It was Harburg who most effectively restructured satiric musical comedy for the age of Hammerstein, emphasizing the contemporaneity that the musical play lacked. *Finian's Rainbow* remains a classic of the socialized musical, supporting ecumenical trade unionism in "This Time of the Year" and "That Great Come-and-Get-It-Day," refuting the work ethic from a working-class point of view in "Necessity," and piquing class distinctions in "When the Idle Poor Become the Idle Rich." Michael Kidd staged a ballet to precede "Idle Poor" in which penniless southern sharecroppers exult in hifalutin outfits ordered by mail on charge account: class now, pay later. It is one of the musical's most commentatively *immediate* images, the very picture of postwar America—but it shows why Harburg's shows have dated so much more than Hammerstein's. Columbia's original-cast *Finian* preserves Ella Logan's mannered rubato—has anyone else ever sung on Broadway with such disregard for metrical bar lines? Still, it works; Petula Clark, excellent in the film version, sings exactly the same way. Victor caught the 1960 City Center revival, so refreshing that it was moved to Broadway so the pious buff could celebrate the mass all over again. (Here, at least, Harburg's racial satire proved still timely.) The revival has Carol Brice, stereo sound, and a bit more of the score, but without Logan and David Wayne's leprechaun it isn't competitive.

Capitol's *Flahooley* includes narrative lead-ins to frame the plot (no notes of any kind on the jacket), but this plot outwits any synopsis. You may wonder what Yma Sumac is singing about in her four solos (not by Fain and Harburg), but listen carefully to the rest, and the Harburgian message will come through. Note the sturdy chording in the choral arrangements, with the sopranos and tenors pushed way up at the climaxes, standard practice at the time. The Capsulanti chorus was Harburg's swipe at McCarthyism—but Capitol deleted the mock Christmas carol, "Sing the Merry," as offensive to popular sentiment. Bagley has it on his Harburg *Revisited*.

Perhaps the R & H era officially ended in 1959, with the beginning of Harburg's flop period, with the last of the "musical plays" by R & H themselves, and with *Gypsy*, often cited as the capstone of the cycle. Columbia's cast album is the item that today's young authors of musicals point to as their inspiration—the work, the place, the people, the record, the idea that urged them to write shows. "I can do that!" No: *Gypsy* is one of a kind, mold broken. But that first excitement stays with us, and reminds us of the recording's significance in our comprehension of the musical. You can't go there again: but you can reckon the visit.

12. *A Newer Style of Heroine*

Nanette Fabray's best role was in *Arms and the Girl,* but the show she is most associated with is *High Button Shoes,* partly because Fabray sang its hit, "Papa, Won't You Dance with Me?" and partly because she and Phil Silvers repeated their roles on television in the 1950s when faithful resuscitations of musicals were popular fare. Decca didn't think much of the Morton Gould–Dorothy Fields *Arms and the Girl* score, cutting only four ten-inch 78s; likewise Victor on the Styne-Cahn *High Button Shoes.* But Fabray sounds fine, even if the choice "Papa" is Doris Day's, on an old Columbia 78.

Helen Gallagher makes a double header with Fabray on *Make a Wish,* but *Hazel Flagg* is a more affable choice, for Gallagher's lead-role prime and a good taste of conventional musical comedy of 1953. She turns up on *Cry for Us All* in only one number, but it's a lulu, "Swing Your Bag." Gallagher buffs like her best in the *No, No, Nanette* revival for the gray fedora she walked in under and her "Where Has My Hubby Gone? Blues," staged in the dark with the chorus boys posed collegiately behind her. I prefer the younger, brassier Gallagher, as on Capitol's *Pal Joey,* wherein she leads all the nightclub numbers.

Julie Andrews is well served by her cast albums. Victor's Broadway cast of *The Boy Friend* is much better than the London original, more complete and orchestrated in gala twenties style. Millicent Martin, later active on Broadway after coming over with *Side by Side by Sondheim,* is heard as one of the "perfect young ladies," and the absurdly pert (not to mention named) Dilys Lay steals side two in "It's Never Too Late To Fall in Love." *My Fair Lady,* like *Kiss Me, Kate,* has two "original cast" discs. There was no stereo available for the first go round in 1956, so Andrews, Harrison, and Holloway rerecorded it in London two years later; Columbia released it with the Hirschfeld cartoon of Shaw working a Harrison puppet working an Andrews puppet that they had used on the mono issue. Columbia also put out Italian and Spanish versions and altogether sold more units of *My Fair Lady* than any label had sold of any other LP title. In those days, the national ear was wired to Broadway. The Richardson-Andreas *My Fair Lady* is also on Columbia, a fine reading with a second Hirschfeld cartoon bringing in two other characters for an "all-star revival." In 1956, Holloway lost a Best Supporting Tony, in 1976 George Rose won as Best Actor—for the same part.

Columbia's *Camelot* gives Andrews not her best part but her "biggest" score, and her crystalline Guinevere knocks down all competition, even from the highly regarded London cast with the impressive Elizabeth Larner, now on Stet. None of Andrews's soundtracks is in class with her show albums, but she made some great recitals for Victor and Columbia in the early days, of show material old and new. *Broadway's Fair Julie* is a sample: Gershwin and Arlen, Weill and Bernstein, *Kismet, Paint Your Wagon,* a touch of Coward. Somehow, she never quite *goes* for it, but *Don't Go in the Lion's Cage Tonight* is a spirited disc, a collection of old music hall tunes. Unlike Joan Morris (or Beatrice Kay, famous in this repertory in the 1940s), Andrews doesn't re-create the old style. Columbia has the Carnegie Hall album with Burnett, which includes a ten-minute medley of show tunes reminiscent of the Merman-Martin marathon, in the form of a history, from *Madame Sherry* and *Naughty Marietta* to "A Boy Like That."

If Andrews's recitals draw on her stage presence, Liza Minnelli's push for a pop kayo in a kind of rock vaudeville. It tells us little of Broadway, though it does help illustrate the gap that has grown between theatre music and the music business. On her early recitals for Capitol in the 1960s, Minnelli looks back to the masters. By the 1970s, she is show biz itself: not in its tradition, but in its destructive narcissism. So she ends up singing "Tropical Nights," which like just about everything else written today is about sating the appetites come who may, and the arrangement—or did I dream this?—includes a disco version of "Bali Ha'i."

Men have left a trail of show albums in all directions. Robert Preston entered late, as a star; Richard Kiley entered early, to grow from youth (in *Kismet*) to star's foil (in *Redhead*) to star (in *No Strings* and *I Had a Ball*) to *padrone* (in *Man of La Mancha*); Joel Grey is the eternal Kid. Capitol's *The Music Man* remains Preston's best role, Kapp's *Man of La Mancha* enshrines the first of Quixotes (despite competition from Continental heavyweights), and Victor's *Goodtime Charley* gives Grey his surest role.

The Big Lady Show throws off a cast album as enthusiastically as it does souvenir programs and t-shirts. The best ones, however, are quite good—Columbia's *Mame* is a joy forever, though I wish they had somehow fit in "The Fox Hunt," one of those concerted pieces in which each of several characters has a solo verse and then everybody sings his part simultaneously. (Harold Rome has used this trick often, in *Call Me Mister*'s "Going Home Train," *Fanny*'s nursery round, and *Destry Rides Again*'s "Are You Ready, Gyp Watson?") Victor's several *Hello, Dolly!*s offer Channing with the best cast, Bailey with the black cast, and Martin with the London cast. The soundtrack has Streisand and new numbers by Herman. *Dear World,* a third Herman score of this kind, comes off much better on disc than it did on stage; this is the kind of music that buffs adore by themselves on dark nights.

What of Lansbury and Channing elsewhere? Lansbury never sang before *Anyone Can Whistle,* but you'd never know it from her confident performance of the Kay Thompsonesque "Me and My Town" or her nonchalant head-voice top notes in "I've Got You To Lean On." Victor put out two different "mixes" of her London-New York *Gypsy,* comparable to Merman's. Perhaps this is the place to mention another *Gypsy,* with Kay Medford on Music For Pleasure, a British label. Having enjoyed a personal success as Mama Brice in the London *Funny Girl,* Medford seemed natural as this other show biz mother. She simply doesn't have the voice for it, but her determination to make it work in the face of catastrophe turns her into a Rose-*verité.* It's worth a listen.

Channing set her persona as Lorelei Lee, so Columbia's *Gentlemen Prefer Blondes* is basic (and far preferable to *Lorelei,* issued twice, in tryout and Broadway versions). However, the 1962 London cast erases the original with a Lorelei (Dora Bryan) who has read Anita Loos, a more complete view of the score, authentic twenties arrangements, the amazing Anne Hart in the sidekick part, and a theatricality typical of the British cast album from day one. It's too bad nobody recorded Channing's 1955 flop *The Vamp,* on silent Hollywood, for this was one of the great strange shows, every choice a wrong one. Steve Reeves, in a small part, thought the overture weak; everyone's a critic. *Show Girl* is little more than Channing's club act.

With Barbara Cook we come to a stream of great scores. Capitol's *Flahooley* and *Plain and Fancy* are treasurable; Columbia's original *Candide* remains one of Broadway's greatest documents. *The Music Man* gives Cook a fine musical scene in "My White Knight," somewhat *recitativo* and a brand-new way of writing one of the musical's most common genre songs (cf., "The Man I Love," "One Kiss," "Just Imagine," "That's Him," "I'll Know," "There Won't Be Trumpets"). Capitol's *The Gay Life* and MGM's *She Loves Me* are the prime Cook albums; note that the former accidentally ended up with two opening choruses, "What a Charming Couple" and "Bring Your Darling Daughter." After the premiere, the first was relegated to the curtain calls, which worked out fine since the show ran in flashback sequence. The major companies didn't want to record *The Grass Harp,* so Bagley issued it; it contains what may be Cook's most beautiful cut, "Chain of Love." Cook herself would probably prefer her two recitals taped in Carnegie Hall on Columbia (1975) and MMG (1980). Both enjoy the marvelous arrangements of Cook's music director, Wally Harper, and it's a relief to note a preponderance of show tunes amid the current pap. On Columbia she refers to *Funny Girl, The Band Wagon, Simple Simon, Mack and Mabel,* and—of course, but much more feelingly than on the cast album—*She Loves Me.* MMG has Berlin, Bernstein, Coward, and a novelty plaint lampooning her Broadway past, "The Ingenue."

Verdon was no singer, but her unique personality carried her through. *Damn Yankees* catches her in musical comedy, *New Girl in Town* in musical play (both on Victor), and while it's hard to imagine anyone else as right in "Whatever Lola

Wants" or "Who's Got the Pain?," it would be a boon to hear a real singer tackle Anna. Columbia's *Sweet Charity* reveals how little this show had beyond its Fosse staging. Perhaps the most satisfying Verdon disc is her early Victor recital, *The Girl I Left Home For,* in which she can elude the vagaries of theatre composition and sing at her pleasure. Here are standards and surprises, all together suggesting a sultry, wiseass I-don't-care. I withdraw the assertion that Verdon was no singer. Her "Ain't Misbehavin' " is tidy and musical, her readings in general attentive to text, her "Jenny" briskly defensive, and she even includes the sensation of a dancebreak in "It's a Hot Night in Alaska"—"Down, boys!" she emits, when the band gets a touch rowdy. Of interest to theatre buffs is the respect for verses in an increasingly verse-bored culture, and the inclusion of rarities from *Gay Divorce* and *Heads Up.* It's late to say so, but I'm impressed.

13. *The Superdirectors*

The superproduction by its nature does not tally on record; hearing it on disc becomes a quest for the *work* beneath the hoopla. With Abbott, there is less of a problem, as one follows the rise of integration in his career. In 1941, *Best Foot Forward* (on Cadence's revival cast) shows a slight plot slant—"Hollywood Story" and "Three Men on a Date" are character songs, "Ev'ry Time" is a relatively suitable torch number, perhaps a little mature for its singer and with a vamp which anticipates that to "Something Wonderful." "Buckle Down Winsocki" fixes school spirit. But everything else is fun fill—kids dating, goofing off, and putting on airs. *The Pajama Game* (on Columbia) is more solidly constructed. Richard Adler and Jerry Ross wrote pop tunes adapting to the stage, more so in "I'll Never Be Jealous Again" and "Think of the Time I Save," less so on "There Once Was a Man" and "Hernando's Hideaway." Abbott is splitting the difference. *The Pajama Game*'s book was reasonably firm, though the cast album reveals incongruities ("Her Is" and "Steam Heat") and tests patience with "A New Town Is a Blue Town." Okay, it's character; but it's dreary.

Once Upon a Mattress, on Kapp, presents a story-turned score by Mary Rodgers (his daughter) and Marshall Barer. It shows off the famous Abbott second act in which little happens—notice how much less urgent the songs on side two are. Still, spoofing "The Princess and the Pea" is a great idea, and Abbott typically chose a cast of youngsters who would reach star (Carol Burnett), reach less than star but work a lot (Jack Gilford, Joe Bova, Matt Mattox, Jane White), or become answers to trivia questions (Anne Jones, Allen Case, Harry Snow). It's too bad no one recorded *Music Is,* the last new Abbott show, in the *Mattress* spirit in its youthful, now becoming prominent cast and melodious score (by Richard Adler). Based on *Twelfth Night* (as was *Your Own Thing,* some years before), *Music Is* had charm and nerve, but it caught New York critics on one of their mean streaks, and they smashed it. Washington had loved it, and New York preview audiences also loved it. Once the reviews came out, the public sat there quiet as death.

Robbins's work doesn't "show" on disc, though his *Peter Pan* turned into one of the finest cast albums, so filled with dialogue, stage business, vamps, cues, dances, and reprises that you can virtually hear the curtain going up and down. Fosse is the opposite of Robbins in that he has had no *West Side Story,* no *Gypsy.* Yet *Pippin,* on Motown, does not sound like an excuse for staging tricks. Dropping a medieval scrollwork of the lyrics to "No Time at All" from the flies and having the public join in may be called a trick; but the song itself is a delightful piece, and the score as a whole sounds intimate. Arista's *Chicago* suggests its production in the vaudeville introductions to the numbers ("And now, Miss Roxie Hart . . ."), and Ralph Burns's slit-eyed, down-and-dirty orchestrations are a show in themselves. Still, the disc tells far more about Verdon, Rivera, or Ohrbach than about Fosse. "Ten Percent" may be heard on Groove Merchant's jazz alternate led by Lee Konitz, unfortunately without a vocal and way under the driving tap tempo David Rounds used on stage.

Champion's obsession with finding the right entry into a number affects his show's records somewhat. *Carnival* might stand as his memorium. MGM's cast album is tight and clean, scarcely suggesting an ensemble show, though the famous opening scene is here. Anna Maria Alberghetti's soprano is delightful, but her diction is so poor I didn't get most of her lines till the London cast came out (after a mere four-week run). Sally Logan is no Alberghetti but she *can* sing English; moreover, the album is considerably more complete, using the musical or textual lead-ins so necessary to Champion's peace-of-mind. We also get a fuller version of the show's best number, "Beautiful Candy," with the vendor's cries that propelled it rhythmically as it opens up to take in the whole carnival, the world.

The *Irene* revival, on Columbia, repudiates everything that made the tidy original such a winner; comparing the two is like witnessing a boxing match between Helen Gallagher and Conan the Barbarian. Only five titles survive from 1919, but there is a fine new song by Wally Harper, "The World Must Be Bigger Than an Avenue," and a wonderful overture that was not used in New York. The recent London cast on EMI attempts to revive some of the original's intimacy, in a variant edition.

The same "new revival" spirit informs Victor's *42nd Street*, with the best and worst of Champion. The best is his shaping of the numbers, assimilated in lead-ins and carried through scene changes, costume changes, story developments. "Dames" for instance, begins at a runthrough in street clothes on a bare stage and concludes in full cry of costumes and set. The worst of Champion is the cardboard portrayals. One minute the director (Jerry Orbach) is callously throwing the ingenue (Wanda Richert) out of his show because the star (Tammy Grimes) says Richert was "out of [the dancing] line." The next minute he's selling her on the "Lullaby of Broadway." This is dishonest. If they have that kind of communication, he wouldn't have fired her just on Grimes's say-so. Producer Shepard, *nolens volens,* has caught the paradox of *42nd Street* on the disc: this is a heartless Broadway show about a big-hearted Broadway.

Bennett's *A Chorus Line*, the last recording Goddard Lieberson produced, has great personal endowment and tuneful pep. If it had been produced in the 1950s, it would have thrown off a mass of singles; but in the 1950s it wouldn't have been so contextual as to defy the single. "What I Did for Love" has traveled widely, but the album is the thing, much bought and too little appreciated. Columbia's *Ballroom* preserves the worst of the show: its composition. And *Dreamgirls,* which radio idiots have been terming a "soundtrack," has come through well enough, though it lacks the lighting towers, the sequins, the curtains, and the *Times* review, all requisite for an appreciation of the show.

14. *The State of the Art*

Here is the musical after Hammerstein, most effectively sampled in Frank Loesser's *Greenwillow*. Released on Victor and reissued, startlingly, on Columbia, the cast album won the smallest of cults. Exhausted by the effort of agitating for *Flahooley*, *Candide*, *The Golden Apple*, and *The Gay Life*, buffs neglect *Greenwillow*, despite excellent performances and a folk pastiche the like of which has not been heard before or since. The setting is a village situated somewhere between Wales and *Allegro*, and in plot premise, characters, sentiment, and moral commentary this is a show Hammerstein might have written if he and Rodgers had split up. In the 1950s, records weren't sealed and customers sampled them in booths; go back in time to sample *Greenwillow*'s opening, "A Day Borrowed from Heaven." Notice how Loesser establishes the show's odd tone in the skewed rhythm; if you tried to dance to it, you'd break your leg. Loesser fans love the snazzy *How To Succeed*, but others could have written it. *Greenwillow* is unique.

After Loesser, Bock and Harnick seem the most Hammersteinian. They come alive on record as in the theatre because their scores are filled with story matter. *Fiorello!* has the winning Ellen Hanley, *Tenderloin* the impressive Wynne Miller, and both scores feature disarming period reconstructions. Bobby Darin made *Tenderloin*'s "Artifical Flowers" a hit single. With *Fiddler on the Roof* one faces quite some choice, what with British, French, German, Dutch, and Hebrew casts among others; even one in Yiddish. London's Topol is the best Tevye, the Netherlands' Enny Mols-de Leeuwe the best Golde, and only foreign casts include the "Bottle Dance." Herschel Bernardi's solo album includes the dropped "When Messiah Comes." Sadly, Bock and Harnick broke up after *The Rothschilds*, one of the most underrated of musicals. Incisive in its sweep and honest in its look at ingrained anti-Semitism in Europe, this group biography gave Hal Linden one of the musical's few male Tony-baiting parts (he won it), enjoyed Michael Kidd's subtle staging, ran on Jewish theatre parties, and was promptly forgotten. Remember it on Columbia.

Sondheim's scores have generally transferred excellently to disc; as with recorded opera, one can settle down with the characters and the music, get closer than in the theatre. Capitol's *Forum* is fine, Columbia's *Anyone Can Whistle* historically notable for Lieberson's decision to record it even though it had only run a week. Industry tradition took a show's cast into the studio the first Sunday after the premiere; this cast played its last performance there. It doesn't sound like a funeral, though two of its three principals, Lee Remick and Harry Guardino, show the effects of months of forcing unmusical voices to sing.

Company's avant-garde score has made it one of the most influential of cast albums. It, too, supposedly had a casting problem in Dean Jones; Jones seems to have agreed, as he left the show early on. He sounds fine on Columbia's cast album, but a second version was issued with the voice of Jones's replacement, Larry Kert, tracked onto the original cuts. On either disc, one can hear two of the most essential Sondheim performances, Pamela Myers's "Another Hundred People" and Elaine Stritch's "The Ladies Who Lunch."

Capitol's *Follies* is the only disappointing Sondheim cast album, much too little of this huge score and no sense of the production. A bit more of the dialogue and something of "Rain on the Roof," "Bolero d'Amour," "One More Kiss," and

"Loveland" would have helped. If Capitol was unwilling to do the whole thing on two discs, it still might have filled out its one more imaginatively. Unfortunately, this *Show Boat* of the postwar era has no aggregation of recordings as our old *Show Boat* has; one longs for a medley, even for dance-band singles. Seek out the rest of *Follies* on the *Sondheim Salute* ("One More Kiss" by the original cast, Justine Johnston and Victoria Mallory, and a cut number, "Pleasant Little Kingdom"), on the British revue ("Can That Boy Fox Trot"), on Victor's *Marry Me a Little* ("Uptown, Downtown" among others), and on Victor's *Stavisky* soundtrack (two cut numbers, "The World's Full of Boys" and "Who Could Be Blue?" and the first version of "Beautiful Girls," all without the lyrics, alas). Victor's Thomas Shepard recorded a 1985 *Follies* concert, a full score and cast to challenge Capitol—and now comes the 1987 London revision.

Columbia's *A Little Night Music* is superb, much better sung and acted than Victor's London cast (which carries over Hermione Gingold). Jean Simmons has spirit, even voice, but she's not as sharp as Glynis Johns, and the others are weak in voice, where the New Yorkers were a kind of new operetta, with a real baritone and soprano in Laurence Guittard and Victoria Mallory, a tenor juvenile in Mark Lambert, and a beguiling Brahmsian quintet. Johns's "Send in the Clowns" is not as famous as the one she delivered, obviously ailing and in distress, in the *Sondheim Salute* (not on the album), but it's still better than versions by Judy Collins, Frank Sinatra, and about a thousand conductors of the Manhattan piano bar. Renata Scotto sings it with more voice, but Johns makes it true. Columbia's soundtrack drops much of the score, but supplies some tasty new lyrics and a marvellous, completely new version of "The Glamorous Life."

The last three Sondheim shows have been Shepard projects on Victor, all fine reproductions of the theatre experience. *Pacific Overtures* is perhaps the desert-island disc, if one had to choose, Broadway's most elegantly concentrated score, beautifully performed by Broadway's most atypical cast. *Sweeney Todd,* musically complete on two records, becomes more effective out of the Minskoff's yawning maw; and of course on repeated listening one can pick out thematic felicities such as the varied, rising three-note theme used in three different songs called "Johanna," one each for her lover, her father, and her despicable father-lover Judge Turpin. His number was cut during previews, but came out on the album and as an appendix to the published piano score. *Merrily We Roll Along* is a triumph, perhaps a vindication, as the recording preserves what worked in the staging and drops the rest. A charming autobiographical moment when the young songwriters audition for a producer: "There's not a tune you can hum," he tells them, almost pleading. And he shows them the kind of tune he means as he goes: "Some Enchanted Evening."

There is no Bagley Sondheim, but Richard Rodney Bennett plays and sings Sondheim rare and familiar on DRG, and *Side by Side by Sondheim* offers a full evening of suave cabaret Sondheim, though Julia McKenzie's famous "Broadway Baby" seems pallid in comparison to what she did for it on stage—McKenzie who turned in one of the greatest comic-singing performances in the musical in London's *On the Twentieth Century. Marry Me a Little,* a two-character *Songspiel* drawn from trunk material, is entrancing, closing such gaps in the repertory as "Happily Ever After," the first version of "Being Alive"; "Bang!," the polonaise seduction from *A Little Night Music,* unfortunately without the assistance of the quintet; and "There Won't Be Trumpets," from *Anyone Can Whistle,* published but cut from the show because Lee Remick got a bigger hand for its lead-in speech than she did for the number itself.

I close in prelude, with Lehman Engel's Columbia album of overtures, *Curtain Going Up.* As with his ballet concert, the selections are disputable—six of the ten pieces included had already been recorded at the time, if cut, and these are generally not the greatest of their kind. *Bells Are Ringing?* Still, the album has a kind of magic, for the overture, the first thing one hears, can be the musical's absolute moment of contact. In *Show Boat, Of Thee I Sing, Wonderful Town, House of Flowers, Gypsy, Funny Girl, A Little Night Music* and *Nine* (both vocal overtures), even in *Annie*'s unassuming, confident solo trumpet, the launching of the spectacular overture is meant as invitation to a spectacular show. An overture can epitomize action (as *Gypsy*'s does) or set atmosphere (as *Show Boat*'s 1927 overture did; the 1946 replacement is just a medley) or paint a unique *colorito* (in *Wonderful Town*'s period pieces or *House of Flowers'* Caribbean scoring). The overture may be the only thing in the musical that has remained a constant since its youth. The top banana is gone, the vaudeville interpolation is gone, the Lillian Russell heroine is gone, the ⁶/₈ comedy hop tempo is gone, even The Girls as Such are gone. When Merman realized that she needed a Porter to help define her—when performers began to collaborate with authors—the Babies made a new Broadway.

Index